MUSIC, SOUND, AND SILENCE IN
BUFFY THE VAMPIRE SLAYER

To Vanessa

Music, Sound, and Silence in *Buffy the Vampire Slayer*

Edited by

PAUL ATTINELLO
University of Newcastle, UK

JANET K. HALFYARD
Birmingham Conservatoire, UK

VANESSA KNIGHTS
formerly University of Newcastle, UK

ASHGATE

© The Editors and Contributors 2010

All rights reserved. No part of this publication may be reproduced, stored in a retrieval system or transmitted in any form or by any means, electronic, mechanical, photocopying, recording or otherwise without the prior permission of the publisher.

The editors have asserted their right under the Copyright, Designs and Patents Act, 1988, to be identified as the editors of this work.

Published by
Ashgate Publishing Limited
Wey Court East
Union Road
Farnham
Surrey, GU9 7PT
England

Ashgate Publishing Company
Suite 420
101 Cherry Street
Burlington
VT 05401-4405
USA

www.ashgate.com

British Library Cataloguing in Publication Data
Music, sound, and silence in Buffy the vampire slayer. –
   (Ashgate popular and folk music series)
   1. Buffy the vampire slayer (Television program)
   2. Television music – History and criticism
   I. Attinello, Paul II. Halfyard, Janet K. III. Knights, Vanessa
   791.4'572

Library of Congress Cataloging-in-Publication Data
Attinello, Paul Gregory.
  Music, sound, and silence in Buffy the vampire slayer / Paul Attinello, Janet K. Halfyard, and Vanessa Knights.
      p. cm. – (Ashgate popular and folk music series)
   Includes bibliographical references and index.
   ISBN 978-0-7546-6041-5 (hardcover : alk. paper) – ISBN 978-0-7546-6042-2 (pbk. : alk. paper) 1. Buffy, the vampire slayer (Television program) 2. Television music–History and criticism. I. Halfyard, Janet K., 1966– II. Knights, Vanessa. III. Title.

ML2080.A88 2008
781.5'46–dc22

2008048627

ISBN 978-0-7546-6041-5 HBK
ISBN 978-0-7546-6042-2 PBK

Bach musicological font developed by © Yo Tomita.

Printed and bound in Great Britain by
MPG Books Group, UK

Contents

List of Figures and Tables   *vii*
Notes on Contributors   *ix*
Foreword by Keith Negus   *xv*
General Editor's Preface   *xix*
Preface by John C. King and Christophe Beck   *xxi*
Acknowledgements   *xxv*

Introduction: "Bay City Rollers. Now That's Music": Music as Cultural Code in *Buffy the Vampire Slayer*   1
Vanessa Knights

PART I   CONSTRUCTING SOUND: MUSIC, NOISE, AND SILENCE

1   Love, Death, Curses, and Reverses (in E minor): Music, Gender, and Identity in *Buffy the Vampire Slayer* and *Angel*   15
Janet K. Halfyard

2   "What's My Melody?" Music and the Deployment of Genre in *Buffy the Vampire Slayer*   33
Louis Niebur

3   Variations on Themes for Geeks and Heroes: Leitmotif, Style and the Musico-dramatic Moment   45
Rob Haskins

4   "What rhymes with lungs?" When Music Speaks Louder than Words   61
Arnie Cox and Rebecca Fülöp

5   Battling the Buzz: Contesting Sonic Codes in *Buffy the Vampire Slayer*   79
Katy Stevens

6   And the Rest is Silence: Silence and Death as Motifs in *Buffy the Vampire Slayer*   91
Gerry Bloustien

PART II OWNING MUSIC: BANDS, FANS, AND POP CULTURE

7   Bronze Things; Things of Bronze: Popular Music Cultures in
    Buffy the Vampire Slayer   111
    Catherine Driscoll

8   More Than a Watcher: *Buffy* Fans, Amateur Music Videos, Romantic
    Slash, and Intermedia   131
    Rob Cover

9   "You're Just a Girl!" Punk Rock Feminism and the New Hero in
    Buffy the Vampire Slayer   149
    Renée T. Coulombe

10 Punks, Geeks, and Goths: *Buffy the Vampire Slayer* as a Study of
    Popular Music Demographics on American Commercial Television   165
    Kathryn Hill

PART III MAKING MUSIC: *BUFFY*, THE MUSICAL

11 Not "The Same Arrangement": Breaking Utopian Promises in the
    Buffy Musical   189
    Diana Sandars and Rhonda V. Wilcox

12 "Give Me Something to Sing About": Intertextuality and the
    Audience in "Once More, with Feeling"   209
    Amy Bauer

13 Rock, Television, Paper, Musicals, Scissors: *Buffy*, *The Simpsons*,
    and Parody   235
    Paul Attinello

Afterword by Anahid Kassabian   249
Bibliography   251
Index   267

List of Figures and Tables

Figures

1.1	The theme from *Buffy the Vampire Slayer*	16
1.2	The theme from *Angel*	17
3.1	Incomplete chord progression in the Buffy-Angel love theme (Christophe Beck)	46
3.2a	Three chords in "Dodgems" (Sound Stage Ltd)	53
3.2b	"Chorus" and compression of original three chords in "Dodgems"	53
3.3	"For the Glory" (Extreme Music) in "The Zeppo"	55
3.4	Four-note motif in "Revelations" (Christophe Beck)	57
3.5	Ascending melodic phrase in "Revelations" (Christophe Beck)	59
4.1	The Buffy-Angel theme (Christophe Beck)	68
4.2	The Buffy-Riley theme (Christophe Beck)	72
4.3	Theme from "The Gift" (Christophe Beck)	77
12.1	Tritone substitution in "I'll Never Tell"	211
12.2	Phrase structure of "What you Feel"	215
12.3	Analytical reduction of verse, chorus, and bridge of "Under your Spell"	218
12.4	Transition from C♯ to E in "Rest in Peace"	220
12.5	Analytical reduction of first verse and chorus of "Going Through the Motions"	225
12.6	Meter shifts in "Something to Sing About"	227
12.7	Ending of "What You Feel" compared to the opening of "Standing"	229
12.8	Phrygian and Dorian modes in "Walk Through the Fire"	230

Table

1.1	A summary of Tagg's observations of male and female characteristics in music	19

Notes on Contributors

Remembering Vanessa Knights

Vanessa Knights, who created the idea for this book with me soon after we met in September 2002, died on 10 March 2007 of a heart attack brought on by polymiositis, an auto-immune disorder with which she had been diagnosed ten years earlier. She was 37 years old; however, despite her long illness and its many difficult symptoms, she had already achieved a remarkable body of work. Indeed, the sheer range of enjoyable things to remember about her is a bit daunting—so much hard work, and so much fun—writing, dancing, shopping, and working with people from all over the world.

There was an endless drive she showed in her research, her teaching, her projects: she was so involved, so energetic. She seemed always to be producing passionately, and politically, committed articles, talks, symposia, concerts—she was always in the midst of things, always doing so much with so many people who could barely keep up with her. Most of Vanessa's research was on Hispanophone culture, particularly music, film, literature, and popular culture, with particular attention to feminism and women's movements, but she collaborated on a number of research areas outside even that wide remit.

Vanessa seemed to know simply everyone: she wasn't only part of every network—across our university, and across several disciplines, continents and time zones; at times it seemed as though she *was* the network, she was what held us all together, flashing around the room, meeting everyone, and introducing them all to each other. I don't know how we'll stay in contact without her—after her death we received a mass of emails from North and South America, Australia, the Caribbean, and across Europe, from people telling us how much fun they'd had meeting her at one conference or another, how lively and interested she was in so many different things, how many ideas and how much support she had given to a wide variety of projects.

An aspect of Vanessa that was remarkable, and one about which I know something: she faced her own health, her mortality, without flinching. Of the people I've known over the past 25 years, including many dealing with terrible illness, Vanessa was among the most clearheaded of them all. She handled hospitals, surgery, doctors, and an obscure condition nobody understood with a firm hand, not allowing them to get to her, or to stop her from living her life. It seemed as though illness and death were just a *thing*: a difficult thing, an annoying thing, but not an important one—less important than life, than the people she loved, than her work—far less important, in fact, than this lively, demanding, strong, affectionate jewel of a woman.

I met Vanessa at a time when *Buffy* fans were presented with an uncomfortable dilemma: to reject the darkness and misery that entered the show in seasons 6 and 7, or to accept and understand them. She and I, both having lived for some years with chronic life-threatening illnesses, were immediately clear which side we were on: we thought it wonderful to see our funny, strong heroine have real and terrible problems, disasters, and my-hat-has-a-cow humiliations, and yet survive. I think Vanessa would have liked to acknowledge that this was one reason for putting this book together: not merely because we enjoyed the topic and had many ideas related to it, but also because we wanted to identify with the show's strength, toughness, and honesty.

Vanessa would have wanted to thank those who helped us to pick up the reins after her death: her beloved husband David Lawtie, who stayed with her throughout her illness, and later allowed us to go through her papers and home computer; her dear friend Anne Davies, who located Vanessa's *Buffy* materials on her office computer and copied them for us; and especially Janet Halfyard, who bravely stepped up from contributor to coeditor, did everything necessary to get this book into print, and did it to the most exacting standards. I like to think that Vanessa is delighted, and proud, with the result.

Paul Attinello
24 August 2008

Paul Attinello is Senior Lecturer in the International Centre for Music Studies at Newcastle University; he has also taught at the University of Hong Kong and UCLA. He has published in *Contemporary Music Review*, *Radical Musicology*, the *Journal of Musicological Research*, *Musik-Konzepte*, *Musica/Realtá*, the revised *New Grove Dictionary of Music and Musicians*, and a number of reference works and collections, including the groundbreaking *Queering the Pitch: The New Lesbian & Gay Musicology*. Current projects include a monograph on music about AIDS and books on Gerhard Stäbler and Meredith Monk.

Amy Bauer Amy Bauer is Assistant Professor of Music at the University of California, Irvine. She has published on the music of György Ligeti, Olivier Messiaen, and modernist aesthetics, and edits the peer-reviewed journal *Lost Online Studies* (loststudies.com). She is currently writing a book on the music of Ligeti and co-editing *Lost in Thought: Critical Approaches to* Lost *the Series*.

Gerry Bloustien is Deputy Director of the Hawke Research Centre for Sustainable Societies, University of South Australia, teaching Cultural Studies and Screen Literacy. Her publications on gender and representation include *Girl Making: A Cross Cultural Ethnography of Growing Up Female* (Berghahn, 2003); studies of *Buffy* and its participatory fan base (*European Journal of Cultural Studies*);

and *Sonic Synergies: Music, Identity and Communities* (Ashgate, 2008). Her co-authored book *Playing for Life* on international music-making by young people at risk will be published by Palgrave in 2009.

Renée T. Coulombe is a composer, improviser, and theorist of audio and digital media culture at the University of California, Riverside. She has published several articles on audio and televisual scoring in *Buffy the Vampire Slayer*.

Rob Cover is Lecturer in Media at the University of Adelaide, South Australia. He researches and publishes on new media, television narrative, and queer theory.

Arnie Cox is Associate Professor of Music Theory at Oberlin College in Ohio (USA). His work focuses on the bodily basis of musical meaning. Publications include "The Mimetic Hypothesis and Embodied Musical Meaning," *Musicae Scientiae*, 5/2 (2001), and "Hearing, Feeling, Grasping Gestures," in Elaine King and Anthony Gritten (eds), *Music and Gesture* (Ashgate, 2006).

Catherine Driscoll is Chair of Gender and Cultural Studies at the University of Sydney (Australia). Her publications include *Girls: Feminine Adolescence in Popular Culture and Cultural Theory* (Columbia University Press, 2002) and *Modernist Cultural Studies* (University Press of Florida, 2008). Her forthcoming publications including a book on online culture, co-authored with Melissa Gregg, and a book on new romance genres. She is a member of the Australian Research Council's Cultural Research Network.

Rebecca Fülöp is a doctoral student in historical musicology at the University of Michigan. Rebecca has contributed to the book review section of *The Journal of Film Music* and is currently at work on her dissertation, tentatively titled "How to Score a Woman: Gender Construction in Hollywood Film Music, 1935–1965."

Janet K. Halfyard is Director of Undergraduate Studies at Birmingham Conservatoire (UK). Her publications include *Danny Elfman's Batman: A Film Score Guide* (Scarecrow, 2004) and essays in *Reading Angel* (IB Tauris, 2005), *European Film Music* (Ashgate, 2006), and collections on horror, animation, and cult TV. Her paper "Singing their hearts out" (*Slayage*, 17) was nominated for *Slayage*'s Mr Pointy award for the best essay in *Buffy* Studies in 2005.

Rob Haskins is an assistant professor of music at the University of New Hampshire (USA). He has published essays on Cage and Glass, and his recording (with Laurel Karlik Sheehan) of Cage's Two^2 was released on Mode Records in March 2008.

Kathryn Hill was a lecturer in twentieth-century music history at the Sydney Conservatorium of Music, 1992–2004. Her specialist area is the history of popular music. She submitted a PhD thesis at the University of Sydney (Australia) in 2008 on the use of popular music on American television, using *Buffy the Vampire Slayer* as a case study.

Anahid Kassabian is James and Constance Alsop Chair of Music at the University of Liverpool (UK); her research and teaching focus on ubiquitous musics; music, sound, and moving images; music and new technologies, especially games, virtual worlds, and pervasive computing; and feminist and postcolonial theories. She is the author of *Hearing Film* (Routledge, 2001), coeditor of *Keeping Score* (University Press of Virginia, 1997), and a past editor of *Stanford Humanities Review and Journal of Popular Music Studies*. With Ian Gardiner, she recently co-founded *Music, Sound and the Moving Image* (Liverpool University Press).

Vanessa Knights was a Senior Lecturer in Hispanic Studies in the School of Modern Languages at Newcastle University (UK). She published on romantic Latin American music, the mass media, and modernity, and was working on this volume, among several other projects, at the time of her death. She was also specialist editor on the board of *Popular Music*, on the advisory board of *Music, Sound and the Moving Image* and on the editorial collective of *Radical Musicology*. She was co-convenor of the popular music research network at Newcastle and one of the co-organizers of the biennial ¡VAMOS! festival of Latin and Lusophone cultures.

Keith Negus is Professor of Musicology at Goldsmiths, University of London. His research engages with all aspects of the production, consumption, and mediation of popular music. He is currently writing a book on Bob Dylan. His books include *Producing Pop* (1992), *Music Genres and Corporate Cultures* (1999), and *Creativity, Communication and Cultural Value* (2004), the latter jointly written with Michael Pickering.

Louis Niebur is Assistant Professor of Musicology at the University of Nevada, Reno (USA). His research primarily concerns avant-garde and popular music of the postwar era, focusing on musics that bridge the categories of high and low culture in society through media technology. He received his PhD in musicology from UCLA with a dissertation on the development of the BBC Radiophonic Workshop, one of the earliest electronic music studios, and his MM from the University of Texas at Austin.

Diana Sandars, PhD, has published on *Ally McBeal* and contributed to the academic journals *Australian Screen Education*, *Idiom*, *Metro*, *Refractory*, *Screening the Past* and *Sensesofcinema*. Her academic and personal passion for the film musical infiltrates the various courses she teaches in the Cinema Studies program at the University of Melbourne and her lectures at the Australian Centre for the Moving Image.

Katy Stevens is a doctoral candidate in Cinema Studies at La Trobe University, Melbourne, Australia. Her primary research theorizes corporeal/aural reception in the cinema, with particular interest in the digital soundtrack. She has taught for several years in Cinema and Television, and is currently coeditor of *Watcher Junior: The Undergraduate Journal of Buffy Studies*.

Rhonda V. Wilcox, PhD, is Professor of English at Gordon College, Barnesville, Georgia (USA). She is the editor of *Studies in Popular Culture*, a founding editor of *Critical Studies in Television*, and coeditor of *Slayage: The Online International Journal of Buffy Studies* (all peer-reviewed journals). She is the author of *Why Buffy Matters: The Art of Buffy the Vampire Slayer* (IB Tauris, 2005, a Mr Pointy Award winner) and coeditor of *Fighting the Forces: What's At Stake in Buffy the Vampire Slayer* (Rowman and Littlefield, 2002) and *Investigating Firefly and Serenity: Science Fiction on the Frontier* (IB Tauris, 2008). She is the co-convener of the biennial *Slayage* Conference.

Foreword

Keith Negus

Music has been integral to television programming since the first public broadcasts were transmitted from London in 1936 and in the New York metropolitan area during 1939. In those early days, with broadcasting hours limited and signals in need of constant retuning, television immediately provided a portal in the home from which emerged performing musicians, singers, and dancers. It also created a box full of opportunities for using music without the musicians visible. After the Second World War, as television became an integral part of domestic family life, the small screen facilitated the widespread appreciation of big band jazz, a new type of solo singer, country, r'n'b, rock'n'roll, and soul, to name the most obvious genres. The pop icons of the North Atlantic—from Little Richard to Madonna, from the Beatles to Beyoncé—have all made it in the marketplace in no small part due to the way television has delivered them into the homes of millions of people. At the same time television has increasingly incorporated pre-existing songs, instrumentals or commissions, integrating the music into interludes, theme tunes, drama, sport, news, documentary, and, in recent years, a wave of "reality" programs.

Despite the continual flow of music from the television set, for many years it was conspicuously absent in textbooks and research studies of television. Histories of twentieth-century music almost completely ignored television. Even histories of rock, which came to prominence with the aid of television, have told us surprisingly little about the importance of the small screen in the making, mediating, and enjoyment of the genre. When music has been mentioned it has usually been in passing, often to register a particularly controversial appearance by Elvis Presley, Jimi Hendrix, the Sex Pistols, Madonna, Public Enemy, or Björk. Little attention has been paid to those pop sounds transmitted without the musicians visible and integral to the rhetorics and representations in drama, soap, sport, and documentary. The test card and interludes that featured so much during the early years of television provided an opportunity for composers such as Eric Coates who have now been recognized for their contribution to light music. During the latter part of the twentieth century, a type of ambient light music—associated with artists such as Brian Eno, Moby, and Air—has featured extensively on television. It has been included to enhance or add sonic momentum to visually predictable programs featuring gardening, holidays, cooking, home makeovers, and so on. Not only has this music been easily incorporated, the sounds coming out of television have also influenced a number of genres of popular music—if you listen carefully you might catch clues and intimations of the influence of television in jazz and rock during the 1960s. You will certainly hear it in electronic dance music and, perhaps most explicitly, in much hip-hop that has been made since the 1980s and 1990s.

No doubt the respective holes in the histories of television and music have come about due to the disciplinary division of labor within the academy. While scholars of classical music ignored television, assuming it to be an insignificant and rather vulgar mass medium, the early pioneers in the study of popular music were concerned with the subcultures on the street rather than the kids on the sofa. Scholars of television were and, to a degree, still are preoccupied with talk and vision, assuming that the hard factual study of "information" is more valuable than the soft, slippery sounds of "entertainment"—even though many of our most profound insights into the world have come from the pleasures of popular art. This collection is not only one more book that challenges the spurious information-entertainment dichotomy, it should provoke mainstream scholars of television to think a bit more about the medium's musicality, and encourage those studying music (art and popular) to think about the way it has become well and truly interwoven with television. The book that follows signals a significant turning point—it is packed with the arguments of scholars who are uninhibited about exploring and speculating across the disciplinary boundaries that have kept music and television separate for so long.

More concretely, this book is important for the way it illuminates how the study of music on television can provide numerous insights into the significance of music as both a cultural form (connecting with subjects and collectivities, values and beliefs), and as a medium of communication (encoding and conveying meaning in quite specific ways). A study of sound in the moving-image media can provide insights into how music works as both a representational and a non-representational form of knowledge and human understanding. By representational I mean the way that music can refer to something other than itself, which we understand via our socially conditioned knowledge of semiotic codes and culturally mediated systems of meaning. Hence, we understand how music can be used as a means of emotional coding—letting us know how the characters are feeling; the sonic conventions that tell us that a character is angry, sad, falling in love, drugged, terrified, or plain bewildered. We grow up acquiring a knowledge of how music can convey cultural codes, often through the use of sonic clichés that enable us to recognize that the action is taking place in an imaginary Scotland, China, or medieval Europe, or the Bronx in the 1950s. Or the music lets us know that we are entering a science fiction story, a haunted house, a tale from the Wild West; or that we are about to hear the evening news. Even with eyes closed we might recognize the use of music to convey drama—the chase scene, the lone individual running down the street, the victim being stabbed in the shower. Music has brought us marching armies, chugging trains, ricocheting gunshots, and waves crashing down on the beach. The audiences for *Buffy the Vampire Slayer* know this, and so too do the directors and producers. As the authors in this collection highlight, a range of recognizable musical and visual codes have been cleverly integrated into the unfolding tale; the significations range from the frivolous to profound, and are at once ironic and highly mannered. The program exhibits a type of knowing intertextuality that seems to play with the very conventions of intertextuality as a device (a kind of post-postmodernism perhaps). *Buffy* has fun with a whole series of genre conventions whilst seeming to set itself the task of inventing its own genre (or transcending genre)—all the while taking advantage of the spectator's love of being manipulated by familiar musical codes; never really forgetting that, in the long run, art often grows out of fun (more often than not it is only furrowed brows and scratched chins that are produced by "Art").

Slightly less obvious, the subject of far less critical attention, and maybe more implied than explicitly engaged in this collection, is the way music communicates as a form of non-representational knowledge and understanding of our world. Here I am referring to a more sensual, an embodied, a less easily rationalized experience whereby human beings acquire knowledge of the world and their place in it through sounds, colors, gestures, and movement. Musically, this can be heard in the way certain pitches, timbres, textures (the tactile quality of sound), melodic patterns, and rhythms can forcibly and physiologically shape our perception of the world, even though they resist attempts to reduce them to easily identifiable cultural codes and social determinants. Silence, a feature of this book and the program, is perhaps one of the most profound representational and non-representational sounds in our lives. John Cage knew this, which is why his ideas still reverberate through popular culture and high art. A lot of state institutions, religions, and commercial corporations know this too, which is why silence is used in all manner of rituals in a way that has a tangible physiological impact on our being—whether it is devotional activity, the sombre appreciation of art in galleries and museums, or the pause for those very long two minutes during which we remember those who have died.

The two modalities—the representational and non-representational—work together. In *Buffy*, we may hear a certain kind of music and this may lead us to assume certain cultural codes; it may suggest a particular time and place, a type of person, a repertoire of significations. At the same time, the music may convey more embodied and sensual meaning through any number of parameters or characteristics—changing pitch, shifting timbres, slips between textures, rhythm, gesture, and movement. None of this is easy to identify and analyze according to scholarly methodologies, but it is recognized by or infiltrates the listener nonetheless. Sound has a material presence—and in *Buffy* that materiality allows us a certain visual and sonic experience of death, resurrection, or romance, one that is far more than simply semiotic or representational. The study of music in television, and the issues raised in the papers here, can contribute to an awareness of the quite profound ways that music gives expression to our lone and our shared worlds.

Any consideration of music in television must inevitably acknowledge the domestic contexts of reception and in doing so it will implicitly challenge some of the assumptions about sound-image relations that have been developed from the study of cinema. There has been a tendency in film studies—and as a result it has seeped into media and communication studies—to treat a film or a television drama as a self-contained narrative; a diegesis that develops and coheres within the screen action. Whilst this may be a quite plausible approach when it comes to understanding films originally made to be experienced in darkened cinemas, it is less convincing when it comes to television programs that are knowingly put together and transmitted to audiences who will be watching within groups of young people or families. This is something that Christine Geraghty highlighted many years ago in her study of soap opera—the diegesis of any soap unfolds as it enfolds the expectations and interpretations of the domestic audience into the development of the story. Television producers know that their public is not going to be sitting in the dark, giving the screen their more or less undivided attention, and they have developed a whole repertoire of subtle or explicit ways of addressing and holding the attention of their domestic audience (they also know how to let you know about something you might not have noticed when you were not paying attention). Just how a particular program or series addresses its audience is best explored through a case study like this rather than via a route into theoretical generalizations. To get at the details and dynamics of the domestic aesthetic of music and television requires a methodology that can do more than register how meaning is conveyed formally through sounds, words, and images; it must seek to embed these within the tangible habitats, encounters, and interpretative strategies through which people actively encounter the program and make it part of their social worlds. Cumulatively this book provides an open non-prescriptive way of doing this, linking text to context, bringing together formalism and hermeneutics.

Apart from all these general conceptual issues, scholarly dilemmas, and diversions, the book is important for the insight it provides into this very particular and idiosyncratic piece of television history. The program was clearly put together by a lot of creative people. It quickly caught the imagination of a young, intelligent, knowing, and self-reflexive audience (a very particular demographic that is also explored, or at least lurks on the sofa, throughout this book). And—maybe because of all this, and the obvious overlap in audience profile—it caught the imagination of academics. The contributors to this collection not only cross the boundaries that have separated the study of music and the moving image; they cross the lines, occasionally play with the codes, that have obliged scholars to separate themselves from the fans.

General Editor's Preface

The upheaval that occurred in musicology during the last two decades of the twentieth century has created a new urgency for the study of popular music alongside the development of new critical and theoretical models. A relativistic outlook has replaced the universal perspective of modernism (the international ambitions of the 12-note style); the grand narrative of the evolution and dissolution of tonality has been challenged, and emphasis has shifted to cultural context, reception and subject position. Together, these have conspired to eat away at the status of canonical composers and categories of high and low in music. A need has arisen, also, to recognize and address the emergence of crossovers, mixed and new genres, to engage in debates concerning the vexed problem of what constitutes authenticity in music and to offer a critique of musical practice as the product of free, individual expression.

Popular musicology is now a vital and exciting area of scholarship, and the *Ashgate Popular and Folk Music Series* presents some of the best research in the field. Authors are concerned with locating musical practices, values and meanings in cultural context, and draw upon methodologies and theories developed in cultural studies, semiotics, poststructuralism, psychology and sociology. The series focuses on popular musics of the twentieth and twenty-first centuries. It is designed to embrace the world's popular musics from Acid Jazz to Zydeco, whether high tech or low tech, commercial or non-commercial, contemporary or traditional.

Professor Derek B. Scott
Professor of Critical Musicology
University of Leeds

Preface

As an aspiring film director, Music Supervisor was a position I would never have considered while continuing to pay my dues as a post-production assistant on *Buffy the Vampire Slayer*. In fact, I had never heard of the position nor knew what it involved until I agreed to take it on. "Get paid for listening to music? Cool!" I thought. It was actually a bigger job than I'd realized.

I built a library of music consisting of independent artists, garage band demos, production library music, and a few big-name artists from my own personal collection. *Buffy* was a mid-season replacement with only 13 episodes ordered by the studio, which meant that our budgets were very small, particularly in the area of music licensing. At first many of the major record companies and publishers denied us use of their material. "Buffy and the Vampires, what?" or "they made a TV show of that movie?" was the typical reaction I would get. But by the end of the first season the buzz about the show was brewing, and the major labels and publishers were starting to see the licensing opportunities, as were the independent artists. The independents knew early on that we favored them over the difficult-to-deal-with majors and began to inundate my office with submissions.

Buffy also periodically required live bands to perform at Sunnydale's local teen hang, the Bronze. This put me into an A&R role where I scoured the local LA music scene, seeking out independent, unsigned bands that might fit into the fledgling "*Buffy* sound." Because Sunnydale was modeled after a small California town, and the Bronze was a small, local all-ages establishment, one would probably not see mega-popular bands, like REM or U2 performing there. Lack of major label permission and budget constraints aside, this became the rationale for discovering more independent artists and, as luck would have it, seemed to work in favor of the show creatively. This added a sense of realism and authenticity to the imaginary *Buffy* universe and became a staple for the show. It also gave those unknown artists an opportunity to become known as the TV audience experienced music they would probably never have been exposed to otherwise.

Eventually, as the show grew in popularity, so did the budgets, and I began to license more popular artists but still kept my focus mainly on those who were still below the radar, or who were on the brink of rising above it, for the Bronze performances, such as up-and-coming artist Michelle Branch, who had performed at the Bronze just months before she hit it big. The only acts which were already hugely popular in their own right before appearing on *Buffy* were Aimee Mann and the Breeders.

Buffy was one of those rare TV shows that had its own instinctual sense of contemporary cool, and lent itself to the creative use of pop songs to help tell the stories. This seemed to occur organically, not relying on them to convince the audience that it was something that it wasn't, or to try to appeal to a certain demographic against its own sensibilities. Simply by the nature of the show and the universal themes it explored, *Buffy* reached audiences of all ages, genders, and backgrounds, and that audience found a deep connection to the music through the experiences of the multidimensional characters they had invested in so heavily.

A new tool called the "Ad card" was introduced by record labels early on and continues to be used by TV shows today. Ad cards are brief, ten-second commercial tags at the end of an episode used as a way to inform the viewer who the artists heard on the show that night were and what the CD cover looks like. Thus, if a viewer liked a particular song, he or she could then go out and purchase that CD. *Buffy* used the ad card thing only two or three times. We stopped mostly because it cut into the show's airtime and tended to diminish the dramatic endings or cliff-hangers that the show would often end on. Since we weren't in the business of selling records, it was more of a priority to keep the dramatic integrity of the show intact rather than to save a few bucks on licensing fees. It separated *Buffy* from the rest, and I think for the most part the audience appreciated that. Even without the ad cards, hardcore fans connected to the music and still found out who the artists were on their own. In fact, there are several websites out there solely dedicated to the music and the artists heard or seen on *Buffy the Vampire Slayer*. These websites actually stirred up enough musical buzz amongst the fans that it inspired two soundtrack CDs (three if you want to get technical), *Buffy the Vampire Slayer: The Album*, and two versions of *Radio Sunnydale*: the US version, and the international version which had nine more songs and was—in my opinion—the better version.

For me *Buffy* was one of the most challenging, educational, and rewarding experiences I've had professionally as a music supervisor. I have not worked on a show since that has encompassed the creative musical sensibility and excitement surrounding the music that *Buffy* had. It truly was a one-of-a-kind show and I'm thankful to have been a part of it.

John C. King

*Buffy the Vampire Sla*yer was a composer's dream. The show itself is very cinematic. Each episode is like a self-contained feature film, with big themes: tragically doomed romance, apocalyptic battles between good and evil, life, death, fate, destiny. Big themes allow for big music. And for a film composer, big music can be flat-out fun to write. The palette was huge. I drew on the long traditions of symphonic film and concert music, as well as more contemporary ideas and experimental sound design. The serial nature of the show allowed for very long-term thematic development: musical seeds planted in one episode could bear fruit in a subsequent episode, or even a subsequent season. This, combined with a visionary writer and executive producer—Joss Whedon—made for an incredibly satisfying sandbox in which to play.

That said, if the show's ideas were big, the resources to produce the score were small. This is the modern television composer's daily lament: not enough time, and—in the case of *Buffy* as well as most other television dramas—no budget for a real orchestra. I often spent as much time polishing the performances of my "fake" orchestra as I did composing.

I wish I could claim that the thematic development in the series was the result of some grand, well-thought-out architecture. On a TV schedule and budget, however, thoughts of grand thematic architectures soon give way to by-the-seat-of-my-pants scrambling. Television composers have the complicated task of producing volumes of music on ridiculous deadlines; reconciling these two opposing situations is our main job. Sometimes, it's just a bit of luck that brings some structure to the musical chaos.

For example, the best known musical theme in the series—the Buffy-Angel love theme—was written for an episode called "Surprise" (2.13), halfway through season 2. The Buffy-Angel love story had been in play since season 1. Since then, a total of three different composers (or teams of composers) had scored the episodes, and no theme had yet been established for the couple. It was almost by accident that the "Surprise" theme ended up being the one that stuck. It was composed in an hour, but developed over the course of the rest of the entire series—and even entirely different shows, too (it was used occasionally in *Angel*). If I had known that that would be the one, I probably would have spent more time on it! But once it became clear that it would stick, I began to relish the opportunity to use it, and did so at every opportunity.

In all honesty, the last thing I'm thinking about when scoring an episode is what a musicologist might think. In fact, if I stopped to think about it, I'd probably be scared or embarrassed, since I'm usually charging ahead without much looking back, in order to make a deadline. So I am incredibly flattered that other musicians and musicologists would find my work worthy of any kind of study (as well as the work of Walter Murphy, Shawn Clement, Sean Murray, Thomas Wanker, Doug Stevens, Rob Duncan, Robert Kral, and others who created the scores for *Buffy* and *Angel* over the course of their production).

I would also like to add that, with regard to music, the show was lucky enough to have Joss at its helm. He is very conscious of music and how it is used, and he's always trying to find new and different ways to implement it into a show. Looking at the way music is used in episodes like "Hush," "Once More, With Feeling" and "The Body" (in which there was no music at all), Joss's commitment to creativity in all aspects of the show is more than clear. It is obviously a pleasure for a composer to work with someone so in tune with musical ideas.

I hope you enjoy this book as much as I enjoyed working on the show.

Christophe Beck

Acknowledgements

The editors would like to thank the colleagues, friends, and members of the *Buffy* community who have assisted in the preparation of this manuscript, in particular Ann Davies, Ian Davis, Johann Hasler, Bennett Hogg, David Lavery, David Lawtie, Leslie Remencus, and Robynn Stilwell. We would also like to thank Heidi Bishop, Rosie Phillips, and the editorial staff at Ashgate for their assistance and advice, and all the contributors to this volume, who have worked so hard and waited so patiently to see the project come to fruition.

A version of Chapter 1 in this volume originally appeared as "Love, Death, Curses and Reverses (in F minor): Music, Gender and Identity in *Buffy the Vampire Slayer* and *Angel*" in *Slayage: the online international journal of Buffy Studies* 4 (2001), available at http://www.slayageonline.com.

Material in Chapter 11 first appeared in Rhonda V. Wilcox, *Why Buffy Matters: The Art of Buffy the Vampire Slayer* (London: IB Tauris, 2005). Reproduced by permission.

Introduction

"Bay City Rollers. Now That's Music": Music as Cultural Code in *Buffy the Vampire Slayer*[1]

Vanessa Knights

To situate the title of this chapter for readers not familiar with the show, in "The Dark Age" (2.8), Buffy is asking Giles—her mentor, or "Watcher"—how his girlfriend, Jenny, is coping after being possessed by a demon who pursued him to presentday Sunnydale from his youthful hell-raising days, both literal and metaphorical:

> [underscore enters under dialogue as Jenny walks away]
> Buffy: Is she okay?
> Giles: Um … The hills are not alive.
> Buffy: I'm sorry to hear that. I think.
> Giles: I don't think she'll ever really forgive me. Maybe she shouldn't.
> Buffy: Maybe you should.
> Giles: I never wanted you to see that side of me.
> Buffy: I'm not gonna lie to you. It was scary. I'm so used to you being a grownup, and then I find out that you're a person.
> Giles: Most grownups are.
> Buffy: Who would've thought?
> Giles: Some are even, uh … shortsighted, foolish people.
> Buffy: So, after all this time, we finally find out that we do have something in common. Which, apart from being a little weird, is kind of okay. [underscore tails off] I think we're supposed to be training right now.
> Giles: Yes. Yes. Um, need to concentrate on your flexibility.
> Buffy: And you know what? I have just the perfect music. Go on, say it. You know you want to.
> Giles: It's not music, it's just, uh, meaningless sounds.
> Buffy: There. Feel better?

---

[1] Most of this introduction was first delivered as "'Bay City Rollers. Now That's Music': Coolness, Crassness and Characterisation on *Buffy the Vampire Slayer*," at the Sonic Synergies: Creative Cultures Conference, University of South Australia, The Hawke Research Institute and IASPM Australia/New Zealand, 17–20 July 2003.

> Giles: Yes. Thanks. Bay City Rollers. Now, that's music.
> Buffy: I didn't hear that.

Music is clearly integral to this excerpt. In response to Buffy's enquiry, Giles picks up on an intertextual reference earlier in the episode by Jenny to the feel-good musical *The Sound of Music* (1965), which she employs as a signifier of happiness and zest for life.[2] The revelation that Giles is not the perfect father figure and has more in common with his teenage charge than might be apparent is poignantly underscored as might be expected for a moment of particular emotional resonance. This stops abruptly as they switch to discussing training, again in terms of music. Whilst their interchange may at first seem to simply signify a generational gap—Buffy gets dance music, Giles is rooted in the 1970s—as the series progresses we learn that they are again not as different as they might seem. In this particular instance, Buffy is appreciating a type of music for its function. As she earlier claims, she requires a beat to aerobicize. Giles is judging it by quite different parameters; he dismisses it for aesthetic reasons, having earlier described it as noise, exclaiming: "I know music. Music has notes." Yet Giles is not the tweedy stuff-shirt he is made to seem here. His musical tastes are admired by the musician (Oz) in the core group of friends who is impressed by his cool vinyl collection. In "The Harsh Light of Day" (4.3), as Oz flicks through the records, Giles admonishes him that there are more important things in life presumably such as combating vampires. However, he is silenced and forced to recognize the importance of music when Oz holds up the album *Loaded* by highly influential The Velvet Underground. We also hear Giles play tracks by Cream ("Tales of Brave Ulysses") and David Bowie ("Memory of a Free Festival").[3] He is later revealed to be an accomplished guitarist and singer in seasons 4 and 5, when we see him performing songs by Lynyrd Skynyrd ("Freebird") and the Who ("Behind Blue Eyes"). He is most clearly coded as belonging to a rebellious 1960s-70s counterculture which could be said to correspond thirty years later to the indie youth culture comprising the majority of the bands Buffy and her friends listen to. This very brief extract serves to demonstrate how popular music, in

---

[2] In the season 3 episode "Beauty and the Beasts" (3.3), Buffy picks up on this reference once more but this time to signify the vivid nature of a dream which she describes as "Three-dimensional, sensurround, the hills are alive…".

[3] His coolness is contrasted to Buffy's mother Joyce who, when she regresses to being a teenager in "Band Candy" (3.6), is a fan of Seals & Croft, Juice Newton, and Burt Reynolds. Giles dreams of putting a band together whilst she muses about watching pay-per-view TV or going to the Bronze. We later discover that he had claimed to be one of the original members of legendary progressive/psychedelic rock band Pink Floyd when he was younger (in "Hush," 4.10). Joyce, whilst eventually supportive of Buffy, is never a core member of the Scoobies (her support network of friends) and is clearly coded as a separate adult figure, as opposed to Giles, who crosses the boundary between adult parental figure and member of the gang.

this case as intertextual reference and diegetic music integral to the scene, along with score function to drive the narrative, nuance characterization and provoke an emotional response.

Surprisingly, given the amount of space devoted to it in interviews and features on *Buffy the Vampire Slayer* (1997–2003) in the SciFi/fantasy/cult television specialist press and the release of four tie-in CDs, relatively little attention has been paid in academic writing to the use of music in the show. With the exception of S. Renee Dechert's "'My Boyfriend's in the Band!' *Buffy* and the Rhetoric of Music,"[4] articles are on the whole limited to online publications such as Jamie Clarke's 2003 article on affective entertainment in *Refractory*,[5] which analyzes the pleasures of consumption, risk, and fandom with particular reference to the musical episode "Once More with Feeling" (6.7), and a number of articles which have appeared in the peer-reviewed online journal for *Buffy* studies, *Slayage*.[6] These include Janet K. Halfyard's analysis of gender and the construction of identity in the theme tunes of *Buffy* and its spin-off show *Angel* in *Slayage*, 4 (2001), which is further developed in this collection; and her essay on performance, sincerity, and musical diegesis in the two shows, published in *Slayage*, 17 (2005), an issue also containing articles by Richard S. Albright on genre in "Once More with Feeling," and Jeffrey Middents on race in the American musical, also in relation to this episode.[7]

Most of the fansites devoted to music, such as Leslie Remencus's now sadly defunct *Buffy and Angel Music Pages* (1997–2003), focus primarily on the songs featured on the show.[8] Although the sites do not always agree, the various compilers have between them provided a wealth of information about music used in the series, and have in turn formed the basis of the comprehensive guide to the

---

[4] S. Renee Dechert, "'My Boyfriend's in the Band!': *Buffy* and the Rhetoric of Music," in Rhonda V. Wilcox and David Lavery (eds), *Fighting the Forces: What's at Stake in Buffy the Vampire Slayer* (Lanham, MD, 2002), pp. 218–26.

[5] Jamie Clarke, "Affective Entertainment in 'Once More with Feeling': A Manifesto for Fandom," *Refractory*, 2 (2003), accessed 12 August 2008 at http://blogs.arts.unimelb.edu.au/refractory/2003/03/18/affective-entertainment-in-once-more-with-feeling-a-manifesto-for-fandom-jamie-clarke.

[6] *Slayage: The Online International Journal of Buffy Studies* (2001–) is available at www.slayageonline.com.

[7] The bibliography of this volume contains full details of papers discussing music in the series.

[8] That is not to say that these websites do not include information on the composers who score episodes. There are also sites dedicated to individual composers such as Robert Duncan's webpage (www.duncanmusic.com), Kevin Manthei's webpage (www.kmmproductions.com), and the Blunt Instrument site dedicated to Christophe Beck (run by Ian Davis) (www.bluntinstrument.org.uk/beck/index.htm), which has an informative page about other composers who have worked on *Buffy*.

show's music that we have composed for the online *Encyclopedia of Buffy Studies*.[9] Similarly, Dechert's essay focuses on this area: she highlights the way popular music confirms the indie aesthetics and credibility of the show and its location on the fringe of the mainstream whilst contributing to the identification between fans and the program.[10] It also provides a thematic backdrop and contributes to characterization. Apart from the considerable discussion of "Once More, with Feeling," relatively little attention has otherwise been paid to the music itself outside Halfyard's 2001 essay, and Neil Lerner's conference papers on thematic scoring in *Buffy*.[11] This should perhaps come as no surprise as, in contrast to the increasing volume of writing on music in film, there is relatively little available on the role of music in television and what exists tends to look, as Dechert's essay does, at the way popular music is used. Meanwhile, as Keith Negus and John Street note in their introduction to the special edition of *Popular Music*[12] on music and television, television has on the whole been conspicuously absent from studies of popular music and vice versa.[13] This is despite, as Tagg has noted, music's almost ubiquitous presence on the small screen.[14] They note that much is to be said about music in soap opera and drama, not just what is used and how but also the processes of sound selection and the imperatives the music has to meet—for example regaining the viewers' attention after an ad break.[15]

The process of sound selection on *Buffy* is slightly different from that of many teen-oriented shows, and is explored in depth here by Kathryn Hill in chapter 10. In his preface to this volume, John King, post-production assistant on seasons 1–3 and music coordinator/supervisor from season 4 onwards, emphasizes that the show did not simply "needle-drop" hits. Tracks featured were chosen for their ability to enhance a scene, their emotional ties to what is occurring and their match

---

[9] The *Encyclopedia of Buffy Studies* is hosted by *Slayage*. The music section is available at www.slayageonline.com/EBS/tables_of_contents/type/music.htm. Originally edited by Vanessa Knights, it is now maintained by Janet K. Halfyard.

[10] Dechert, "My Boyfriend's in the Band!", p. 219.

[11] Neil Lerner, "Christophe Beck and Buffy's First Romances: Paradoxes of Musical Scoring in *Buffy the Vampire Slayer*," paper presented at *Slayage* conference on the Buffyverse, Middle Tennessee State University, Nashville, Tennessee, 28–30 May 2004; and "The Buffy-Riley Leitmotif and Musical Evidence for the Romantic Conflation of Angel and Riley," paper presented at SC3: *Slayage* conference on the Whedonverse, Henderson State University, Arkadelphia, 5–8 June 2008.

[12] Keith Negus and John Street, "Introduction to 'Music and Television' special issue," *Popular Music*, 21/3 (2002), pp. 245–8.

[13] Ibid., p. 245.

[14] Philip Tagg, "Music Analysis for 'Non-Musos': Popular Perception as a Basis for Understanding Musical Structure and Signification," paper presented at the Conference on Popular Music Analysis, University of Cardiff, Cardiff, 17 November 2001, accessed 18 August 2008 at www.tagg.org/articles/cardiff01.html.

[15] Negus and Street, "Introduction," p. 248.

with particular characters. In other words, they were not just chosen on the basis of lyrics: subtext and vibe were also important.[16] Furthermore, King and Whedon have a preference for unsigned bands. Apart from being cheaper than licensing tracks (from song-sourcers or libraries of ready-made temp tracks and back catalogues from production companies), there is also an ethos of giving exposure to marginal groups which fits in with Dechert's argument about the indie aesthetics of the show and its location on the cult fringe of the mainstream.[17]

In studies of television music, *Miami Vice* (1984–89) is frequently cited as setting a precedent for the use of contemporary pop in conjunction with stylish visuals.[18] In contrast to John Fiske's assertion that the use of top 20 songs interrupts the narrative and rarely advances understanding of character, plot, or setting,[19] Robynn Stilwell persuasively argues the opposite with examples of pop music contributing to the diegesis of the show, setting mood and providing intertextual resonance (1996).[20] *Ally McBeal* (1997–2002) has also been analyzed for the use of pop music to reinforce its iconic and social status.[21] In *Buffy* both dramatic scoring and source music (music produced within the implied world of the show) contribute to the diegesis, mood and setting of the show.[22] Source music would include all the music we hear being played at the Bronze club where Buffy and her friends hang out, or the records and CDs characters listen to. It rarely matches cues although it may respond to events. For example, bands at the Bronze routinely break their performances when vampires attack (Jonathan's swing band stops its performance in "Superstar" (4.17) when Karen rushes in after being attacked). In other words, groups which appear at the Bronze are not simply the band of the week chosen for commercial reasons, in contrast to bands appearing in the club P3 at the end of most episodes of the Warner Bros series *Charmed* (1998–2006). Another clear example is the closing of "Tabula Rasa" (6.8), where Michelle Branch is on stage at the Bronze performing "Goodbye to You"—which is source

---

[16] Dechert, "My Boyfriend's in the Band!", p. 219.

[17] Furthermore, the placement of the core characters at the margins, or their outsider status, confers them with more power to deal with evil than had they remained at the center (ibid., p. 218).

[18] Julie Brown, "*Ally McBeal*'s Postmodern Soundtrack," *Journal of the Royal Musical Association*, 126 (2001), pp. 275–303; K.J. Donnelly, "Tracking British Television: Pop Music as Stock Soundtrack to the Small Screen," *Popular Music*, 21/3 (2002), pp. 331–43; Robynn Stilwell, "In the Air Tonight: Text, Intertextuality and the Construction of Meaning," *Popular Music and Society*, 19/4 (1995), pp. 67–103.

[19] John Fiske, *Television Culture* (London, 1987), p. 255.

[20] Stilwell, "In the Air Tonight."

[21] Brown, "*Ally McBeal*'s Postmodern Soundtrack"; Donnelly, "Tracking British Television," p. 333.

[22] In the case of the episode "I Only Have Eyes for You" (2.19), the plot is actually driven by the Flamingos' track which lends its title to the episode (see Dechert, "My Boyfriend's in the Band!", p. 220).

music for Buffy and Spike, who are at the club.[23] However, the music actually starts when Buffy and Spike are still outside and continues over a set of jump cuts and dissolves, where we also see Tara, Willow, and Dawn at the Summers's home, and Giles on a plane to England. The song is therefore also functioning as scoring, matching the emotional nuances of the scenes but also the narrative in its lyrics, Branch acting as an almost extra-diegetic narrator or Greek chorus, commenting on the events unfolding and guiding the audience's emotional response. All of the characters are upset and either leaving or saying goodbye, whether it is to relationships or the past that they knew. Music here is working in conjunction with the camerawork as dissolves and camera angles help to clearly identify the characters with one another, and the atmospheric blue lighting of Branch on stage intensifies the melancholic mood. As Stilwell argues for the use of song in *Miami Vice*, "the unspecific in the song is realized by connection to specific characters and situations."[24] The segment is similar to the MTV-style playouts of *Ally McBeal* episodes analyzed by Julie Brown in that images without dialogue succeed each other to draw together various story lines with remarkable economy. The disembodied voice of Branch attaches itself to the different characters we see, switching "I-you" subject position according to the visuals. As Rob Cover discusses in chapter 8 of this volume, this type of use of popular music extends into intermedial uses when fans begin creating their own music videos, drawing on music from the series and also drawing other music as commentary into the Buffyverse through their own songfics and filk-sings.

Even more closely tied to narrative function are the songs which were composed specifically for the show. In the season 4 finale "Restless" (4.22), Giles sings the rock-opera-style "Exposition Song" backed by Four Star Mary on drums, guitar, and bass, with the composer Christophe Beck on piano. Giles is performing his usual role of explaining the supernatural events but this time through the medium of song, foreshadowing the musical episode in season 6, in a performance that also provided the opportunity for the usually invisible band and composer to be made visible in a knowing nod to fans. Finally, although this event takes place within a private dream space it also signifies a turning point for Giles. Whereas he has previously been identified as lacking in confidence and has confined himself to playing his guitar at home, he will move out into the public space of the Espresso Pump, to the shock of the younger characters, in season 5.

The soundtrack to *Buffy* does not, however, just consist of pop songs. Indeed, the quality of the scoring by composers such as Christophe Beck has been noted as enhancing the often filmic quality of the show as opposed to the use of stock music in most television, particularly the standardized repeated cues often found

---

[23] This song also featured in the centennial episode of *Charmed*, in which one of the sisters (Paige) is whisked into a parallel universe. Whilst the song does not match the visuals, it could be seen to be related to the main theme of the episode in which Phoebe is finally rid of her ex-husband Cole.

[24] Stilwell, "In the Air Tonight."

in generic television.²⁵ Beck estimates that each episode may have 19–20 minutes of scoring.²⁶ In particular, action, comedic moments, and moments necessitating a particular emotional range are often scored, and this latter area is discussed by Arnie Cox and Rebecca Fülöp in their chapter here on the emotional affect of scoring in *Buffy*. There are three key innovative episodes in this respect, all written and directed by the show's creator Joss Whedon, and several chapters in this collection focus on these including those by Paul Attinello, Amy Bauer, Gerry Bloustien, Katy Stevens, and Diana Sandars and Rhonda Wilcox. "Hush" (4.10), scored by Christophe Beck and featuring *Danse Macabre* by Camille Saint-Saëns, is notable for 25 minutes without dialogue; "The Body" (5.16) starkly lacks any music and the sonic landscape is therefore focused on aspects of sound design, most conspicuously the use of ambient silence; and "Once More, with Feeling" otherwise known as "*Buffy* the Musical" takes the series into new musical territory altogether.

Many writers about music have historically contended that it is non-representational or non-referential. Although this view increasingly has less currency in musicological discourse, it has never been a credible position to take in relation to film and television music, where production music libraries clearly exist indexed by categories such as mood, geography, period, genre, structural function, and action. Clearly there is some sort of communicative system at work here dependent on cultural associations with particular musical signifiers. The empirical research done by Philip Tagg and Bob Clarida on listeners' responses to title themes from film and television indicates a certain degree of consistency between encoding and decoding.²⁷ The scoring of *Buffy* both uses and plays ironically with these conventions: for example, in the teaser for "Flooded" (6.4), the audience is falsely cued by Thomas Wanker's score and the camera work to expect the monster of the week. We are in a darkly lit place, a basement reminiscent of *A Nightmare on Elm Street*. We hear the dramatic scoring of low, atonal strings with no discernible rhythm, typical of a horror build-up. There is a low rumbling sound which is possibly diegetic or part of the horror-coded score. We then hear a drip … and this is, in fact, the villain of the week: Buffy's domestic problems, a leaking pipe, highlighted by the comic reveal of Buffy saying "So, we meet at last, Mister Drippy" as the pan discloses the stairs up to the rest of the Summers's house. Conventional musical coding from film and audience expectation are used to comic effect.

---

[25] See Donnelly on *Star Trek* and *Dr Who* in "Tracking British Television," pp. 334–5. Beck won an Emmy for Best Dramatic Score for "Becoming, Part 1" (2.21).

[26] Nancy Holder, with Jeff Mariotte and Maryelizabeth Hart, *The Watcher's Guide* (New York, 2000), vol. 2, p. 434.

[27] Philip Tagg, "An Anthropology of Stereotypes in TV Music?", *Swedish Musicological Journal* (1989), pp. 19–42, accessed 12 August 2008 at http://tagg.org/articles/xpdfs/tvanthro.pdf.

According to Dechert, one of the primary functions of music on the show is to establish character identity.[28] Characters are coded by the music they listen to and sing.[29] The matching of different styles of music to particular characters and the role of music in reinforcing a communal identity between characters, the show, and fans bring up a series of key questions about the construction of identity, meaning in music, and popular aesthetics which are the central issues examined from different perspectives in Catherine Driscoll's and Kathryn Hill's chapters. Which kind of music is preferred by the show and why? How does the audience identify with the characters through their musical tastes? All of the characters comprising the main Scooby gang (Buffy and her core support group) are coded as having "cool" musical tastes regardless of generational differences. The music they prefer could be described as belonging in the margins of youth culture or within particular sub- or countercultures which have evolved since the 1960s. Weinstein notes the rhizomatic nature of youth culture is such that, although it is co-opted by consumer culture, new shoots constantly emerge.[30] So, Giles is located in 1960s' and 1970s' youth counterculture; Spike (despite his Victorian origins as a middle-class poet) is clearly identified with an amoral, disaffected violent punk-rock aesthetic through his love of the Sex Pistols and the Ramones, and his quoting from songs by the Clash ("Rock the Casbah" in "The 'I' in Team," 4.13) and Alice Cooper ("School's Out" in "Chosen," 7.22). All of the younger Scoobies are identified with the indie bands that play at the Bronze and campus parties. They are deliberately positioned outside the mainstream of pop, which is coded as crass. Buffy's friends are shocked when Spike reveals she wanted "Wind Beneath my Wings" as their first dance in "Something Blue" (4.9), and she has to explain it away as the influence of the spell.

Meanwhile, Kathy Newman's penchant for Cher, Celine Dion and other "VH1 divas" in "Living Conditions" (4.2) signifies that she does not fit in with the Scoobies. The Viacom music channel VH1 prior to 2001 explicitly targeted an older demographic than MTV, aiming its brand at 25–49-year-olds.[31] Whilst appearing to be a typical co-ed, Kathy is in truth a dimension-hopping Mok'tagar

---

[28] Dechert, "My Boyfriend's in the Band!" p. 219.

[29] Xander's fantasies in "Teacher's Pet" (1.4) convert him into a phallically empowered, Hendrix-like rock-god. In reality he is a virgin teenager drooling in class and has to be rescued later in the episode by Buffy. Cordelia in "The Puppet Show" (1.9) reveals her self-obsessed nature through her choice of the song "The Greatest Love of All" (for herself) for the talent show. The song later ironically reoccurs in an intertextual nod for fans of both shows when she is an amnesiac in season 4 of *Angel* and sings it to try to recall who she is (see Halfyard, "Singing Their Hearts Out," 30–31).

[30] Deena Weinstein, "Youth," in Bruce Horner and Thomas Swiss (eds), *Key Terms in Popular Music and Culture* (Oxford, 1999), p. 110.

[31] Norma Coates, "Music Television or Television Music? Pop Music on American Television as the Implementation of Contemporary Business Trends and Strategies," paper presented at the 12th Conference of IASPM, McGill University, Montreal, 3–7 July 2003.

demon and some three thousand years old (although this is young for her species). Her repeated playing of "Believe" by Cher tortures Buffy through incessant repetition, although it is also possible to see in the lyrics an echo of Buffy's loss of Angel at the end of season 3 and her apparent lack of strength as season 4 begins. By saying that she and Buffy, in contrast to Kathy, put the "grrr" in girl, Willow not only references their empowerment and strength in demon hunting but, as Renée Coulombe discusses in this volume, she also references the Riot Grrrl bands featured elsewhere on the show, who are often held up as an indication of its feminist ideology as well as further evidence of its indie aesthetics.

Character is also set up through the use of leitmotif in the score, which is the focus of Rob Haskins' essay. These feature particularly heavily in relation to the melodramatic aspect of Buffy's love relationships, such as Christophe Beck's Buffy-Angel love theme in season 2, the Buffy-Riley theme (season 4) and Spike's theme (season 6). However, leitmotifs are not restricted to score. The Four Star Mary track "Pain" occurs in three different episodes. It first occurs in "Bewitched, Bothered and Bewildered" (2.16), where it ironically indicates Willow's joy at having a boyfriend in the band playing the Valentine's Day Dance at the Bronze (her exclamation is the source of Dechert's title). This contrasts directly with Xander's pain at being dumped by Cordelia, Cordelia's pain at his betrayal and her ostracism by the popular set, and Buffy's pain as her boyfriend Angel turns evil. In "Deadman's Party" (3.2), Buffy's pain and estrangement from her friends is central to the episode and, as Whedon has noted, the show is more interesting when Buffy is in pain.[32] Indeed, pain seems to be a central trope in the show, particularly the pain of growing up and learning who you are. Finally, in "Living Conditions" it signifies the Scoobies' difference from the demonic Kathy as her Celine Dion poster is replaced by a Dingoes Ate My Baby poster, but at the same time indicates that again, as a season opens, Buffy is alienated from the world around her. Having lost the love of her life at the end of the previous season, she is finding the adjustment from high school to college hard to make. In contrast, Xander's pain at being rejected by Buffy in the season 1 finale "Prophecy Girl" (1.22) is ironically played down by his over-indulgence in what he describes as the "music of pain" as he repeatedly listens to "I Fall to Pieces" by Patsy Cline.

Intratextual allusions and quotations also help set up character: for example, an invisible Buffy whistles "Going through the Motions" from "Once More with Feeling" as she leaves the social worker's office in "Gone" (6.11). Indeed, since she came back from the dead she seems to be going through the motions, lacking in feeling and regard for others, as Spike points out to her. Allusions can also have a clear narrative function. The "Buffy-Angel" theme cues alert listeners that he has called Buffy from Los Angeles in "Anne" (3.1) when she answers the phone but gets no reply; and after Joyce's funeral in "Forever" (5.17), Giles listens to "Brave Ulysses," which he had previously listened to with her in "Band Candy"

---

[32] FilmForce, "An Interview with Joss Whedon," *IGN.com*, 23 June 2003, accessed 17 July 2003 at http://filmforce.ign.com/articles/425/425492p1.html, p. 8.

(3.6). These intratextual allusions are all very specific to the musical history of the series, but musical allusion works at a wider intertextual level through the score's references to filmic musical genres. This also contributes significantly to our understanding of narrative and characters, which is the focus of Louis Niebur's essay in this volume.

An intertextual borrowing from outside the series is used to set up Jonathan's alter-ego in "Superstar" (4.17). In the teaser (and altered opening credits) he is visually and musically coded as one of his idols, James Bond, through the retro-sounding "spy chord"[33] and brass stab. His image of suave sophistication is identified with the actor we later discover to be his favorite Bond, Roger Moore, and he is also ironically figured visually as Angel in the altered credits for this episode, wearing the long duster coat identified with the final shot of the *Angel* credits. However, the teaser also functions to tell us that all is not right in this world through the generic horror strings and overhead shot as the Scoobies approach his desk, and Jonathan swings round in a manner more reminiscent of the baddie Blofeld than Bond. Here the sound and image work in counterpoint to each other for an audience informed by the popular cultural references of generic horror and Bond films. His polished Sinatra-style performance as a swing singer later in the episode also signifies his artificially enhanced condition, further emphasized by the fact that actor Danny Strong is lip-synching singer Brad Kane of Royal Crown Revue. Indeed, as well as the close identifications between off-center youth culture and the main characters, music is often used ironically or parodically to indicate changed character. When Xander has been magically converted into the object of every woman's desire in "Bewitched, Bothered and Bewildered," he strides through the school corridor to the Average White Band's "Got the Love" in a slow-motion sequence reminiscent of John Travolta's strut in *Saturday Night Fever* (1977).[34] Of course, without the spell Xander is no sex symbol and, despite the lyrics "Got the love/Got to make it work on you/Got the love/Just can't keep it hid," the one person the spell has not worked on is the girl it was cast for, Cordelia.

Intertextual musical and pop culture references abound throughout the show. Music references range from opera (Puccini), through English folksong ("Early One Morning"), World War I soldiers' anthems ("It's a long way to Tipperary"), dialogue references to musicals (*Porgy and Bess*, *The Sound of Music*), musical films (*The Wizard of Oz*, *Mary Poppins*, *Song of the South*), and references to pop from the 1950s on. Understanding these requires a particular cultural capital from the *Buffy* fan community. This capital circulates outside the text through internet sites, chatrooms and boards, printed texts, and communities who meet both virtually and physically to engage with the show. The intensity of their exchanges indicates how much music matters and the pleasure derived from the engagement with meanings experienced and shared.

---

[33] Tagg, "Music Analysis for 'Non-Musos'."
[34] Dechert, "My Boyfriend's in the Band!", p. 220.

Giles's reference to the Bay City Rollers which opened my introduction, whilst apparently setting him up as "uncool" for a teen viewer, may have the opposite effect for late twenty-somethings who caught the Rollers's revival tour in the early 1990s, or nostalgic thirty- and forty-somethings who were fans first time round of the 1970s teen pop idols. The meanings produced by music and references to it depend on the identification processes between the music and audience which will involve their social and cultural contexts, their personal histories bound up with particular memories and emotions, as well as receptional competences—that is, "the ability to recall, recognize and distinguish between musical sounds as well as between culturally specific connotations and social functions."[35] An example of multiple meanings ascribed to one piece of music would be the aforementioned use of Camille Saint-Saëns's *Danse Macabre* in "Hush." The connotations of death and macabre humor may be evident to those familiar with the piece or the musical conventions it employs. To British audiences it may be more familiar as the theme tune to the unusual mystery series *Jonathan Creek* (1997–2004) with its connotations of magic and the supernatural as mysteries to be solved by a male-female duo (in this case Buffy and Riley). Fans of both shows may appreciate the insider knowledge that Anthony Stewart Head, who is playing the music to accompany his exposition of the problem, appeared in *Jonathan Creek* in 1997 as the magician Adam Klaus.[36]

The essays that follow in this collection will further elucidate the pivotal role of music in Whedon's Buffyverse through an in-depth analysis of the work of the composers, lyricists, musicians, music executives, and producers involved, and the audience reaction to music, sound, and its absence. The three sections organize this material into three broad categories of musical activity and engagement in television in general and in *Buffy* in particular. Part I focuses largely on the composed music and sound design of the show and the way this is involved in the production meaning within the *Buffy* text through mechanisms of psychological and emotional affect, and various types of cultural musical and sonic codes. Part II focuses on popular music, both that used within the show and the musical fan communities that surround it, examining ways in which music is used to identify, position, and explore characters and narratives, and also the way viewers have used music to extend the Buffyverse for themselves as fans. Part III then looks exclusively at "Once More, with Feeling." This is the musical area of *Buffy* that has been most discussed in existing literature already, but the three essays here offer three distinct perspectives, presenting a musical analysis in Amy Bauer's essay, which illustrates how the musical structure of the songs supports narrative interpretations; Diana Sandars and Rhonda Wilcox's examination of its problematic

---

[35] Tagg, "Music Analysis for 'Non-Musos'."

[36] The show revels in extratextual in jokes for the informed viewer. For example, when Buffy refers to the "Time Warp" in "Band Candy" to conjure up wacky party dancing as well as a slip in time, fans of Anthony Stewart Head will also be reminded of his acclaimed stint as Dr Frank-N-Furter in the 1990 London revival of *The Rocky Horror Show*.

relationship to the utopian Hollywood film music in essay; and Paul Attinello's concluding expansion of the field of enquiry to other televisual experiments with musicals.

The essays here do not in any way attempt to have the last word on music in the Buffyverse, but this is certainly the first time a collection of essays dedicated entirely to the music of one television show has been published. Television as an area of study has made enormous gains in the last few years: from a steady representation in journals since the late 1990s to more recent collections and monographs, many from scholars associated with *Buffy* studies, in particular David Lavery, Rhonda Wilcox, and Stacey Abbott. Music, however, still remains on the fringes of the discourse. In the several collections edited and overseen by Abbott for I.B. Tauris on *Angel*, *Farscape*, *Alias*, *Charmed*, and *Firefly*, only the two volumes dedicated to Whedon's work contain essays on music, and in the growing number of volumes dedicated to particular TV series it is still common for music to be omitted from their discussion. This present volume demonstrates how important music is in our understanding of and engagement with a television series. At the time of writing, another volume dedicated to music in *Buffy* has already been announced, but while *Buffy* is a particularly rich text for musical study it is not the only one. It is, therefore, our fervent hope that this volume will be the first of many examining the contribution to television made by music.

PART I
Constructing Sound: Music, Noise, and Silence

Chapter 1
Love, Death, Curses, and Reverses (in E minor): Music, Gender, and Identity in *Buffy the Vampire Slayer* and *Angel*[1]

Janet K. Halfyard

Music plays an important role at a number of different levels in *Buffy the Vampire Slayer* (1997–2003). There is a great deal of diegetic music in the series, mainly issuing from the Bronze, which forms part of the characters' sense of identity, a youth sub-culture defined by its music.[2] However, the non-diegetic music also plays a role in the construction of identity in the series, and this process begins in the opening credit sequences of both *Buffy* and its companion series, *Angel* (1999–2004), with the theme tunes that are closely identified with not just the series but with their eponymous characters. This music can be looked at from two different perspectives: in terms of the relationship of these themes to each other and to other music associated with horror genres, including vampire films; and in terms of how music itself can communicate information to the audience about the identity of the character it represents.

The Theme Tunes in *Buffy* and *Angel*

The importance of theme music lies in its ability to establish and reinforce a series's identity, positioning it in relation to the cultural musical codes that are a major part of how music generates meaning in film and television contexts. In his commentary for "Welcome to the Hellmouth" (1.1), Joss Whedon reveals that a composer was originally employed to write a theme song for *Buffy*, but Whedon did not feel that the result effectively captured the essence of the show and of Buffy herself. Instead, Nerf Herder—suggested to Whedon by Alyson Hannigan—was

---

[1] An earlier version of this chapter was published in as "Love, Death, Curses and Reverses (in F minor): Music, Gender and Identity in *Buffy the Vampire Slayer* and *Angel*," *Slayage*, 4 (2001).

[2] See S. Renee Dechert, "'My Boyfriend's in the Band!' *Buffy* and the Rhetoric of Music," in Rhonda V. Wilcox and David Lavery (eds), *Fighting the Forces: What's at Stake in Buffy the Vampire Slayer* (Lanham, MD, 2002), pp. 218–26; and the chapters in Part II of this volume.

one of several bands considered to write a new theme.[3] There are a number of ways in which their theme can be read which illustrate why Whedon chose this one and what he was intending the title music to say about the series and its central character.

The first four notes of Nerf Herder's theme for *Buffy*'s opening credits are played on the organ and carry a wealth of intertextual associations (see Figure 1.1).[4] The organ has long been a signifier for horror, starting with its explicit diegetic use in *Phantom of the Opera* (1925) and *Dr Jekyll and Mr Hyde* (1932), in which Dr Jekyll also plays the organ. The sound of the organ then became synonymous with Hammer Horror in the 1960s and 1970s, and subsequently with the horror genre as a whole. More recently, the use of the organ has become both a comic and ironic gesture, found in films such as the comedies *The 'Burbs* (1988) and *Dracula: Dead and Loving It* (1996), as well as more obvious Hammer successors such as *House on Haunted Hill* (1999).

Figure 1.1   The theme from *Buffy the Vampire Slayer*

The theme of *Buffy* starts with this organ horror signifier, but then instantly changes its message. It removes itself from the sphere of both classic horror and its spoofs by replaying the same motif, the organ now supplanted by an aggressively strummed electric guitar, relocating itself in modern youth culture and relocating the series in an altogether different arena. Whedon himself confirms this reading, observing that the title sequence begins

> with this scary organ and then devolves instantly into rock and roll, which is basically trying to tell people exactly what the show is in the credits—which is "here's a girl who has no patience for a horror movie, who is not going to be a victim, who is not going to be in the scary organ horror movie. She's going to bring her own sort of youth and rock and attitude to it." ... I very much wanted to state the mission up front.[5]

---

[3]   Joss Whedon, "Welcome to the Hellmouth" audio commentary, *Buffy the Vampire Slayer: Season One Collector's Edition* (2000).

[4]   The earlier version of this chapter in *Slayage* gives the key as F minor: this is due to the fact that in the process of making DVDs for the European market, the masters are produced using the NTSC format versions, resulting in the episodes playing 4 per cent faster. This has the effect of transposing the music up by a slightly flat semitone. To viewers of the DVDs in PAL format, the theme tune therefore appears to be in F minor.

[5]   Joss Whedon, "Welcome to the Hellmouth" audio commentary.

Darling Violetta's theme for *Angel* is, on the surface, entirely different from that of *Buffy*: tempo and texture are certainly noticeably different from the driving forces of Buffy's music. However, not only are both themes in the same key, E minor, but the first four notes, which in *Buffy* are the notes from which the entire theme tune is derived, are also the first four notes of *Angel's* theme, the fourth note (D) being transposed up an octave in *Angel's* music, rising instead of falling as it does in *Buffy* (see Figure 1.2).

Figure 1.2   The theme from *Angel*

Buffy's basic theme is too short to really be called a melody; rather, it is a four-note motif. Angel's theme is a considerably longer melody, and where the opening four notes echo the pitches of Buffy's motif, the final four notes echo its shape. The similarities of key and motif between *Buffy* and *Angel* might be read as a thinly disguised means of reasserting the eternal bond between the two characters—although they are separated (into two series, apart from anything else) they will always be connected. The shared motif stands as a symbol of their common mission, of the emotional connection between them and also of their separation. The differences between these themes, however, are just as interesting and speak more clearly to the idea of music as identity.

One of the most striking differences between the two theme tunes is their mood. Buffy's theme is played by an amplified rock band and the melodic line is carried by an increasingly frenetic electric guitar. Angel's theme is more obviously lyrical, less frenetic, and although the guitars and drum kit of the rock band are included in the ensemble, they are not foregrounded so dramatically. Instead, acoustic instruments are also present, with the piano and cello dominating the melodic line. One could easily argue the appropriateness of this on the grounds that Buffy is a modern girl, and therefore more likely to listen to the kind of music heard in her theme, identifying with it as well as being identified by it on grounds of her youth and cultural environment, in particular the Bronze. Angel, meanwhile, is an eighteenth-century Irish vampire: rock music is certainly not his music in terms of his somewhat unusual age group or culture and so a more classical and arguably Irish-traditional sounding theme is one that he might identify with more readily. This is also a quite specific aspect of his coding as a vampire in musical terms, and moreover, his coding as a specific type of vampire, the—literally—soulful, tragic-hero vampire as opposed to the devil-may-care, blithely vicious vampire typified by Spike. This typology of vampires and their music is duplicated in Neil Jordan's film version of *Interview with the Vampire* (1994). Louis, referred to in the film as "the vampire with a human soul" is, like Angel, a brown-haired, eighteenth-century vampire whose lyrical musical theme is carried primarily by cellos.[6] Lestat, like Spike, is a blond vampire who embraces the modern era and its music. One of the underlying themes of *Interview* is immortality and the problems of surviving it, the difficulty of adapting to the passing of eras; music, both source and underscore, is often used to indicate how well a character is integrated into a particular era. Lestat, thoroughly acculturated into his contemporaneous setting, draws on his ability as a musician and his familiarity with contemporary repertoire as part of his hunting tactics in the early nineteenth century, using music to win the trust of his victims; Louis dances to a nineteenth-century waltz as he embraces the *fin de siècle*, but after this he seems to get stuck in the romantic orchestral sound world of the score, his music never fully embracing the music of the twentieth-century society he inhabits. The final time-locator is the Rolling Stones song "Sympathy for the Devil" sung by Guns'n'Roses that closes the film. Lestat, having attacked Louis's interviewer in a moving car, takes over the steering wheel and switches on the radio, where he finds the rock song. Symbolically, he appropriates not just his victim's car, but also his century and his century's music, moving away from an archaic orchestral sound to embrace the new and modern world of pop and rock.[7]

As I have discussed elsewhere, Louis, Dracula in Coppola's 1992 film version, and Batman, in Tim Burton's 1989 vampiric version of the superhero, all share a very similar musical theme written in a minor key with classical Hollywood orchestral scoring that marks them out as tragic, romantic heroes.[8] Angel's cello connects him to this musical sound world, in comparison to the aggression, youth, and vigor of the rock and punk music that is associated with Lestat and Spike.

However, aside from the temporal codings in the music, it can be argued without much difficulty that Buffy's music is coded male and Angel's is coded female. Some of the most systematic work on audience reception of film and television music has been done by Philip Tagg with Bob Clarida and Anahid Kassabian. Tagg's reception test is impressively straightforward: ten theme tunes taken from a range of film, TV, and popular music are played to an audience who are asked to write down any verbal-visual associations (VVAs) that occur to them in response. This test was carried out between 1979 and 1986 with groups of students in Sweden (92 per cent were Swedish); 70 per cent of them had no formal musical training and had largely not encountered this music before, so could not have

---

[6] The music for *Interview with the Vampire* was composed by Elliot Goldenthal. Louis is generally represented by strings, usually cellos, and the lyrical cello theme heard in the cue "Born to Darkness" is used for scenes involving voiceovers by Louis, narrating his past to the interviewer, and is therefore specifically identified with him.

[7] In Rice's sequel, *The Vampire Lestat* (New York, 1985), Lestat goes a step further, becoming a rock star.

[8] For a more detailed discussion of Burton's Batman as a vampire and the musical connections between the themes of these three films, see Janet K. Halfyard, "The Dark Avenger: Angel and the Cinematic Superhero," in Stacey Abbott (ed.), *Reading Angel* (London/New York, 2005), pp. 149–62.

been influenced in their responses by knowledge of the films and TV programs for which the music had been written.[9]

The test generated considerable data from which various analyses have resulted, including Tagg's 1989 paper, "An anthropology of stereotypes in TV music?"[10] This puts forward an analysis of gender-associative responses to certain kinds of music by establishing which tunes produced VVAs of a man or men, which of a woman or women, and which of mixed-sex groups. To summarize, from this it appeared that four of the ten tunes might be characterized as feminine, in that they produced significantly more female VVAs than male; that the VVAs of four of the other tunes were predominantly masculine; and that two could not clearly be categorized. Using the four "male" and four "female" tunes, the music's characteristics were analyzed to see if there were qualities common to the two groups. Bearing in mind the music of *Buffy* and *Angel*, table 1.1 shows a summary of some of Tagg's findings.

Table 1.1   A summary of Tagg's observations of male and female characteristics in music

Musical parameter	Male characteristic	Female characteristic
Tempo	Faster	Slower
Note values*	Shorter (therefore appearing faster)	Longer (therefore appearing slower)
Rhythm	More rhythmic irregularities (e.g. syncopations, repeated notes)	More regular: normal dottings and divisions of note groups.
Phrasing	Staccato, quick repeating notes	Legato, smooth and flowing
Dynamics	Same volume throughout	Phrases get louder, then softer
Instruments (melody)	Electric guitar, synthesizer, trumpet, percussion	Strings (e.g. violin and cello), flute, piano
Instruments (accompaniment)	Strumming guitars, brass, synthesizers, percussion	Strings, piano, woodwind

Note

*   *Note values* refers to how the basic beat of the music is subdivided. If the basic beat is a crotchet (quarter note) this can be subdivided into smaller values such as two quavers (eighth notes) and four semi-quavers (sixteenth notes). The smaller the note value, the more sounded notes there are per measure and the faster the music appears to be.

---

[9]   See Philip Tagg and Bob Clarida, *Ten Little Title Tunes* (Lima, OH, 2003), pp. 107–120.

[10]   Philip Tagg, "An Anthropology of Stereotypes in TV Music?" *Swedish Musicological Journal* (1989), pp. 19–42, accessed 12 August 2008 at http://tagg.org/articles/xpdfs/tvanthro.pdf.

The summary is, in many ways, a fairly accurate description of the two theme tunes under discussion here, but with Buffy's corresponding far more closely to the male category and Angel's to the female. In particular, the audible pulse of the *Buffy* theme is around 200 beats per minute, whilst that of *Angel* is closer to 120. The strumming of the guitars in *Buffy* creates accompaniment note values that are noticeably shorter than those in *Angel*. The basic pulse of *Buffy* is subdivided throughout the accompaniment (most noticeably in the drum track) and also in the final stages of the melody line, creating the illusion that the tempo of the music increases toward the end. Angel's music is smooth and flowing, with a dynamic shape to the phrases, and a melodic line that concentrates on cello and piano; Buffy's music remains at a similar volume throughout, although it gradually gets higher in pitch, and it uses the rock-band line-up implied by the male side of Tagg's analysis. In terms of rhythm, it has both masculine and feminine qualities in that it is characterized by "male" repeated notes (strumming) and "female" regularity, although there is some subtle syncopation in the melodic line. Angel's melody also has characteristics associated with male rhythm, in that it is slightly syncopated (i.e. the note does not fall on the beat but between beats).

Tagg also describes the shape of the melodies in his study. Male-identified melodies tend to have their highest notes on the first accented note of the complete motif, which is hard to argue for the theme of *Buffy*, and neither does it describe *Angel*'s melody. However, female-identified melodies, Tagg observes, have either an "up-and-back-down" or "down-and-back-up" contour, and have what he describes as "generally descending tendencies." Angel's theme is clearly of the "up-and-back-down" variety and the trajectory of the melody is very much downward, the final note being considerably lower than the starting note. While Buffy's theme is made up of four-note motifs which often end on a note lower than the starting note, the theme as a whole has an unquestionably rising tendency; thus while the melodic shape does not altogether fit the male pattern, it does not have the obviously female qualities that Angel's has.[11]

---

[11] Tagg makes it clear in his paper that the analysis and its conclusions apply to the eight tunes that he is considering; and he acknowledges that there is quite often a crossover between what he describes as "female" music and music that is sometimes used to describe heroic men within film soundtracks. However, both Tagg and I are analyzing not underscore music here but theme tunes, which rely on our enculturated knowledge of music to provide a great deal of information about the nature of what we are about to watch. Like film, TV genres are associated with particular musical genres and the music gives us coded information about the narrative that is to follow.

Gender Reversals within the Narrative of *Buffy*

This musical gender reversal leads to the question of whether it is a reflection of similar reversals in the characters' coding and positioning within their narratives, and also highlights other role reversals that surround how the series as a whole positions itself from the outset, reversals that are at the heart of Whedon's stated mission to counter the figure of the "little blonde girl who goes into a dark alley and gets killed in every horror movie,"[12] with a little blonde girl who instead takes on the vampires. These inversions of our expectations are apparent even before the theme music is heard for the first time: the opening scene of the first episode presents a nervous blonde girl and an evidently mischievous—possibly dangerous—boy sneaking through the school at night. As Matthew Pateman observes:

> This neat and utterly expected opening soon presents its own inversion ... the sweet blonde victim turns out to be the vampire and it is she who sinks her fangs into the boy. Apart from debunking the generic expectation of the girl as victim ... this opening also asserts the ways in which the less obvious generic aspects of the show will also be either (perhaps too easily) inverted or (much more interestingly) confused, intermingled and made complex.[13]

These processes of challenging our expectations are present at all levels of the narrative, and very much present in the construction of Buffy herself, highlighting a variety of observations in relation to her as a hero and how she rewrites the rules of the heroic in relation to the female. In fact, some of the innovative positionings in *Buffy* as a whole become more apparent when it is set alongside a superficially comparable series such as *Charmed* (1998–2006). Both have strong female protagonists with special powers and a mission to protect the world from evil; both are supported by supernatural men whose very nature makes normal romantic relationships highly problematic, Leo the White Lighter[14] being the rough equivalent of Angel, although Leo also combines this role with characteristics of a Watcher.[15]

---

[12] Whedon, "Welcome to the Hellmouth" audio commentary.

[13] Matthew Pateman, *The Aesthetics of Culture in Buffy the Vampire Slayer* (Jefferson, NC, 2006), pp. 89–90.

[14] A White Lighter is a guardian angel, appointed by Elders to protect good witches and future White Lighters. Leo has a variety of magical abilities and is immortal. His relationship with Piper is initially forbidden, fraught with obstacles, and further complicated by his ascension to Elder status at the close of season 5.

[15] Some of the ideas here are really only true of *Buffy* in seasons 1 to 3: after this, relationships and the balance of power within the Scooby gang become increasingly complex. This is a feature of the development of the narrative and the growth of the characters that has been seen in other areas, such as Anthony Bradney's observations on Buffy's relationship to law and *Buffy*'s relationship to the cop show genre, both of which

Musically, there are similarities too: the theme tune of *Charmed* is a rock song, sung by the male lead singer of Love Spit Love. However, this song is extraordinarily deceptive on a number of levels. Written and recorded by the British group the Smiths, "How soon is now?" was originally released in 1985. Love Spit Love's cover was later used in the trailers and as part of the soundtrack for the film *The Craft* (1996) with which *Charmed* has an obvious connection, both being concerned with teenage witches in California. However, the theme song of *Charmed* uses only extremely carefully edited sections of this cover, pasted together to make it appear a coherent lyric. If one does not know the Smiths' version (or, indeed, the full Love Spit Love cover), what one is likely to hear when one watches the opening sequence of *Charmed* is: "I am the sun/ I am the air/ I am human and I need to be loved." Notwithstanding that it is sung by a male voice, and quite aggressively in the style of American rock songs from the third line onwards, this is still a seemingly apt lyric for the Halliwell sisters with its invocation of celestial bodies and elements (even if *moon* might have been more obviously mystical than *sun*), and the sense of wanting to be normal despite the abnormality of magical gifts. However, the actual lyric is "I am the son/I am the heir/Of a shyness that is criminally vulgar," which has very little to do with three sisters who are clearly not sons and are anything but shy. It would seem that the sisters have appropriated a masculine music, as Buffy can be argued to have done, but they have had to alter and manipulate it to make it fit them, whereas Buffy's appropriation is much more direct and less contrived. There is also an almost immediate retreat from the masculinely coded music of the opening credits in *Charmed*: quite consistently, the theme song is immediately followed by a second song at the start of each episode. This second song is usually more lyrical and ballad-like, and also often sung by a female voice, as if to balance and even counter any lingering possibility that the sisters might be seen as too masculine or aggressive. The second song serves to alter the tone of the series, normally softening it back into a more obviously female model. The end credits of *Charmed*, unlike *Buffy*, do not return to the opening theme but substitute a much gentler and more lyrical piece of instrumental music, heavily informed by timbres of world music. *Buffy* reestablishes its male-coded, heroic musical identity at the end of each episode, whereas *Charmed* retreats from it into more evidently feminine musical timbres and gestures.

Other aspects of Buffy's position in relation to the Halliwell sisters are also revealing in terms of Buffy as a female hero. While *Charmed*'s heroines are a trio of young women with mutually complementary powers who work in collaboration, the nature of Buffy's calling means that essentially she is required to work alone. This idea is suggested in the opening sequence, which (in the early seasons) begins with the observation that "she alone will stand against the vampires," and where

---

also change after season 3. See Anthony Bradney, "Choosing Laws, Choosing Families: Images of Law, Love and Authority in *BtVS*," *Web Journal of Current Legal Issues*, 2 (2003), accessed 27 October 2003 at http://webjcli.ncl.ac.uk/2003/issue2/bradney2.html.

the final image of the opening credits is always of Buffy on her own. This is also referred to directly in the narrative, from Giles in season 2 saying to Willow and Xander that "your help will be greatly appreciated, but when it comes to battle, Buffy must fight alone" ("School Hard" [2.3]), to Buffy herself in "Selfless" (7.5):

> Buffy: At some point, someone has to draw the line, and that is always going to be me. You get down on me for cutting myself off, but in the end the Slayer is always cut off. There's no mystical guidebook. No all-knowing council. Human rules don't apply. There's only me.

The principal members of the Scooby gang support her, but their role is often peripheral or takes the form of providing distractions, particularly in seasons 1 to 3. Willow's use of the internet and her spell-casting both fall into this category before she acquires power on a grander scale from season 4 onwards; Xander is frequently perceived as a hindrance and his best form of help often comes from his passive pseudo-memory of tactical knowledge rather than any ability to act; Giles's designation as Watcher is explicitly passive, and his function is cast as that of walking reference library. His comments demonstrate that he often sees himself as a liability or an obstacle, such as his remark to himself "Oh, good show, Giles … at least you didn't get knocked out for a change" in "Buffy versus Dracula" (5.1) and his song "I'm standing in your way" in "Once More, with Feeling" (6.7).

In contrast to Buffy's solitary position, the *Charmed* trio's mutual interdependence (they can only perform advanced magic together, drawing on "the power of three") reinforces the idea of women as sociable creatures who work best in cooperative groups, while Buffy's apparently solitary position corresponds more closely to conventional ideas of the male hero. Heroes tend to have support networks of friends who provide them with information, and technical and emotional support, as well as providing distractions to create opportunities for the hero to act, but when it comes down to the moment of confrontation, the hero, be he Beowulf or Superman, must prevail alone. This scenario is repeated in the relationship between Buffy and her gang as well as in the perpetual problem of her superpowers being a source of friction in her relationships.

The whole question of power and agency is defined differently between the Halliwells and Buffy. The sisters' strength is supernatural, magical, a power of mind and spirit which seems a more obvious type of power for a woman to possess, because in terms of physical strength, women cannot compete with men—except, of course, that Buffy can. Her power lies in preternatural strength which is therefore defined not as magical but out of the ordinary course of nature: she is superhuman, not a witch. Her agency lies not in the mind—there is always a measure of surprise when Buffy gets good grades—but in physical strength, again putting her more clearly in the realm of male action heroes rather than teenage heroines.[16]

---

[16] Buffy's physical strength and determination have some clear predecessors in *Xena: Warrior Princess* (1995–2001) and in the heroines of science fiction films, notably Ripley

Buffy's Theme Tune as Underscore

The role of the theme tune in *Buffy* outside the credits is somewhat atypical for television, where the theme is often an integral and regular part of the underscore, as, for example, in the series of the *Star Trek* franchise. *Buffy* makes only occasional and very specific use of its theme at the end of season 1 and again in season 2, where it preempts the love theme that emerges for Buffy and Angel in the middle of the season. Right from her inception, Buffy has embodied both the hero and the heroine—the normal girl the hero is expected to save—and at times these two roles become polarized in a way that draws attention to the difficulties she faces in finding a balance between them. The uses of the theme on these occasions are intimately bound up with Buffy's identity in terms of masculine and feminine codings, and the tension between Buffy as hero and as "normal girl."

The first time this polarization is overtly articulated is in the finale of season 1. She discovers a prophecy that she will die in her great confrontation with the Master, and in the moment that she believes the prophecy to be true, she becomes the heroine, the damsel in need of rescue. This transformation is underlined by the way she dresses for the final battle: she is wearing her prom dress, a marvelously semi-classical confection of white, floaty layers which she wears incongruously with a modern and less obviously feminine leather jacket, a visually overt juxtaposition of hero and heroine that draws attention to itself by its very oddness.

She is killed by the Master, but then brought back to life by Xander performing CPR. Where before the hero and heroine aspects of her identity were uncomfortably juxtaposed, now they merge. Buffy loses the leather jacket at the moment of her death so is now, visually, entirely the heroine; but, psychologically, the hero-aspect reasserts itself as she realizes that her death has turned out to be temporary. Looking like the heroine but acting as the hero, it is at this point that the theme music is heard. Followed by Angel and Xander, she marches back to the high school, full of drive and purpose, and clearly in control of the situation: despite the fact that between them Angel and Xander have just saved her life, they are visually relegated to the position of back-up team rather than positioned as her equals.[17] After Buffy has momentarily become the embodiment of the "the little blonde girl" Whedon created her to challenge, the theme tune is played in its original form outside the credits on only this one occasion in the entire 144-episode span of the series, re-establishing her as the hero, the site of narrative agency that the male-coded theme indicates.

---

in the *Alien* quartet (1979–97) and Sarah Connor in *Terminator II* (1991), although she has no obvious predecessors in pure horror or even superhero film genres, where the function of women is mainly to be saved by the male heroes.

[17] The positioning is reiterated regularly in the various opening credit sequences of both *Buffy* and *Angel*, where the title character is generally seen at the front of the group as they walk purposefully forward.

However, after Buffy has defeated the Master, the theme is brought in again for the final scene in the library as the Scoobies contemplate their victory. Rather than being joyous and celebratory, the music is lyrical and reflective, and by simply altering some of the key parameters of instrumentation, accompaniment, tempo, and rhythm, it is converted into a classically female-coded theme, according to Tagg's criteria. The electric guitar is replaced by piano, the repeating notes of the accompaniment's strumming are eliminated and the drum kit removed; the tempo is slowed down enormously, the syncopation disappears, and now the up-and-back-down shape of the melody serves to emphasize gentle, lyrical femininity as a quality of this melody that we have not previously heard. Buffy has fulfilled her role as hero, a role which makes extreme demands of her, including requiring her to die in order to win—a scenario that will be repeated in season 5. The music in this final scene of season 1 is very clearly identified with Buffy, who seems dazed, almost shocked that the battle is over and she has won. There is some difference between her mood and that of her companions at this point, who seem much more upbeat—Xander's demeanor, in particular, seems somewhat at odds with the tone of the music. At the end of the scene, in a direct reversal of the usual positioning, Buffy trails behind the group as they leave the library. The others are laughing, but she still seems more subdued. This is the calm after the storm: her heroic mission has been completed and so the heroic cast of her theme tune has been removed to reveal her instead as "just a girl," and one who has perhaps not quite come to terms with the fact that she has survived.

The basic melody of the theme, out of the context of its rock-band rendition, is used on more than one occasion in season 2: in "The Dark Age" (2.8), for example, it plays briefly in the underscore against Giles in his moment of despair when he realizes that the demon he raised in his student days is stalking him. He has just turned Buffy away from his apartment without telling her what is going on, and the subtle use of the theme at this point might indicate his knowledge that he needs her and her heroism but cannot bring himself to tell her what he has done.

A more elaborate use of the theme is its reworking in a major key as a lyrical, wistful theme for Buffy as she waits for Angel at the ice rink in "What's my Line? Part 1" (2.9). It accompanies her as she skates alone and—as with the use of the reworked, female-coded theme at the end of "Prophecy Girl" (1.12)—once again the theme in this new form represents Buffy's dual roles as superhero and teenage girl by using the Nerf Herder theme in another female-coded version. The conflict between her two identities is never more clearly pointed than in this moment as both she and her music attempt to distance themselves from the heroic identity, and yet the fact that she can never separate herself from this identity is underlined by this still being clearly recognizable as the same theme, albeit seen from a different musical angle. Whether major or minor, aggressive or lyrical, coded male or female, it is still the theme that both identifies and defines Buffy the Vampire Slayer. This idea is underlined at the end of "What's my Line? Part 2" (2.10), as Buffy says goodbye to Kendra. The major key version of the theme plays again, musically mirroring what Kendra tells Buffy "You always do that ... You talk about slaying like it's a job. It's not. It's who you are."

Buffy's theme, like Buffy herself, negotiates a path between male and female codings: one is not compromised by the other. Instead, the coexistence of masculine and feminine traits within Buffy and her music creates a context in which a woman is able to retain her conventional femininity but still be perceived as equally, if not more, competent and capable as a male hero would be in similar circumstances. More than that, the theme reveals itself to be about who she is rather than about what she does: its general absence from the underscore accentuates the extent to which it specifically identifies her more than her actions on the occasions that it is used outside the credits.

Buffy's Musical and Narrative Influence on Later TV Shows

Two other post-*Buffy* series that bear a strong imprint of its influence are *Alias* (2001–2006) and *Dark Angel* (2000–2002).[18] Both of these series have a central female character who takes on the characteristics of a hero in the same way that Buffy does, possessing superpowers in the form of technological gadgets or genetically engineered advantages,[19] isolated by their differences, unable to be with the men they love, acting alone but supported by friends, and battling the occult forces in the form of prophecies (*Alias*) and mystical evil organizations (*Dark Angel*), despite both series being positioned as much more scientific than supernatural in their general approach than *Buffy*.

In terms of gender roles and their subversion, both have central female characters who, unlike Buffy, have gender-ambivalent names, Sydney and Max respectively; but like *Buffy* their theme tunes also deflect straightforwardly feminine coding. *Alias* uses extremely fast, repetitive techno music both for its titles and much of its underscore, putting it in a very similar musical category to *Buffy* in terms of its gender implications. *Dark Angel* is more obviously electronic in approach, reflecting its futuristic setting, integrating sounds and images in a way that leaves the material of the title sequence ambivalently positioned between ambient noise and music. It includes the sound (and image) of an accelerating motorcycle engine and layers of other environmental sounds such as breaking

---

[18] Even the title of *Dark Angel* appears to make direct allusion to the Buffyverse, and its first series was programmed back to back with *Angel* on Sky One in the UK, the program trailers advertising both series together, with an evident assumption that viewers of one could be expected to want to watch the other.

[19] Richard Reynolds, in his empirical definition of a superhero, identifies one of their common characteristics as being the possession of superpowers that defy normal human capabilities (e.g. Superman) or the equivalent in terms of gadgets (e.g. Batman). Buffy and Max fall into the first category, whilst Sydney falls into the second. See Richard Reynolds, *Superheroes: A Modern Mythology* (London, 1992), p. 16.

glass, alongside more conventionally musical ones such as the fast drum track. This places it more in the realms of electroacoustic music, implying an idea of masculinity if only because the genre was and still is largely dominated by male composers and technicians. However, the most prominent conventionally musical sound is a wordlessly singing female voice and, in terms of gender coding, this theme is rather more oblique than those used by *Buffy* or *Alias*. In fact, as in the case of *Charmed*, there is a musical deception at work. The full theme, as heard on the series's album, is written and performed by Chuck D (from Public Enemy) and the female rap artist MC Lyte, and it has extensive spoken lyrics from both male and female voices. Hannah Bosma has observed the tendency in electronic music for female voices to be used more often than male voices, and that female voices tend to sing, often wordlessly, whereas male voices tend to speak.[20] By eliminating the speaking voices altogether and leaving only the female singer, the theme for *Dark Angel* potentially falls into a form of gendered coding much associated with electronic music, where the female voice is frequently rendered inarticulate within a male-coded electronic sonic environment. Here, however, both the masculine and feminine characteristics of the theme can be attributed to Max, because the use of the motorcycle acceleration sample is a sound that obviously belongs to her—both with the image of her on her motorcycle in the credits and the fact that this remains her favored mode of transport during the series. The dynamic is different to Buffy's, where there are no obvious elements of "femininity" about her theme tune, but where the extreme femininity of her name, with its assonant and alliterative allusions to "fluffy" and "bunny," acts as an effective counterbalance to the masculinity of her music. In *Dark Angel*, the theme embraces both Max's femaleness through the use of the voice and her appropriation of masculine territory through the sonic image of the motorcycle. Despite the differences between the two shows, in both *Dark Angel* and *Alias* there is a clear positioning of Max and Sydney in terms of character and series identity as established in the theme music which owes a debt to *Buffy* and the appropriation of male musical codes by a female hero.

---

[20] Hannah Bosma, "Male and Female Voices in Computer Music," *Proceedings of the International Computer Music Conference 1995* (San Francisco, 1995), pp. 139–42, accessed 18 August 2008 at http://cf.hum.uva.nl/~hannah/icmc95.htm. While these gender codings became established in electroacoustic music in the 1950s and 60s, Bosma's work looks at composition through to the 1990s, and there is ample evidence both in her work and in my own experience as a singer working in electroacoustic music that the general trend towards using female voices in relation to sung wordlessness and linguistic fragmentation remains strong in contrast to the use of male voices.

Gender Reversals in *Angel*

Angel's equally unconventional positioning is also reflected in the ambivalence of his music. Again, much is revealed by returning to the comparison with both *Buffy* and *Charmed*. Buffy's gang is a rather amorphous body: there are the four main characters, but also a variety of hangers-on, which include Angel himself, Faith, Anya, Jenny, Cordelia, Tara, Oz, Riley, Dawn, and Spike, plus the group of potential Slayers that join them in season 7. Angel's associates, however, are much more stable and consistent, established in season 1 as a group of three, even if as a different three in the first and second halves of the season, Doyle being replaced by Wesley. Roles within the team are more formalized and professional, including the fact that they are paid for the work they do. In subsequent seasons, new characters are gradually added to the team: Gunn in season 2, Fred in season 3 and Lorne in season 4, although the clear delineation of each role continues and is brought into even clearer definition when they take over the Los Angeles branch of Wolfram and Hart and are assigned their own departments. Once they have joined, characters do not leave, even if Wesley's actions lead him to be ostracized for a time and Jasmine's presence causes temporary rifts in the group in season 4. Nor do they bring their partners into the group as temporary members, as happens in *Buffy*. Wesley's two girlfriends, Virginia and Lilah, are never part of the gang; Gunn and Fred reduce any possible complications by having a relationship with each other, while Angel's son Connor never truly manages to mesh with the group at all. In both seasons 3 and 4, he remains on the periphery, always a potentially disruptive element rather than—ironically—a member of the "family." His participation in the events of the final episode of season 5 are clearly a one-off contribution: he does not stay to fight in the final confrontation that ends the series.

The profile of *Angel*'s season 1 trio, especially after Doyle's death, is surprisingly similar to that of *Charmed*. "Seriousness" runs in direct correlation to age, with Angel and *Charmed*'s Prue positioned as the most serious characters, holding the position of most responsibility and authority within each group. Cordelia and Phoebe, the two youngest characters in each trio, are both viewed (without necessarily a great deal of evidence) as the most prone to irresponsibility; and Wesley and Piper hold the middle ground, displaying varying levels of both sense and silliness—although the difference is most dramatic in Wesley, where his fluctuation between competence and incompetence is frequently used to comic effect.[21]

The same pattern runs true on an active-passive power scale. Angel and Prue have the most developed powers and greatest physical strength derived from supernatural sources. Prue's telekinetic power enables her to hurl people against walls, in addition to which she can astrally project herself—she is the first of the

---

[21] This holds true after Prue's death and the arrival of a new youngest sister. Piper takes on the role of most responsible sister, while Paige is automatically positioned as the most irresponsible and rebellious of the trio, recasting Phoebe in the middle sister role.

sisters to acquire a second power. Piper can "freeze" everything and everyone around her, so whilst she cannot act directly, she can prevent (or delay) others acting against her. This develops into a more aggressive form in later seasons, but while she can therefore act more directly on events, it often results in her exploding things unintentionally, which undermines her ability to act effectively. Comparably, Wesley has the Watcher's knowledge (which can serve a similar preventative purpose) and a fair degree of physical strength with which to make an impact, if a less impressive one than Angel. Meanwhile, Phoebe and Cordelia share a near-identical and entirely passive gift: each is subject to visions of innocents in need of help, although like Piper's, Phoebe's gift also later develops into a more active form. In later seasons, the new characters in *Angel* enhance the existing functions fulfilled by these three without bringing an entirely new type of ability to the group. Fred adds to the specialist knowledge of the group, complementing Wesley's Watcher role with scientific knowledge, while Gunn adds to the physical strength of the group, supporting and complementing Angel; Lorne's empathic ability acts as a parallel to Cordelia's visions, allowing for passive interventions that give insight into the future.

Where Buffy ultimately acts alone, Angel is more dependent on his group in order to act. Cordelia (and later Lorne) provides him with the impetus for action before events have occurred, whereas Buffy tends to respond to danger after it appears. Likewise, where Buffy's group tends to shift to include temporary and occasional members, Angel's more fixed group works more like the cooperative female group of the *Charmed* sisters. Likewise, although both the *Angel* season 1 and *Charmed* trios have a support group of friends, particularly police contacts, none of the supporters are ever truly brought into the group; they may assist, but they always remain outside the core.[22] This is also an explicitly female construct: heroes may work as duos, where one is the hero and the other is the "sidekick" (Batman and Robin, Hercules and Iolaus, and, in the same mould, Xena[23] and Gabrielle), but not normally in trios (perhaps another reason that Warren, Jonathan, and Andrew's trio proved to be so dysfunctional). Meanwhile, supernatural females have been working in groups of three since the Greeks: the Fates, Gorgons, Graeae, Hesperides and Furies are all trios of magical sisters, and the model for others throughout Western history from the three witches of Shakespeare's *Macbeth* to recent film and television manifestations such as *The Witches of Eastwick* (1987), *Hocus Pocus* (1993), and the three of *Charmed*.

---

[22] The oldest and most serious members of each trio have personal relationships with their police contacts: there is definitely a hint of a romantic connection between Kate and Angel, which is highly problematic and fails to develop; and Prue is involved with her detective, Andy, a relationship that is ended by his death.

[23] The masculine-feminine dualities in the musical construction of Xena through her own theme tune and battle music have been discussed by Carolyn Bremer in "Duality and Completeness: An Analysis of the *Xena: Warrior Princess* Theme Music," *Whoosh!*, 20 (1998), accessed 26 August 2008 at http://www.whoosh.org/issue20/bremer1.html.

Even the familial aspect of the various "three sisters" can be carried over to Angel's realization at the end of season 1 that he, Wesley, and Cordelia are themselves a family unit. Whereas Buffy and her friends know (even if they do not like it) that she must and ultimately will act alone, when Angel does this in *Angel* season 2 in his attempt to combat first Wolfram and Hart and then Drusilla and Darla, it is positioned as an aberration, a betrayal of the family unit, and a possible descent into evil for the vampire with a soul.

This formation of a cooperative, mutually interdependent group, then, is one aspect of female coding in *Angel* that can be seen mirrored between the musical and narrative constructs.[24] However, like Buffy, the combination of male and female qualities is also apparent at other levels of his character's construction. In addition to his distinctly gender-ambivalent name, some of the feminizing qualities that are most obviously attributed to him relate to his curse, which simultaneously prevents him from functioning either as a vampire or as a human. His moral code, imposed on him by the acquisition of a soul, means that he cannot bite, and he cannot have sex with the woman he loves lest it allow him a moment of pure happiness which would remove his soul and turn him evil. Given that the vampire's bite is conventionally seen as a sexual metaphor, a sublimation of the erotic impulse, Angel is effectively doubly castrated—voluntarily on both counts, as it turns out—which, whilst not making him female, certainly does not permit him to act as a classically romantic male heroic character. Quite the contrary in fact: he is only able to have sex when love is not involved. He is forbidden both his primary functions as vampire and as the romantic lead; in both cases "getting the girl" is not an available option. Yet, just as Buffy is all woman, if a new kind of heroine, so Angel is clearly a romantic-heroic male figure within both narratives. Spike, with his jibes about Angel being "poncey", a "nancy boy" and "prancing away like a magnificent poof" ("In the Dark" [A1.3]), may acerbically highlight the extent to which his masculinity is undermined, but Angel is nonetheless desired by Buffy, Cordelia, Faith, and Darla, envied by Doyle and Wesley, and swooned over by the Furies; and the music does, in fact, remind us of this. During the title sequence of *Angel*, at the point where David Boreanaz's own name credit is shown over several shots of Angel in action, the (female) cello is replaced as the principal melodic instrument by the (male) electric guitar. This substitution lasts exactly as long as David Boreanaz's personal credits, the cello taking back the melody after four measures as Cordelia's image appears.[25] The ambivalence of Angel's various dualities—man/vampire, lover/celibate, vulnerable/immortal—are clearly reflected in the male/female duality of his music's construction.

---

[24] As the group expands beyond the initial trio, it becomes increasingly like a comic-book superhero consortium such as the X-Men, Fantastic Four, or the Justice League.

[25] This sequence is disrupted in subsequent seasons where the addition of new principal characters to the opening credits means that the guitar is still playing when Cordelia's image appears, but the original intention and rhythm of the relationship of music and image is nonetheless very apparent in season 1.

In conclusion, *Buffy* and its spin-off, *Angel*, have attracted attention because of the way in which they transgress boundaries. This is nothing so simple as blurring: if a boundary, such as male and female codings in music, is blurred, then it loses its ability to reveal anything meaningful. Instead, *Buffy* and *Angel* acknowledge and even rely on the fact that the boundaries are there but cross them anyway in order to reveal a world more subtle and complex in its construction than film and TV horror narratives have historically allowed. On one hand, this reflects the subtleties and complexities of the world in which we ourselves live, and the extent to which the perception of gendered roles has changed. Given that the mainstream cultural shifts with regard to real-world gender roles originated in the 1960s and 70s (if not arguably rather earlier), the moment for art to catch up with life in presenting female toughness and male sensitivity in a constructive and sympathetic light was perhaps overdue, but it is nonetheless a tribute to the innovation and creativity of Joss Whedon and his team of creative collaborators that they succeeded in capturing the popular imagination with characters and scenarios that challenge the status quo so effectively. The subversion of long-maintained constructs appears to extend to every level of *Buffy* and *Angel*; and so it should doubtless not surprise us that it can also be found so clearly in the music that identifies the title characters.

Chapter 2
"What's My Melody?" Music and the Deployment of Genre in *Buffy the Vampire Slayer*

Louis Niebur

One of *Buffy the Vampire Slayer*'s (1997–2003) greatest skills was its ability to mimic or adopt the generic conventions of many genres, shifting between them at will, often combining them. *Buffy*'s screenwriters artfully mixed elements of fantasy, science fiction, comedy, teen drama, and epic adventure. They rarely stayed within the confines of one particular genre for an entire episode, but rather deployed genre moment by moment, creating a form of generic collage. Because of this unique quality, *Buffy*'s music supervisors and composers faced the challenge of accommodating this schizophrenia in a way that musically unified the end result. The musical options available to the show's composers were many: they could adopt themes and cues from the original film upon which *Buffy* was based, as in the series derived from the film *Stargate* (1994); they could adopt a leitmotivic approach, with evolving themes for situations and characters, as in Christopher Franke's epic *Babylon 5* (1994–98) scores; or they could rely mostly on popular music to act as backdrop for the characters and situations, following the example of many 1990s teen dramas such as *Party of Five* (1994–2000), *My So-Called Life* (1994–95), and *Beverly Hills 90210* (1990–2000). *Buffy*'s production team ultimately settled on an equal mixture of popular and orchestral (or synthesized orchestral) music, with each standard episode using orchestral music to punctuate action sequences or comedic moments. This scoring is rarely melodic, but orchestral music is also used to add gravitas to high-stake dramatic scenes, often employing leitmotifs in these situations. Popular tunes then serve to highlight more domestic moments related more often to typical teenage dilemmas, such as relationship issues. This broad pallette of options enabled the composers and supervisors to move easily between the various genres as needed without feeling constrained by a "house style."

Within this generic musical background, however, the constantly changing character of the music served as a commentary on more than the literal action on screen. Rather, the program vitally used music to help decode these shifting generic references to the audience, disguising its revolutionary use of genre. As a viewer (and listener), one could identify through music how one was meant to interpret a scene based on the expectations one had for a certain genre as represented on the program. This genre would be musically depicted while the action took place. Fascinating as this is, however, the potential remained for the program to lack a sense of internal coherence with all this generic diversity, a pitfall common to much contemporary postmodern television. However, instead it was the generic diversity itself that evolved into one of the most remarkable hallmarks of the program, using the sturdiness of film music's traditional semiotic code structure as a stabilizing force. This supposed incoherence given identity by music mirrors the contemporary individual in postmodern society, which Royal S. Brown refers to as "a materialistic nonentity waiting, like the filmic character, to become an image given affective substance and dramatic importance by music."[1] Genre is used in *Buffy* as shorthand: the merest suggestion of a particular archetype or archetypal sound refers the knowledgeable audience toward its understanding and expectation of the standard resolution of generic situations. *Buffy*, then, like much postmodern media, begins its discourse from the start at a distanced position—relying on its audience's expectations, often subverting them, but always depending on them. In this respect, music is a kind of mortar holding the referents together, not only linking them but uniting them. Thus the juxtaposition itself becomes a vital element of the program. These multiple and multivalent genres reflect a general tendency in postmodern discourses, according to media scholar Jim Collins, who observes that "once conflicting, often contradictory interpellations are at play simultaneously within a given social formation, stylistic differences as visible signs of differences between discourses are themselves *interpellative*."[2] The musical definitions supporting these discourses are not intended to be read as "real" or as manipulating the audience into believing what they are seeing is real. Instead, they allow the audience to guide their expectations for the program or scene's dénouement.[3] It is an indicator of the success of this practice that, throughout its seven-year run, *Buffy* rarely appears directionless, but rather effectively disguises this disjunction through a virtuosic manipulation of genre. To demonstrate this, I will offer several examples from throughout the series, each of which displays this flexible, open-ended approach to genre.

Once deployed, this technique guides the audience through the minefield of genre, alerting us to vital issues such as tone, suspense and intensity. But this is not where the function of the music stops. What of those cues that seem to contradict what is occurring on the screen? In addition to this primary role, music often fulfills a secondary role as well, entirely dependent on the first but existing outside of its control. How do we understand those cues that deliberately evoke genres that

---

[1] Royal S. Brown, *Overtones and Undertones: Reading Film Music* (Berkeley, 1994), p. 245.

[2] Jim Collins, *Uncommon Cultures: Popular Culture and Post-Modernism* (New York/London, 1989), p. 86.

[3] An important exception includes genres for which this function is essential, such as the French New Wave style of "The Body" (5.16)—but of course here there is absolutely no music at all.

are obviously not what are visually represented? After *Buffy* carefully defines each musical genre—or relies on popular definitions—and casually deploys stereotyped evocations of them, it enables the use of these tropes for external, ironic purposes. The same musical ideas that help cue the audience for (detached, stereotyped) "sincere" emotions can be evoked as external commentary on the internal fictional world of Buffy and her friends. Occasionally, this commentary manifests itself as if the music were emerging from within the minds of our characters, often in a way we have been led to believe is not a "real" part of the fictional world of *Buffy*, an example of what Claudia Gorbman calls the metadiegetic.[4] Just as often, this musical play is used to comment externally on the absurdity of the depicted situation. Either way, these musical cues depend for their success on the preexisting knowledge of this music's function in a more "authentic" way in the program.

One way *Buffy* is able to construct such sophisticated musical meanings is by taking advantage of television's extended serial format. Over a particular series, audiences come to know characters, feel close to them, remember their past, and, equally importantly, learn how they are meant to be interpreted. These characters can change, evolve; in fact, this is one of the greatest joys of *Buffy*, seeing "our" characters progress through childhood insecurity to the confidence of adulthood. Xander, Willow, Spike, and above all Buffy herself change over the series's run, and the program takes advantage of our collective memories of their past by drawing on our musical memories of this journey. A fragment of leitmotif, a comedic snapshot of 1970s funk or battle music, all combine to contribute to the "thickening" of these fictional characters. As popular culture scholar Alexander Nehamas notes, one of the fundamental qualities a television serial brings is this ability to construct characters over the long term:

> Character ... is manifested through particular occurrences in particular episodes; but each manifestation is thin and two-dimensional, until we realize that thickness and depth are added to it if (and only if) it is seen as a manifestation of character which can be understood and appreciated only over time and through many such manifestations.[5]

Music conspires with script over the seven-year run of *Buffy*, reminding us of past encounters, romances, and events, enriching our encounters with familiar characters, while making easier in the process the ability to play against established character traits through music. Fundamentally, ironic commentary is made easier through the pre-established knowledge of a character, situation, or theme's typical portrayal in literature, television, and most particularly, the specific genre evoked.

---

[4] Claudia Gorbman, *Unheard Melodies: Narrative Film Music* (Bloomington, IN, 1987), pp. 22–3.

[5] Alexander Nehamas, "Serious Watching," in Ruth Lorand (ed.), *Television: Aesthetic Reflections* (Oxford/New York, 2002), p. 49.

Sincerity

For the first year, as the production team worked to find the correct tone for the show, the program's original music, like many low-budget cult television shows, suffered under an extremely limited budget and consequently was realized mostly on rather cheap sounding synthesizers. Most importantly, much of *Buffy*'s first season music closely resembles other programs' approaches at the time: pathos is represented by slow, heavily echoed clarinet or piano/keyboard melodies, drawing upon sounds familiar to any viewer of the then hugely successful young adult drama *Ally McBeal* (1997–2002), and rapidly declining night-time soap *Melrose Place* (1992–99). Walter Murphy's synthesized vibraphone scores, particularly to "Angel" (1.7), cannot help but strike the listener with hindsight as odd, giving little away about Angel's character or his coming significance. Indeed, for the first truncated season of only 12 episodes, *Buffy*'s music is remarkably noncommittal, and Murphy's use of the signature tune in his non-diegetic score at the end of season finale seems to wrap the series up nicely as nothing more than a particularly long film. In that case, only the series itself is represented by its score: it is a self-contained entity, and as such the incidental music is not required to offer anything other than a summary of the series at the end. Other than this finale music, the internal score for the whole of the first season reflects *Buffy*'s identity as quirky, serious, and suspenseful, without the sense of structural (or musical) irony that would become such a large part of the series. This is all the more remarkable given the ironic tone of the opening credits, juxtaposing musical and visual horror tropes, depicted as serious, against an indie rock beat and images of trivial teenage high-school life, an unexpected combination potentially leading an audience to expect much more in the way of self-referential knowingness.

It is also worth noting that seven of the first season's episodes were self-contained stories, such as "Nightmares" (1.9) and "The Puppet Show" (1.10). By the second year, however, as *Buffy*'s success became apparent to the production team, they realized the show had the potential to tell larger, more elaborate stories. Different musical techniques emerged from this newfound approach, particularly in scores written by increasingly confident composer Christophe Beck. Chief among these new techniques was the use of the leitmotif, reminiscent less of Richard Wagner and nineteenth-century opera, and more the adoption of this technique by Hollywood film composers of the 1930s and 1940s, particularly those for melodramas like Max Steiner's *Now, Voyager* (1942) and *Gone with the Wind* (1939). The heroic male leads of the series, Angel, Riley, and, towards the end of the series, Spike, were each represented by musical themes of their own, in the best leitmotivic tradition of the classical Hollywood Golden Age score, with each theme nuanced to represent the nature of their relationship to Buffy. Right from the start, though, rather than representing a standardized episodic scoring practice these musical themes were acting as markers of genre. In other words, the "Buffy and Angel Love Theme," for example, first heard in season 2's "Surprise" (2.13) captures quite literally the melodramatic tone of the encounter depicted, standing in as a representation of the emotion between Buffy and Angel, itself a manifestation of the generic sonic stereotyped notion of soap opera or romance. In this way, the music in what was otherwise quite a scary episode fulfills a vital role in defining for the audience the type of program watched *at that moment*: a shift from horror to melodrama. This *bricolage* process, while unusual in contemporary television, is reminiscent of the discontinuity created by silent film accompanists, jumping from one piece to another, one style to another, a technique that was abandoned with the advent of synchronized sound and a much more precise ability to merge music continuously with the image.

Using the language of Hollywood film scores to represent the overwrought drama of the American soap opera is a tradition that dates back at least to late 1970s and early 1980s night-time serials. *Dynasty* (1981–89), in particular, also after an initial musically ambiguous first season, quickly developed a complex series of leitmotifs for each main character. In that case, the reference to 1930s Hollywood melodramas was overtly made in all aspects of the production; costume, hair, over-the-top dialogue and plots, and, above all, music. In *Buffy*, this choice is only one of many but clearly signposts the soap moments and maintains a clear distinction from other aspects of the score as the only melodic style of composition chosen. The three men who each develop relationships with Buffy represent the more serial aspects of the program and as such are given the musical material to match. Spike's music demonstrates this perfectly. Although a character introduced in the second season, Spike only receives his own leitmotif in the sixth, as he falls in love with Buffy and the relationship becomes more generically soap-like. That is, his music reflects this new persona evoking the conventions of the night-time serial. A more striking example, perhaps, because it was so short-lived, was Willow and Xander's love theme, which arrives in "Band Candy" (3.6), is carried through to "Revelations" (3.7) and is only present during those few brief moments of romance between them.[6]

Another technique brought to the forefront in *Buffy*'s second season was a specific kind of percussive action music. This generic designation applies to the final or penultimate act of any *Buffy* episode, at those moments when the featured threat is being dispatched usually through Buffy's abilities as the Slayer. This plot aspect is as distant from the romantic angle of the leitmotif as is possible and is musically quite different as well. Here, percussion and dissonance dominate the score: the brash timbres of brass instruments accompany each act of slaying, and the complex polyrhythmic accompaniment to action is what characterizes this particular genre.

A third and final genre designation for *Buffy*'s original non-diegetic music is horror, as this sound has evolved since the rise of the slasher genre in the late

---

[6] Thank you to Rob Gokee for pointing this example out. See Rob Gokee, "Buffy the Vampire Slayer 3.06: Band Candy," *Resource Site for Chris Beck @ Blunt Instrument*, 19 June 2005, accessed 29 February 2008 at http://www.bluntinstrument.org.uk/beck/buffy/3-06/bandcandy.htm.

1970s and early 1980s. Primary referents here include John Carpenter's electronic score for *Halloween* (1978), and Harry Manfredini's *Friday the 13th* (1980), but often references are made to earlier films such as Bernard Herrmann's *Psycho* (1960), or the intense dissonance of Bronislau Kaper's 1950s horror films such as *Them!* (1954). This genre sounds different from the action genre in its distinct lack of rhythmic tension. Instead, tension is created through the use of high, dissonant strings combined with low pedal points, often augmented by atonal stingers in brass or other "stabbing" instruments.

Finally, since the very beginning, one of *Buffy*'s primary stylistic referents was the high school drama, and accordingly the expectation is met by filling these teenage moments with largely diegetic rock and pop songs taken from real, not-yet-broken-though bands of the type to which our fictional characters are presumed to listen. Non-diegetic popular music also fills out the texture of these scenes, using cinematic techniques exemplified by John Hughes's Molly Ringwald vehicles such as *Sixteen Candles* (1984), *The Breakfast Club* (1985), and *Pretty in Pink* (1986).

One way of looking at these varying depictions of genre is to decide what the function of each genre is in the first place. What is being suggested by the use of melodrama, action, or horror? It may seem like a rather obvious observation, but first we must acknowledge that a fundamental aspect of each musical device, the very reason for its success, is that the musical genres themselves have built into their nature the ability to reflect the type of drama they are depicting. In its most straightforward sense, the diegetic music of the Bronze is quite literally the soundtrack to our characters' lives and requires the least justification from a theoretical viewpoint. When heard diegetically, this popular music is both creating a sense of realism for the teen drama (one of the genre's key requirements) and providing emotional support for the dialogue occurring over it (also one of the genre's key requirements). The non-diegetic score often functions in an equally uncomplicated way. For example, the rhythmic nature of action music is a synchretic depiction of the rhythm or motion displayed on screen, to borrow a term from sound theorist Michel Chion.[7] For Chion, the synchretic represents any sound for which there can be seen a literal sound source, such as the crack of contact between a baseball and bat shown on screen, or a violin's melody emerging from a visualized violin player. *Buffy*'s action music synchretically attempts to mirror the visualized violence. The situation becomes more complicated when we attempt to understand other genres like melodrama or horror. Here, music may be understood to either portray an inward or outward perspective directing the audience's attention to the intended point of view. As Brown observes about the score for *Double Indemnity* (1944), for example:

---

[7] Michel Chion, *Audio-Vision: Sound on Screen*, ed. and trans. Claudia Gorbman (New York, 1994), p. 63. Chion coined the term "synchresis" by combining the terms synchronism and synthesis, using it to describe the "spontaneous and irresistible weld" created in the audience's perception of simultaneous audio and visual on-screen events.

rather than involving us emotionally with specific characters and their specific situations, *Double Indemnity*'s score basically allows us to experience its characters only through the eyes of its ... protagonist ... It is therefore as if much of the music in *Double Indemnity* springs from the character's imagination to back the drama he is creating.[8]

His suggestion is that in some scoring society is reflecting its desires through music onto characters, as in the music used in classic Hollywood melodrama, where culture's melodic outpouring of acceptance for that kind of romantic love is on display. In other genres, for example, *film noir* or horror films, the score is in some sense controlled by the anti-social or deviant individual, resulting in what is read as ugly, anti-social music. This shift and loss of control—the removal of musical control from our protagonists and onto villains, a move from outside to inside, and the subsequent shift from tonality to dissonance—is one of the main devices through which contemporary film scoring achieves its power. It also considerably strengthens *Buffy*'s ability to shift between genres quickly: with so little similarity between these sounds, it is difficult to confuse the many options or approaches.

"Faith, Hope and Trick" (3.3) offers an example of many of the procedures I have been discussing. The episode deftly juggles genre throughout, moving carefully from popular music to action and suspense music, and large-scale orchestral sounds. Immediately after the familiar title credits, the story is centered on the Bronze. This space is almost always used in combination with popular music, either live or non-diegetic, to depict Buffy's life as a typical teenager. Accordingly, Third Eye Blind's "The Background" plays as Buffy and Angel dance and she tells him "I miss you." The lyrics to the song—"Everything is quiet since you're not around/And I live in the numbness now in the background"—mirror the situation depicted, as is typical of both film and television uses of popular song. This scene is revealed as a dream when the action shifts to Angel's home and a scene several episodes earlier is shown—Buffy driving a sword through Angelus. Here pop is replaced by suspense horror music, recapturing the fear of that prior situation. Buffy suddenly wakes from her dream and looks at the Claddagh ring given to her by Angel in the previous season, and, as she does, first two, then four notes of their love theme emerge from the fading suspense cue. This reference is enough to evoke both Angel and the melodrama of their original encounter in "Surprise". Instantly, this melodrama replaces all sense of suspense or horror (seen earlier as the threat of the unstable), as the subject position of the music returns to the safety of tonality. Later, towards the end of the episode, as "normal-guy" Scott unknowingly tries to give Buffy an identical Claddagh ring to the one she and Angel exchanged, this reference triggers the theme again—vaguely, and just for a few seconds—before morphing into suspense music at the appearance of Giles. Giles is almost always involved in the horror or suspense portion of each episode, and this new cue alerts the audience to the shift in genre again, from melodrama to

---

[8] Brown, *Overtones and Undertones*, p. 133.

suspense. At the end of the episode loyal viewers are rewarded for their constancy by the fulfillment of the earlier teasing references to Buffy and Angel's love theme as Buffy tells Giles and Willow about Angel being cured of his demonic possession at the end of the last season. Here, as Buffy recollects the events leading up to her "killing" him, and the pain of their relationship, we are presented with a full, lush version of their theme, one that recreates the original atmosphere of their feelings in all its Hollywood romance. This is followed moments later by Buffy entering Angel's mansion, and, dialogue-free, she says goodbye by removing her ring and placing it on the ground, evoking their love theme as it was heard for the first time in "Surprise" in ironic full circle, a bare clarinet replaced by an even more empty-sounding piano melody, echoing with reverb. Our concluding shift in genre, though, occurs seconds later, when suspense music returns to herald the return of Angel in a lightning burst of energy, returning viewers to the supernatural realm of the program. Of course, even this isn't the final shift in genre in the episode—this is reserved for the closing credits music, the hard guitar punk-pop tune functioning as a concluding jolt back to the realm of teen drama.

Irony

I would argue that one of the primary themes of the series throughout its seven-year run was the exploration of identity all adolescents face in high school and college, a "trying on" of different identities and personalities. This situation is exaggerated in the series often by its realization through supernatural means. The heightened character malleability *Buffy* offers facilitates equally exaggerated musical commentaries. Occasionally this music is used comically, is self-consciously extradiegetic, but just as often *Buffy*'s music enacts a synchretic manifestation of the action on screen.

What, then, of that music that evokes genre in an ironic or more self-conscious way? Or of those cues that ironically contradict the onscreen action? How are viewers meant to understand genre in the context of these more complex evocations? The issues raised by these questions reflect a larger issue in postmodern philosophy, chief among them the anti-modernist notion that "everything has been done before," articulated by Jameson's fear that:

> the writers and artists of the present day will no longer be able to invent new styles and worlds—they've already been invented; only a limited number of combinations are possible; the unique ones have been thought of already. So the weight of the whole modernist aesthetic tradition—now dead—also "weighs like a nightmare on the brains of the living" as Marx said in another context.[9]

---

[9] Fredric Jameson, "Postmodernism and Consumer Society," in E. Ann Kaplan (ed.), *Postmodernism and Its Discontents: Theories, Practices* (London/New York, 1988), p. 28.

This fear of a tired continual play of played-out referents is directly challenged by *Buffy*, with its resuscitation of archetypes for both comedy and drama. In this, I am arguing against Catherine Belsey, who, using Althusser, suggests that television, among other arts, operates in a "classic realism" mode, emphasizing the "illusionism" preferred in the medium, disguising its artificiality and enforcing "a single privileged discourse which contains and places all the others."[10] It is exactly the lack of a single privileged discourse in this era of satellite television that makes the medium such a dynamic force in minority interest programming in the new millennium, with *Buffy* only one among many examples.

I would argue that the program's standard method of referencing specific musical genres is what enables the comedic practice of ironic interpellation. We get the joke because we are familiar with these musical markers from their more serious usages in this same program, often in the same episode. A few examples will demonstrate this phenomenon. For each "serious" character or relationship there is often a comic mirror relationship. Xander, as Buffy's least capable assistant, is most often set in opposition to her legitimate emotions and confrontations. In "The Initiative" (4.7) Xander has taken over Buffy's cemetery patrol and encounters the vampire Harmony (the comic equivalent to the more serious Spike). Their scratching, kicking, flat-palmed slapping fight is depicted in mock-epic slow-motion and scored with completely serious action music highlighting the absurdity of the situation, while at the same time referencing earlier authentic fights Buffy has had herself with more legitimate opponents. From what subject position is this music coming? In the diegesis of *Buffy*, the audience knows that vampires are a real danger, that Buffy risks her life each night when she patrols and that Xander could potentially face life-threatening encounters if he substitutes for her—but extradiegetically the audience knows that Xander's encounter with the incompetent Harmony contains no threat whatsoever. The musical commentary to the fight draws attention to the production process, that the director and composer want the audience to know that *they* know how silly the characters are. Just as each serious battle contains in it the reference to all the genre films that came before it, here we face multiple layers of reference, resulting in a comic effect. Ultimately, this process relies on a kind of intertexuality common to most postmodern discourse, a discourse in which Pierre Macherey believes that:

> to explain the work is to show that, contrary to appearances, it is not independent, but bears in its material substance the imprint of a determinate absence which is also the principle of its identity. The book is furrowed by the allusive presence of those other books against which it is elaborated; it circles about the absence of that which it cannot say.[11]

---

[10] Catherine Belsey, *Critical Practice* (London, 1980), p. 92, quoted in Nehamas, "Serious Watching," p. 48.

[11] Pierre Macherey, *A Theory of Literary Production* (London, 1978), pp. 78–80.

But of course, in *Buffy*, the audience is required to say what is absent: it must recognize the absent source, or the joke will not be funny.

In "Bewitched, Bothered and Bewildered" (2.16) music is again used in a way that potentially highlights the production aspect of its construction. Xander's newfound supernatural sexual desirability is demonstrated by a slow-motion strut down the corridor of Sunnydale High School accompanied by funk music, the Average White Band's "Got the Love." This is a generic scene borrowed from countless films, most specifically a combination of the opening tracking shot in *Saturday Night Fever* (1977), featuring a strutting Tony Manero (John Travolta) and the later scene as he enters the disco, desired by all women.[12] The music here, however, has been shifted from disco to funk, possibly to account for the cultural relocation disco has undergone, from heterosexual to homosexual, since the release of that film. Determining how this is funny is a bit complicated and again depends on a knowledge of the program and Xander's traditional role as comic relief. It is initially inconceivable in this scene that he could be sexy to women based on his reception from them in the past. While on the one hand 1970s funk is often portrayed as still containing the essence of "funkiness," on the other it is hopelessly unfashionable, a remnant of an embarrassing age of ostentatious sexuality totally at odds with the more restrained sexuality of a contemporary teenage generation. This double meaning combines to give the music its ironic charm. If Xander were truly irresistible in a sincere way, it is hard to imagine this is the music he would have been given; rather, it is more likely that a contemporary pop song would have been used reflecting sincere emotions. In fact, an excellent parallel exists in season 3 when Scott approaches Buffy in "Faith, Hope and Trick" at the Bronze and Darling Violetta's "Cure" plays behind his authentically romantic banter.

There seem to be two ways to approach this scene with Xander. First, one could compare it to the fight with Harmony: a campy reference to other bad teen movies, with all the self-conscious awareness on the part of the production team that this implies. Slow-motion camerawork highlights the montage's "don't take this part seriously" effect, as if this section could be removed from the realism of the rest of the episode. We are, in essence, laughing at Xander, laughing at *Buffy*, laughing at teen drama.

Another possibility exists, though. This additional meaning does not discount the earlier reading, but complicates it, and that is the fictional reality of the situation. Because of a love spell, characters are still threatened by the outcome of this situation, as humorous as it is. This is a "real" love spell with the potential to destroy our characters. Ironically, of course, despite the lyrics "Got the love/Got to make it work on you/Got the love/Just can't keep it hid," the one person the spell has not worked on is the girl it was cast for, Cordelia. The music must be taken seriously on this account. It is emerging from the diegesis as some subconscious

---

[12] S. Renee Dechert, "'My Boyfriend's in the Band!' *Buffy* and the Rhetoric of Music," in Rhonda V. Wilcox and David Lavery (eds), *Fighting the Forces: What's at Stake in Buffy the Vampire Slayer* (Lanham, MD, 2002), p. 220.

manifestation of Xander's attractiveness, a sexiness that in other, equally real genre films is represented in the same way. According to the traditional makeup of this scene, the slow-motion is to be understood, like the music, as a concentration of feeling, a distillation of the intensity this spell has created.

Either way this scene is approached, however, one thing remains; the character of Xander never breaks through the "fourth wall": he remains trapped in his environment and has no conscious awareness of non-diegetic music. He is either truly a victim of his own spell and the music is recasting him as a genuine if hitherto unsuspected sex symbol (we are laughing with him), or he is a tool of an omnipotent director, manipulated for our pleasure (we are laughing at him).

Another example of this self-conscious toying with the characters (and audience) occurs in "The Zeppo" (3.13), where Xander finally loses his virginity, to Faith. The scene is played with total seriousness, and the music is passionate, romantic, sensual. Suddenly, the director cuts the music and the image to Xander standing outside Faith's apartment, her saying, deadpan, "that was great, I gotta shower," and throwing him out of the house. Is this Xander's impression of the event? Incredibly moving to him until the moment Faith abruptly chucks him out the door? Or is it the director having fun at Xander's expense, interrupting him before anything too graphic is shown, a pawn in the director's game?

Xander is not alone in this musical treatment. Dawn, normally a serious character, finds herself on the opposite side of this equation in "Him" (7.6), when, under the influence of a love spell, she fawns over the school's quarterback to the strains of Max Steiner's theme from *A Summer Place* (1959). Again, we are either mocking Dawn and all those for whom the theme from *A Summer Place* could actually represent true romance; or we are meant to think of that hackneyed tune as a legitimate expression of her feelings, heightened, like the song, to ludicrous extremes because of the spell.

One final demonstration will show how virtuosically a director can move between genres, while negotiating the delicate boundary between irony and sincerity. The episode "Something Blue" (4.9) contains all of the genres under discussion here, beginning with a dramatic, romantic leitmotif representing Willow's grief over the loss of Oz, her ex-boyfriend. Heard whenever Willow expresses her feelings of loss in private, the theme swells with lush strings and a simple piano melody (in an orchestration practically identical to that used for Buffy and Angel's love theme). Clearly, the music is evoking the genre of melodrama. The second time this motif is heard, however, it is transformed halfway through into a carefully crafted suspense reference as Willow casts a spell to try and cure her breaking heart. So far, so *Buffy*. Unfortunately, the spell does not work and instead has the effect, among other things, of making Buffy and Spike fall in love. As before, the non-diegetic music treats this artificial love as just as real as any more legitimate relationship we have seen thus far. This means that when Buffy and Spike announce their engagement to Giles the music swells to a joyous climax, a slightly dated chromaticism in the harmony, evocative of old fashioned Max-Steiner-esque Hollywood scoring potentially betraying its function as satire, but still using the same orchestration as before.[13] Our only serious indication that something is wrong occurs at the end of this cue when the camera shifts to Giles. As the perspective shifts from Buffy to Giles, suddenly romance morphs into horror, augmented by the addition of the piano, which had been previously associated with the legitimate emotions of Willow and was entirely absent from Buffy and Spike's love theme. Moments later, Buffy asks Giles to give her away at her wedding, and the music that accompanies this scene is every bit as sincere as Willow's earlier heart-breaking scene, with tender strings and an emotional piano melody. It is obvious that for a second Giles is buying into the emotion before snapping back into reality. Real, fake, inward, outward—all of these cues relate to their function as representation of genre.

As these examples show, *Buffy*'s composers constantly negotiated the complex range of musical options allowable when the program itself refused to limit its options to a single genre. Rather than letting this ambiguity trouble them, they turned this into a virtuosic display of generic dexterity. By inserting a constant play between sincerity and irony into the music as well as the drama, composers, particularly Christophe Beck, were given an exceedingly uncommon gift in television: the chance to allow their music to define, strengthen, and often contradict the action on screen.

---

[13] Chromaticism as a harmonic tool is largely associated in film and television scoring with the overwrought compositional style of Golden Age Hollywood, a kind of heightened emotionality which is unfashionable, but perfectly understandable in a parody of romance.

Chapter 3
Variations on Themes for Geeks and Heroes: Leitmotif, Style and the Musico-dramatic Moment[1]

Rob Haskins

Buffy the Vampire Slayer (1997–2003) is justly celebrated for the important role music plays to heighten the series's unusual blend of the supernatural, romance, melodrama, and comedy. The strident theme song sets the tone for the series as vital and youth-oriented, one that is cool and current. Source music that the characters hear at the Bronze becomes the soundtrack of their lives. Dramatic scoring serves a number of familiar functions: for instance, to accentuate moments of conflict and tension, as in the frequent, elegantly choreographed fight scenes; or to offer an emphatically formal punctuation of an episode's structure, as in the orchestral stinger—the violent, fragmentary orchestral cue—that often precedes the fade to black before a commercial break.

Once *Buffy* hit its stride in its second season, however, dramatic scoring assumed even greater significance through the contributions of Christophe Beck, one of several individuals who replaced Walter Murphy as composer. Murphy's dramatic scoring was competent but rarely inspired and sometimes relied heavily upon rather artificial-sounding samples of instruments and predictable synthesizer sounds.[2] Beck, who scored 12 of the season's 22 episodes and went on to score all of seasons 3 and 4, combined electronic sounds with fine samples of acoustic instruments, and he augmented the vitality of the recordings by hiring session musicians; the quality and variety of his orchestrations far exceeded Murphy's; and he developed several important leitmotifs, generally understood in film or television music studies as a musical idea that accompanies the entrance of a particular character, a reference to a particular activity, or an emotional state experienced by particular characters—the haunting and lyrical cue that signified the love between Buffy and Angel is one well-known example. Beck's work won an Emmy in 1998 for the episode "Becoming, Part 1" (2.21) and arguably set the

---

[1] This paper is for Robert Cobert and Christophe Beck, and *in memoriam* Dan Curtis.

[2] As an example, consider the cue accompanying Buffy's descent to the Master in season 1's "Prophecy Girl" (1.12): faux-portentous brass chords are reinforced with a reedy synthesizer patch and overly artificial reverb, and the chord progression is hackneyed and totally forgettable—style without substance.

tone for the remainder of the series. For instance, Thomas Wanker's scores for seasons 5 and 6 owes such a debt to Beck's orchestration and expressive orientation that Beck could have written them himself.

More interesting is the character of the music itself, a diverse but orderly assortment of idioms including: indie rock; modernist classical music with dissonant harmonies and angular, asymmetrical rhythms, recalling Stravinsky's *Rite of Spring* (1912); and the more harmonious, repetitive postmodernist classical music that emerged in the 1980s, a style resembling, for instance, the final movement of John Adams's *Harmonielehre* (1984) or Michael Nyman's soundtrack for *The Piano* (1993). Many of these diverse cues were written by Beck, while others were selected from the libraries of various commercial houses by music supervisor John C. King. Beck's orchestrations lend added warmth to his musical ideas, which often include lyrical, well-formed melodies and unusual, colourful harmonies that, nevertheless, rarely stray far from the major and minor triads familiar in Western classical music. Nonetheless, the harmonies surprise because they are used in unconventional ways, sometimes with unexpected chromatic shifts. Many of the other cues are equally euphonious and inventive.

The subtleties of Beck's Buffy-Angel love theme offer a straightforward example (Figure 3.1). The chordal progression that accompanies the lyrical melody follows a pattern familiar in tonal music, but the progression breaks off before its expected completion; then the four chords of the incomplete progression recur. Meanwhile, the melodic line that it accompanies gracefully descends during the first statement of the progression, then begins a more poignant ascent for the repetition. All these elements beautifully evoke the unconventional nature of the relationship between Slayer and vampire—the heartbreaking impossibility of its full realization, but also its enduring passion.[3]

Figure 3.1   Incomplete chord progression in the Buffy-Angel love theme (Christophe Beck)

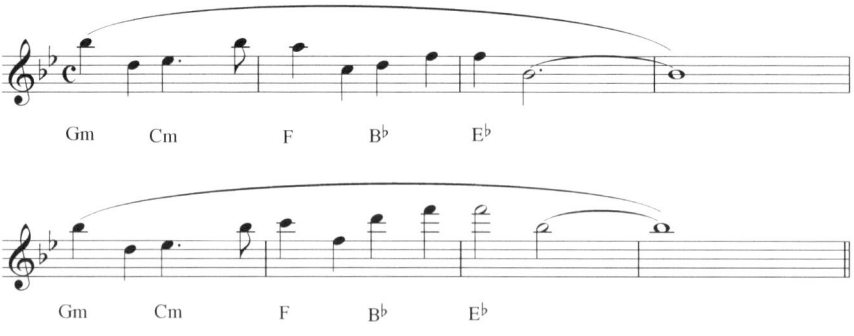

---

[3] Beck creates nascent forms of the theme in various early episodes of season 2, and the theme appears in various keys throughout the series. One of the first appearances of the complete theme occurs in "Surprise" (2.13) in the key of F minor.

Buffy's Avuncular Elder: Dark Shadows

Buffy's heavy reliance on memorable music is not unprecedented and was in fact equally important in a much earlier television serial, *Dark Shadows*, which aired on the ABC network Mondays through Fridays from June 1966 to April 1971. The two series share certain affinities. Like *Buffy*, *Dark Shadows* explored the general theme of the supernatural in modernity (and postmodernity); and, like *Buffy*, the earlier series enjoyed a diverse audience that ranged from teenagers to academics.[4] A brief comparison of the two series will help provide a context for understanding the richer, more engaged listening experience that I believe *Buffy*'s soundtracks offer to audiences.

The brainchild of producer-director Dan Curtis, *Dark Shadows* began as a Gothic soap opera that told the story of a beautiful governess, Victoria Winters, who worked for the wealthy Collins family living in a sprawling mansion in Maine.[5] In time, however, this story arc was abandoned in favor of sustained attention on the character of Barnabas Collins, a noble, guilt-ridden vampire who had been chained inside his coffin in 1796 and unexpectedly released by an itinerant ne'er-do-well in 1967. Thereafter, the dramatic situations of the series depended upon pointed interactions between magic and modernity. Dr Julia Hoffman, a blood specialist and psychiatrist who had fallen in unrequited love with Barnabas, attempted to cure him through a series of unconventional experiments and later applied the same skills to treat several other supernatural creatures. Time travel (to both past and present) formed a staple of the series, and two story lines even explored the notion of parallel universes; such phenomena were often ably explained by Professor T. Eliot Stokes, who taught occult studies at the local college.

Some of these elements also figure prominently in the *Buffy* mythos. Buffy herself resembles the intrepid Victoria Winters before Barnabas's arrival: the central character who cleverly ferrets out all the mystical oddities plaguing the community and her loved ones. Angel offers a distant echo of Barnabas. Both are vampires who agonize over their state but ultimately find purpose battling the forces of evil; Angel loves Buffy but cannot consummate the relationship, while Barnabas loves Victoria, who cannot return his love. Rupert Giles, the librarian and custodian of arcane knowledge, reminds some viewers of Professor Stokes. And Willow Rosenberg, the waif-like computer whiz who initially addresses her shyness around men through intellectual pursuits, stands in as a kind of Dr Hoffman.

But there are important differences, too. After Barnabas arrives, for instance, Victoria becomes increasingly incapable of dealing with the supernatural forces around her; and neither she nor other pivotal characters, such as Professor Stokes,

---

[4] For more, see Kathryn Leigh Scott (ed.), *The Dark Shadows Companion* (Universal City, CA, 1990).

[5] Throughout the series, the writers borrowed liberally from various literary classics; the Victoria Winters story line, for instance, owed some of its content to Charlotte Brontë's *Jane Eyre*.

ever realizes Barnabas's true nature. In *Buffy*, however, the protagonists are all equally aware of the supernatural forces they fight and know they must work together in order to succeed. The series differ, too, in their treatment of magic and modernity. In *Dark Shadows*, magic was often placed in opposition to science, and in such a way that science could in some cases effectively discipline magic. In *Buffy*, science is a tool that the characters sometimes use to harness magical forces, but there is never an instance in which rationality conquers magic. For this reason, Willow and her early role model Jenny Calendar combine the two pursuits in their work, and Jenny identifies herself as a techno-pagan. It is hard to imagine the staid Dr Hoffman engaging in such behavior.

The role of music in *Dark Shadows* and in *Buffy* also reveals further similarities and differences. In the earlier series, music was almost ubiquitous; it frequently gave the series the quality of melodramas, music-theater pieces of the eighteenth and nineteenth centuries in which actors spoke text simultaneously with instrumental music. A series of musical cues, composed by Robert Cobert and available on long-playing records, were selected by the series's musical supervisor, Sybil Weinberger. These were used to accompany certain stock situations such as a visit to the local cemetery, the act of hypnosis, or the casting of a spell. In addition, certain of these cues were, from the series's beginnings, associated with specific characters. As the series gained in popularity and characters remained constant, this simple leitmotivic quality became increasingly important. For instance, one melancholy cue associated with Barnabas was so heavily identified with his character that it was used during an unusual period of several weeks in which he did not appear, in order to remind viewers of his presence.

Although Cobert wrote a handful of additional cues as the series progressed, most of them were in place when the series began, and most were used repeatedly during its five-year run. This gave the series a certain formal quality that occasionally complemented its dramaturgy. One of the most telling instances of this formalism occurred in the so-called transition moments before commercials: at these points, an unusual revelation is made and the characters freeze while the camera lingers on them in extreme close-up, all of which is accompanied by music. Such a frozen close-up can last up to ten seconds. In episode 815, for instance, Quentin Collins asks a powerful sorcerer, Count Petofi, if he will release the Collins family from a spell that the Count has cast with his magical hand. Petofi's equivocal response, "There are some things I will not ask this hand to do," implies a refusal, and the camera alternately focuses on the Count's face (frozen with a smug smile), on Quentin's, and Barnabas's (both frozen with expressions of hyperbolic fear) for a transition that lasts ten seconds. Cobert's menacing musical cue, scored for strings and timpani, culminates on the dissonant interval of a minor second.[6] The aforementioned orchestral stingers that punctuate a sequence preceding a

---

[6] See *Dark Shadows: DVD Collection 15* (2004), episode 815. The transition begins at 9:21.

commercial break on *Buffy* are similar; they often show a character motionless, or nearly so, but they rarely last more than one or two seconds.[7]

The use (and reuse) of pre-recorded musical cues in *Dark Shadows* also, of course, gave the series a rather static quality, which was further reinforced by the fact that characters' personalities rarely changed unless they were under the influence of evil forces. It also stressed the low-budget aspects of the series that gave it the feeling of a guilty pleasure—or, in Joyce Millman's memorable description, the opportunity "to feast on camp-a-licious flubbed lines, awkward silences, wandering boom mikes, misfiring props and special effects along the lines of dime-store vampire teeth and rubber bats on a string."[8] Even so, the music for the series showed an impressive level of sophistication for its time. All the cues were orchestral and many included the novel sound of the theremin, which was relatively new in television scoring at the time: the majority of musical cues for daytime serials of the time were still performed on electronic organ. Moreover, the music associated with the series exemplified various musical styles: a modernistic style with extended tonal triads and frequent dissonance supplied the usual fare, but Cobert also created nineteenth-century parlor and cabaret songs, jazz and rock tracks, all to be treated as source music for the various time periods in which the story lines were set.

Buffy's musical cues resembled those of *Dark Shadows* in their pervasiveness, in the use of leitmotifs, and in stylistic variety. But whereas the cues in *Dark Shadows* were nearly always limited to repetitions of various tracks from pre-existing recordings (a practice referred to in the industry as needle dropping), many of the cues for *Buffy* seem to be recorded anew for each episode; sometimes a leitmotif is rescored and subtly varied each time it appears in an episode, for example the various appearances of the Buffy-Angel love theme in season 2's "Surprise" (2.13). Other dramatic scoring obliquely varies material from a well-known theme in order to comment on a dramatic situation in the script. In season 3's "Revelations" (3.7), an act 1 scene shows Buffy and Angel touching as they perform T'ai Chi; their feelings have begun to reignite, and the music presents a salient fragment from the love theme—not enough material to qualify as a variation, but something more akin to a brief allusion that foreshadows events yet to come. The variety of musical styles in *Buffy*'s dramatic or source scoring also reveals other aspects of the characters, such as their social status or their position in the unfolding drama. In particular, indie-style rock often appears as a marker of Buffy's peers at Sunnydale High or in the Bronze.

---

[7] Compare the transition in season 3's episode "The Wish" (3.9) at the conclusion of act 1, which accompanies Anya's menacing "Done!" after Cordelia wishes that Buffy had never come to Sunnydale.

[8] Joyce Millman, "Dark Shadows," *salon.com*, 20 May 2002, accessed 20 June 2006 at http://dir.salon.com/story/ent/masterpiece/2002/05/20/dark_shadows/index.html. Indeed, several memorable musical cues at wrong moments provide the musical equivalent of misfired props or flubbed lines.

From Opera to *Buffy*: Contextualizing Musico-Dramatic Techniques

Both of these modes of musical discourse—subtle or overt thematic variation and/or development of thematic ideas, and the use of style as a marker of character and dramatic situation—have a long history in opera. In particular, Mozart has long been recognized for his penchant to depict characters and dramatic situations through music as clearly as his librettists did through their poetry. His Italian operas from the 1780s and 1790s draw on a treasury of shared musical styles and dance rhythms to give the audience insight into his characters, their psychology and their social status. As Wye Jamison Allanbrook points out, Mozart's audiences would have recognized these stylistic references and used them to understand elements of the character or drama that were not made explicit in the operatic libretto. For example, in *Don Giovanni*, Mozart evokes the age and conservatism of the Don's jilted lover Donna Elvira by writing an aria for her in the style of Handel, a style in vogue some sixty years previously. Furthermore, Mozart accompanies the Don's utterances throughout the opera with the rhythms and characteristic figurations of dances from various socioeconomic strata in order to illustrate his chameleonic ability to appeal to any sort of woman he desires.[9]

In the late nineteenth century, Wagner created a new kind of opera in which he imagined that the voices would not take precedence over the orchestra; rather, both would participate in a mode of musical unfolding that resembled the purely instrumental tradition of the nineteenth-century symphony. In this new type of music drama, as it has come to be called, Wagner used a series of recurring musical ideas which were also called leitmotifs. Successive appearances of the leitmotifs in Wagner's music dramas, however, were not identical but instead could be reorchestrated, extended, lightly varied, and made to accompany activities other than the ones with which they were originally associated. As a result, the musical ideas took on a life of their own and contributed to an evolving sense of the drama rather than one which was purely static.[10]

As I will discuss later, these methods of allying music with drama make important contributions to *Buffy*, but they are neither the only ones nor the most notable instances of the series's imaginative approach to the soundtrack. A variety of novel relationships between dialogue and other soundtrack elements (with or without other dramatic action) appeared so frequently during the course of the series that they became almost as important as the ongoing narrative itself. Examples include the co-existence of dialogue and dramatic scoring as equals (indeed, season 6's "Once More, With Feeling" [6.7] sets dialogue *as* music, in the manner of musical theater); long sequences of images accompanied only by dramatic scoring

---

[9] See Wye Jamison Allanbrook, *Rhythmic Gesture in Mozart: Le nozze di Figaro and Don Giovanni* (Chicago/London, 1983), pp. 235–8 and 218–20.

[10] For more, see Carl Dahlhaus, *Richard Wagner's Music Dramas*, trans. Mary Whittall (Cambridge, 1979), pp. 61–4. The various nascent forms of the Buffy-Angel love theme mentioned in n. 3 function in a similar manner.

(season 4's "Hush" [4.10]); even extended sequences containing neither dialogue nor music (season 5's "The Body" [5.16]), in which silence joins with *mise-en-scène* to assume a greater importance in the drama than usual. As a result, viewers could respond to many of these soundtrack elements as decisive conveyances of dramatic significance or nuance rather than as elements that supplement or augment dramatic moments conveyed primarily by the agencies of the actors alone through, for instance, dialogue, facial expression, or body language.

Of course, these shifting relationships between narrative and soundtrack mirror the polysemic quality of the major characters. Angel, the vampire with a soul, emerges early on in the series as a mysterious figure whose ultimate motives are unclear, but his alliance with the forces of good eventually becomes plain. An unexpected turn of events occurs when Buffy and he make love and he reverts to the evil character, Angelus, that he had been in the series's prehistory. Even after his return from this unexpected descent into evil, his character maintains abundant contradictions, doubts, even occasional malevolence. The development of Willow's character is even more dynamic. From her nerdy beginnings, she matures into a powerful witch, comes out as a lesbian, and develops a dangerous addiction to magics that brings her close to total annihilation. By the series's end, however, she seems to find a way to overcome this addictive trait and emerge as the character most responsible for facilitating the defeat of the evil forces that are about to destroy the world.

The complexity and paradox of these characters invite us to turn similarly detailed attention to the complexity and paradoxes of the musical score. In order to show what kinds of insights we might gain from such attention, I want to describe how music functions in two pairs of related scenes from episodes in *Buffy*'s third season as they might be heard by what I will call meticulous listeners. Such listeners would, first and foremost, be omnivorous, able to recognize musical styles from a variety of popular and classical traditions: in short, they can savor the stylistic variety implicit in Beck's music and other source and dramatic scoring. Meticulous listeners would probably be responsive to subtle elements of harmony in these musical styles and sensitive to such aspects of compositional design as variation technique and the development of thematic ideas, whether or not they know the technical vocabulary traditionally used to describe them. Such listeners could also appreciate the finest nuances in the development of plot lines in the *Buffy* world—nuances that are also reflected through subtle signals from dialogue or body language—and understand other soundtrack elements as intimately bound up with such signals. I acknowledge that *Buffy*'s viewers comprise a diverse cross-section of humanity that may or may not have access to and literacy in a variety of classical musical styles (although they probably have a sophisticated understanding of musical conventions in music for film and television generally). I hope my limited use of technical language and musical examples will not deter any readers.

Musical Style Transformed: Xander's Progress in "The Zeppo"

Most of *Buffy*'s characters matured and deepened as the series progressed. One of the first to show this growth was Alexander (Xander) Harris. Though he would end the series as a self-assured, resourceful, even heroic, young adult man, Xander began his journey as a geeky, wisecracking misfit who developed a crush on Buffy shortly after her appearance in Sunnydale. This relationship could not be consummated—partly because of Buffy's higher calling, partly because of her stronger romantic attraction to Angel—and so Xander stumbled into a series of improbable demonic infatuations and his almost inexplicable early relationship with the class queen, Cordelia Chase. Though he never lacked courage, he often had very little strength or special knowledge to add to the activities of the Scooby gang.

Even though Xander's role in season 3 rarely extended past his reliable contributions of comic relief, audiences began to see evidence of his progress toward the heroic. In "The Zeppo" (3.13), these two traits of Xander—the comic and the heroic—come together in a stunning fashion, as he first becomes the unwitting chauffeur for a band of zombified high-school bullies and ultimately acts as the agent that prevents them from realizing a plot to destroy the school with a massive explosion. Two of the musical cues help to delineate Xander's essential nature—as perhaps the most prominent Everyman character of *Buffy*—through a musical style evoking indie rock or pop. But subtle variations in the content of the two cues also illustrate his progress toward the heroic and do so without violating the boundaries of the musical style that represents him.

By the time of "The Zeppo," the secret liaison between Xander and Willow has long been revealed. The mortified Cordy has banished Xander from her life, and Xander is aimless, unsure of himself once again. The episode opens with an ensemble scene in which he is not prominent, and which contextualizes the more important scenes to follow. He appears in his usual status as the bumbling low man on the totem pole of the Scoobies as they face a trio of particularly virulent demons in a dark cave. Each character except Xander clearly has an important role to play: Willow casts a spell that obscures the cave in a thick fog; Buffy and Faith work together with their superhuman strength to dispatch the demons; and Giles helps to manage and produce the entire event, although as usual his production skills fall just a bit short. After the fight is concluded, Xander emerges from a pile of debris, where it seems he had been knocked unconscious. The remaining Scoobies express some concern over his safety, and ultimately Giles suggests that Xander might do better by holding up the rear in subsequent battles. In other words, Giles tells Xander that he should not try to participate; he should remain an observer and almost entirely out of harm's way.

This situation is immediately echoed in the first scene following the opening credits. We see the familiar exterior of Sunnydale High, where Xander attempts to join a game of catch that two jocks are playing. The musical cue ("Dodgems," by

Sound Stage Ltd)[11] confirms both Xander's Everyman status and his clumsiness (Figure 3.2a). Scored for an ensemble of guitars and drum kit, it closely resembles a verse of an indie rock song without lyrics. Three chords appear in a continuous cycle that sounds four times: the first chord briefly establishes a home key, while the second and third outline a progression that facilitates a smooth transition back to the initial chord. The emotional affect of this cycle sounds familiar and unassuming, and the cyclical repetition sets up a groove or pattern of expectation that nicely reflects Xander's desire to participate in the game.

Figure 3.2a   Three chords in "Dodgems" (Sound Stage Ltd)

Figure 3.2b   "Chorus" and compression of original three chords in "Dodgems"

Shortly afterward, the indie rock song shifts its pattern to suggest a chorus (the change occurs almost simultaneously with Xander's entreaty, "Les, buddy!"); the chords are nearly the same as before, but now the first alternates once with the second and the third has expanded to twice its original length, a device that

---

[11] Rob Gokee, "Buffy the Vampire Slayer 3.13: The Zeppo," *Resource Site for Chris Beck @ Blunt Instrument*, 25 August 2005, accessed 30 June 2006 at http://www.bluntinstrument.org.uk/beck/buffy/3-13/thezeppo.htm. Thanks to Christophe Beck for this reference.

prolongs our expectation for the return of the cycle and effectively complements Xander's increasingly impassioned entreaties to join the game, to belong, to matter (Figure 3.2b). During this first hearing of the new cycle, one of the jocks finally throws the ball to Xander. The chorus cycle begins again as Xander attempts to catch it. But shortly after the repetition begins, the ball collides with the lunch of school bully Jack O'Toole—soon to be revealed as a zombie who participates in a scheme to plant a bomb in the school's basement. The three chords of the original cycle are now compressed from the comfortable four-beat rhythm of the original cue into a symmetrical series of smaller beat patterns (Figure 3.2b, mm. 5–6), and the cue ends without tonal closure. Xander is left to cope with the social damage that he has suffered without the benefit of music. His attempts to assuage Jack are mostly ineffectual, and after Jack promises to do Xander bodily harm when he assembles his gang, a brief, menacing cue (by Beck) plays that rapidly transforms the comedy of the scene.

Shortly after extricating himself from this lame performance, Xander is approached by Cordelia, who has observed the entire incident and who effectively reduces him to dust:

> Cordelia: It must be really hard when all your friends have, like, super powers—Slayer, werewolf, witches, vampires—and you're just, like, this little nothing … Xander, you're the *useless* part of the group; you're the Zeppo.

Xander attempts to counter Cordy's attack with his trademark witty comebacks, but by the end of the scene it is clear that his humiliation is complete. As she walks away, Cordy exults: "There was no part of that that wasn't fun!"

But Xander's subsequent (and predictable) misadventures in the episode progress in an unexpected way. Believing that he needs to become cool, Xander decides that acquiring a gimmicky accessory would offer the quickest route to coolness and arrives at campus the next day in a vintage 1957 Chevrolet Bel Air convertible that he has borrowed from his uncle. Through a twist of fate characteristic of his hapless luck, he finds himself acting as the driver for the zombie gang that Jack has resurrected. The situation comes to a head when the gang members urge Xander to become a full-fledged member—and zombie—himself, courtesy of Jack and Jack's knife, "Katie." Xander manages to escape, and discovers the gang's plot; unable to enlist the assistance of the other Scoobies, he sets out for the school on his own. Along the way he manages to kill two of the zombies, confronts Jack, engages him in a charged game of intimidation over the ticking time bomb, and ultimately coerces Jack into deactivating it.

In the final sequence of the episode, the Scoobies minus Xander reflect on their own brush with death—their successful battle to prevent the Hellmouth from opening through the efforts of the Sisterhood of Jhe. Willow muses on the cluelessness of the world around them: "No one will ever know how close it came to stopping—never know what we did." When Xander enters, he elects not to tell his friends about his own important contribution to the eradication of last night's danger. In the episode's final scene, he walks across the lawn of Sunnydale High and encounters Cordelia once more; she continues her attempts to demolish Xander's self-esteem. His response is to say nothing: he smiles knowingly at her, and Cordy looks away nervously. In a reversal of the opening scene's camerawork, the camera follows Xander as he walks away. Cordy now recedes into the background, unable to say anything but "What!?" three times.

The musical cue here—"For the Glory," by Extreme Music—subtly indicates the beginnings of Xander's transformation, already hinted at by his strong, silent reticence with the Scoobies (Figure 3.3). It begins as Xander smiles enigmatically; the cue resembles the indie-style rock that opened the episode and recalls the memory of Xander's ignominious failure on the lawn when the episode began. Now, however, the indie rock moves toward a different conclusion. The chord progression contains the three chords of the opening cue, but adds three additional chords that complicate the straightforward sense of direction in the first cue's cycle.[12]

Figure 3.3   "For the Glory" (Extreme Music) in "The Zeppo"

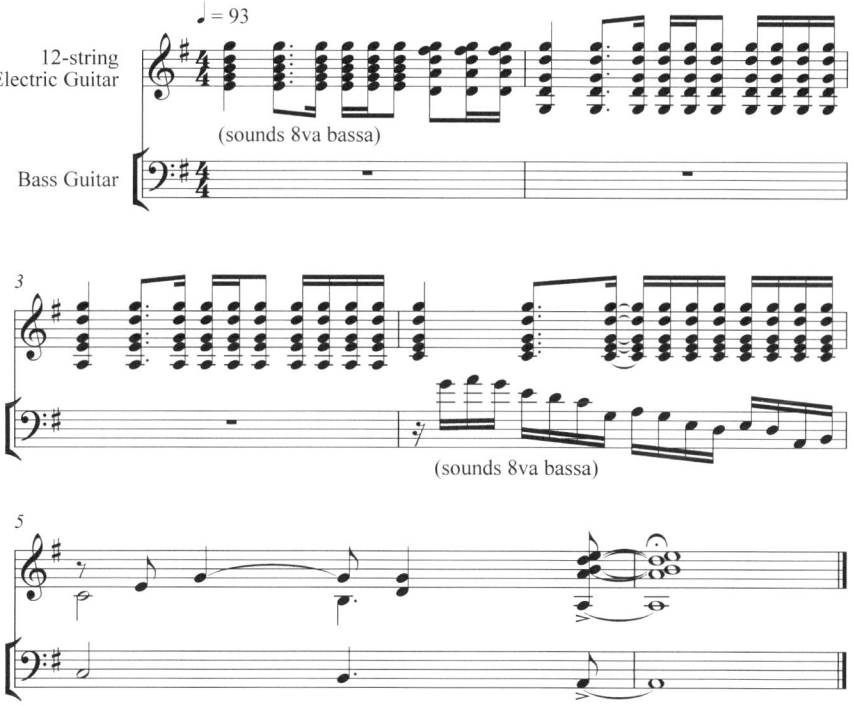

[12] The salient chords are E minor, D major, G major, A minor, C major, and A minor—vi, V, I, ii, IV, and ii in G major. The pitch class G sounds through all the chord changes, including D major.

Indeed, this cue contains no cyclic repetition at all. When the final phrase of the cue begins, the dialogue has ended and the music, preceded by a sudden explosion of melodic activity in the bass guitar, surges into prominence and evokes a sense of exhilaration as Xander continues confidently to walk away.

The final sonority (which overlaps with Joss Whedon's executive producer credit) again leaves the music without a conventional sense of closure, yet this time the euphonious quality of the chord and its volume is sufficiently strong on its own to suggest a kind of breakthrough moment.[13] Certainly, it implies something of Cordelia's inability to understand Xander's transformation (expressed by her repeated question, "What!?"). But it indicates something even more important: Xander—even though he remains Everyman—has finally come into his own as a character with his own agency and purpose. More fully than ever before in the series, he has acknowledged his own particular abilities, his own strengths, and his own singular kind of knowledge—knowledge that no other member of the Scooby gang possesses. Listeners who attend carefully to the two cues will apprehend that the second modifies the quite usual strains of indie rock to support a psychological passage somewhat ambiguous yet resolute, even courageous.

Variations on a Theme of Betrayal: Two Cues in "Revelations"

The two cues in "The Zeppo," strictly speaking, do not share salient melodic material; what they have in common is the same key, instrumentation, and general style. They also accompany two important scenes that centre on Xander's sense of self. Hence, it is possible to consider them as a pair and to draw comparisons between them that show how their musical differences function to fulfill a greater dramatic purpose. In the earlier episode "Revelations" (3.7), two related musical cues—both composed by Beck—again appear at pivotal moments in the drama that comment on each other. And here, because each cue shares melodic material, it is possible to understand the two cues as different expressions or variations of the same theme: indeed, it is as if elements of the first musical cue take a different course in the second and point to essential dramatic differences between the two.

The episode's principal theme is of secrets held, which lead to feelings of betrayal; the bitterness of trust misplaced; and the salvation that true trust offers. A rogue Watcher arrives in Sunnydale, ("Mrs") Gwendolyn Post. Her aim is to retrieve the mystic glove of Myhnegon, which will give her limitless power. She fools Faith into trusting her by playing on Faith's own insecurities that she does not truly belong in the Scooby gang. Meanwhile, Buffy keeps secrets of her own: Angel has inexplicably returned from a hell dimension and, after a short period under her observation, appears to make a transition more or less restored to his original, soul-imbued state. She senses her old love for him returning with

---

[13] The chord is the unusual A9sus4, a chord with three instances of perfect fourths or fifths.

increasing passion, and she has continued to keep his reappearance in Sunnydale a secret from the other Scoobies. Xander and Willow also continue to nurture their illicit affair, the strain of which is clearly wearing them down.

This complex tapestry of secrets begins to unravel when Xander discovers that Angel is alive, sees him kissing Buffy, and informs Giles. As Buffy checks in with the gang the following morning, she is subjected to an intervention in which the other members of the gang share their feelings of being deceived and their fears concerning Angel's return. Giles abruptly calls an end to the proceedings and dismisses the Scoobies, leaving Buffy to think that he understands what she has done and is not angry. However, Giles brusquely silences her:

> Giles: Be quiet. I won't remind you that the fate of the world often rests with the Slayer. What would be the point? Nor shall I remind you that you've jeopardized the lives of all you hold dear by harboring a known murderer. But sadly, I must remind you that Angel tortured me … for hours … for pleasure. You should have told me he was alive. You didn't. You have no respect for me, or the job I perform.

Giles's words underscore the sense of betrayal that can result from secrets withheld. The cue that accompanies this scene is brief but potent. Its scoring for strings, synthesized brasses, and winds contrasts markedly with the indie rock style of "The Zeppo." It more closely resembles a kind of neo-romantic concert music and, as such, helps to set the more serious, heroic tone of this episode.

The cue revolves around a brooding, four-note melodic idea (Figure 3.4), which begins in one key, is repeated with some momentary harmonic alterations, and finally arrives in a new but related key. The music oscillates between two chords in this new key but does not lead to complete tonal closure.[14] The elegiac quality of the leitmotif clearly augments the feelings of betrayal that Buffy's friends now feel; they heighten her own sense of loneliness in her world, and underlie the frustrating, unrequited love that she knows is her fate to share with Angel.

Figure 3.4   Four-note motif in "Revelations" (Christophe Beck)

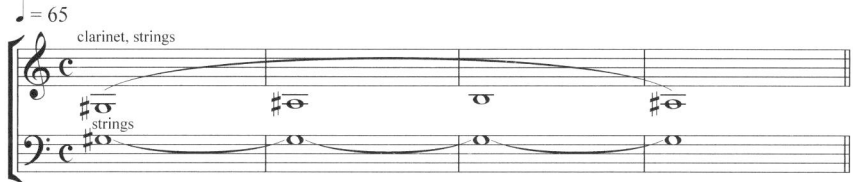

---

[14] The idea begins in G♯ minor; it is transposed up a fifth and harmonized with an F♯ minor chord, which acts as a pivot to an arrival in C♯ minor; the oscillation is simply a repeated half-cadence in this new key.

As in "The Zeppo," musical changes within the cue are perfectly timed to coincide with Giles's nuances or turns in the dialogue. The four-note motif's simple transformation occurs when Giles mentions his torture at Angel's hands, and the harmonic arrival coincides with his sad acknowledgement that Buffy does not respect him. More important, the cue's lack of harmonic closure suggests a question that awaits an answer—and a later scene that will revisit these emotions to explore their consequences further.

The theme of betrayal and of truths withheld continues to develop throughout the episode, and the major characters continue to suffer from deception, ulterior motives—and from the revelations that could eventually provide healing and stability. Mrs Post earns Faith's trust, only to be revealed as a renegade Watcher who wishes only to acquire the glove of Myhnegon. The romantic affair between Xander and Willow remains a secret; but, as Willow attempts for the first time to share the secret with Buffy, it is clear that the secret cannot remain hidden for much longer. Faith's suspicion that the Scooby gang has not completely accepted her as a member leads her to attempt to kill Angel. In the end, Giles is seriously wounded by Mrs Post, and Buffy and Faith face off against each other, allowing Mrs Post to claim the glove. Luckily, Buffy and Faith quickly adapt to this shocking change of events and work together to save the day.

Nevertheless, as Buffy herself acknowledges in the penultimate scene of the episode, the feelings of betrayal continue to have a negative impact on the Scoobies. The offer of true trust returns—along with a reprise of the important cue from the earlier scene—in the final sequence of the episode, a poignant meeting between Buffy and Faith. Having been bested in battle, and having been betrayed by Mrs Post, Faith has returned to her Spartan accommodations at a seedy motel in Sunnydale. Buffy visits and tries to reassure her that she is a friend, that Faith belongs in the circle that includes Buffy and the other Scoobies. But Faith—stoically wounded—rejects Buffy's offer.

We hear a near-literal reprise of the betrayal music that appeared earlier as Buffy tries to assure Faith that she is trustworthy with the following dialogue:

> Faith: Yeah, well, you can't trust people. I should've learned that by now.
> Buffy: I know this is gonna sound funny coming from someone that just spent a lot of time kicking your face, but you can trust me. [cue begins]
> Faith: Is that right?
> Buffy: I know I kept secrets, but I didn't have a choice. I'm on your side.
> Faith: *I'm* on my side. That's enough.

The cue changes as Buffy replies, "Not always," with the addition of a flowing piano part that gives the music a softer dimension, more lyricism and depth. The increased lyricism helps underscore Buffy's realization that she needs a community of loved ones to help her accomplish her mission. As the reprise reaches the same harmonic goal as before, Buffy turns to leave, much as she did after Giles's rebuke. But then the scene—and the music—takes an unexpected turn. Faith seems to reconsider Buffy's offer but, in the end, rejects it. Buffy's expression changes from hope to despair as the music returns to its original key and a final repetition of the brooding four-note motif. In what remains, Beck adds a new musical idea: a slow, ascending melodic line in the woodwinds and high strings (Figure 3.5). The music accompanies two separate shots: the first shows Buffy outside Faith's hotel room. She begins to walk down the stairs with a strong, unreadable expression; she pauses after a few steps, her face softens and she appears to be in deep thought. Then, as the melodic idea continues to ascend, the camera returns to Faith. She is looking out of the window; the melodic ascent seems to suggest the possibility that she might accept Buffy's offer of friendship and rebuild the trust between them. The rich succession of chords that accompanies the melodic ascent move the listener rapidly through a kaleidoscopic succession of harmonies that has not appeared elsewhere in the episode and that seems to evoke Faith as she considers this hopeful possibility.

Figure 3.5   Ascending melodic phrase in "Revelations" (Christophe Beck)

But the series of harmonies and melodic ascent inevitably reach a very different conclusion. Faith looks down in despair just as all the other instruments fall silent except for the high strings sustaining the final note of the melodic ascent. Finally, she returns to the television she has been watching: she rejects the possibility of reconciliation. All the instruments return to sound the final, unexpected, somber chord, which returns us to the minor tonality with which we began.[15] With this chord we have our first powerful sense of Faith's sadness, a sadness that she cannot overcome, not even with all of her considerable powers as a Slayer. And in the tragic-sounding chord, which swells into the soundtrack, we also begin to sense that things will not turn out well for her: these are in fact the first presentiments of her turn to evil and ultimate tragedy that culminate at the end of the season.

Although thematic elements in the script suggest a relationship between these two scenes, the correspondences are not explicit: for instance, Buffy and Giles are involved in the first scene, while Buffy and Faith are involved in the second. But the varied appearances of a single musical cue confirm these ambiguous correspondences so decisively that the two scenes come to be united. Furthermore, the musical technique of variation makes the thematic connections of betrayal of trust and reconciliation overt in a way that the dialogue cannot.

More importantly, the key dramatic moments in both episodes occur without any dialogue whatsoever. Xander overcomes his vulnerability to Cordelia and

---

[15]   E (no third), B major, C minor, G major, and finally G♯ minor.

reaches a new psychic plateau by abandoning words altogether; his silence confounds Cordelia and takes away the chief source of her power over him. Music alone confirms Xander's new-found faith in himself. Similarly, the consequences of Buffy's betrayal and her attempts to make amends in "Revelations" become tangible and momentously poignant through the melancholy music that we hear. In such moments, music gains parity with the actors' expressions and movements and arguably exceeds them in a manner strongly evocative of opera.

These examples—rare in television, to be sure—set the stage for many other amazing discoveries of the intimate relationships between sound and drama in *Buffy the Vampire Slayer*. They invite our ongoing attention, demand that we carefully scrutinize them: not merely as effective but ultimately subsidiary dramatic scoring, but also as a consciously evolving alchemy of sound, sight, and word. We might do well to hear all film or television sound—dialogue, scoring, and Foley effects—as a unified musical continuity, not as complementary elements forged through the magic of post-production. In so doing, we help to develop a new understanding of a vital electronic art form, one that offers a vital source of expressive sustenance.

Chapter 4

"What rhymes with lungs?"
When Music Speaks Louder than Words

Arnie Cox and Rebecca Fülöp

> Angelus: Dear Buffy. I'm still trying to decide the best way to send my regards.
> Spike: Why don't you rip her lungs out? Might make an impression.
> Angelus: Lacks … poetry.
> Spike: Doesn't have to. What rhymes with lungs?
>
> (from "Bewitched, Bothered and Bewildered")

Introduction: Lyricism and Pathos; Words and Melodies

Humor in *Buffy the Vampire Slayer* often serves to balance the intense drama of the show, but just as often it also highlights the inadequacies of verbal communication. For example, in "Some Assembly Required" (2.2), when Giles begins his romantic pursuit of Jenny Calendar, Buffy offers some advice:

> Buffy: You also might wanna avoid words like "amenable" and "indecorous," you know. Speak English, not whatever they speak in, um …
> Giles: England?
> Buffy: Yeah. You just say, "Hey, I got a thing, you maybe have a thing, maybe we could have a thing."
> Giles: Oh, thank you, Cyrano.

Actions, as an alternative to language, sometimes speak louder than words; however, actions often lack an aesthetic dimension. A case in point is the exchange between Angel's evil alter-ego and pre-ensouled Spike in the epigraph to this paper. Spike advocates the immediacy of violent action, but Angelus wants a deeper aesthetic component to his Valentine's Day activities.[1] Taking a hint from Angelus's complaint, Spike invites us to entertain an absurd blend of violent action and poetry. While such a blend of words and deeds is practically impossible, Angelus does find a way to hurt Buffy by hurting Giles, in a deed that is at once cruel and poetic. In the subsequent episode ("Passion" [2.17]) Angelus prepares a scene that leads Giles to expect a romantic tryst with Jenny, with candles and roses

---

[1] In addition to a desire, presumably, to maintain his reputation, he wants to hurt Buffy because of the love that he shared with her as Angel.

and the operatic music of Puccini,[2] only for Giles to discover what the audience already knows—that Jenny has been killed by Angelus. In lieu of the lyricism of poetry, Angelus has integrated the lyricism of music with his violent actions, which adds something beyond the reach of words.[3]

By analogy, the show's production team regularly makes similar aesthetic choices in adding music to heighten the pathos of scenes already fraught with emotion. Our task in this essay is to offer an account of how the musical soundtrack achieves its effects in these types of scenes, including, for example, Oz and Willow's break up in "Wild at Heart" (4.6), Buffy's sacrifice in "The Gift" (5.22), and Giles's discovery of Jenny's body in "Passion." These scenes are emotionally moving in their own right, but their pathos is magnified by the accompanying non-diegetic musical soundtracks, all of which have one thing in common: a lyricism which invites a particular sort of engagement on the part of the audience. To account for this engagement and the emotional affect that it generates, we will consider some basic features of embodied music cognition which have been heretofore largely overlooked in musical analysis, but which play a crucial role in the construction of musical affect, partly because of the subtlety of their operation. In scenes of the type that we will examine, this usually involves the wordless lyricism of instrumental music composed especially for the show; however, occasionally it involves music with words, especially songs imported from outside the show that offer a kind of consoling commentary on the action (for example, Sarah McLachlan's "The Prayer of St Francis" at the end of "Grave" [6.22]). The lyrics of a song, because of their semantic content, and because they are conveyed by the human voice, generate a different kind of affect than does the lyricism of instrumental music. Our discussion will focus not on the use of this form of musical expression, but instead on that of the instrumental score.

Mimetic Participation: Perception and Cognition

Humans are imitative creatures. In the cradle our first lessons in being human involve imitation of those around us, along with their imitation of us, and throughout our lives overt (actual) and covert (imaginary) imitation remains basic to communication and our understanding of one another. Because imitation gradually becomes more covert as we grow older, the claim that adults rely on imitation to understand other humans may seem counterintuitive, but there is a great

---

[2] The duet "O soave fanciulla" from *La Bohème*, which we examine below.

[3] The first impression is that Angelus has left the music on inside Giles's apartment but, as we discuss below, the conclusion of the scene complicates this view of things. Also, although there are in fact words for this music, they convey no semantic meaning to the majority of the intended audience, owing to the language (Italian) and the idiom (opera); therefore, what is added here is much more *lyricism* than lyrics.

deal of evidence that cognition of observed actions relies on imagined imitation.[4] Because acts of imitation result in actual or imagined participation, we can refer to this aspect of human cognition as *mimetic participation*. In what follows we try to show how different kinds of observed human behavior motivate different kinds of participation. With respect to music, this means that different kinds of music, and different aspects of music, motivate different kinds of participation. For our purposes here, the crucial detail regarding mimetic participation is that it generates a visceral, affective response. To understand how different kinds and features of music affect us, we have to understand the kinds of mimetic participation that they afford and motivate.

The basic theory of mimetic participation is that when we see and/or hear someone else doing something, part of how we understand their actions involves imagining doing the same thing ourselves. This is akin to *empathy* or *projection*, but explained from a different perspective. Four details of the theory are that:

1. imitation can be actual (overt) or imaginary (covert);
2. it can occur in real-time or in reflection;
3. it can be conscious or unconscious; and
4. the strength of imitation will vary from person to person.

Evidence for this theory comes from various areas of inquiry, including infant studies, motor imagery studies, speech imagery studies, and musical imagery studies for both song and instrumental music.

As infants, we learn to understand others by imitating the facial gestures, gross motor gestures, and vocalizations of those around us. As we become better practiced, such imitation can be accomplished more or less entirely in the imagination, although occasionally it takes an overt form. In musical experience, for example, we can feel the music without any overt participation, but we often tap our toes or nod our heads, and we may occasionally conduct, or play air guitar.

In order to understand the relevance of motor imagery studies for music, one must understand that music is most often produced by human motor actions—that is, the bodily actions of singing and playing instruments. From this perspective, musical sounds signify the motor actions that produce them, and our reading of these signs at the most immediate level involves motor imagery. Among the studies of motor imagery, perhaps the most compelling are those involving *mirror neurons*.[5] Mirror neurons are unusual in that they fire both when an action is

---

[4] Evidence in music and in other domains of experience is presented in Arnie Cox, "The Mimetic Hypothesis and Embodied Musical Meaning," *Musicae Scientiae*, 5/2 (2001), pp. 195–209. The basic idea is not new in music, but the extent of its relevance, and the evidence brought to bear, are novel in this hypothesis. Rather than cite all of the relevant studies in the present essay, we refer the reader to this earlier essay.

[5] There is extensive and wide-ranging scientific coverage of this area, including Andrew Meltzoff and Wolfgang Prinz, *The Imitative Mind: Development, Evolution, and*

performed and when it is observed. Although they have yet to be observed in musical experience, it may be that part of what we feel when listening to music is the result of mirror neurons firing in response to observed (seen and/or heard) actions of performers—such as the finger and arm movements of guitarists and the vocal contractions and articulations of singers.[6]

Speech imagery studies apply to music when one acknowledges that song is, in effect, sung speech. According to work done by Alan Baddeley and Janet Larsen, part of speech comprehension involves *subvocalization*.[7] Subvocalization is the "inner" speech that one hears while reading, recalling spoken words, and rehearsing words, but also while listening to spoken words. The theory is that while listening to someone speak, we covertly (and unconsciously) imitate the words heard. This suggests a way of accounting for how spoken words generate affect; to the extent that song is sung speech, the theory also has implications for music.

We subvocalize not only when we listen to song, but also when we listen to instrumental music. This occasionally manifests in singing aloud with an instrumental melody, as well as "beat boxing" (imitating the percussion sounds of rap). What is particularly interesting is the implication that music in general is comprehended, at least in part, in terms of our own vocal exertions, so that part of what we feel when listening to music involves imagining what it would feel like to sing it. The lyricism that we analyze in the examples below taps deeply into the process of subvocalization by offering especially singable melodies, whether vocal or instrumental.

But there is another form of mimetic participation that is perhaps the most important and yet the most elusive: the amodal exertions we feel when listening to and recalling music. By amodal exertions we mean the interior "clenchings" that are not goal-oriented and are not obviously related to observable motions of

---

Brain Bases (Cambridge, 2002), and Marco Iacobini, *Mirroring People: The New Science of How We Connect with Others* (New York, 2008). One recent application linking mirror neurons directly to music is Arnie Cox, "Hearing, Feeling, Grasping Gestures," in Elaine King and Anthony Gritten (eds) *Music and Gesture* (Aldershot, 2006), pp. 45–60; and a theory similar to the mimetic hypothesis is proposed by Istvan Molnar-Szakacs and Katie Overy in "Music and Mirror Neurons: From Motion to 'E'motion," *Social Cognitive and Affective Neuroscience*, 1/3 (2006), pp. 235–41, which provides a very good summary of recent relevant findings from outside of music.

[6] A number of essays have appeared recently which explore the implications of mirror neurons for musical meaning, but we have not found a study of mirror neurons observed during specifically musical behavior. One study that comes close is Stefan Koelsch et al., "Investigating Emotion with Music: an fMRI Study," *Human Brain Mapping*, 28/3 (2005), pp. 239–50.

[7] This is our reading of Baddeley's *phonological loop*. See Alan Baddeley, *Working Memory* (New York, 1986); and Janet Larsen and Alan Baddeley, "Disruption of Verbal STM by Irrelevant Speech, Articulatory Suppression, and Manual Tapping: Do they Have a Common Source?" *The Quarterly Journal of Experimental Psychology A*, 56/8 (2003), pp. 1249–68.

the body. For example, in listening to a guitarist, we would empathetically feel something of the relevant finger and arm movements and we would comprehend the sounds produced in part via subvocal imitation, but we would also feel something more visceral and ineffable that is not located in the specific modalities of limb, digit, and vocal exertions. This "gut" response is nevertheless an aspect of motor imagery: a comprehension of the musical exertions seen and heard which is manifest in inner, visceral exertions. We suspect that this feeling is physiologically connected to vocal experience, since vocal production involves contractions of the muscles of the torso. But whatever the specific workings may prove to be, there are two key points: in listening to and recalling music we empathize with the exertion dynamics that we see and hear, and this empathy is part of a broader process of human comprehension via mimetic participation. With respect to the music of *Buffy*, the theory of mimetic participation provides a way of accounting more precisely for how the music engages us and generates affect.[8]

Mimetic Participation and Affect: Some Basic Analytical Tenets

We can set forth a few basic theoretical guidelines based on the principle of mimetic participation. The first is that all of the music heard motivates mimetic motor imagery. When the music is (ostensibly) produced by a diegetic source (e.g., a band at the Bronze), the added visual stimuli provide a more concrete motivation (if also at a price of a reduction in subtlety). It is important to note that in each case the imagery is motivated but not guaranteed, and that the strength of the imagery and the visceral-emotional response will vary from person to person. For example, imagery for guitar music will be stronger in listeners who play the guitar. Among those who do not play guitar, imagery will still be stronger for those with experience imitating guitar sounds gesturally (air guitar) and/or vocally (singing guitar solos with recordings and from memory). So, while music motivates mimetic motor imagery, its strength and form will vary.

Additionally, we should note that soundtracks also employ musical devices with constructed meanings—for example, a quiet string tremolo to signify danger or apprehension. If we ask how this signification works, we might simply note the external association with all of the scenes in movies and television (and radio) in which these devices are used. But this overlooks a crucial part of the structuration

---

[8] The question of precisely how a physical response motivates an emotional response is beyond the scope of this discussion. However, along other lines, the theory supports S. Renee Dechert's point regarding music as a community-building device in *Buffy*, and affords a more explicit understanding of how music seems to exert a power that "transcends language" (Dechert, "'My Boyfriend's in the Band!' *Buffy* and the Rhetoric of Music," in Rhonda V. Wilcox and David Lavery [eds] *Fighting the Forces: What's at Stake in Buffy the Vampire Slayer* [Lanham, MD, 2002], pp. 218–60). The theory would also extend to comprehension of the observed actions of the characters. For example, not only are the stunts understood in part via mimetic participation, but so are facial gestures and tears.

process: that such associations must make some intuitive sense in the first instance, and that it is an identity between our visceral-emotional responses common to dramatic experience and musical experience that makes possible and motivates these associations. The analyses that follow are meant in part to show how such meaning construction operates.

Willow and Oz

As we watch Oz saying goodbye in "Wild at Heart," we empathize with Oz and Willow in part by implicitly projecting ourselves into their situation, and this projection probably involves some measure of (non-musical) mimetic participation—for example, comprehension of facial gestures, postures, and speech would involve some measure of subconscious imitation. As we are engrossed by this drama, the instrumental music invites—and perhaps motivates—us to participate as well, but this invitation is much subtler than that of the drama we are witnessing: the music is invisible, the source of the music—that is, the performance—is invisible, and there is no semantic content demanding attention. The final scene begins with a high, soft, sustained string unison, signifying apprehension to help convey Willow's state of mind as she finds Oz packing his things. Part of how this works is that listeners feel what it would be like to produce this soft, sustained sound—probably not in terms of the bowing involved, and perhaps only partly by subvocal imitation, but more likely in terms of a subtle, amodal exertion: a feeling of suspense resulting from a feeling of sustaining an exertion that would produce such a sound; a feeling that, at a basic level, is akin to holding one's breath.

When Oz expresses his doubt about the separation between the wolf and the human within him, we hear a piano accent—which then turns into the first statement of the fragmentary theme. But the strings still hold the tension until Willow asks, "Oz, don't you love me?" Then the strings are finally set free from their sustained note; and when Oz tells her he has never loved anything else, we are finally given some relief from the tension, in the form of the warm sound of the English horn, a modulation, and an orchestral swell to support their embrace. The change of timbre here marks the evolution of the mood—the reassurance of love by Oz, despite his need to leave—and the English horn as a wind instrument affords a stronger invitation to participate subvocally. Its sound is richer and more plaintive than that of other woodwinds, and we experience this warmth as listeners and participants. Similarly, the orchestral swell is not only a sound that comes at us, but also an action that we take part in, in conjunction with the rush of emotion sympathetically generated as they finally embrace. This soon subsides, however, and the music modulates back to its earlier state, supporting the return of our attention to the fact that Oz is actually leaving.

The moment when Oz exits the house could also have been a good place for a song to begin, although this would undoubtedly have changed our experience of the scene. The instrumental scoring here allows an affective flexibility that operates quite differently from the processes of commentary and affiliating identification discussed by Anahid Kassabian, for although songs occasionally have more than one mood, having more than two is rare.[9] There is clear evidence that this flexibility was precisely what Whedon required, although he initially wanted a song for this scene. Christophe Beck reports that "they looked for weeks for a song. Ultimately nothing quite gave Joss the satisfaction he needed and the emotional range he needed there. So at the last minute I sort of came in and, I guess, did some kind of rescue job. But apparently everyone was happy with it."[10] The English horn statement of the theme allows us to keep our attention not only on the action but also on what has just been said, providing an avenue to express our affective response non-conceptually and focusing our attention on the dramatic action.

Buffy and Angel

Buffy and Angel's recurrent musical theme takes advantage of instrumental music's capacity for subtle and powerful reuse, whether as a whole or in part. Not only might a song be too blunt for this purpose, but an instrumental theme has the advantage of greater flexibility and is better able to match the real-time emotional dynamics of the drama. Before examining the theme's use in various contexts, let us consider how it achieves its central affect.

Like many themes used in *Buffy*, this one is simple and unobtrusive: trochaic gestures in a gently rocking four-four meter in four-bar phrases; diatonic melody and harmonies (using only the notes belonging to the key); and, at least in its first occurrence, a spare two-part texture of melody and accompaniment on an acoustic piano (Figure 4.1).[11] The melancholy of the minor mode is juxtaposed with the optimism of the major mode, with each phrase beginning in E minor and concluding in C major, and then with a final tag in E minor. The major is, however, tinged with a hint of instability in the form of a harmonic ninth

---

[9] Anahid Kassabian, *Hearing Film: Tracking Identifications in Contemporary Hollywood Film Music* (New York, 2001).

[10] Nancy Holder with Jeff Mariotte and Maryelizabeth Hart, *The Watcher's Guide* (New York, 2000), vol. 2, p. 433.

[11] The theme is performed in various keys (but mostly in D major/F♯ minor) in its different occurrences in the show. Our transcription is in C major/E minor. The theme can also be heard as modal, which helps to locate it within the vernacular of traditional musics and which, in turn, establishes a measure of innocence appropriate to a relationship involving someone as young as Buffy. In these ways the theme is distinguished from other thematic music, particularly the Buffy-Riley theme and the use of Puccini's "O soave fanciulla" for Giles and Jenny, both of which are discussed below. Beck's manuscript of this theme in is also reproduced in Christopher Golden and Nancy Holder *The Watcher's Guide* (New York, 2000), vol. 2, p. 434.

on each C major arrival (marked with a box in Figure 4.1). The listener is encouraged to expect a degree of harmonic and metric stability on the third bar of each phrase, but this subtle dissonance, in a context nearly devoid of any other dissonance, keeps the music from stalling by denying the establishment of complete stability. When the theme abruptly closes with a return to E minor, the hopeful associations of C major are denied; the music tells us that this couple cannot escape its melancholy doom.

Figure 4.1   The Buffy-Angel theme (Christophe Beck)

The foregoing reading objectifies the music, treating it as a text whose meaning we can extract from a quasi-objective standpoint, but this overlooks basic features of musical experience that engage us and move us. Because the theme is simple and quiet, its effect is subtle; however, in addition to exterior associations, we also feel this music through mimetic participation. The arpeggiations of the accompaniment invite us to move in concert with it—not to the point of actual movement, but at least to feel a vicarious exertion that is congruent with it. The changing states of the melody—its "forward motion"—similarly invite us to exert vicariously and covertly as if moving, then pausing and holding when it reaches its sustained notes in the third bar of each phrase. In the second phrase, when the harmonic ninth is featured in the melody, we are invited to feel this instability: *we are now taking part* in the production of the semi-unstable sound whose gentle dissonance is amplified by its arrival at the metric place of stability. This is why the passage not only sounds beautiful but also *feels* beautiful—a little instability, a little delayed fulfillment of our expectations, a little prolongation of desire. And when the final melodic pitch of E changes context from the more optimistic C major to the more nostalgic E minor, we take part in this metamorphosis.

As the capacity for empathy varies from person to person, so does the strength of mimetic participation; the subtlety of this theme, and its secondary role as dramatic support, somewhat attenuate the effects of mimetic participation as compared to listening to the music in isolation from the visual image. It is, of course, possible to be unmoved by this theme but, for those who are moved, we suggest that it occurs in part through the process we have described. In fact, we would argue that even a feeling of aversion to this or any other music involves the same processes.

Functions of the Buffy-Angel Theme

The numerous uses of the Buffy-Angel theme in seasons 2 and 3 of *Buffy* (as well as in season 1 of *Angel*) can be sorted according to four main functions:

1. the theme helps to establish the relationship between Buffy and Angel;
2. it serves as a nostalgic symbol of Angel, particularly from "Innocence" (2.14) to "Becoming, Part 2" (2.22) while he is the soulless Angelus;
3. it engenders a nostalgia in season 3 for a romance that they gradually realize cannot be sustained; and
4. it comments ironically on the action.

We are introduced to the Buffy-Angel theme at the turning point of season 2, "Surprise" (2.13). The episode opens with Buffy's surreal, prophetic dream, which moves her to pay an early morning visit to Angel. The theme begins at the point when Angel kisses her, and the rest of the scene consists of the two attempting to control their rising passion. The sweetness and simplicity of the theme not only establishes the sincerity of this relationship, but also tells us how we are supposed to feel about it. In contrast to the more adult theme used for Buffy and Riley later on in the series, the Buffy-Angel theme encourages us to look upon this romance with the same innocence and naivety with which the 17-year-old Buffy sees it. The theme recurs several times throughout the episode, each time at a key point in the development of the relationship: when Angel tells Buffy that he has to leave her, when they say goodbye and he gives her the Claddagh ring (which will become an important symbol well into season 3), and just before they finally sleep together. The theme thus develops associations not only with Buffy and Angel generally, but also with some of the features specific to their relationship: impediments to their happiness, the ring as a symbol, and the physical consummation of their love, with the consequential changes in both characters and the plot lines.

Because of the associations that accrue to the theme during its first few appearances, once Angel has lost his soul and the relationship is defunct, it begins to serve a new purpose. At this point it becomes a symbol of what Buffy has lost and also reinforces visual reminders such as the ring. In re-experiencing this music, we remember its previous contexts and thereby empathize all the more strongly with Buffy. One of the first times that this occurs is in the episode that follows their consummation ("Innocence"), after Buffy realizes what has happened to Angel. The scene takes place in the library with the entire Scooby gang trying to make sense of the situation. The camera pans across the group, finally landing on Buffy, whom we see looking at the ring as we hear the theme once again. While the visual cue alone might suffice to indicate that she is thinking of her relationship with Angel, the music makes our participation more visceral. There is a similar scene later on in "Becoming, Part 1" (2.21), when Buffy is talking on the phone to Willow and accidentally uncovers the ring lying in a drawer. As her voice falters and the theme enters, the music lets us feel how difficult it will be to follow through with her resolve to kill Angel. Near the end of "Becoming, Part 2," Willow, Oz, and Cordelia manage to restore Angel's soul, but Buffy realizes that she must nevertheless kill Angel in order to save the world. The theme here, extended and with a grander, more "cinematic" orchestration than in its previous incarnations, achieves perhaps its greatest power as it draws us back into her feelings of love, at the same time that it reminds us that she must sacrifice that which she desires most. Only a theme that has accrued so many prior associations could generate such pathos.

Once Angel has thus been re-ensouled, killed, and subsequently brought back to life (in "Faith, Hope and Trick" [3.3]), the possibility of a renewed relationship with Buffy seems to present itself. We know, as do they, that this can never happen, because a second consummation of their love would lead to Angel's reversion, but their passion makes abstinence a torture. During this period (up to Angel's departure in "Graduation Day, Part 2" [3.22]), the theme takes on a new meaning—a nostalgia for a dream that can never be fulfilled. One of the clearest examples occurs in "Choices" (3.19) when the Mayor lectures the lovers, forcing them to face the paradox of their desire for and devotion to one another as well as the impossibility of having a life together. The fragment of the theme played here makes our experience of the paradox visceral by reharmonizing the opening with a destabilizing, chromatically descending bass: the melody that was once pure and simple is put into a context that is dissonant, unstable, and complex.

In "The Wish" (3.9) we get another kind of distortion of the theme. In the reality of this alternate Wish-verse, Buffy has never met Angel until she finds him in a cell in the basement of the Bronze, now the Doppelgangland hangout of the vampires. He is nevertheless still the vampire with a soul and he recognizes her, so that when she discovers him we are invited to hope that she will instinctively know him and that their love will transcend the boundary between the two realities. But the music tells us that this cannot happen, as we hear and feel a skewed, atonal fragment of the Buffy-Angel theme. The cruel irony of seeing these two thus separated is enhanced by the music: as they are still related to their usual selves, the theme has the same slow rhythm and tempo, a similar contour, the same spare texture, and the same orchestration (acoustic piano). But as they do not feel the love we have come to expect, the melody is distorted and non-diatonic, and the harmonies are unstable and cold. In hearing the recognizable elements skewed in this way, we feel not only the distortion of the characters (musical and dramatic) but also the irony of their being so close and yet so far apart.

We should also remark on the somewhat conspicuous absence of the Buffy-Angel theme during their wordless goodbye at the end of season 3 ("Graduation Day, Part 2"), when Angel leaves Sunnydale. The original theme could have been used to summarize their relationship in Sunnydale, but the new theme introduced for the last three episodes of season 3 points to the fact that their relationship is now in a new state. All the pain and struggle associated with the old theme are now in the past, and here we have music that, while just as sentimental, is also more mature, with strings and harp and a more indirect mode of expression. This theme also achieves something that the original theme could not easily accomplish: it offers an untroubled closure in the major mode, articulating a quiet acceptance of what must be.

Buffy and Riley

We first hear the Buffy-Riley love theme in "Hush" (4.10). In the commentary for that episode, Joss Whedon compares the Buffy-Riley theme to the Buffy-Angel theme:

> I think it's actually, for my money, better than the Buffy-Angel love theme, which is very straight-ahead romantic. This has a plaintive quality that's a little bluer and stranger—maybe it points to the way their relationship is gonna go—but to me it's more adult than the very straightforwardly romantic Buffy-Angel theme.[12]

In making sense of this interpretation of the Buffy-Riley theme, we can begin by noting the difference in the choice of instruments. The piano of the Buffy-Angel theme is an instrument that many people are able to play, and the theme is simple enough that it could be played by the least experienced pianist. By contrast, the strings of the Buffy-Riley theme are more specialized instruments, and it is also not music that an individual can recreate alone.

In addition to differences in instrumentation, the indirect, poetic expression will generally be experienced as more sophisticated or more adult: in fact, nearly every aspect of the Buffy-Riley theme is less direct, less straightforward, than the Buffy-Angel theme. Although it initiates a binary oscillation as does the Buffy-Angel theme, the music loses momentum in measures 5–9, sitting on the dominant of F minor, and bar 6 is inserted to disrupt the oscillating pattern (Figure 4.2). Harmonically, the Buffy-Riley theme plays with the same ambiguity between the major and minor modes that is so prominent in the Buffy-Angel theme, but it also

---

[12] Joss Whedon, "Hush" audio commentary, *Buffy the Vampire Slayer Season Four DVD Collection* (2002).

employs a third mode (Lydian) whose distinct affect adds another dimension.[13] The first phrase (mm. 1–9) begins in A♭ major and then moves toward the relative F minor. However, instead of actually going to F minor, we get only as far as its dominant (mm. 5–9), with the typical delaying embellishment of the 4–3 suspension (the melodic F–E♮ in m. 5).[14] The music sets up a desire for F in the melody supported by its tonic F minor harmony, but we get neither the expected melody note nor harmony, only a reiteration of the 4–3 suspension (m. 8), which prolongs the state of desire.

Figure 4.2   The Buffy-Riley theme (Christophe Beck)

Note that we are not interpreting this as the *music's* desire, nor are we suggesting a fanciful interpretation of tonal instability as the listener's desire. According to the mimetic hypothesis, the audience participates vicariously in this melody, via mimetic participation, and the traditional tonal dynamic of stability/instability that this music draws on creates the expectation of, and the desire for, specific tonal and

---

[13]   The Lydian mode is similar to the major scale, but the fourth note (fourth scale degree) is raised a half step.

[14]   For readers unfamiliar with this terminology, a suspension is a note that begins as a member of one chord, where it is consonant and stable, but which is then sustained over a new chord of which it is not a member, where it becomes dissonant and unstable. This instability then generates a desire for consonance and stability. The "4–3" simply identifies the intervals between the bass (the lowest note of the chord) and the suspension and its resolution: the 4 is the dissonance (instability) and the 3 is the consonance (stability). In Figure 4.2, the 4 is marked with a box along with the other dissonant, destabilizing intervals.

harmonic states. With this in mind, we can understand Whedon's anthropomorphic description of this theme as "plaintive" as being motivated by the vicarious experience of the music's tonal instability, slow pace, and quiet dynamic level, and the downward contour of its principal melodic gesture: it is not only the sound of a plaint, it is the feel of a plaint.

The second phrase (mm. 9–16) is a restatement of the theme a fifth higher, in E♭ major/C minor, but reharmonized. The melodic D♮ (m. 10) over the A♭ major harmony brings in the feel of the Lydian mode, which in recent years has come to be associated with tender and often saccharine moments in movies and television.[15] A more usual and mundane D♭ here would have been felt as having a strong tendency to descend to C, much like the F descending to E♮ in mm. 5–9 of the first phrase. By contrast, the D♮ instead motivates a more neutral or even opposite feeling: it could ascend to E♭ just as well or better. This felt upward tendency, which then goes unfulfilled as the D♮ descends to C after all, is nicely congruent with the as-yet unfulfilled desire felt by Buffy and Riley. In this context, the hint of the Lydian mode introduces its motion picture associations at one level while also engendering the strangeness that Whedon refers to: this raised fourth scale degree (D♮) is foreign to the major and minor modes. The sound here is exotic yet familiar, since there is only one strange note in an otherwise familiar sound world.

Perhaps the greatest difference between these two themes is that the Buffy-Riley theme contains much more harmonic dissonance (as marked with boxes in Figure 4.2), and is thereby saturated with the dynamics of dissonance/resolution, instability/stability, and desire/satisfaction. In the larger context, this concentration of dissonance gains its effect through contrast with other music heard on the show, and more broadly with television and pop music generally, which normally has less dissonance and/or does not feature it as this theme does. More specifically, these dissonances are featured through gaining accents: the most salient ones are the top notes of the melodic gestures, and they occur on downbeats against a new harmony (mm. 1, 3, 8, 10, 12, and 14). Downbeats are normally felt as moments of stability—these are the moments of weight, as opposed to the upbeats—and when a dissonance occurs on a downbeat it is thus foregrounded and becomes a subtle yet salient moment of instability. The conflict generated by these downbeat dissonances is then resolved in each case by a relaxing, downward stepwise motion into the weaker second half of each bar. In classical music parlance these are melodic "sighs"—so-called not only because of their somewhat analogous sound, but also because of their analogous feeling: an initial tension that is dissolved in an outward, descending gesture of the voice. This use of dissonance lends an indirectness of expression and an intensity of affect that is lacking in the more straightforward Buffy-Angel theme, and it is perhaps this feature which is most responsible for Whedon's response to the theme.

---

[15] This practice goes back at least to the 1960s, as in the denouement of *To Kill a Mockingbird* (1962; music by Elmer Bernstein).

Giles and Jenny and the Music of Grown-Ups

Although the focus of this essay is not on songs and singing, the use of Puccini's duet "O soave fanciulla" in the second season's "Passion," at the point when Giles finds Jenny Calendar's dead body, constitutes another special case that merits discussion here. We hear the duet begin as Giles arrives at his home; the timbre suggests that it is coming through the door and is thus diegetic. Although Giles does not yet know that Jenny is dead, we already know this (we saw her killed by Angelus in an earlier scene), which leads us to believe that Angelus has included the music along with the roses and the wine in the apartment as part of his cruel joke. The crescendo to the climax of the duet is timed to match Giles's ascent up the stairs and discovery of her body. Then a subtle and artful thing happens. The camera cuts to Giles standing outside his front door talking with the police, but the music does not jump in a similar fashion. Not only does the music smooth the transition between scenes, as is common enough, but it also shifts into a non-diegetic position: it seems at first that the diegetic recording has simply continued—with Giles too devastated to turn it off—but the timing is wrong, since we have jumped ahead while the music has continued seamlessly; the music fades out about twelve seconds into the scene.[16]

A portion of the audience will never have heard this duet before, but it will at least be recognized as opera with all of the associations that this brings. Likewise, even without knowledge of the text, it is likely to be recognized as, or interpreted as, a love song. Depending on one's response to operatic music, this duet might serve both to pull in and push away the audience, but for those who are moved by this music, the mimetic hypothesis helps explain how. The music invites us to feel the powerful expenditure of energy evident in the climax. Here are two humans in effect screaming in a musical way, and we feel this energy both as second-person listeners and as imagined first-person singers. The empathy that results from mimetic participation takes the form not only of the specific vocal exertions but also an ineffable, visceral clenching. Although this experience is similar to what one might experience in other musical contexts, this particular instance is unique for *Buffy* in several respects. First, with one purely comic exception, we do not hear operatic music elsewhere in the series.[17] Second, high-energy diegetic singing is relatively rare, as is such close integration with a character's emotional

---

[16] For those who know the duet, the spell may be disturbed earlier because of the cut-and-paste job done on the score: the portion we hear at first actually comes later than what follows here. The music editor (Fernand Bos) creates a smooth loop from the end of the excerpt back to its beginning, and the excerpt ends at the point where it began.

[17] Willow is known to have issues with opera following her disastrous attempt to sing the role of Madame Butterfly in "Nightmares" (1.10). Here, although the performance is again of a famous Puccini love duet, the male opera singer is clearly positioned as obnoxious and unattractive. One might easily read an intratextual allusion into these two uses of Puccini duets at nightmarish moments. [Ed.]

state, and the combination of these two (as in this case) is rarer still. Third, only instrumental music normally metamorphizes so quickly, aligning itself with the dynamics of the on-screen action. Finally, this is one of the rare occasions in which the music changes from diegetic to non-diegetic.[18] This may be the only occasion with so much at stake where opera could have been used without obvious irony, and this transition is perhaps the only way it could be used so effectively. As non-diegetic music, opera would normally be far too intrusive because of its stylistic conspicuousness. If it were used as diegetic music, there would be no way to cut between scenes without cutting the music, and because of our engagement with the music this would be too jarring: to engage the audience at this level only to cut them off would violate their emotional commitment. By instead carrying the music across scenes while transcending the diegetic world of the narrative, we are allowed to stay with the feeling a little while longer as the narrative moves inevitably forward.

The Special Case of No Music: "The Body"

The music in the soundtrack guides us towards what and how to feel. It invites us to engage with its lyrical commentary, occasionally with words but most often without. It usually reinforces the affect of the drama, although it may be ironic or otherwise oblique. However, in "The Body" (5.16), the only episode of *Buffy* that lacks a musical soundtrack, we get no such guidance, and in its absence we have the opportunity to feel how even instrumental music is a distraction from, as well as a complement to, the central narrative. By omitting non-diegetic music, this episode moves away from the dramatic technology usually employed by television and toward the world of dramatic theater. Without music's acoustic balm, all of our empathetic attention is on the characters and their state of bewilderment—especially on Buffy's. Music here would provide a conceptualization and a catharsis, as it did in "Wild at Heart," but a catharsis at this point would in some measure trivialize the loss; it is difficult to imagine what kind of music would not detract from the emotional impact. Let us consider more carefully how this lack of music achieves its effect.

---

[18] Another example occurs in "Tabula Rasa" (6.8), where the music in the Bronze stays with us as we move through a montage of the various troubled characters before finally returning to the Bronze. This technique has been used in film, as in the opening of Quentin Tarantino's *Pulp Fiction* (1994), where Dick Dale's recording of *Miserlou* (1962) takes us from the coffee shop to the radio in Jules and Vincent's car. Ken Garner discusses such diegetic/non-diegetic migration, and also discusses the Dick Dale example from a different perspective in "'Would you Like to Hear Some Music?' Music in-and-out-of-control in the Films of Quentin Tarantino," in K. J. Donnelly (ed.) *Film Music: Critical Approaches* (Edinburgh, 2001), pp. 188–205.

From one perspective, a lack of music can rightly be understood as the removal of an element in the dramatic object, thereby concentrating our perceptual energies on the characters and their actions. The lack of music, from this perspective, constitutes a missing source of associations, which would otherwise help to generate greater aesthetic distance. From another perspective, the lack of music also moves the drama one step closer to real life. These perspectives notwithstanding, the view which we are advocating is that mimetic engagement with the music would provide a conduit for the expression and release of tension. Without this conduit, whatever tension one might feel in response to the drama does not have this aesthetically integrated source of release, and so we are left in a state nearer to the unrelieved state of shock and grief portrayed by the characters. On another level, the lack of music in this episode helps to dramatize this development in the overall narrative of the series: something so disturbing has happened that music—and the release that it provides—is not solemn enough to be a part of it.

It is important to note that one need not be aware of the lack of music in order for it to have its effect; in fact, by operating on a subconscious level, the effect might be greater than it would be otherwise. Another example where music is excluded occurs in a similarly potent event, the rape scene in "Seeing Red" (6.19). It may be easy to imagine some sort of appropriate music which would magnify the drama by inviting us to empathize with its energy, but while this might heighten the experience in one respect, it would again provide a covert (subconscious) outlet for whatever tension we might feel in response to the observed violence. By denying the audience this aesthetic release, the tension is more concentrated and disturbing: with no music to empathize with (that is, mimetically engage with), our empathy remains more focused on the characters and the emotional states they are portraying.

"The Gift"

We could not conclude this essay without coming to terms with what is perhaps the most moving music from the entire series, the theme for Buffy's sacrifice in "The Gift" (5.22). As much as or more than anywhere else, the dramatic context demands a dynamic instrumental music capable of reflecting both the personal and the epic aspects of this event (Figure 4.3).

One of the most important features of the music is its slow tempo. The strong-weak rhythmic pattern between the accompaniment and the melody invites a particular pattern of exertion: slow, regular, binary, and, at the start, with a low level of motor intensity. This pattern of exertion has its own feel, but it will also motivate the memory and imagination of experiences that involve analogous exertion patterns. Because the onscreen drama demands the greater part of our attention, the imagery motivated by mimetic engagement is likely to remain unspecific, and this is part of music's subtle power: we feel something that is at once definite (mimetic engagement) and yet mysterious and largely non-conceptual.

Figure 4.3   Theme from "The Gift" (Christophe Beck)

Another salient feature of this theme is the sense of being pulled inevitably and irresistibly forward. The continuity of the melody invites a feeling of continuous, sustained effort. At a level beneath the particular physical modalities of walking or pulling is the feeling of continuous exertion, articulated by the strong-weak pattern of the accompaniment and the syncopated rhythms of the melody. The stepwise motion of the accompaniment, especially the bass (in most of the four-bar phrases) also motivates a sense of striving. The fact that the bass line ascends in most instances, especially at the climax, magnifies this feeling to the extent that one is subvocally engaged, as it takes greater effort to ascend in singing and speaking than to descend. The muscular tension involved in this effort becomes part of the blended feelings generated by this music.

The rhythm and the contour of the melody contribute to this sense of striving. The accompaniment's weak-strong pattern establishes the downbeat as the most stable position, and the middle of the bar (beat 3) as the next most stable. The melody at first reinforces the stability of the downbeat but then uses it as a springboard to emphasize the unstable beat 2 in creating syncopation. By leaping upward, landing on a weak-beat harmonic dissonance, and then sustaining this dissonant note across the new chord in the middle of the bar, the music emphasizes instability and generates a desire for a return to stability (somewhat like the Buffy-Riley theme). The regular half-note pulse of the accompaniment provides a stabilizing force, but it is also the rhythmic structure against which the syncopations of the melody are contrasted.

Finally, in addition to the surface associations of the orchestration—the epic strings, brass, timpani, and cymbals, and the plaintive oboe and clarinet, all of which invoke the world of movie scores—the various instruments and combinations invite different sorts of participation that shape the affect of this musical experience. The solo piano at the beginning is simple and gentle. The ambient sounds are attenuated when the music comes in, allowing us to focus on Buffy and Dawn, with this simple melody in the background gently inviting the kinds of covert participation we have described. When the full orchestra enters in the third phrase, the music gradually expands, adding more participants (musical performers) and thereby becoming a massive utterance: the swelling voice of many speaking as one. The swelling and fading both engages and overwhelms the participating audience, immersing us and shaping our response to the events we are watching.

Conclusions and Implications

We have tried to show how instrumental music engages us, and what its affective results and functions in *Buffy* are. The key element in our account is the principle of mimetic participation, which we believe accounts for much of our immediate, intimate, visceral response to music and thereby to the narrative with which it is combined, a view that can easily be applied to other television shows and films. On another level, mimetic engagement with a film's music, whether diegetic, non-diegetic, or somewhere in between, is a part of how the viewing experience generates identifications. Anahid Kassabian's distinction of affiliating and assimilating identifications (involving songs versus composed scores, respectively) results in part from the kind of visceral engagement we have described; we believe that score analysis such as Kassabian offers can be more revealing if it accounts more explicitly for how the audience engages with the music in an immediate, visceral way.[19] The variability in the strength and modalities of mimetic participation also supports Kassabian's point that identities are afforded (or perhaps motivated) but not guaranteed: one reason that identities are not guaranteed may be that mimetic engagement with the music is overridden by other factors, such as personal or cultural associations attached to the music. For example, a given musical style will motivate a more or less specific bodily engagement, but an individual listener may be uncomfortable with the embodiment thus invited and so find little or no identification with the music. Finally, if we think of music as inviting mimetic participation, this offers a way of understanding how different kinds of music afford different kinds of affective experiences. As we have seen in the case of *Buffy*, this view also offers a way of understanding how music shapes our response to television and film, in ways more direct and powerful than words alone ever can.

---

[19] Kassabian, *Hearing Film*.

Chapter 5
Battling the Buzz: Contesting Sonic Codes in *Buffy the Vampire Slayer*

Katy Stevens

> I start babbling, and he starts babbling, and it's a babble fest
> (Buffy in "Hush")

For *Buffy the Vampire Slayer* pre-existing textual conventions were so often a source of tension against which to distinguish what was new and different about itself. At its very foundation, *Buffy* was a series designed to challenge the hegemonic notion of the passive female, a familiar trope of the horror and fantasy narratives that underpin it. And just as *Buffy* engaged repeatedly with these conventions of gender and genre throughout its life, so too did it seek to challenge and toy with what the televisual medium itself had long been. In "Hush" (4.10) and "The Body" (5.16) the primacy of the "flow" or "hum" which informs the very basis of the sonic codes of television are reworked for their affective potential. Each episode in turn throws into sharp relief the soundtrack conventions at work within TV drama, and in doing so contributes to the already manifold ways in which *Buffy* has staked its claim in pop culture history.

Television is subject to more rigid sonic constraints than the cinema for it is bound by rules of seeking and ensuring constant engagement with its easily distracted audience. While the cinematic spectator is literally immobilised and enveloped by the architecture of the theatre, the television audience is a transitory and fickle subject, inclined to distraction and channel flicking. The domestic sphere in which television addresses its audience marks it as a wholly different audiovisual experience from the cinema: while its ubiquity is certain, the television (and its texts) must compete for the attention of an audience occupied with other quotidian distractions. Consequently television is reliant on the mobility of sound and the resonance of voice to engage its audience, to distract them from cooking their evening meal or screaming at their hyperactive siblings.

In *Visible Fictions* John Ellis notes the centrality of the soundtrack in the medium:

> The role played by sound stems from the fact that it radiates in all directions, whereas view of the TV image is sometimes restricted. Direct eye contact is needed with the TV screen. Sound can be heard where the screen cannot be seen. So sound is used to ensure a certain level of attention, to drag viewers back to

looking at the set[.] ... Sound holds attention more consistently than image, and provides a continuity that holds across momentary lapses of attention.[1]

The spatial dislocation and mobility of sound is perhaps one of its most definable features—it is never locatable; it shifts, moves, and travels. It can be perceived in more complex fashions than the visual, for one need not be in direct line of sight or have an adequate degree of light in order to receive sensory product. We can hear through walls and around corners, behind us and above us because sound permeates material and diffuses accordingly. What is ignored so often in investigations of the work of sound in the arts is the capacity for the body to receive and register sound. Sound travels in a manner alien to the image: whereas light constitutes the path along which a visual object travels to the subject, sound is, by its very nature, a path in itself. Sound is vibration traveling through air, so it is *felt* by the body as well as being interpreted in greater detail and complexity by the ear and brain. The body, in turn, is a sensory object located in a space and state of arousal, responsive to external stimulus.

What this collection of physical sonic characteristics provides for television is an opportunity to constantly "hail" the audience even when they may not be fixed in front of "the box." What comes of this scenario (a flow of sonic stimulus) is a degree of continuity that the televisual image can never provide owing to its need to be perceived by a subject in direct line of sight. As John Ellis has remarks, "sound carries the fiction [in broadcast television, while] ... the image has a more illustrative function."[2]

What lies at the foundation of this observation is the idea that sounds bears the weight of meaning in the televisual text, distinct as it is from cinema. It is the "major carrier of information"[3] and consequently also the most important means of attracting and retaining the attention of the audience. Michel Chion has quite rightly likened popular television to illustrated radio,[4] prioritizing the voice, and particularly the vocal volley of dialogue, within a sound mix that attempts to hook the audience as they go about their domestic routine. As a result, it is the human voice that must facilitate both sonic and narrative continuity.

The technical limits of the televisual soundtrack must not be underestimated in a consideration of the play of the voice within the medium. While undoubtedly influenced by the textual and technical conventions of the cinema, the gradual improvement of home theatre systems and their increasing presence in Western economies of consumption, the production context of television must still account for and cater to the lowest common denominator—the most basic television set in an average lounge room in suburbia. If sonic meaning cannot be conveyed with

---

[1] John Ellis, *Visible Fictions: Cinema, Television, Video* (London, 1982), p. 128.
[2] Ibid.
[3] Ibid., p. 128.
[4] Michel Chion, *Audio-Vision: Sound on Screen*, ed. and trans. Claudia Gorbman (New York, 1994), p. 157.

a degree of clarity through these basic low-fidelity systems then the televisual text is not working within established, acceptable modes of TV production. As a consequence, sets will switch channels or be turned off altogether and programs will disappear from scheduling. The commercial foundation of television dictates that the sound mix must operate along lines acceptable to transmission through the minuscule built-in speakers on an average set. The primacy of the voice in television largely ensures that these technical concerns are adhered to, for just as the human ear is designed to garner optimum reception of frequencies surrounding those of the range of the human voice, so too are conventional speakers configured to project these frequencies with a clarity not afforded to much higher or lower frequencies.[5] Even with the recent migration to digital television in numerous Western markets, as well as the centrality of the DVD format to methods of televisual consumption, the dynamic range at work in the soundtrack of TV texts still seems to adhere to these principles of portability across various technological environments—from the handheld A/V device to the standard television set to the elaborate high-definition home-theater system.

Since the dominance of the human voice in televisual texts makes simple the conformity to the rudimentary technical limitations of the medium, the voice becomes imbued with the responsibility of communicating as much sonic information as possible—both narratively and emotionally. Those peripheral sound objects that might slip out of the frequency or volume range of television set speakers are often reasserted and validated through verbal recognition. So the voice often takes on the responsibility of embodying and bringing to life the complex acoustic environments within the text. In this sense the human voice becomes accountable for materializing the "liveness" of the originating body of utterance (the subject) and the surrounds it inhabits.

This reliance on voice, or vococentrism, is generally abided by mainstream television series, dependent as they are on a gaggle of voices to capture and communicate action. *Buffy* is no stranger to this employment of, and reliance on, vococentrism—the wit of the dialogue and canny exchanges confirm the appreciation of the vocal nature of the medium. The publication of a dictionary of *Slayer Slang* attests to the interest in the show's formal manipulation of language,[6] while in their essay "Staking in Tongues: Speech Act as Weapon in *Buffy*" Overbey and Preston-Matto support this linguistic curiosity in remarking that the Scoobies "are on the cutting edge of language, creating new expressions, constantly manipulating older expressions in order to update them ... or completely circumventing the expected use of language."[7]

---

[5] Ellis, *Visible Fictions*, p. 128.

[6] Michael Adams, *Slayer Slang: A Buffy the Vampire Slayer Lexicon* (Oxford/New York, 2003).

[7] Karen Eileen Overbey and Lahney Preston-Matto, "Staking in Tongues: Speech Act as Weapon in Buffy," in Rhonda V. Wilcox and David Lavery (eds) *Fighting the Forces: What's at Stake in Buffy the Vampire Slayer* (Lanham, MD, 2002), p. 74.

Much like this inventive treatment of language, the show's engagement with the sonic "rules" of the medium is not always a complicit one, at times manipulating and exploiting the import of the voice in television for affective potential. To listen critically in the Buffyverse is not only to appreciate the linguistic dexterity of the Scoobies and the menagerie of Monsters-of-the-Week, but to probe the very sound of the space—to put one's ear up against the television speakers, and to consider the radical potential of the *Buffy* soundscape. "Hush" and "The Body"—two episodes written and directed by series creator Joss Whedon—represent pinnacles in the distortion of the sonic conventions of television. Though entirely dissimilar episodes in terms of both their subject matter and emotional resonance, each installment uniquely challenges television's acoustic orthodoxy to its own textual and narrative ends.

At a basic level, "Hush" operates as a televisual homage to silent cinema, which in fact was hardly ever silent, always accompanied by a musical soundtrack or various forms of sonic accompaniment.[8] From major movie palaces with their permanent orchestras to the traveling roadshow and its solo pianist, the cinema had always been an audiovisual spectacle, albeit "deaf" to the real sound of the story, for it possessed "no ears for the immediate aural space, the here and now of the action,"[9] a condition Willow suspects early on in "Hush" (her first reaction being a fear that she has become deaf).

Early cinema was, more accurately, voiceless or "mute" as it is still referred to in Latin Countries.[10] Muteness too best describes "Hush," for the soundtrack is rarely silent, laden as it is with Christophe Beck's evocative score and the direct reference to its formal ancestor, the silent film, with the inclusion of Saint-Saëns's iconic *Danse Macabre*. As far as television is concerned, this voiceless sound track—this muteness—represents a serious threat to the quotidian relevance of the medium. Recalling Michel Chion here, it is the human voice which bears the weight of hailing and retaining the television audience. By refusing to abide by this fundamental rule of television, "Hush" operates in direct opposition to popular narrative televisual texts and significantly in contrast to the bulk of other *Buffy* episodes—a veritable "babblefest" as Buffy describes the natural state of the Buffyverse. "Hush," however, takes issue with the vococentrism of the medium and mobilizes a succession of critical engagements with the voice and its arrangement in both audiovisual media and notions of subjectivity.

---

[8] See, for example, film theorist Norman King, who cites numerous historical commentaries on the early cinema in support of such a claim ("The Sound of Silents," in Richard Abel (ed.) *Silent Film* (London, 1996), pp. 31–3).

[9] Michel Chion, *The Voice in Cinema*, trans. Claudia Gorbman (New York, 1999), p. 7.

[10] Ibid., p. 7.

"Hush": Muteness and Vocal Indexicality

This season 4 episode enacts the materiality of voice as an embodied object through the visualization of its theft by supernatural villains, the Gentlemen. Only ten minutes into the episode's running time the entire cast are rendered mute. As the town lies asleep at night the omnipresent camera weaves in and out of rooms of sleeping bodies, the inhalation and exhalation of the townspeople's breath the only discernable movement within the frame. A sinister looking Gentleman opens a small wooden box from his position high within the town clock tower. As he does so the camera returns to the sleepers, where we now see a fine cloud, elongated and shadowy, drift from their open mouths. These clouds sail across the town toward a central point—the clock tower—where they are captured within the small wooden box cradled by the monster. As the last fragment of mist enters the container, a skeletal hand closes it shut, and the entire town is left voiceless.

The cloudy mist used to indicate the disembodiment and "theft" of the voice directly mimics visuals used earlier in the same season in the episode "Living Conditions" (4.2) in which Buffy is seen to be having her soul stolen by a demonic college roommate. This correlative pairing of images asserts the preoccupation that the voice represents something of the "essence" of a subject, and its materiality brings to life an enigmatic element of the individual. This visualization of voice, disembodied from its source but still "live," marks a clear appreciation for the voice as a material body in itself—a physical trace and a distinct object. During the eventual emancipation of these entrapped voices, the collapsed mist of voices once again fissures into discrete clouds rapidly returning to their originating bodies. This sense of connection and ownership of voice is enacted within this moment as an otherwise undifferentiated mass parts and distinguishes itself into individual packages to return to their respective bodies.

As Kaja Silverman observes, the voice has come to represent the very essence of presence in subject theories ranging from Plato to Cixous.[11] The human voice is never standardized, always made up of individual flavors and textures. This unique assemblage of tone, timbre, pace, pitch, sustain, and volume shapes the indexical nature of the human voice and enables the conception of a corresponding enactment within audiovisual media.

The voice is registered in audiovisual media usually in relation to the originating body and its image. This notion of a diegetically embodied voice is what gives rise to an appreciation of utterance as subjective trace, as an indexical object in its own right. Still, even the voiceover emanating from a visually absent body is imbued with the presence of a body through its articulation of flesh. Whether visually embodied or not, the voice, unlike the image, is not contained by the boundaries of the screen's frame. It travels across several trajectories within the textual system, first from the body of utterance to the recording device—the microphone—where it

---

[11] Kaja Silverman, *The Acoustic Mirror: The Female Voice in Psychoanalysis and Cinema* (Bloomington, IN, 1988), p. 43.

is transformed into electrical vibration much as the body becomes a cinematic image through the casting of light onto film and the chemical reactions that constitute the celluloid processing mechanics. The apparatus produces the impression that the line between microphone and sound projector is a direct one, though of course any number of re-recordings, edits, dubs, and post-production manipulations may have occurred. What is important to this reading, however, is that the textual system of audiovisual media and the context of reception naturalize this process, this transformation, so that what is produced is a cognitive link between the body of the performer, their projected image, and the resounding voice.

The very language of recording the human voice is imbued with the connotations of entrapping a body. To "capture" the voice with a microphone and analog tape or digital medium expresses an investment in seizing an object, a body. This language operates in direct contrast to the essentially ephemeral nature of sound and, of course, the voice itself. What this capturing, this recording, marks is an attempt to retain the body as voice through the mechanical apparatus of recording and playback. This analogy of entrapment acknowledges the flesh of the voice and its enmeshed relation with the body of utterance. As a body in itself, though inextricably bound to the originating body through a relay of signs that mark it as such, the human voice operates as an object to be seized and projected through the apparatus. In "Hush," it is the ornamental box treasured by the Gentlemen that serves such a purpose, diegetically enacting the very process that the sonic landscape of television values above so many others: the relay and mediation of the human voice.

Within this episode the issue of televisual reliance on the voice and the corresponding investment in the utterance as indexical trace is enacted at multiple points in the diegesis. On realizing the communal muteness of the town, Riley and Forrest—two characters involved in a secret government operation—rush to enter their underground headquarters. On entering the electronically protected elevator the two men are directed by an awkward computerized voice to "Please enter vocal identification." Seconds pass and the same inhuman voice speaks again: "Vocal identification not accepted. Please enter vocal identification." Riley panics, exhales, and pants hopelessly into the microphone panel in the elevator wall. As he is unable to produce his acknowledged vocal patterns for verifiable identification, the mechanized pod transporting the two men shuts down and proceeds to emit a poison gas. Of course, the two recurring characters are returned to safety but what is of issue here is that within a mechanical operation (or apparatus if you will) the subject was considered Other and hostile without his voice in its unique configuration to identify him. The absence of his voice rendered his embodiment incomplete and consequently undermined the wholeness of his subjectivity. This commitment to the truthful indexicality of the voice finds itself enacted repeatedly within "Hush," both diegetically and formally, indicating the medium-specific dependence on vocal performance.

At the climax of the episode Buffy is once again armed for combat as her scream is mystically returned to her and resounds through the tower and out onto the street. The Gentlemen suffer prophesized defeat as their monstrous heads tremble then explode from the power of her now embodied voice. In a television episode empty of human voice save for several minutes at the outset, Buffy's scream returns the diegetic world of Sunnydale, and the televisual medium itself, to its natural order—to a babblefest. Her scream is one of mastery operating in direct opposition to the claims of Michel Chion in "The Screaming Point," in which he asserts that the female scream, the woman's cry, represents a misfortune and a sexual vulnerability available for the pleasure of the male spectator.[12] Buffy's scream is more in line with what Chion describes as the male "shout," imbued as it is with power and mastery.

Buffy wields this masculine shout as she does the phallic stake: both are her weapons for penetrating and obliterating the Other—the monster, the demon. Critical work done on the violence and power of the speech-act in the Buffyverse usually concentrates on the linguistic prowess of the Scoobies, constructing sharp, savvy dialogue as a combat tool.[13] However, the resonance of the voice and its acoustic presence also mark an exercise in dominance and command for our heroine. And as we see two seasons later, Willow too assumes this power, as her scream of fury ruptures the integrity of the mythical form of Osiris in "Villains" (6.20). Evidently, this power is too great for the witch to wield as she quickly descends into the form of the now infamous Dark Willow.

In regard to the status of voice in television, however, Buffy's scream represents and performs a distinct re-embodiment of the vococentrism of the medium and a return to the natural order of the babblefest. Buffy's voice made flesh once again reanimates the vocal obsession of television. Formally "Hush" does not abandon the power and investment in the voice, although it does skillfully draw attention to it. Rather, it transfers its weight and import to the elevation of non-diegetic musical scoring within the soundtrack. This reliance on music operating within the internal logic of the text formally aligns the episode with pre-talkie cinema and its enactment of character muteness as opposed to filmic silence. The screening of silent film conferred importance and weight upon an extradiegetic musical accompaniment. From the professional orchestra down to the traveling pianist, the musical score was relied upon to accent and convey both narrative and emotional meaning to an audience. By matching and detailing action through live performance, the soundtrack supplemented the spectacular and immersive potential of the onscreen narrative. It ensured a sensory continuity that served to capture and maintain the emotional attention of the audience. In "Hush," the same principal applies: the prevalence of the musical score operates as a ubiquitous narrator for the voiceless emotion as it is played out and in turn solicits the empathy of the audience through its affective devices.

The season 5 episode "The Body," however, directly rejects this affective potential of musical scoring in favor of constructing a sparse vocal soundscape,

---

[12] Chion, *The Voice in Cinema*, p. 77.
[13] Overbey and Preston-Matto, "Staking in Tongues," passim.

opting for the complete rejection of diegetic and non-diegetic music throughout the show (with the exception of the opening Christmas flashback scene), notable for the fact that the series is usually heavily laden with both. Instead, the human voice takes on a more performative, live quality that accents the indexical nature of the voice in quite different ways to those of "Hush."

"The Body" of the Voice

> The connection between a vocalized signifier and the signified is a mode of transparency, not a *connection*, since in this formulation there is no space between the two elements. Meaning *is* the sound of the voice.[14]

"The Body" is an unusual televisual text. In its unnatural ordering of sound objects, use of aural point of view, denial of omnipresent sonic access, and long periods of silence intercut with close-miked voices, it manipulates the sonic conventions of television in unnerving ways. Like "Hush" it takes issue with the investment of voice in television as both subjective essence and tool of exposition, but unlike the earlier episode it makes particular use of both silence and the potential proximity of voices as affective devices.

The episode centers around the death of the principal maternal figure in the ensemble of characters—Buffy's mother, Joyce Summers. The death constructs a *mise-en-scène* of relative stillness, only occasionally broken with frenetic movement such as the anxious response of Buffy's discovery of her mother's body, or the vampiric attack in the morgue. Notably this visual stillness and static composition is reflected and extended through the soundtrack. It is the relative quiet of the soundscape, coupled with the unusual elevation of diegetic sounds[15] and the favoring of extreme close-ups that weights the episode with its affective yet unnerving resonance. Silence in television is dangerous and consequently uncommon for it initiates the danger of losing the viewer in the absence of the flow of acoustic spectacle inherent to the traditional televisual text—for example, the laugh track in sitcoms is a sonic assurance that silence will never intrude on the "hum" for very long.[16] "The Body" enacts a distinct rejection of this reliance on sonic cues and objects for its enactment of story, emotion, and spectatorial identification with onscreen bodies.

---

[14] Charles Affron, *Cinema and Sentiment* (Chicago, 1982), p. 105.

[15] The atmospheric sounds outside the Summers' home or Xander's punch into the wall are two such examples.

[16] Serge Daney uses this word "hum" casually to describe the typical flow and make-up of the television soundtrack in Serge Daney and Bill Krohn, "Les Cahiers du Cinéma 1968–1977: Interview with Serge Daney," trans. Bill Krohn, *The Thousand Eyes*, 2 (1977), accessed October 2002, at http://home.earthlink.net/~steevee/Daney_1977.html. It highlights the role of the television in contributing to the daily soundscape of the domestic space.

What this manipulation of televisual sonic conventions achieves is a paradoxical reliance on the soundtrack, but less on the flow of noise and more on the expanse it can provide through silence and its juxtaposition with sonic density. The voice becomes an explicit sign and enactment of liveness realized through the specific vocal performances of the actors and the recording techniques employed in production. To consider this through a lens borrowed from Roland Barthes, the voice here becomes "language lined with flesh, ... a whole carnal stereophony."[17] The audience is admitted into an intimate space, in which language is ineffectual and the body incapable of maintaining balance, expressed through the uneven and breathy voice. Such an impression is arrived at through deliberate manipulation of both the apparatus and the conventions of voice recording.

The majority of the episode sounds as though it is recorded using close-miking techniques whereby the recording apparatus (typically a magnetic microphone) is held in close relation to the mouth of the performer. This aesthetic device is usually employed through visual pairing with close-ups, or through the use of voiceover or post-dubbing. "The Body" is shot largely in (off-center) close-up and two-shot, possibly enabling the positioning of the onset boom close to the body of the performer. However, the use of body-mikes is also able to produce such a technical effect. What is ultimately created through close-miking techniques is a sense of density and proximity of the voice to the ear of the audience. It constructs a sensation of presence, in which the traditionally undesirable qualities of the recorded voice (the pops, spitting, and hissing) are brought to the fore and are felt literally to breathe into the ear of the audience. Distance is all but obliterated in the cognitive path between mouth and ear, as it is between the mouth and the recording device of the apparatus. However, like the out-of-context extreme visual close-up, the acoustic close-up can serve to subtly distort the voice through the very closeness of it. Natural modes of hearing rely on distance between sound-source object (in this case, the mouth) and the ear in order to establish perspective. Once perspective is problematized through the close-up, the relationship between object and perception is altered.

The acoustic close-up in "The Body" obliterates distance between performing body, apparatus, and spectator body. The proximity of the voice opens up intimate access to its textures, intonations, and delivery that reveal a "liveness" not otherwise accessible. Voices cracking—as Willow's does several times as she fruitlessly frets over finding the correct ensemble for the unfortunate occasion— become interchangeable with bodies physically breaking down. In a sense, the voice becomes a performing body in itself, acting in and for the originating body. To quote Roland Barthes, who perfectly expresses the liveness of the acoustic close-up, "the cinema capture[s] the sound of speech close up ... and make[s] us hear in their materiality, their sensuality, the breath, the gutterals, the fleshiness of the lips, a whole presence of the human muzzle."[18]

---

[17] Roland Barthes, *The Pleasure of the Text*, trans. Richard Miller (New York, 1975), p. 66.

[18] Ibid., p. 67.

For an audience subjected to such intimate access, the "presence" of the naked and vulnerable voice draws one into the emotional space of the text. Proximity of voice aids this textual immersion, and when the narrative is one predicated on grief and psychological disintegration, as "The Body" is, the effect on the audience is comparatively distressing. The voice, as the primary constituent of the television soundtrack, carries the weight of both narrative and emotional continuity, and in this case it is manipulated for utmost affective potential, literally embodying the emotional drive of the narrative.

As in "Hush," there is the firm resignation that bodies and these tactile voices belong together, for those that aren't paired together are untrustworthy, or even uncanny. The use of aural point of view in "The Body" constructs a number of situations in which bodies and their voices become detached, impossibly separated. As Buffy is being advised by the doctor that her mother's death would have been "quick and painless" there is a brief moment in which his voice of authority is breached. His mouth utters soundless words while Buffy's aural point of view projects and constructs new words for him: her distrust of his authority compels her to fabricate a "truth," uttered in his voice but not from his mouth. The shapes he mouths conflict directly with the sounds projected through Buffy and into the soundtrack. It is through his voice that she constructs what she believes to be an unmentionable truth—her culpability in her mother's death—for in the logic of audiovisual media, it is the voice that reveals and exposits.[19]

In another instance, aural point of view prevents access to one of the most traditionally valued exchanges in television, when Buffy tells her younger sister Dawn that their mother is dead. The scene is shot from behind a pane of glass as the girls stand outside a school classroom. Their bodies are visible through the barrier but their voices are muted and inaccessible from the audience's point of view. Both bodies are still, facing one another, Buffy gesturing with hands only. Dawn collapses out of the frame but the camera does not move to take her in. The silence is left unbroken. This silence constructs an expanse that runs for several minutes. Scene changes effect no change in the soundtrack as mouths do not utter a noise, and diegetic sounds are muted to the point of indiscernibility, whereas in earlier scenes the sonic hierarchy was reversed with incidental sounds such as car engines and windchimes brought forward in the mix. When at last there is a voice within the sparse soundscape (Willow's nervous fretting) it is intrusive and too close and intimate, for it resembles a body in crisis, its nasal and crackled texture revealing too much of the subject, in stark contrast to the usual polish of the recorded TV voice. It is through this juxtaposition between (near) silence and proximate voices that the episode constructs its affective resonance, in direct opposition to popular conventions of television.

---

[19] The verbal exposition in Buffy is a staple of its narrative structure, parodied so well in "Restless" (4.22), as Giles sings rather than speaks his role as the primary expositor in the episode's long-form dream sequence.

"That's enough small talk, don't you think?"

> I think that television is not taken seriously by anyone … Its principal impact resides in the fact that it becomes a background noise which keeps you from hearing other sounds.[20]

Buffy is a text as challenging, complex, and adventurous as its namesake heroine. The constant undertaking of playfully and earnestly manipulating televisual form and expectations has earned it a valuable place in the audiovisual canon, even while it still struggles to earn a place of stature in the industry it operated within. What is certain is that in its seven years on the air it made an indelible impression on the medium and made possible its reinvention. For *Buffy* is not simply a cinematic show brought to life or perhaps resuscitated on television (an apparent compliment to its formal achievements). Its form is unmistakably situated within a long history of serial television, yet it thrives in challenging its form.

Close consideration of the televisual soundscape is an important tool for enlivening and decoding the emotional and textual power of *Buffy*. By restructuring the valued position of the voice and the "hum" imperative of the medium, the series drew attention to the conventions of the medium and sought to challenge their stranglehold on the texts produced within it. In discussing Godard's televisual work, French film and television critic Serge Daney argued that by challenging the sonic codes one is able to "break the hum" of the medium, consequently demonstrating "that television, far from making people passive, demands from them on the contrary to produce a kind of work that the journalists don't produce [for them],"[21] empowering the audience to make meaning and to perform their own unmediated analysis. Joss Whedon and the creative team behind Mutant Enemy clearly challenged the *Buffy* audience in an equivalent way, acknowledging their familiarity with television form and actively working with those expectations. In doing so, the series performed dangerous and dexterous sonic feats against the monolith of the television convention. May its legacy be lasting and audible.

---

[20] Daney and Krohn, "Les Cahiers du Cinéma 1968–1977."
[21] Ibid.

Chapter 6
And the Rest is Silence: Silence and Death as Motifs in *Buffy the Vampire Slayer*

Gerry Bloustien

> Silence has become the indicator of an unusual intensity of feeling—emotional intensity in the Hollywood film; public solemnity in the two-minute silence on Veterans' Day; the one-minute silence before kick-off in which to honor someone's death.
>
> (Simon Frith, "Music and Everyday Life")

> Thus, from whichever direction we approach it, music in our societies is tied to the threat of death ... Everywhere in fact, diversity, noise, and life are no longer anything more than masks covering a mortal reality: Carnival is fading into lent and silence is setting in everywhere.
>
> (Jacques Attali, *Noise: The Political Economy of Music*)

"The hardest thing in this world is to live in it":[1] Silence as Death in *Buffy the Vampire Slayer*

The world of *Buffy the Vampire Slayer* is replete with noisy representations of death and dying—excessive music and language underscore the demise of vampires, demons, humans, and hope. Over its seven years, as in the narrative conventions of some of the most enduring dramas and soap operas, where narrative death is never quite as final as it would seem, two of the main characters in *Buffy* died and returned to life: Angel from hell or purgatory; while Buffy herself died twice and the second time was brought back from heaven through magic.[2] And yet, despite the recurring accounts of rebirth and redemption, the sense of menace, doom, and

---

[1] Buffy's last words to Dawn in "The Gift" (5.22), which Dawn then repeats back to her in "Once More with Feeling" (6.7). The allusion to Hamlet's final words to Horatio (5.2. ll. 357–8) in the title of this essay is used sarcastically in *Buffy* by Giles in "The Dark Age" (2.8) as he describes Buffy's music choice as "noise."

[2] Within the long narrative arcs and generic conventions of daytime soap operas, particularly some exceptionally long-running ones originating in the USA such as *Days of Our Lives* (1965–), *The Bold and the Beautiful* (1987–), *Passions* (1999–), *As the World Turns* (1956–) and *The Young and the Restless* (1973–), death (although sudden and violent) is often not as final as it would seem. Many characters in these series become victims of

anxiety never quite disappeared but remained like a never-ending underground rumble. I argue that this sense of doom, the unanswerable threat that did not go away, was represented most poignantly in the series not through noise and music but through the gaps and silences.[3] In the original *Buffy* film (1992), Whedon himself twice articulates the link between silence and death using Hamlet's final words to Horatio, "the rest is silence": once by Merrick (Donald Sutherland), Buffy's Watcher, as he lies dying and then by Buffy (Kristy Swanson) who repeats the line to Lothos toward the end of the film when she realizes what it means.

As the two quotations that head this chapter indicate, many cultures still use stillness and quiet in informal customs and in more formal rituals to capture and reflect on peace, human frailty, and mortality. While these are moments of truth and self-awareness, when the participants step out from their everyday world of turmoil and uncertainty into a utopian space of peace, they are also moments that highlight the ephemeral nature of our everyday existence. Perhaps for this reason, the concept of silence itself can be slippery and hard to pin down. It never simply means absence of sound but connotes a range of feelings and beliefs. It has been defined (when used as a noun) as the state of being silent (as when no one is speaking); yet the absence of sound can not only indicate peace and quietness but also muteness or a refusal to speak when expected. It can thus also connote secrecy, the deliberate act of keeping things hidden. When used as a verb, silence can also mean to force quietness or speech upon oneself or on others, so to repress or to keep from expression. Silence has also been defined as white noise: sounds that we choose not to, or have forgotten how to, hear; that which prevents us from hearing significant sounds or from communicating effectively. At its most extreme silence signifies nothingness, loss of subjectivity and consciousness, "to be no more," a total powerlessness, a yielding up of the self to the ultimate oblivion of otherness, the universal cosmos, death.[4]

In a series where music and language are so central, this chapter explores their obverse, the narrative role of gaps and silences that underscore the inescapable paradox of death as that which is both desired and feared. Although the characters speak of and might even positively experience an after-life, death for all of the protagonists is seen as an avoidance of the necessarily difficult process of

---

severe accidents or trauma resulting in (near) death, disappearances, or comas, and they often make spectacular recoveries or reappearances.

[3] For other related interpretations of the use of silence in *Buffy* see Kelly Kromer, "Silence as Symptom: A Psychoanalytic Reading of 'Hush'," *Slayage* 19 (2006); and Patrick Shade, "Screaming to be Heard: Reminders and Insights on Community and Communication in 'Hush'," *Slayage* 21 (2006).

[4] The works of Harold Pinter (1930–) and Samuel Beckett (1906–1989) have both explored the use of silence in dramatic texts; the musical work and theoretical explorations of John Cage explored the idea of silence in music and poetry, perhaps most famously in his 1952 work *4'33"*, during which the performer makes no intentional sounds. See John Cage, *Silence: Lectures and Writing* (London, 1987).

living. That is, it is seen as a poignant desire to return to an existence devoid of responsibility or, in Derrida's terms, a return of the "orgasmic" or "demonic." Derrida argues that, despite modernity's belief in control and order, the seductive demonic is always threatening to re-emerge.[5] By "demonic," Derrida implies a re-emergence of the pre-Platonic state, an extension of what Freud has called the "the death instinct"[6] and Roger Caillois called "*le mimetisme* [mimesis]."[7] The relinquishing of responsibility may mean a life without agency, yet the payoff can also seem attractive.

In *Buffy*, the recurring motif of silence can be seen in four main modes as representing the protagonists' fears along a continuum of unease—from small niggling doubts to full-blown anxiety. None of these modes is used exclusively, of course, but they are frequently combined or juxtaposed within an episode. However, when some modes are particularly dominant and extended in a sequence, such as in "Hush" (4.10) or "The Body" (5.16), they lend a particular emotional feel to the episode, as explained more fully below.

The first mode of silence is its most common occurrence in that, throughout the series, we can identify interrupted speech flow, which occurs in the form of pauses, stuttering, and faltering dialogue. These moments, which we might call mini-silences, are often part of an endearing or humorous aspect of characterization such as that of the self-deprecating, unconfident Willow, Tara, or Giles. Yet these mini-silences also signify moments when self-control and self-possession are lost for all of the characters. This is particularly salient for it is yet another way in which the series deviates from the usual American teenage drama: in the majority of similar programs that mainly target teenage viewers, nearly all of the main characters are fluent, articulate, and witty in their complex speech acts.[8] In *Buffy*, however, alongside the humorous wit are many moments of inarticulateness when the snappy comeback fails, highlighting those times when the social masks and illusions slip, and the doubts and anxieties about personal worth and sense of self re-emerge. While most of the protagonists share the ability to play with language humorously and intelligently, they all also indicate their personal insecurities at various times by their halting speech, repetitions, and stammering. In such situations they use their language as a shield, using humor together with their self-deprecating speech, as when Willow explains her fear of expressing her feelings

---

[5] Jacques Derrida, *The Gift of Death* (Chicago, 1995), p. 35.

[6] Sigmund Freud, *Beyond the Pleasure Principle* (New York, 1991), p. 244.

[7] Roger Caillois, "Mimicry and Legendary Psychasthenia," *October*, 31 (1984), p. 25. Freud defines the *Trieb* or drive (which is translated as "instinct" by Strachey), to be "an urge inherent in organic life to restore an earlier state of things which the living entity has been obliged to abandon under the pressure of external disturbing forces" (Freud, *Beyond the Pleasure Principle*, pp. 46–9).

[8] Karen Eileen Overbey and Lahney Preston-Matto, "Staking in Tongues: Speech Act as Weapon in *Buffy*," in Rhonda Wilcox and David Lavery (eds) *Fighting the Forces: What's at Stake in Buffy the Vampire Slayer* (Lanham, MD, 2002), p. 83.

in the opening episode, "Welcome to the Hellmouth" (1.1): "No, no, no, no. No speaking up. That way leads to madness and sweaty palms." Or her explanation to Buffy in the same episode when they first become friends about her lack of a boyfriend:

> Willow: I–I–I don't actually date a whole lot ... lately.
> Buffy: Why not?
> Willow: Well, when I'm with a boy I like, it's hard for me to say anything cool, or, or witty, or at all. I–I can usually make a few vowel sounds, and then I have to go away.

Willow's lack of confidence is taken to the extreme in the episodes "The Puppet Show" (1.9), "Nightmares" (1.10), and "Restless" (4.22), where she is struck dumb by stage fright and forgets her lines completely. Similarly, Giles's stammer could arguably indicate his upper-class affectations but also his personal anxieties.[9] For example, in numerous season one and two episodes, he reacts in a way similar to that described by Willow whenever he tries to talk to Jenny Calendar, particularly when he attempts to ask her out on a date in "Some Assembly Required" (2.2). This central insecurity remains even when the outward bodily façade suggests otherwise. For example, when in "A New Man" (4.12) Giles is turned into a monster and speaks in Fyarl, Spike not only translates Giles's demon tongue into English but, with his usual insight, can also see through the grim exterior to the real (far less scary) man beneath:

> Giles (as monster): You help me and I don't kill you.
> Spike: Oh, tremendously convincing. Try it again without the stutter.

This use of mini-silences runs throughout the seven seasons, serving as an ongoing backdrop to the other three, more complex ways in which silence is used within the over-arching narrative.

The second mode in which the motif of silence is used is what might be called "wordless silence"—that is, when all dialogue is removed, replaced by diegetic and non-diegetic sounds. The episode "Hush," a well-acknowledged example of this use of silence, is also significant for demonstrating the ways in which spoken language can sometimes mask genuine communication, becoming instead white noise blocking out interpersonal contact and truth. Several other episodes also have long wordless sequences in line with the common generic convention of soap operas and melodramas, the gap left by the lack of dialogue being filled

---

[9] When we see Giles transported back to his wayward adolescence in "Band Candy" (3.6) we not only see a more childish Watcher but hear a very working-class British accent that perhaps indicates a youthful affectation, an attempt to appear "more cool" by distancing himself from the upper-class origins implied by a name like "Rupert." Thank you to Janet Halfyard for this suggestion.

with a plaintive non-diegetic score.[10] Such moments—as when Dawn prepares herself for her own sacrifice in "The Gift" (5.22) by painstakingly folding her clothes—create a hiatus in the pace of the story and aim to increase the pathos and tension for the audience. This is just one of the myriad ways in which musical cues such as Nerf Herder's overall *Buffy* signature tune, Christophe Beck's themes for the Buffy-Angel relationship, or his score for the supernatural atmosphere in "Hush" deliberately create specific emotive qualities in the series. Sometimes the ambient music begins as a live performance in the Bronze such as those by Angie Hart, the songwriter and lead singer from the band Splendid, who appears three times in *Buffy* in "I Only Have Eyes for You" (2.19), "The Freshman" (4.1), and "Conversations with Dead People" (7.7). What begins as diegetic performance can shift to serve a non-diegetic function, as the music and lyrics continue to play in the non-diegetic background of the scene when the character moves outside of the nightclub space, as in "The Harsh Light of Day" (4.3) when the music of the band Bif Naked is used in this way. In some cases the use of music moving from diegetic to non-diegetic can be seen as acting as a metadiegetic soliloquy,[11] for it could be argued that, apart from its emotive quality, the music could be interpreted as being replayed in the character's head.

The third mode of silence is what I call "empty silence" when the sequence is completely devoid of sound, so that there is neither dialogue nor musical score. Lack of sound on television for an extended period of time is dramatically untenable even for the transgeneric world of *Buffy*, as it clearly flouts cinematic and televisual narrative convention and disturbs audience expectation.[12] For this reason this type of silence is usually sandwiched between moments of distorted or dislocated sound or followed by very limited, ambient sounds. While "The Body" presents the most obvious and sustained example of this mode of silence, there are also several other key moments in various episodes such as "Restless" or "Normal Again" (6.17) when diegetic sound alone carries the narrative or when the sound is deliberately dislocated from the image to reinforce the surreal atmosphere, such as in "Restless" when the voices in Xander's dream are dubbed into French.

---

[10] One of Willow's skills, used strategically at key moments, is her ability to use telepathy to convey her thoughts soundlessly and thus privately to Xander and Buffy. See for example "Showtime" (7.11).

[11] See Claudia Gorbman, *Unheard Melodies: Narrative Film Music* (Bloomington, IN, 1987), pp. 22–3.

[12] The sonic discomfort created by extended lack of dialogue and lack of emotive score recalls sections of Hitchcock's *The Birds* (1963), David Lynch's *The Straight Story* (1999), and much of Jane Campion's work such as *A Girls Own Story* (1984) and *The Piano* (1993). Only a few television writers/directors have regularly played with sound in this way: Dennis Potter comes to mind, some of his most well-known television series for the BBC being *Pennies from Heaven* (1978), *The Singing Detective* (1986), *Christabel* (1988), and *Blackeyes* (1989).

The fourth type of silence in *Buffy* is in a reflexive mode, when that which has been silenced or that which cannot be spoken, such as a taboo, is made overt and forced into articulation through a more foregrounded and reflexive thematic device. Such examples can be seen in hyperreal or surreal episodes such as "Restless," "Normal Again," or "Once More, with Feeling" (6.7) as described in more detail below.

In each of these four overarching modes, the motif of silence becomes a powerful negative presence, the fissure in the illusion of control which points to the limits of language.[13] Indeed, as Wajnryb reminds us, "it may be that messages refracted through silence are the more powerful."[14] Before looking more closely at examples of each of these modes, it is necessary to understand why the motif of silence works so effectively overall. To do this we need firstly to revisit the role of noise itself and then consider the concept and narrative device of mimesis which underpins the series as a whole.

"Don't speak Latin in front of the books":[15] Noise, Magic, and Mimesis

The use of noise—excessive sound, burlesque, histrionics, music, humor—as a masking or distancing strategy, is hardly new or unique. Literature and other more recent media are replete with examples of humor and excess being deployed to explore and to avert the terrifying concept of human mortality, that over which we have no control. The gently humorous exchanges in *Buffy*, such as the following from "Prophecy Girl" (1.12), neatly capture this sense of uncertainty:

> Master: You were destined to die. It was written!
> Buffy: What can I say? I flunked the written.

Or (perhaps more poignantly) in "Lie to Me" (2.7):

> Buffy: Nothing's ever simple anymore. I'm constantly trying to work it out. Who to love, or hate... It's just, the more I know, the more confused I get.
> Giles: I believe that's called growing up.
> Buffy: I'd like to stop then, okay?
> Giles: I know the feeling.

From Plato to writers and artists of today, such reflexive depictions of our everyday real-life anxieties and fears have been noted and analyzed, as for example in the

---

[13] Jacques Derrida, *Writing and Difference* (London, 1978), p. 54.
[14] Ruth Wajnryb, *The Silence: How Tragedy Shapes Talk* (Sydney, 2001), p. 35.
[15] Giles to Xander in "Superstar" (4.17) when Xander's careless and inappropriate use of Latin creates a spell that causes the books to burst into flame.

works of numerous writers.[16] The defensive use of humor and excess has also been recognized as such by contemporary readers and audiences everywhere for, as reflected in the many website posts, "might it be that truth is scarier than all the collective monsters put together?"[17] As I have argued elsewhere, in *Buffy* these anxieties are frequently more chronic than acute.[18] They are fears, usually expressed as "a rumbling paranoia rather than once for all fits of panic"[19] reflecting a general sense of menace that, despite the humor and the lively fight scenes, is central to the show's "mirrored realism"[20] and echoes our lived experiences in late modernity. As such, the sense of menace represents both the constant irritations of life, as well as the greater manifestations of evil, combining the banal and the catastrophic, the minor difficulties and greater dangers, and thus it epitomizes the chaos and unease of life in the early twenty-first century. As a rumbling paranoia it waits in the wings for moments when the noise of distraction stops, knowing that it is the silence of loneliness, isolation, and oblivion that represents humanity's greatest fears. These are the moments when we can no longer fool ourselves or lull ourselves into our usual state of security by trying to convince ourselves, as Taussig caustically explained, that "we live facts not fictions."[21]

The mimetic faculty expressed through art, magic, or ritual is the vehicle by which all cultures interpret and attempt to control these fears of the uncanny, attempting to keep in check the irrational and the inexplicable. At its most straightforward level of meaning, mimesis can be interpreted as the symbolic transfer of power or energy from an object or person to its representation so we might imagine through the creation of the copy—a drawing, a photograph, a joke, a story, a play, or a nursery rhyme—that we have control over the real thing that frightens or disturbs. Most cultures still attribute great power to the photographic or recorded image, as for example is the case with many indigenous Australian

---

[16] Mikhail Bakhtin, *Rabelais and His World* (Cambridge, MA, 1968); Georges Bataille, *Visions of Excess: Selected Writings, 1927–39 (Theory and History of Literature)* (Minneapolis, MN, 1985); Peter Stallybrass and Allon White, *The Politics and Poetics of Transgression* (Ithaca, NY, 1986); Marina Warner, *No Go the Bogeyman: Scaring, Lulling and Making Mock* (London, 2000); Don Handelman, *Models and Mirrors: Towards an Anthropology of Public Events* (Cambridge, 1990); Michael Taussig, *Mimesis and Alterity* (New York, 1993).

[17] Tracy Little, "High School of Hell: Metaphor made Literal in *Buffy the Vampire Slayer*," in James B. South (ed.) *Buffy the Vampire Slayer and Philosophy: Fear and Trembling in Sunnydale* (Chicago, 2003), p. 285.

[18] Gerry Bloustien, "Fans with a Lot at Stake: Serious Play and Mimesis in *Buffy the Vampire Slayer*," *European Journal of Cultural Studies*, 5/4 (2002), pp. 427–51.

[19] Boyd Tonkin, "Entropy as Demon: Buffy in Southern California," in Roz Kaveney (ed.) *Reading the Vampire Slayer: An Unofficial Critical Companion to Buffy and Angel* (London/New York, 2001), p. 43.

[20] Brian Wall and Michael Zryd, "Vampire Dialectics: Knowledge, Institutions and Labour," in Kaveney (ed.), *Reading the Vampire Slayer*, p. 53.

[21] Taussig, *Mimesis and Alterity*, p. xv.

and American groups.[22] Consider also the way all cultures seem to create jokes or satire in times of greatest stress or fear, which Freud identified as having two functions—aggression and exposure[23]—but which others have argued are also used to protect and shield the self.[24]

Although the process of mimesis is often interpreted as straightforward imitation or copying, to do so underestimates the complexity of meaning and power in the concept, particularly through its literary, anthropological, and social dimensions. Taussig, for example, likened the process of mimesis to sympathetic magic, arguing that it is the faculty that enables us to "explore difference, yield into and become Other,"[25] a process of transformation by which a copy of something draws power from the original in order to assume the power of the original. Walter Benjamin, from whom Taussig draws his understandings, saw mimesis as an innate human quality, "the powerful compulsion in former times to become and behave like something else."[26] It alters and re-emerges in each era,[27] at times—including now in late modernity—confounding "the boundaries of the subject … the mirror of representation is refigured in terms of nauseating synthaesthesia."[28] The words "nauseating synthaesthesia" point to the visceral power of mimesis, which overloads the senses in its awesome possibilities of separateness or "alterity" within similarity,[29] a reaction that was captured in Buffy's very physical, human response to her mother's death.

On a more banal but equally significant level, mimesis can be seen underpinning the power of advertising: we know that the product will not deliver the magical properties it seems to promise—beauty, prowess, attraction, wealth, or recognition—and yet somewhere subconsciously we seem to believe that the product does have the potential to deliver its promises and, despite our rational

---

[22] These prohibitions are not universal, however, and many are undergoing change, permitting photographs of the deceased to be published, for example, if the deceased has expressly given permission. See Chips Mackinolty and Jamie Gallacher, "A note on referring to deceased Aboriginal people—and the use of the term "kumanjayi" and its spelling and linguistic variants," *ABC Television: Media Watch* (2005), accessed 6 August 2006 at www.abc.net.au/mediawatch/img/2005/ep07/mackinolty.pdf.

[23] Sigmund Freud, *Jokes and Their Relation to the Unconscious* (New York, 1963).

[24] See, for example, Chaya Ostrower, *Humor as a Defense Mechanism in the Holocaust* (PhD thesis, Tel-Aviv University, 2000).

[25] Taussig, *Mimesis and Alterity*, p. xiii.

[26] See Walter Benjamin, "On the Mimetic Faculty," in *Reflections: Essays, Aphorisms, Autobiographical Writings*, ed. Peter Demetz (New York, 1986), p. 333.

[27] Mark Hansen, *Embodying Technesis: Technology Beyond Writing* (Ann Arbor, 2000).

[28] Sheli Ayers, "Virile Magic: Bataille, Baudelaire, Ballard," *Speed: Electronic Journal of Science and Re-Enchantment*, 1/2 (2001), accessed 18 August 2008 at http://proxy.arts.uci.edu/~nideffer/_SPEED_/1.2/ayers.html.

[29] Taussig, *Mimesis and Alterity*.

judgment, we purchase. It is through the power of mimesis that we are moved empathically, sometimes even physiologically, by art or religion and it is the process of mimesis that underlies our belief in the efficacy of ritual, music, magic, and spirituality through its possibilities of transformation, protection, and power. As the means for cognitive and emotional immersion in the imaginary worlds of texts, mimesis underpins the audience's affective responses to any art form, for it plays "a critical role in nearly all areas of human thought and action, our ideas, our speech, writing and reading."[30]

Language, spoken or written, represents one of the most powerful vehicles for the mimetic faculty, bridging the cognitive and affective gap between self and other through the use of words. But, while such bridging is about empathy (blurring of the me and the not-me), such intersubjectivity can be utterly terrifying. In *Buffy* one such example occurs in "The Killer in Me" (7.13) with the metamorphosis of Willow into Warren, the man that she killed, through her double sense of guilt: for his death and for "killing Tara" again, by her moving on into a new relationship: "I let her be dead. She's really dead. (Breaks down into tears) And I killed her."

While we most frequently lose the sense of being a separate individual through the experience of extreme ecstasy (sexual or spiritual love) as we feel the self seeming to merge with the other, we also signal our belief of the utter finality of death through our rituals that stress the merging of self and the cosmos. In the narratives of the Buffyverse these two states of utter abandonment are shown to be inexplicably tied together.

In all cultures, language is one of the main ways in which we try to regain control, to overcome the overwhelming fear of the not-me, using words to name, label, separate, and divide, and to re-present the imaginary power of individual self. In the *Buffy* narratives it is the very materiality of the language through the literal metaphors and the "palpable power of words and utterances"[31] that serves this purpose. For example, as Adams perceives, particular language styles and linguistic patterns are not only used in *Buffy* to protect the self as a shield but also to attack the other as a weapon.[32] As Overbey and Preston-Matto put it: "Any Slayer can brandish a weapon, but for Buffy the Vampire Slayer, the tongue is as pointed as the stake."[33] We can see this not only in Buffy's famous puns, which other characters such as Xander, Willow, and the Buffybot fail to replicate when they assume her Slayer duties, but also in the language of the other characters such as Cordelia's sarcastic barbs in seasons one and two.

When language becomes the voice of seemingly rational or scientific reason it can become an even harsher form of weapon, often literally mechanized in *Buffy*

---

[30] Gunter Gebauer and Christopher Wulf, *Mimesis* (Berkley, CA, 1992), p. 1. See also Steven Shaviro, *The Cinematic Body* (Minneapolis, MN, 1993).

[31] Overbey and Preston-Matto, "Staking in Tongues," p. 73.

[32] Michael Adams, *Slayer Slang: A Buffy the Vampire Slayer Lexicon* (Oxford/New York, 2003).

[33] Overbey and Preston-Matto, "Staking in Tongues," p. 84.

as in the communication tools of the Initiative (see "Hush"). Here, again, language clearly indicates its potential to separate the self from the other, forming and underpinning social hierarchies and social capital. In more benign scenarios, even Giles's characteristic, British-inflected pomposity—he is described as "a textbook with arms" in "Welcome to the Hellmouth"—often leaves the young people's comprehension far behind as he waxes lyrical about the mythology of demons:

> Giles: There is a fringe theory, held by a few folklorists, that some regional stories have actual, very literal antecedents.
> Buffy: And in some language that's English? (Gingerbread, [3.11])

Giles, who is less comfortable in social discourse, especially when anxious or embarrassed ("Prophecy Girl", "Helpless" [3.12]), comes into his own when he needs to refer back to ancient languages, texts, or knowledge. Language as social capital, of course, always works to segregate the dominant from the subjugated, tending to separate the adult from the child, but it can work the other way as when the younger Scoobies' innovative, creative, and manipulative "slayerspeak" leaves certain adults and peers outside of the accepted circle.[34]

In its most transparent and mystical representation of mimesis, language is the vehicle through which spells and other magical incantations enable the individual to attempt to gain control over the natural (and unnatural) universe. It is the link between the real and the symbolic, in which the figurative becomes concrete or literal, that underpins the metanarrative and central conceit of *Buffy* as well as much of the humor and the drama of the series.[35] This use of the literal metaphor is a perfect example of the way mimesis is applied to language in the series so that, through symbolic association and magic, the cognitive becomes concrete. Thus, high school actually becomes hell-like; the overlooked students literally become invisible; the "hot" cheerleader really catches on fire; the mother who longs to relive her childhood indeed swaps bodies with her daughter;[36] and the daily often melodramatic "routine" or "arrangement" of Buffy's life becomes a musical soap opera in "Once More, with Feeling" and her friends provide back-up through songs. When Buffy tells the First to "get out of my face" in "Chosen" (7.22) she means it both metaphorically and literally. It is worthy of note that when Willow is at her most powerful she no longer needs to speak the incantations out loud: she and the dark magic become one. The mimetic blurring is complete; there is no more division. As Giles explains in "Lessons" (7.1), "It's inside you now, this magic. You're responsible for it."

---

[34] Rhonda Wilcox, "'There will Never Be "a Very Special" *Buffy*': *Buffy* and the Monsters of Teen Life," *Journal of Popular Film and Television*, 27/2 (1999), pp. 16–23.

[35] Ibid.

[36] See "The Witch" (1.3), "Out of Sight, Out of Mind" (1.11), and "Storyteller" (7.16).

In all of these ways the mimetic faculty helps to hold back the anxieties of everyday life, constraining the underlying fear of mortal reality. However, when reality under the flimsy veil of containment threatens to become too overt, then the noise has to become greater and metaphor needs to become excessive to drown out the fear through burlesque, humor, irony, or caricature. Freud's analyses of jokes or Bakhtin's description of the carnivalesque revealed the ways the terrifying realities of life had to be transformed and distanced through exaggeration, excess, or self-deprecating humor.[37] Similarly, in the Buffyverse, the ultimate fear of mortal reality is deflected through distancing techniques. These more excessive exaggerations, as in "Hush" and "Once More, with Feeling," always point to the moments when "contradictory realities coexist, each seemingly capable of cancelling the other out."[38] Sometimes such strategies fail, and the fear becomes so acute that no humor is possible.[39] In the Buffyverse, as I indicated above, several episodes such as "Restless," "The Body," and "Normal Again" particularly express this poignancy and anxiety, demonstrating the myriad ways in which the mimetic silence of death and loss of self is both represented and concealed in varying degrees of intensity. Leaving aside the mini-silences, it is to the first of the other three overarching modes of silence that I turn my attention now.

"Won't say a word":[40] The Mode of Wordless Silence

For an episode that is renowned for its use of silence, the first quarter of "Hush" is full of demonstrations of talk as an ineffectual masking strategy, with several amusing incidents showing spoken language as noise rather than communication and, indeed, as avoidance of genuine communication. For example, despite the episode's opening dream sequence, which clearly reveals Buffy's unconscious desires to herself as well as the viewers, Buffy and Riley in their waking states avoid any physical contact and thus any expression of their mutual sexual attraction. Instead, they engage in their usual "babble fest." Xander and Anya argue in public because Anya refuses to distinguish between public and private conversations and Xander cannot articulate his love and commitment, a failure that is to have more disastrous consequences later in the series. Giles and Olivia initially engage in inconsequential chat rather than physical affection after a long separation until Olivia calls a halt: "that's enough small talk, don't you think?" Meanwhile, Willow attends a Wicca group where the "blessed-wanna-be" members derisively dismiss

---

[37] See Freud, *Jokes and their Relation to the Unconscious*; Bahktin, *Rabelais and His World*.
[38] Richard Schechner, *The Future of Ritual* (London, 1993), p. 36.
[39] Stallybrass and White, *The Politics and Poetics of Transgression*; Bloustien, "Fans with a Lot at Stake."
[40] Buffy's teasing words to Riley at the beginning of "Hush" (4.10) prove to be prescient.

any talk of magic and spells as disempowering stereotypes, preferring to discuss their cake stall and fundraising.

When the Gentlemen arrive in Sunnydale shortly afterwards, bringing death and silence into the town by stealing hearts and voices, their appearance also removes much of the possibility of both communication and miscommunication, although not all. As speech cannot be used, the characters revert to other methods of expressing thoughts and commands such as gestures, drawings, posters, music, signs, and written messages. Professor Walsh, for example, types into an electronic speech machine, its mechanical (and masculine) voice devoid of emotion and intonation, reinforcing its pragmatic purpose as a vehicle for maintaining order. Because these methods are less sophisticated than speech, where clarification can immediately be sought and given, we see several humorous examples of misinterpretation especially during Giles's childlike illustrations of the Gentlemen's gruesome purpose and methods.[41] Yet, when the dialogue stops, moments of genuine interpersonal connection do occur during this silent time: Buffy and Riley finally kiss, expressing their growing attraction for each other, and reveal their respective secret identities of Slayer and fighter for the Initiative; Xander demonstrates (through his frenzied attack on Spike) that he does truly care for Anya when he believes mistakenly that she is Spike's victim; Tara and Willow, through their clasped hands and shared focus, reveal and combine their mutual magical powers, demonstrating that their combined force is more than the sum of their separate selves and heralding their future romantic and sexual unity.

"Hush" also demonstrates the ways in which silence can hide something that is too frightening to articulate: that which has been "silenced." In the UK Channel 4 countdown of the *100 Greatest Scary Moments* (2006), "Hush" came in at a respectable 25. As Joss Whedon explained in his interview for the program, "silence is the essence of horror." In the same program TV critic Angie Errigo referred to "Hush" as epitomizing the uncanny. As Giles realizes, the characters of the Gentlemen are straight from fairy tales and dreams, from the world of the hidden, the taboo, and the unconscious, where extreme fears are repressed and submerged under the babble of the everyday.[42] Through the musical score of "Hush" composer Christophe Beck deliberately references the work of two renowned cinematic artists of the grotesque: writer and director Tim Burton and composer Danny Elfman (whose collaborative work scored all but one of Burton's

---

[41] Misunderstandings occur in other episodes too with humorous results due to the lack of a mutual spoken language, as for example in "First Date" (7.14) between Giles (whose "Mandarin is thin" and whose Cantonese is "a little thinner") and Chao-Ahn, the Chinese potential who only speaks Cantonese. Thanks to Vanessa Knights in personal communication for reminding me of this.

[42] Rosemary Jackson, *Fantasy: The Literature of Subversion* (London, 1981); Warner, *No Go the Bogeyman*. Also see "Gingerbread," where Giles had already pointed out that "fairy tales are real," or "Killed by Death" (2.18), where Buffy agrees with the small children that "there are real monsters."

films). The work of these two artists frequently expresses the unconscious fears underlying polite society. The satiric film *Mars Attacks!* (1996), while not drawing on Gothic horror, as in "Hush," certainly uses its science fiction plot to create a parodic but still gruesome scenario of attacks by outsiders, alien invaders who also reflect our fears and paranoia. The narrative resolution of "Hush," exploding the heads of the Gentlemen by Buffy's discordant scream[43] is certainly also more than a nod to the similar technique used in the Burton film where the yodels of Tom Jones produced a parallel effect for the Martians. As in "Hush," where lone heroes, reason, and technology fail to overcome the evil invaders, discordant sound and human collaboration succeed.

"It's mortal and stupid":[44] The Mode of Empty Silence

While "Hush" is an excellent example of wordless silence, other episodes illustrate the use of complete or almost complete silence, as explained above, where all but ambient sounds are removed. In "The Body," Buffy discovers the body of her dead mother, dead not by the hand of any supernatural monster or phenomenon, but from natural causes. As Giles noted much earlier in "Killed by Death" (2.3), death and disease are "possibly the only things that Buffy cannot fight," such knowledge reinforcing recognition of both the heroine's and our own human frailty and mortality.[45] The following extract from the episode was transcribed online by a self-identifying fan:

> Buffy turns and walks toward the kitchen, putting down the phone on a table. She gets to the back of the living room just before the kitchen door. Suddenly she falls to her knees and vomits on the floor. We hear the sound of wind chimes over the retching noises.
>
> Buffy stands up slowly, her back to the camera. She puts a hand on her stomach, walks through the kitchen to the back door, opens it and looks out. We hear birds

---

[43] Interestingly, several online fans and critics have commented that Buffy's scream in "Hush" was in sharp contrast to the way female screams on screen usually connote vulnerability. Rather, this one was "in line with what Chion describes as the male 'shout' which is imbued with power and mastery." See Katy Stevens, "Vocal Indexicality in *Buffy the Vampire Slayer*" (2002), accessed 15 August 2005 at http://www.katystevens.com/essays-buffybazin.html. Also see Michel Chion, *The Voice in Cinema*, trans. Claudia Gorbman (New York, 1999).

[44] Anya, the ex-demon Anyanka, describes death in her struggle to understand mortality in "The Body."

[45] This is said early in the series. Later the show demonstrates that there are several aspects of evil that Buffy cannot fight alone; to overcome them she requires the combined efforts of all of her key friends, "the source of our power" ("Primeval" [4.22]), with their respective cognitive, spiritual, and emotional strengths and skills.

singing, distant voices, ordinary city noises. Close-up on Buffy's face, sweaty and pale. She stands there for a moment, then turns back inside, leaning on the door for support. She looks at the kitchen island, goes over to it and takes a bunch of paper towels off the roll. Leaving the back door open, she goes back into the living room and puts the paper towels over the spot on the carpet where she vomited.

Lingering shot of the paper towels on the carpet as the moisture begins to seep through.[46]

Where words fail, Buffy's body emits its own non-verbal reminder that, despite her superhuman powers, she is still mortal, vulnerable, and fragile. The physiological reaction of vomiting indicates the loss of self-control and power. Note that the only sounds the viewer hears in this episode are heightened diegetic ones: Buffy's footsteps across the kitchen floor, the wind chimes as she opens the door to the garden, the sounds of the street and everyday life continuing from birds and the children's shouts, and the sound of Buffy's own retching as she vomits on the floor.[47]

While the scene described above is particularly poignant, it is reinforced by other long silences and half-finished sentences but again without non-diegetic sound in various scenes in the episode. For example, when Buffy calls Dawn out of her art class to inform her younger sister of the death, the scene is filmed through the glass window between the classroom and the corridor. Just as in the art classroom, where the students are told to focus not on the body in front of them but "on the negative space around the object," the viewer too at this moment is led to a very different perspective on grief. Instead of a privileged close-up to the intimate moment, which is the usual framing in a television drama, the viewer is kept with the teacher and the classmates at a helpless and painful distance, behind the glass, listening only to the muted cries of the teenage girl. Similarly, when Xander, Anya, and Tara meet with Willow in her room before the funeral, they struggle to come to terms with Joyce's death in their own particular non-verbal ways. Willow anxiously tries to find the right outfit to wear, one that "Jo-Joyce really liked," one that shows she is supportive of Buffy, one that shows she can cope as a mature adult and "dress like a grownup … can't I be a grownup?" Xander's dramatic punching of a wall is his way of expressing his pent up feelings of impotence:

Willow: Did it make you feel better?
Xander: For a second there.
Willow: A whole second?

---

[46] Extract from *Buffy Episode #94: "The Body" Transcript* transcribed by Joan the English Chick, accessed on 16 October 2005 at http://www.twiztv.com/scripts/buffy/season5/buffy-516.htm.

[47] Thanks to Vanessa Knights who pointed out that these sounds, although diegetic, are hardly realistic, being isolated and louder than usual and exaggerated by the extreme close-ups and odd camera angles.

Anya, who with her demonic background regularly fails to adhere to politically correct conventions, refers to the Joyce they knew as "a dead body," an object that can be "viewed" and "cut open." After Willow's appalled rebuke—"Would you just … stop talking? Just … shut your mouth. Please …"—and her admonition that "it's not okay for you to be asking these things," Anya painfully articulates what the others have covered up in their avoidance and coping behaviors:

> I don't understand how this all happens. How we go through this. I mean, I knew her, and then she's, there's just a body, and I don't understand why she just can't get back in it and not be dead anymore. It's stupid. It's mortal and stupid.

If Anya alone among the friends is able to voice the ineffable in waking hours, the one place where fears are always expressed for everyone are in visions and dreams. Nightmares or "the dreams" have always been regarded as one of the defining characteristics of the Chosen One, as revealed in "Welcome to the Hellmouth" (1.1), but in "Restless" Buffy, Xander, Willow, and Giles share their anxieties through their dreams and are all visited by the spirit of the First Slayer.[48] In "Goodbye Iowa" (4.14), the friends realize that the only way to defeat Adam, a "kinetically redundant, bio-mechanical demonoid," is to magically combine their powers. It was a necessary step as Adam with his internal power source of Uranium 235, unlike other monsters that Buffy had faced, had also crossed genetic boundaries between demons and humans:

> Adam: I'm aware. I know every molecule of myself and everything around me. No-one—no human, no demon has ever been as awake and alive as I am. You're all shadows. ("Superstar" [4.17])

The mystical combination of mind, spirit, heart, and hand evoking the power of the First Slayer by Willow's magic counters Adam and Spike's attempt to isolate Buffy from her friends in "The Yoko Factor" (4.20) and allows the newly empowered Buffy to defeat Adam. However, the spirit of the First Slayer, affronted by this evocation, brings fear and death to the entire group in their dreams. While the specific anxieties and paranoia about self-worth in the episode are directly linked to the characters themselves—such as Willow's latent social inhibitions, Xander's anxieties about his sexuality and commitment and his lack of direction, and Giles's feelings of failure about his role as Watcher—the audience can empathize because these concerns are easily identifiable and applicable to reality outside of the text. This insight brings us to the fourth mode of silence in *Buffy* where reflexivity highlights the deliberate engagement with audience and increases the fear to such an extent that the narrative vehicle has to become mimetic excess.

---

[48] "Restless" in turn refers back to "Nightmares" (1.10), in which each of the Scoobies was forced to confront and articulate their hidden anxieties and worst fears.

"It's all about subterfuge":[49] The Mode of Reflexive Silence

This self-conscious, self-reflexive mode, especially when framed within the formal structures of a televisual text, simultaneously proposes "a scepticism not only towards supernatural experience and superstitious belief but towards all naïve forms of credulity."[50] That is, the narrative pace slows as the audience is taken into a new space of discovery, a new confrontation of dramatic possibilities, removing as it does so the audience's sense of privileged observer. The real source of the terror, as becomes increasingly clear as the series develops, is not external to the characters (or the audience) but within. In *Buffy* the real hero is ultimately not Buffy but the combined force of the Slayer and her close companions—and of all potential Slayers everywhere by the end of season seven. Just as the Scoobies have to combine emotionally, sometimes mystically, losing the individual self in each other in order to defeat the all-encompassing evil, so too, in such moments, the boundaries between good and evil merge. It becomes clear at those moments that the First Slayer and the First Evil share the same foundation and in many ways the same goals. As Spike clearly and perceptively explained to Buffy in "Fool for Love" (5.7),

> Death is your art. You make it with your hands, day after day. That final gasp. That look of peace. Part of you is desperate to know: what's it like? Where does it lead you? And now, you see, that's the secret. Not the punch you didn't throw or the kicks you didn't land. Every Slayer ... has a death wish. Even you.

At such moments of revelation, the separation between the self and the other becomes too blurred for comfort. Intimacy means loss of separateness, loss of hiding, or silencing those parts of ourselves that we desperately want to conceal—even from ourselves.

Several episodes including "Restless" use a combination of total silence together with sequences of surreal imagery and dislocation of sound from image to express this in-built anxiety about faltering or lost sense of identity. This is particularly highlighted by repeated reference to hiding, concealing, naming, and labeling things, as in Buffy's comment to Willow: "Your costume is perfect. [whispers] Nobody's gonna know the truth. You know, about you"; or later in Giles's explanation of the purpose of the play: "Acting is not about behaving; it's about hiding. The audience wants to find you, strip you naked, and eat you alive, so hide. It's all about subterfuge."

In "Restless", this reflexive mode—revealing each character's hidden insecurities, dramatized through performances that are judged and the bizarre incidents that stress watching—is heightened by a number of silent sequences. As the threat becomes too extreme for comfort, the non-diegetic music and

---

[49] Giles in "Restless" (4.22).
[50] Markman Ellis, *The History of Gothic Fiction* (Edinburgh, 2000), p. 14.

the behavior of the characters—which often underscores (and exaggerates) the seriousness of the situation—is then swiftly undermined, either by physical humor, mainly through the characters' facial expressions, or the timed delivery of the lines, or the use of wit and puns. The extreme juxtaposition of the humorous with the more conventional language of terror, such as Giles's singing denouement at the Bronze—accompanied by his appreciative audience holding up lighters, a rock-concert convention for particularly soulful or "iconic" numbers indicating the listener's involvement and identification with the emotion of the song—is immediately followed by his gruesome "scalping" by the First Slayer.

The quintessential reflexive episode in terms of taboos and silences is "Once More, with Feeling." In this episode the whole community of Sunnydale is affected by a spell that is in many ways the obverse of the one that created havoc in "Hush." This time everyone is compelled to vocalize through song their innermost feelings but also their concerns and anxieties, especially the ones they would prefer to keep hidden. Buffy sings of the meaningless routine of her life, which is just "going through the motions" and why "she came from the grave much graver." While her friends believed that they had brought her back to life from a kind of hell dimension, she has in fact been pulled out of heaven. She has regained life but she confesses that now she feels emotionally dead. The deliberate use of the slurring semi-tone shift as she sings "heaven" is discomforting, offering again a musical equivalent to the stutter, noted above. Spike's response and admonition to her about the need to "go on living/So one of us is living" repeats the same emotionally discordant break.

Xander and Anya admit in song that they are terrified of their coming marriage commitment for they could "really raise the beam in making marriage a hell!" Even the romantic song "Under Your Spell," performed in an idealized pastoral setting by Tara, has darker connotations with its ambiguous lyrics. As Tara herself comes to discover later in the episode, Willow has literally been "playing with [her] memory." She has bewitched her lover into forgetting any discord between them: "Willow, don't you see/There'll be nothing left of me," a poignant reference back to her literal loss of self, dependence, and extreme vulnerability in season five when, as a victim of Glory's gruesome attack, she was deprived of her mind and reason. Giles sings of his realization that Buffy will always remain childlike, emotionally dependent on him if he stays in Sunnydale and then both he and Tara are heard in harmony although singing separately about the painful necessity of leaving Buffy and Willow. Spike's song laments his frustrated sense of unrequited love for Buffy with his plea that she should let her (un)dead lover "Rest in Peace."

The ways in which the humor and the music are used in this episode exemplify the reflexive mode of mimetic excess, discussed above. The episode not only makes explicit the taboos and secrets that have been silenced throughout the series so far but it also deliberately implicates the audience in the performance. The regular viewer understands the *double entendres* of the lyrics and is overtly invited to step back from their usual emotional enmeshment in the diegesis. The conventional dramatic fourth wall, where the audience is allowed to be a separate, omniscient observer of the performance, is removed by the unconventional soap opera opening credits, the several direct incidents of address to the camera such as "and you can sing along," and by references made by the characters themselves to their roles as actors, such as Xander's "this is my verse, hello!" or Anya's awareness that "It was like we were being watched ... Like there was a wall missing ... in our apartment. Like there were only three walls and not a fourth wall"; or Willow's plaintive "I think this line's mostly filler."

While this episode has rightly been acknowledged as exceptional in its transcending of both its genre and the medium[51] it needs to be recognized also for the way it again highlights the darkness, tragedy, and silence of the Buffyverse that underlies the music, humor, and excess.

A recent article by the Australian novelist Marion Halligan described the concept of death as something that underpins all art and popular culture as the "powerful shaping narrative," the "defining fact of life," and a "marvellous liberating secret."[52] As she argues, drawing on examples that range from classical literature to contemporary television, while we accept that death is necessary to life, we do not want to face it just yet. Instead, as Joss Whedon also eloquently illustrates, we build up a mountain of strategies, masks, masquerades, and euphemisms, "from the bathetic to the solemn" to block out the silences that we fear will overwhelm us.[53] This chapter aims to further these insights by demonstrating the complex role of "silences" in the *Buffy* series, achieved through four different narrative techniques: interrupted speech flow or "mini-silences"; "wordless silence" where some form of diegetic sound but no words are used; "empty silence" where anxiety and fear are underscored through a lack of all diegetic and non-diegetic sound; and finally the foregrounded reflexive use of silence, where the inescapable paradox of death as that which is both desired and feared is articulated, made overt, faced through the surreal, the hyperreal and mimetic excess. Together these examples illustrate attraction and (ironically) the longevity of the Buffyverse, for its enduring attraction for its fans is not simply its fun, its intelligent though dark humor, and its music but ultimately because it dares to state and clarify what we all know and fear—that "ripeness is all; the rest is silence."

---

[51] See Rhonda Wilcox, *Why Buffy Matters: The Art of Buffy the Vampire Slayer* (London, 2005), pp. 191–205; John Kenneth Muir, "Cult TV Friday Flashback #9: Buffy the Vampire Slayer: 'Once More With Feeling'" (2005), accessed 26 June 2006 at http://reflectionsonfilmandtelevision.blogspot.com/2005/09/cult-tv-friday-flashback-9-buffy.html.

[52] Marion Halligan, "He Kindly Stopped for Me," *The Weekend Australian* [Review section], 19–20 August 2006, p. 9.

[53] Ibid.

PART II
Owning Music:
Bands, Fans, and Pop Culture

Chapter 7

Bronze Things; Things of Bronze: Popular Music Cultures in *Buffy the Vampire Slayer*

Catherine Driscoll

```
Intro
e-------------------------------------------------------|
B-------------------------------------------------------|
G-9--11--12--7--7-7-9-11-7------------------------------|
D-9--11--12--7--7-7-9-11-7----------PICK SLIDE----------|
A-7--9---10--5--5-5-7-9--5------------------------------|
E-------------------------------------------------------|
Then Kick in Full Distortion With Drums and Bass
e-------------------------------------------------------|
B-------------------------------------------------------|
G-9----11-12--7-----9-11--7-----------------------------|
D-9-X6-11-12--7-X14-9-11--7-X8--------------------------|
A-7----9--10--5-----7-9---5-----------------------------|
E-------------------------------------------------------|
```

(Anonymous tab for Nerf Herder's *Buffy* theme)

Welcome to the Hellmouth

The theme track to *Buffy the Vampire Slayer* firmly locates the series within a particular musical field.[1] It is not that Nerf Herder's original track written for the series defines it as belonging to the same aesthetic or even audience as "rock," "alternative rock," or still less the far more specific niche of "nerd core."[2] Rather, the music underwriting the title sequence, in conjunction with its series of young faces turning to camera (ready for audience identification), anchors the series in the broad, contested terrain of youth-directed popular culture. Moreover, given the disjunction between the audiences for "nerd core" and fresh teen faciality, it anchors the series in the contradictions integral to popular youth culture.

---

[1] Thanks to Paul Attinello for the invitation to write this piece, to Janet Halfyard for her insightful comments on my draft, and to my son Sean for coming round to *Buffy* in the end and helping me hear it differently.

[2] It is this track's attachment to *Buffy*, rather than fan relations to Nerf Herder, that propel its distribution on multiple open access guitar tab sites.

The predictable framing of conventionally attractive and overwhelmingly young actors both plays against and points to the extratextual conventions of popular music as it is identified with "youth" and establishes the series within that field of conflicts and assembled partial identifications rather than for any specific genre or audience.

Noticing this invocation of youth culture makes no claim about the role of any specific demographic in *Buffy*'s production or consumption. Both youth and youth culture here are ideas available to diverse audiences and for many different purposes. *Buffy* draws out several key points of tension from the idea of youth culture, each of which is especially visible in the field of youth-directed popular music.[3] In this essay I argue that youth-directed popular music cultures, indexing a broader field of popular music cultures, are deployed in *Buffy* with an emphasis on these tensions and contradictions which serve the narrative and aesthetic functions that are central to *Buffy*'s production, consumption, and distribution.

Nerf Herder is not the first thing we hear on *Buffy*. The first episode, "Welcome to the Hellmouth," opens on near silence, building into an atmospheric score that tags the show as belonging to a horror genre. When the formulaic horror set, replete with skulls and other threatening shapes, quickly transforms into a science classroom, we have in no way left that genre. Instead, this shift merely refines the kind of horror we are watching to the teen horror film with the institutional management of youth as a conventional narrative frame. Though this opening invites us to believe we are entering the story alongside the figure Carol Clover refers to as the "final girl"—the character with whom the teen slasher genre traditionally begins and ends—the pretty blonde in an iconic school uniform who climbs through a window into this first shot quickly turns out to be the monster.[4] It is as she transforms into a vampire and attacks the boy teasing her with sex and horror that we are thrown into the theme tune, dislodging any more precise generic placement for the series than "youth culture."

In this first episode the theme fades out with Buffy's upward glance from the shadows to the light. She is not looking at us but this is still a look of power, leaving the audience firmly located with the right "final girl" when the title sequence ends. In the next scene the narrative shifts to yet another register in which it again insists that *Buffy* is a narrative about youth culture. Buffy's teen girl bedroom, watched over by her mother's authority and framed by both popular music and school, presses the story into another highly recognizable scenario for the relationship between youth and popular music: the girl pop fan and her domesticated bedroom culture.[5] After the opening vignette, the title sequence, and the introduction to

---

[3] See Andy Bennett, *Popular Music and Youth Culture: Music, Identity and Place* (London, 2000).

[4] See Carol J. Clover, *Men, Women and Chainsaws: Gender in the Modern Horror Film* (London, 1992).

[5] The gendering of the "mainstream" through and in popular music cultures is a crucial context here, but it is also worth noting that *Buffy* partly degenders the mainstream

Buffy's home life, we have a fourth beginning, as Buffy is dropped off for her first day at a new school. Through this scene, the generic inflections of Dave Aragon's "No Heroes" stress for us exactly how little Buffy's story will accord with the nice day at school version of teen life her mother clearly wants, and it also dislodges any neat identification we might make between Buffy's life and the musical taste regimes which would more predictably oppose "cheerleader blonde" to "vampire slayer."

While *Buffy*'s placement as youth culture weakens in later seasons as Buffy and her friends take on more adult roles, the association set up in the first season continues, especially through its use of popular music and the implications of that for the audience it claims. S. Renee Dechert suggests that the series uses music in three ways: to set the mood, to "establish the identities of characters," and to "reinforce the communal identity" established between *Buffy* and its fans.[6] I want to consider the complexity and contradictions of these deployments of popular music and make some further claims for the importance of popular music cultures in *Buffy*. Taken as a whole, the first episode's sequence of openings insists that we approach *Buffy* through a set of conflicting claims about genre and style firmly anchored in debates about youth and music. Having thus laid out musically the contradictions and continuities between "the Vampire Slayer" and "Buffy," it remains one of the subtle strengths of *Buffy the Vampire Slayer* that it does not limit the story to that dynamic opposition. Instead it deploys the conflicts embedded in the conceptual field of popular youth music and its audiences to problematize this and all other dichotomous narratives, even that between good and evil on which the series initially appears to be premised. It is by acknowledging the complexity of popular music cultures, beyond the reference points of individual songs or artists, that the series uses music to further its complications of realist, romantic, and supernatural story lines.

Buffy's high school is one nexus for the complex popular musical location of the series. Cordelia's "coolness test" exemplifies this in the first episode, setting Buffy's story within a mass-produced and institutionalized popular culture that nevertheless crucially, and at times painfully, negotiates identities through taste and style. This is a common production strategy for television directed at younger audiences, drawing on the conventions of teen film that coalesced in its most influential form in the 1980s and set the parameters for "teen television" including

---

by positioning girls as equally likely to exceed its boundaries and boys—like Xander, Andrew, Jonathan, and Warren—as the most enthusiastic popular culture fans. See Catherine Driscoll, "Girl Culture, Revenge and Global Capitalism: Cybergirls, Riot Grrrls, Spice Girls," *Australian Feminist Studies*, 14/29 (1999), pp. 173–93.

[6] S. Renee Dechert, "'My Boyfriend's in the Band!' *Buffy* and the Rhetoric of Music," in Rhonda V. Wilcox and David Lavery (eds) *Fighting the Forces: What's at Stake in Buffy the Vampire Slayer* (Lanham, MD, 2002), p. 219.

groundbreaking series like *Beverly Hills 90210* (1990–2000) and *Buffy*.[7] In line with these conventions, scenes in the school corridors, in particular, are frequently given coherence by an alternative music fragment. That is, the music used in such scenes—to open, close, or completely frame any shared school space—is usually a fragment of a newly released or unreleased popular song. The temporally specific currency of these fragments works to fix the cultural "now" of the audience and, by implication, also the characters; and their never-quite top-40 status tags them as "alternative" both by that opposition and in the post-MTV sense of being caught in the hybrid zone between rock artistry and commodified pop. When *Buffy* intersperses selections from independently circulated music releases with sections of original score it does so as a post-MTV text, and the music video genre is crucial to *Buffy*'s use of popular music as narrative and to its integration of audio and video components in that both music and visual images simultaneously tell stories about each other.

These alternative fragments set the school scene as being not only the fictional Sunnydale High but also the "real life" field that circulates popular music as youth culture. That these are fragments, never beginning at the beginning or the end of the track but in the middle, emphasizes their role of setting the scene amidst a musical culture rather than as independent works of art. These fragments are both exegetical, giving additional information about the meaning of the spaces and the lives of the characters, and they narrate a location for the series itself, identifying an audience presumed by the non-fictional currency of those songs. This is further emphasized by the fact that they tend not to be strictly diegetic. They rarely belong directly to the story line of an episode or a specific moment for the characters. They tell another story than that; a story about the cultural resonance of the narrative, the tracks, and *Buffy* as cultural artifacts that circulate in an audience comprised of the characters on screen, the audience for the series, and the musical peers of both.

This relation also structures promotion for the series and its fan culture negotiations, for example in the release of CD collections of alternative music as series soundtracks, in the performance of the Goo Goo Dolls at the season 6 relaunch of *Buffy* on the UPN network, in Whedon's having invited Nerf Herder to write the *Buffy* theme based on the current musical tastes of the young cast, and in the importance of the songfic genre to *Buffy* fan fiction (which I will return to below). But some reflection on the importance of sound to television will be useful here. Drawing on Christian Metz's classic recognition that "off screen" sound in fact denotes the *image* of the sound's source being off screen[8] we can see

---

[7] Adrian Martin discusses the 1992 *Buffy* movie's relation to this genre in "Teen Movies: The Forgetting of Wisdom," in *Phantasms* (Ringwood, 1994), pp. 63–9. See also Thomas Doherty, *Teenagers and Teenpics: The Juvenilization of American Movies in the 1950s* (Philadelphia, 2002); and Catherine Driscoll, *Girls: Feminine Adolescence in Popular Culture and Cultural Theory* (New York, 2002), pp. 219–23.

[8] Christian Metz, "Aural Objects," in Leo Braudy and Marshall Cohen (eds) *Film Theory and Criticism*, 6th edition (Oxford, 2004), pp. 366–9.

multiple layers of presence for music in *Buffy*, ranging from music not directly linked to the narrative or to the visible *mise-en-scène* to the staged and screened "live" performance of a track. But, as John Ellis notes, television "sound holds attention more consistently than image, and provides a continuity that holds across momentary lapses of attention."[9] Television sound thus has "a more centrally defining role" than in cinema and music must play its part in television's emphasis on immediacy and on the present tense identification between audience and broadcast program.[10] It is thus both not enough and in practice inaccurate to discuss the soundtrack of a *Buffy* episode as "behind" or "beneath" or in any way secondary in the episode, and variations in the use of music have enormous importance for the reception and meaning of any episode.

As these alternative fragments narrate an ongoing story about the central characters' relation to cultural fields that ground the show's real world appeal they assemble music in *Buffy* as a mode of *interpellation*.[11] Recognizing one's taste, or a taste with which one has an important cultural relation, means being named by a text as an audience for which it has meaning. In this way the use of popular music is powerfully different from that of other musical fields. Like all popular music cultures after the rise of mass-produced recording and the gradual but dramatic identification of popular music with youth culture, popular music in *Buffy* simultaneously plays with familiarity and difference/rebellion, with authority and community, and with distinction and enthusiasm. *Buffy*'s deployment of popular music cultures comprised of songs, performances, styles, genres, industries, and audiences is not monolithic even in this complex form. Different strategies are engaged for different narrative ends and even these shift across the series in line with its longest narratives of social and personal change and supernatural conflict. In fact, social and personal change and supernatural conflict are often coded as cultural changes and conflicts presented in both iconic and narrative terms through popular music cultures. Only some of the importance of music to *Buffy* can thus be encompassed by listening to the soundtrack of the compiled episodes.

The Bronze is a key space in which characters and plots directly interact with those alternative fragments and with popular music cultures more generally. I will return to the strange status of the Bronze as a music venue but, like most other crucial thematic locations for the *Buffy* narrative, we encounter the Bronze in the first double-length episode ("Welcome to the Hellmouth" [1.1], and "The

---

[9] John Ellis, "Broadcast TV as Sound and Image," in Braudy and Cohen (eds) *Film Theory and Criticism*, p. 396.

[10] Ibid., pp. 397–9.

[11] While interpellation is often relegated to the structuralist past of critical and cultural theory because of its singular reference to "the Law," it remains a useful tool for considering the way in which audiences, as individuals but also as groups, are hailed by a range of statements. Interpellation requires that you already understand yourself to be necessarily included in a statement but this is true of many ways people recognize themselves in certain cultural forms and practices.

Harvest" [1.2]). In fact, the first major battle and victory for Buffy occurs not only at the Bronze but for control of the Bronze. As Buffy enters it for the first time, the focusing track is invested with a strict diegetic context and thus becomes something other than a fragment. Sprung Monkey are "playing" the Bronze that night, and their "live" performance is our first interior shot of the club. The Bronze is thus immediately associated with live music, with access to live music venues and thus youth culture that escapes institutional structures like family, school, and industry formatting, and is in turn associated with the authenticity attached to the live (witnessed) performance (experience) of music. The Bronze is situated by and as a popular music culture that is rarely associated with girls like Buffy or Cordelia despite their insistence that the Bronze is "the only place to be," and the Bronze thus references both the association of chart pop music fandom with girl culture and the association of live "alternative" music performance with dangerous pleasure. We could take Sarah Thornton's opposition of "mainstream" and "hip" as another terminology for this opposition,[12] but here I keep the denigrated category of *pop* to which the "hip," the "subcultural," and even the most mass-distributed and commercial "rock" remain *alternative*. The Bronze both represents and exceeds the musical tastes of the central characters, who are also the characters we most often see at the Bronze, and thus comes to stand in for the whole of popular music and its associated cultural fields.

Across the series, supernatural dimensions line up with popular cultural elements to prove the significance of the latter as well as the reality of the former. This applies clearly to the overarching self-reflexive metaphor of *Buffy* for the first five seasons—that adolescence is hell.[13] In the opening double episode, the high school and the Bronze are the sites for the first vampire attacks we see. Spanning institutional and counter-institutional uses of popular music as youth culture, these venues are set against the ancient cavernous sunken church (become prison for a Master vampire) from which evil ensues in this foundational narrative for the series. The Hellmouth is literally placed in the school, but encounters with the supernatural are just as centered on the Bronze (and not in just the high school years). After the supernatural emergence of "Welcome to the Hellmouth," the return to *Buffy*'s normal world—to the way things are still the same in spite of all the supernatural drama—is marked in "The Harvest" by kids just hanging out in the schoolyard to the accompaniment of another alternative fragment.

Setting both *Buffy*'s status quo reality and its most pervasive conflicts in the realm of youth culture almost necessitates a dominant role for popular music as a field of conflicts. Within and without the field of popular music production, youth-

---

[12] Sarah Thornton, "The Logic of Subcultural Capital," in Sarah Thornton and Ken Gelder (eds), *The Subcultures Reader* (London, 1997), pp. 204–209.

[13] In this I am elaborating on Whedon's insistent analogy between high school and hell in the first three seasons of *Buffy*. Adolescence is understood here loosely as personal and social development in relation to the set of subject positions comprising a culturally specific idea of "youth." See Driscoll, *Girls*, pp. 48–53.

directed music is a site of both veneration and dismissal, and within and without the field of youth culture, popular music is a highly fragmented and heavily invested set of forms, practices, identities, and communities. Moreover, youth and youth culture as ideas are often summarized by popular music in hierarchized and hierarchizing debates about culture and identity. As Robert Hullot-Kentor paraphrases the dominant Adornian critique of youth-directed music as defining popular music:

> Neither movies nor—certainly—the plastic arts can possibly inculcate themselves as commercial necessities in the everyday structure of life on the scale of music, in the ease with which music's intensities of sound, feeling, and rhythmical order can—for instance—be mobilized in the promise of expressive immediacy, accompanying presence, ecstatic transcendence, sexual assertion, devoted obedience, or registered complaint; as regression in the service of the ego; as a dogmatic, rhyming wisdom–literature for the otherwise unadvised; as a carping–thumping motivational device for suppressing expression; or for cocooning and masking painfully disruptive psychological states.
>
> Commercial music is truly the snake oil of adolescence, and given the absurdity of what the bottle dispenses—the music itself—its broad application would be comic were it not meant to salve the most legitimate and urgent needs a person has.[14]

Counter to this kind of dismissal, cultural studies work on both youth culture and popular music has stressed, sometimes to the exclusion of all institutional and economic constraints, the production of meaning, identity, community, taste, and style through popular music. *Buffy* certainly takes up these debates but not without recognizing they are as important within the field they describe as they are outside it.

The weakness of the Adornian critique is not, as writers like John Fiske might claim, that consumers of popular music are creative in their relations to popular music, because Adorno's argument does not necessarily exclude that.[15] Instead, Adorno's argument that popular music exemplifies the false diversity sold by

---

[14] Robert Hullot-Kentor, *Things Beyond Resemblance: Collected Essays on Theodor W. Adorno* (New York, 2008), p. 51. Adorno, or at least the influence of his essays "On Popular Music" and on "the culture industry" (the latter especially shaped by his earlier work with Horkheimer), remains the pivotal figure in debates over consumption, authenticity, and popular music. As Leppert claims, "music criticism has retained the aesthetic query that lies at the heart of Adorno's concern: is the music 'authentic'?" See Leppert in Theodor W. Adorno, *Essays on Music*, ed. Richard Leppert (Los Angeles, 2002), p. 346. However, this interest has also retained Adorno's political focus. See also Lawrence Grossberg, "Reflections of a Disappointed Popular Music Scholar," in Roger Beebe et al. (eds), *Rock Over the Edge: Transformations of Popular Music* (Durham, NC, 2002), pp. 25–59.

[15] John Fiske, *Understanding Popular Culture* (London, 1989).

"the culture industry" neglects the way that the everydayness of popular music provides a space for disseminating shared narratives and images in relation to which cultural positions take place at the level of community. *Buffy* notices that popular music not only validates but produces powerful discourses—for example, "Lots of people lose themselves in love. They write songs about it." ("Beauty and the Beasts" [3.4])—that provide a network of distinction, so that Xander can ask whether a particular romantic moment involved "Wild monkey love or tender Sarah McLachlan love" ("Wild at Heart" [4.6]). Popular music is field of strategic possibilities as well as a regulated system of differences, and in both senses it works at the levels of industry, community and personal identity simultaneously.

Doing it His Way

> Joyce: Do you like Seals and Croft? [Giles gives her a look] Yeah, me neither. [Joyce accepts a cigarette from Giles] Thanks. So how come they call you Ripper? ("Band Candy" [3.6])

The episode "Band Candy" exemplifies the way that, as Dechert discusses, *Buffy* uses popular music to further characterization. Music cultures are used as a narrative shorthand to develop, distinguish, connect, complicate, and historicize characterizations which form the ground for further narratives—in short to refine characterization as a mobile position in the field of cultural production. In this episode, the adult population of Sunnydale is transformed by cursed candy bars into a range of walking youth stereotypes that is nevertheless given a degree of credibility by being aligned with an already implied backstory for Giles.[16] It relies on the premise that "youth" is a set of practices—principally behaviors and attitudes—that are manifest in the taste for youth culture. This youth culture is not confined to music, but the relationship between the two is used to shortcut through exposition of why youth culture itself may be a danger to Sunnydale.

The transformed Giles is first seen crouched on his living-room floor, his usually neat clothes askew, turning over a record album in his hand. It is his relationship to popular music that first signifies the crucial difference of candy-cursed Giles when, now lying on the floor smoking a cigarette, he is distracted from his conversation with Joyce by a need to participate more intensely in listening to Cream's "Tales of Brave Ulysses." While smoking, drinking, and sexual attraction are important signs of his juvenilization, it is music that most spectacularly signifies youthful Giles and sets up a frame for the episodic crisis brought about by youthful "attitude." Divesting himself of all responsibility for others, not only unable to recognize the significance of the crisis at hand but even

---

[16] Xander summarizes this backstory in "Beer Bad" (4.5) as "Mr I spent the sixties in an electric Kool-Aid funky Satan groove" only to be corrected by Giles that "it was the early seventies."

of his relationship with Buffy, Giles paces to the mirror, worrying about his hair as he enthuses that he has "got to get a band together."

For most of the adults, there are two options for this cursed night—the Bronze and nothing. This emphasizes what the series has repeatedly suggested about youth culture in Sunnydale. Outside the requirements of home and school life there is hanging out, whether in parks, cemeteries, or libraries, and there is the Bronze. For cursed Giles—and the irony remains sharp when viewed across the complete series—the Bronze is "dead." His musical taste is more classic rock than dance club: he yearns for his own band and implies that he is too cool for the Bronze as a music venue (it's not clear if, in his young Ripper persona, he thinks the Bronze was ever alive). Meanwhile, at the Bronze, Oz as the younger generation's index of musical cool is performing with his band, Dingoes Ate My Baby. But this is a taste stratification rather than a periodization of youth culture and Giles's workplace antagonist Principal Snyder is wildly impressed by the cool scene at the Bronze.

The Bronze this night is packed with cursed adult party animals who alarm the regulars (our regular "youth" characters) by seeming like a disturbing mirror of themselves. The episode as a whole, and this scene in the Bronze in particular, works on a stark opposition between the youth-directed popular musical "now" and an assembled collection of past instances of that music: the rock and roll standard, "Louie Louie" (1955, 1963, etc.); the Cream track (1967); the singularly mid-1970s Seals and Crofts; Billy Joel, who can be placed across the 1970s and 80s; the very 1981 Juice Newton; and Kiss, one of the platinum acts of the mid- to-late 1970s. Significantly, however, this history is not nearly so straightforward. "Louie Louie" took on its strongest youth culture cachet from its deployment as a youth-as-party theme in *Animal House* (1978), even though in "Band Candy" it is sung on stage by men who would have been around thirty when that film was released. This mismatch is paralleled in Principal Snyder quoting the late 1970s television hit *Welcome Back Kotter* as an icon of teenage boy cool, even though he is clearly too old to have been part of its fan base, and by the elderly Miss Barton using hippy argot to signify her youthful attitude even though she would have been solidly middle-aged when it was fashionable. This assembled field is a roughly 1970s-centered vision of youth culture, which might be shaped by Ethan's magic—he's around the right age—but is too dispersed across incompatible taste categories to represent any individual and instead best represents the period, most marked in the early 1970s, in which "rock" was established as "authentic cultural expression."[17]

The gulf between "then" and "now" is crucial to "Band Candy." Current tracks are juxtaposed with these older youth music reference points, exemplarily in the Bronze when Every Bit of Nothing's "Slip Jimmy" (1998) is interrupted by the late-middle-aged men who invade the stage half-dressed to perform their slurred

---

[17] See Motti Regev, "Producing Artistic Value: The Case of Rock Music," *The Sociological Quarterly*, 35/1 (1994), pp. 85–102.

drunken rendition of "Louie Louie." In the audience, Oz, Buffy, and Willow look on in horror as the late 1970s retrofitting of a 1960s' pop track is brought into conflict with the youth music "now" of their venue and indeed their band. The fragment of "Louie Louie" can thus signify decades of changing and often incompatible forms of youth music culture, setting out the ethical, dramatic, and comic terrain of the rest of the episode. The same historical layering is offered in the closure of the episode when Principal Snyder, restored to all his mean maturity, orders the Scoobies to clean the school lockers of graffiti reading "KISS ROCKS." While Willow is initially puzzled, along with the audience, she has to get the reference eventually, because the "KISS Alive" reunion tour was one of the smash successes of 1996. This clash of tastes, audiences, generations, and music cultures is what needs to be cleaned up and swept away at the end of the episode in order to return us to our usual field of musical associations for the series.

"Lover's Walk" (3.8) also plays with the generationalization of popular music but to very different ends. The score and the story for this episode are framed by the reprise of one song. As he stumbles into the ruins of his old Sunnydale residence near the beginning, the drunkenly maudlin Spike sings a snatch from "My Way," a song most famously associated with Frank Sinatra (1969). But the episode closes with Spike clearly singing along to Gary Oldman's 1986 cover of Sid Vicious's 1978 cover of the Sinatra classic. This layering of musical renovation succinctly foregrounds the importance of what sociologist Pierre Bourdieu calls "the field of cultural production" to understanding character in *Buffy*.[18] The character of Spike was always premised on a popular cultural image of "Brit Punk" (painted in very broad strokes). Spike's loose coagulation of Cockney street cred and punk rock iconography—with, at least at the outset, a nazi punk connotation as well—was almost incidental in a late 1990s California context when Spike was designed to be a minor series villain. But the character's success, drawing heavily on the long currency of Brit Punk as an image of youthful male rebellion, ensured Spike's first return in "Lover's Walk," where his musical reference points were more coherently fixed around the image of punk by representing Spike's personal triumph in the recasting of a Sinatra classic as a cover of a cover of a Vicious classic.[19]

The seven-way romantic crisis of "Lover's Walk" does not matter to my argument here except insofar as it participates in this field of popular music cultures defined as youth culture. High school dramas and hopes are opposed to the perverted adolescence of the un-aging vampire—in Cordelia's terms, the only kind of "moron" who would want to come back to Sunnydale. It is a tenet

---

[18] See Pierre Bourdieu, *The Field of Cultural Production*, trans. Randal Johnson (New York, 1993).

[19] This use of style sourced from popular music is not contradicted but complemented when Spike's unstable cultural location is retrofitted in season 5. In "Fool For Love" (5.7), it is revealed that Spike's pre-vampire human form was a middle-class English fop, who later adopted a pseudo-working-class and then pseudo-punk persona as a negotiation of appropriately impressive vampire identity.

of the series that vampires are endlessly drawn to the Hellmouth that is high school/the Bronze/adolescence. Spike's pain and his tantrums are as much a part of this permanent signification of adolescence as his punk sensibilities, but no more than Angel's poised moodiness. That Buffy and Angel's love is "eternal, literally," as Spike says, is as much a high teen fantasy as never aging, and this love like blood "screaming inside you to work its will" can clearly also be read as love like adolescent hormones. But the romance narrative as apostasy of youth remains inseparable from the positioning of characters within a field of cultural distinctions. Bourdieu argues that any field of cultural production is a "space of positions and [a] space of the position-takings in which they are expressed."[20] Within such a field,

> no cultural product exists by itself, i.e. outside the relations of interdependence which link it to other products. Michel Foucault gives the name "field of strategic possibilities" to the regulated system of differences and dispersions within which each individual work defines itself.[21]

As *Buffy* routinely demonstrates, the same regulated field of strategic possibilities frames the self-representations of individuals, and popular music works as one regulatory apparatus marking out strategies and identities.

Within the love tangle of "Lover's Walk," Spike and Angel as potential partners are distinguished by their differential positioning in the field of cultural production. Spike drunkenly staggers to a window and looks in at Angel reading by the fire. Angel's high-culture credibility is reinforced not only by his comparative sobriety but also by what he is reading—Jean-Paul Sartre's *La Nausée*—while Spike slurs abuse, swigs from a bottle and collapses in a heap. His black leather duster coat, his junk-filled blacked-out car, his irrational non-life-threatening behavior, and the Mayor's comments on his unpredictable troublesomeness all help resurrect Spike's off-the-rails Brit Punk inflection as problem adolescent. Perhaps the Sinatra version of "My Way" is just as possible as a reference point when Spike is reminiscing about Drusilla and bemoaning Angel's role in alienating them. However, a Sinatra reading of Spike here is more available as nostalgia or kitsch for the audience invoked by *Buffy*.

Bourdieu stresses that "the meaning of a work (artistic, literary, philosophical, etc.) changes automatically with each change in the field within which is it situated for the spectator or reader."[22] This is not only exemplarily true here of Sinatra, transformed into a nostalgic self-indulgence that is powerless in comparison to

---

[20] Bourdieu, *The Field of Cultural Production*, p. 30. It is crucial to understanding the consumption of popular music to see it in these terms, especially how "the structure of the field, i.e. of the space of positions, is nothing other than the structure of the distribution of the capital of specific properties which governs success in the field" (ibid.).

[21] Ibid., pp. 32–3.

[22] Ibid., pp. 30–31.

Angel's silent existentialism. It is equally true of Spike's closing reprise of "My Way," now framed by his repositioning as the one who knows about the passions of love, life, and youth. In Vicious's version of the song, Sinatra's mix of plaintive farewell and triumphant memorialization is recast as a threat and a promise. It is as a punk as much as a vampire that Spike can tear off along a "long and lonely highway," always at the end of his own life, but now also established by the confrontational authenticity of punk as happily in charge of his own destiny. In this way the use of a single song establishes narrative layers and trajectories and extends characterization by manipulation of where it sits in the field of popular music validated by the series as a whole. Thus not only the dramatic segmentations of popular music culture into niches and clusters of taste and style but also the pervasive inculcation of popular music into the everyday lived experiences of the audience sustain it as an effective shorthand for characterization.

This technique of extended characterization through popular music is employed most succinctly across the series in moments of identity change and/or crisis. Xander's hyena presence in "The Pack" (1.6) is brought home first to his friends in the way he occupies the Bronze, to the accompaniment of the Dashboard Prophets, and then to the school in his slow-motion prowl glossed by Far's "Job's Eyes." In "Who Are You?" (4.16), the transformation of Buffy to Faith-in-Buffy is always tentative until she decides to take on some version of Buffy's life, a transformation which of course can only be celebrated at the Bronze, where Faith-in-Buffy embraces her rewritten Buffy potential by dancing to Nerf Herder's "Vivian," appropriating what might be understood as Buffy's band.[23] In "Smashed" (6.9), the extent of Willow's willingness to use magic for her own personal satisfaction is dramatized by her changing the entire Bronze scene from college rock with party boys to post-Riot-Grrrl band with caged dancing boys.[24] Dechert discusses this use of music as "a motivational force," with reference to scenes like the sexy dance in "When She Was Bad" and to the centrality of the Flamingos' "I Only Have Eyes For You" in the episode of that name (2.19).[25] This observation could be extended to consider how popular music is positioned in *Buffy* at an intersection of the plot, the characters, and the audience, calling in the latter case on their own relations to popular music as well as to particular characters or scenes.

---

[23] This is also the episode in which Willow introduces Tara to Buffy and to her slaying life via the representative role of the Bronze. The girls concur that the scene is "cool," meaning inseparably Willow's life viewed through the Bronze, and the Bronze itself.

[24] Virgil play three songs while Amy and Willow assess the Bronze and find it less than girl friendly. Willow transforms Virgil into the Halo Friendlies performing "Run Away." The allusions around this transformation include reference to the Riot Grrrl interventions in the gendered space of music venues, sometimes insisting the mosh pit usually dominated by men be a girls-only space.

[25] Dechert, "My Boyfriend's in the Band!" p. 220.

Dingoes Ate My Baby

> Dingoes Ate My Baby play their instruments as if they have plump polish sausages taped to their fingers ("Earshot" [3.18])

Calling Nerf Herder "nerd core" exemplifies the niche formation of audiences and tastes within popular music, but it is equally important to popular music that such niche labels do not prevent circulation of the track outside the taste communities that use it. Individuals in turn move through and attach to different taste communities, and what is summoned by "popular music" and in *Buffy*'s use of popular music is never a single taste community or even a relevant set of communities but the entire field of cultural production—classifying and clustering via the inevitably self-reflexive mechanisms of taste. As Bourdieu famously summarizes this idea,

> Taste classifies, and it classifies the classifier. Social subjects, classified by their classifications, distinguish themselves by the distinctions they make, between the beautiful and the ugly, the distinguished and the vulgar, in which their position in the objective classifications is expressed or betrayed.[26]

This is precisely why Anya, ever the monitor of capital distribution in the later series, is concerned to find that her duet with Xander in the musical ("Once More With Feeling" [6.7]) is a "retro-pastiche" that is "never going to be a breakaway pop hit." The effects of musical taste are not usually quite so overtly performed and recognized as they are by Anya's annoyance. Buffy's concern at being caught up in a "training montage from an 80s movie" is more typical, leaving unstated what is at stake for her or anyone else in being associated with such a soundtrack.

The last sequence before the Spike-centric tag to "Lovers' Walk" includes a shot of Oz playing his guitar, almost as if he were the one playing the melancholy music centering that scene and thus almost as if he were in charge of the music and its commentary on the plot. Oz's character commands all fields of musical knowledge—or at least all the ones in relation to which we seem him placed. This is partly because he is the only major character to be specifically identified as a (semi-professional) musician, but this is also Oz's function in *Buffy*'s games with knowledge and authority, within which Oz stands in as a figure for popular cultural "cool." This is one reason why Oz rarely shares narrative space with either Angel or Spike, who are antagonistic figures of coolness or style that do not leave room for Oz's more contemporary knowingness. Instead, Oz's command of popular culture, and especially popular music, is a counterpoint to other figures who know in the changing present tense, and especially for Xander and Giles.

This "cool" is anchored to the now of the series by its use of contemporary tracks and its claims to the immediacy of live performance, and thus remains closely tied

---

[26] Pierre Bourdieu, *Distinction: A Social Critique of the Judgement of Taste*, trans. Richard Nice (Cambridge, 1986), p. 6.

to its generationalizing narrative. As Thornton points out, age is the dominant demographic factor influencing positions in the cultural field of popular music.[27] In "Welcome to the Hellmouth," Giles refers to the Bronze's music culture as a "din," but in "Wild at Heart" he visits the Bronze looking for company and appreciating Veruca's live presence as valuable in that context. Veruca's sexy stagey presence is directly opposed to Willow's lack of alternative sophistication—to her warm and familiar attitude to the Bronze as "one place that you can come back to where everything's predictable" and to her ignorance of hip "musicianese" talk about amp brands and models.

Oz not only has hip credibility amongst his musical peers but also appreciates Giles's record collection ("The Harsh Light of Day" [4.3])[28] and can comment appreciatively on genres like jazz and marching bands in "Beauty and the Beasts." This musical knowledge and credibility does not exclude him from other forms of knowledge—as is the case, for example, with Xander's knowledge of popular culture. The same conversation has him positioned as academically brilliant, acing the final of "senior bio" simply by showing up. Oz's detachment from the social and cultural capital of education is directly juxtaposed with his attachment to music. In "Beer Bad," for example, Oz misses class because the band is practicing, and this episode and the next, "Wild at Heart," make it clear that the authority and power of education is not as effective in some contexts as the authority and power gained from specific relations to popular music. Thornton would call the latter "subcultural capital." She argues that

> Bourdieu does not talk about these popular "distinctions" as "capitals". Perhaps he sees them as too paradoxical in their effects to warrant the term? In response, I would argue that clubs are refuges for the young where their rules hold sway and that, inside and even outside these spaces, subcultural distinctions have significant consequences.[29]

What critiques and exposes cultural capital in *Buffy*, however, is nothing subcultural but, instead, cultural eclecticism.[30]

The concise form in which Oz expresses his knowledge contributes to his "cool." When speaking of music, or culture more broadly, Oz's concise expression

---

[27] Thornton, "The Logic of Subcultural Capital," pp. 203–204.

[28] The dialogue recording this is worth noting: "Oz: Okay, either I'm borrowing all your albums or I'm moving in. / Giles: Oz there are more important things than records right now. / Oz: (Holding up a record.) More important than this one? / Giles: Well I suppose an argument could be made for …" ("The Harsh Light of Day").

[29] Thornton, "The Logic of Subcultural Capital," p. 202.

[30] Clashes between cultural capital and youth culture are only satirized in Giles's antagonism towards the culture of Buffy and her friends, and crises which pit cultural capital against the cultural eclecticism of "the Scoobies" center on The Watcher's Council itself—and Buffy and eclecticism clearly win.

implies certainty.³¹ This attributes to him the power to distinguish for himself and others. However, Bourdieu used the term "distinction" to talk about those who "know" in ways that give them cultural capital—privileged positions based on knowing what the most economically advantaged believe is culturally valuable. Oz's taste, like *Buffy*'s taste, is more eclectic, aligning both with the "cultural goodwill" Bourdieu associates with the middle classes, who are caught between knowing about culture and their uncertain access to it. Although Thornton does not phrase it that way, this is the ground upon which she can discuss the "classless autonomy of hip youth."³² Like *Buffy* itself, Oz does not have to hate uncool or passé things, knowing about and appreciating jazz, 1970s rock, and old movie scores. Neither Oz nor *Buffy* needs to conform to clichés about musical credibility like that conjured up in Xander's fantasy of himself as a rock god ("Teacher's Pet" [1.4]).³³ Oz's knowledge thus extends across the field of cultural production, for example in the following exchange about celebrating Buffy's return to Sunnydale:

> Oz: We should figure out what kinda deal this is. I mean, is it a gathering, a shindig or a hootenanny?
> Cordelia: What's the difference?
> Oz: Well, a gathering is brie, mellow song stylings. Shindig: dip [nodding to Cordelia, who smiles], less mellow song stylings, perhaps a large amount of malt beverage. And hootenanny, well, it's chock full of hoot, just a *little* bit of nanny. ("Dead Man's Party" [3.2])

At this hootenanny-come-zombie film, and in a selection of episodes from seasons 2 to 4, Oz's band, Dingoes Ate My Baby, appears to mark out an important trajectory from high school through college and an extension of the series narrative through and about popular music. I want to focus here on two elements of the Dingoes' place in *Buffy*—the authenticity claims of "live" "rock" and the interplay between *Buffy* and its fan cultures over music. The band's first role is to articulate a range of coolness factors, most of which center on investing Oz with cultural authority,

---

³¹ Oz does show uncertainty in highly personal contexts—with reference to his werewolf self and with reference to his relationship with Willow—but not when speaking of culture. His place as a musician, above everything else, gives him a position from which to speak of culture comparable to Michel de Certeau's discussion of academic expertise, although the fact that Oz thus speaks from within the field of culture about which he speaks makes all the difference. See Michel de Certeau, "The Place from Which One Deals with Culture," trans. Tom Conley, in Luce Giard (ed.), *Cultural in the Plural* (Minneapolis, MN, 1997), pp. 123–31.

³² Thornton, "The Logic of Subcultural Capital," p. 206. As Regev explains this eclecticism, "the ability of musicians to cross genres and musical languages … while preserving an authentic rock 'drive' (as judged by critics) has become an aesthetic value in rock music." Regev, "Producing Artistic Value," p. 97.

³³ See Dechert, "My Boyfriend's in the Band!" p. 221.

but some of which devolve from the authenticity of live music performance onto Dingoes as more "live" than a fictional band can usually be because they are "played" by a "real life" band, Four Star Mary. The authenticity of having a real band behind the fictional band only operates for a specialized audience—it is an apparently trivial *Buffy* fact that only has significance for fans. Even the musical coherence of having the same group of musicians playing Dingoes' music does not require they be a "real life" band rather than session musicians. What Four Star Mary enable is a special place for Dingoes amongst the knowledge games of *Buffy* fans.

The name of Oz's band is itself a kind of in joke, clearly a reference to the fact that Oz is a werewolf but also giving another "rock band" inflection to "baby" than that invoked in the citational dimension of the name.[34] But Oz was a musician before he was a werewolf, even if his werewolf nature dominates his part in the supernatural and romantic dramas of the series. While the fact that the only other characterized werewolf in the series is also a musician suggests that the conjunction of musician and werewolf might be something more than a coincidence, being a musician is more fundamental to Oz's character: to his singular personal style. This might conform most closely to Thornton's model of subcultural capital insofar as Oz's credibility as a musician, and the authenticity of his relation to music, only operates within a limited social field—the field intersecting youth and popular music.[35] Oz's cultural style embodies the Bronze's sense of cool although neither the Bronze nor Oz represents the audience's presumed musical tastes so much as they each provide a space for the audience to interact with *Buffy*'s knowledge of popular music.

Oz's role thus needs to be considered in relation to the Bronze's status as the site and the index of cool—"they let anyone in, but it's still the scene," Cordelia says in "Welcome to the Hellmouth." It is nevertheless a strange and, as I suggested above, eclectic music venue. Placed "in the bad part of town," it evokes a transient underground club with its warehouse district setting. The early denizens of the Bronze seem to be young adults or older teens than Buffy when the series begins, and the music, while varied, is never "chart pop." The Bronze also serves alcohol and checks the ID of patrons at the door in some episodes, but it nevertheless admits 15-year-olds. At different times it sports a disco floor, pool tables, shabby second-hand lounges, and dining tables. It always has a long bar, a stage and some sort of dance floor. Although they are absent from Bronze scenes as often as not, there are also multi-level mezzanines that look over the club as a whole. Regardless of these generic shifts, accentuated by shifting demographics represented in the extras cast, socializing and coolness rather than music per se are the attractants at the Bronze. The last appearance of the Bronze is in "Empty Places" (7.19), where it stands as both a summary of adolescence—the shift from underage inexperienced girls to

---

[34] The band is at one level named after the famous cry by Australian Lindy Chamberlain whose baby Azaria went missing in 1980, presumably taken by a wild dog (dingo).

[35] Thornton, "The Logic of Subcultural Capital," p. 203.

woman with both knowledge and authority—and the life of pleasure and everyday danger that is slipping away around the central characters.

Whenever the series offers a comparison or competitor for the Bronze this works as a kind of coolness competition, with the alternate venue being used to claim a specialized kind of cool. A selection of these venues appears in "Beer Bad," where the comparison between the Bronze and other places to be runs parallel to a comparison between live bands and different investments in popular music. This is the first episode in which the female werewolf Veruca appears, as the singer for Shy, a band playing the Bronze. Oz is there to affirm that they are worth watching—"I know their drummer, he's cool." Again, the band is "played" by a "real life" band, in this case THC, and fan discourse about the two episodes in which Shy appears turns in part on articulations of coolness—as do the episodes themselves. Veruca's cool is more closely aligned with Thornton's discussion of subcultural capital—she's cool as and for her specific genre of popular music. And these episodes frame Willow and Oz's separation as not only about sexual infidelity and werewolf angst but also over the distribution of cool. Next to Veruca, Willow feels uncool, and her role as Oz's girlfriend compounds this. She complains about the perceived inauthenticity of her relation to music when she mocks herself through parodies of Veruca and Oz's attitudes: "My name is Veruca, I'm in a band. I'm Oz, I'm in a band. Oh and this is Willow. Oh how fun, a groupie." ("Beer Bad").

Willow refuses to identify with this inferior position when she declines attending the band's next rehearsal and despite Oz's gesture at understanding—"I guess I can see how it would be … dull for you"—his delivery positions this as an unforeseen problem of taste between him and Willow. Willow is not outside the taste regime centered on live and alternative bands, but occupies a lower place in the hierarchy proper to the live-band authenticity scene. Buffy herself is actually marginal to this scene. Instead, she knows music television and the exchange between Willow, Oz and Veruca takes place when Buffy, transformed by cursed beer into cavegirl-Buffy, is watching chart pop videos. What cavegirl-Buffy knows, in her literally primitive frame of mind and thus as a commentary on the relation between pop style and band style, is that chart pop is "shiny."

Chart pop is never a focus in *Buffy* as even the uncool teens manage to have more niche musical tastes. Cibo Matto playing an out-of-the-way venue like the Bronze in a parochial location like Sunnydale, or a group of Californian high-school kids all knowing and appreciating Cibo Matto, is as unlikely as attack by vampires. Although it has a commercial logic tied to promotion of the band, as Dechert discusses, these selections present a hip taste that makes a claim for the location of the series as a whole in the field of popular music.[36] She points out that there are solid commercial reasons for not including major pop hits in the series, but financial exigencies do not explain the specific taste conjunctions of music selection on the series, which pitched *Buffy* to a demographic who could

---

[36] Dechert, "My Boyfriend's in the Band!" pp. 222–4.

appreciate the distinction between "pop" and hip/alternative and the authenticity invested in "live" music.

The Bronze was also the name for the best known online *Buffy* fan community, originally hosted on the Warner Bros. (WB) site and given special authority by regular visits from Whedon and other members of the writing and production team. Although the declared purpose of the Bronze chatroom was to form a community for responses to the series, what dominated the action there was a sense of hanging with those who knew—those with knowledge of a very specific cultural field. Across the range of chatrooms, discussion boards and other online communities spawned by *Buffy*—a series which marks a shift in the usual practices of dedicated TV fandoms because of its timing in relation to the expansion of internet usage—knowledge about *Buffy* is the central currency. Across forums like *The Buffy Cross & Stake*, more focused communities like *The Kitten Board* (dedicated to Willow and Tara), and the range of new Bronze chatrooms that appeared when the WB site was taken down as the series moved to UPN, the kind of *Buffy* fan one might be is articulated not only by opinions of the series but by the kinds of knowledge one has and deems appropriate to discussing *Buffy*. A many-layered set of connections frame discussions of *Buffy* music in these forums, but always with an emphasis on popular music rather than the original scoring.

Like Xander and Willow's game of guessing movie lines in "When She Was Bad" (2.1), these exchanges and assessments of knowledge for pleasure are a way of affirming shared knowledge and thus the cultural parameters of community. Whether exchanging files or tabs of the *Buffy* theme, comparing preferences and dislikes, or mapping associated consumption, these fan practices usually involve arranging a series of musical objects—not necessarily in a hierarchy because of the avowed eclecticism of *Buffy*—and always make a statement about the speaker through that arrangement. We could starkly call this "name dropping." While such games distinguish some fans as more knowledgeable—and thus as accruing local authority—they do not articulate any subcultural capital because that formulation requires a more coherent cultural field than is provided by consumers of popular culture even in the tight frame of fan communities. Just as "buyers of the same records do not necessarily form a coherent social group [because their] purchase of a given record may be contextualized within a very different range of consumer choices; they may never occupy the same social space,"[37] *Buffy*'s appeal is not *to* a specific social group or space but rather *via* a set of cultural positions.

Different taste communities nevertheless shape ways of using popular music to be a *Buffy* fan. Knowing about references to the theme from *A Summer Place* within the series is a different kind of knowledge claim and a different cultural position than knowing that the actor Anthony Stewart Head, who plays Giles, had previously performed in musicals and "really" sings in more than just the musical episode of *Buffy*. Another kind of position again is involved in recognizing Giles's acoustic performance in "The Yoko Factor" (4.20) as a rendition of

---

[37] Thornton, "The Logic of Subcultural Capital," p. 205.

Lynyrd Skynyrd's "Freebird" or knowing that Head released an album, *Music for Elevators* (2002), with George Sarah of THC, the band behind Veruca's band.[38] While these specific types of knowledge bring different kinds of authority to a fan community, fan communities also form around particular tastes in being a fan. On the Bronze (in any of its incarnations) and across the breadth of online *Buffy* fan communities, fan hierarchies have formed around modes of *Buffy* fandom deemed superior to others on the basis not only of what a fan knows but also how they practice their fandom. Within the normative hierarchy of fandom, fan-fiction writers are positioned near the bottom, and within the hierarchies of fan fiction in turn, one of the least distinguished modes of fan production is the songfic genre, which provides an interesting further comment on the place of popular music in the field of *Buffy* fandom. Fan fiction would appear, from the outside, already to be relegated to the most derivative margins of popular cultural production, but within fan fiction excessive attachment to or foregrounding of popular music is itself dismissed as immature and derivative.[39]

The most foregrounded or "present" representations of popular music on *Buffy* function as a type of atmospheric lyricism, such as the performances by Cibo Matto, Michelle Branch ("Tabula Rasa" [6.8]) and Aimee Mann ("Sleeper" [7.8]). This mode of using popular music on *Buffy* is often associated with its most angst-ridden plot turns, and that strategy is taken up by some fan-fiction genres, within which the songfic is the most striking example. Although the songfic genre was by no means invented by *Buffy* fandom it is more common there because of the importance of popular songs to *Buffy*. In general a songfic takes the lyrics of a song—sometimes a song a character is listening to or even singing but very often one included only as an epigraph to the story—and uses them to frame a story based on the characters, settings and/or events of a "source text" which is not the song (so a *Buffy* songfic might quote a Sarah McLachlan lyric as a way of

---

[38] Still more obscurely, the photograph of Giles as bass guitarist in "The Dark Age" (2.8) superimposes Head's face on an image of Sid Vicious (Dechert, "'My Boyfriend's in the Band," p. 222). The incorporation of such details as academic research exemplifies the tendency for *Buffy* scholars to participate in fan knowledge games discussed by Henry Jenkins and John Tulloch with reference to *Star Trek* fans and then extended in interesting ways to the relationship between fans and academics by Matt Hills. See Matt Hills, *Fan Cultures* (London, 2002), and Henry Jenkins and John Tulloch, "Beyond the *Star Trek* Phenomenon: Reconceptualizing the Science Fiction Audience," in John Tulloch (ed.), *Science Fiction Audiences: Watching Star Trek and Dr Who* (London, 1995), pp. 3–24.

[39] The subgenres of fan fiction are rarely attended to in detail in scholarship, but years of ethnographic work in fan-fiction communities supports this observation as well as the recurring convention of apologizing for writing and publishing a songfic. As one LiveJournal poster puts it, "I am myself a shameful perpetratrix of the dread songfic on occasion. I try to keep the lyrics to a bare minimum, though, because I do know that they're annoying as fuck."

framing or exploring Buffy's or Xander's feelings for Spike).[40] The denigration of songfics relies on both their tendency toward melodrama and their central utilization of two source texts resulting in production of less "original" content. As Motti Regev argues, in a discussion of cultural capital within popular music, "belief in the ideology of autonomous art still determines the struggle and defines the prizes in the field of cultural production."[41] Dismissing songfics as inadequate to authentic expression and incapable of aesthetic originality clearly mirrors the dismissal of pop music in the broader terrain of music cultures. Songfics not only provide a fan commentary on the way in which songs are used within *Buffy* but on the similarities between how *Buffy* and popular music are circulated by fans, and on the intertextual relations between popular songs and *Buffy* that are produced by the audience at the edges of the series itself.

It is thus possible to shift the discussion of how popular music cultures work in *Buffy* onto the fan cultures predicated on the series. In the fan communities as much as in the series, popular music identifies narrative patterns and knowledge games that form taste communities and assert distinctions. Specific tracks, bands, performances, allusions, or interpretations are components of both knowledge of (experience in) the series and modes of forming (sub)communities. They also show how *Buffy* not only circulates similarly to popular music but is more explicable through the insistent but changeable taste regimes of popular music than is television in general.

Buffy takes up a range of key issues for thinking about popular music as they appear in academic studies, fan activities, and other popular discussions of music, including the relation between alternative and popular music cultures, the production of coolness through musical subcultures, the generational organization of fashions in music, and the disputed connections between authenticity and live musical performance. *Buffy* not only uses popular music but works hard to resemble popular music at its most eclectic, while still remaining anchored to familiar contradictions of the relations between youth and popular music. All such negotiations rely on the commodified cultural field through which one's place in the world is articulated, and such negotiations operate not only in the consumption of cultural artifacts but also in communities that operate at a tangent to commodities themselves. Fan communities predicated on *Buffy* form taste communities around the different ways of positioning *Buffy*, including as "youth culture" and as pop eclecticism.

---

[40] The "source text" is the text on which fan-fiction communities base their original stories. While fan fiction has multiple forms and is disseminated via different media, since the late 1990s it is most commonly original fiction based on a literary or media text with a narrative centered on a romantic or sexual pairing. See Kristina Busse and Karen Hellekson (eds), *Fanfiction and Fan Communities in the Age of the Internet: New Essays* (New York, 2006).

[41] Regev, "Producing Artistic Value," p. 87.

Chapter 8
More Than a Watcher:
Buffy Fans, Amateur Music Videos, Romantic Slash, and Intermedia

Rob Cover

Cheese Slices

In the final episode of *Buffy the Vampire Slayer*'s fourth season, "Restless" (4.22), a mysterious and inexplicable figure appears in a dream sequence, stating only that he has "made a little space for the cheese slices." It has sometimes been pointed out that *Buffy* is a text which avoids romantic, emotional, cheesy material[1] except occasionally as farce—for example, the sweeping orchestral score to a scene in which Buffy and Angel both argue for self-sacrifice over the other, as seen from Xander's point of view in "The Zeppo" (3.13). "Cheesy" music is identified here—and reacted to in *Buffy*—as a particular genre of popular romantic, couple-oriented, love-inflected, emotional material that is often considered commercial and suburban. Indeed, a statement on cheesy music is made in the opening of the fourth season in which Buffy objects to her new college room-mate's taste for the popular releases of Celine Dion and Cher ("The Freshman" [4.1]), her posters eventually replaced with the text's own signifier of alternative sound, Dingoes Ate My Baby or, in the extra-textual sphere, Four Star Mary ("Living Conditions" [4.2]). However, Joss Whedon himself does claim to be delighted with "the amount of cheese that we can sort of get away with."[2] The signification of cheese is represented not only in the content of the plot, but in both image and, most importantly, the score.

In this chapter, I want to draw together various strands of analysis around *Buffy* in order to show the ways in which as a text it must be understood as *intermedia*—that is, as a narrative comprised of, or fused between, moving image and sound, audio which includes dialogue, effects, incidental, and narrative-related

---

[1] Mary Alice Money, discussing the bluntness of Cordelia and Spike in "The Undemonization of Supporting Characters in *Buffy*," in Rhonda V. Wilcox and David Lavery (eds) *Fighting the Forces: What's at Stake in Buffy the Vampire Slayer* (Lanham, MD, 2002), p. 103.

[2] David Lavery, "'Emotional Resonance and Rocket Launchers': Joss Whedon's Commentaries on the *Buffy the Vampire Slayer* DVDs," *Slayage* 6 (2002), 6–7.

music—and that, as a text, its meanings are located only through the intermedial relationship of these components. They are thereby open to transformation in the reconfiguration of intermedial components: where the cheese as romantic, couple-oriented, love-inflected emotional material comes in is not in the text but in its availability to be read by fan audiences. "A little space for the cheese slices" is made in the active reading and art production by various categories of fan audience, and a slightly greater space is opened up by active fan audiences utilizing not only the form of slash fiction in order to disseminate radical readings of the text, but newer interactive technologies in order to circulate on the internet a new type of politically recuperative slash in the form of re-mixed cheesy amateur music videos. These often utilize still and moving images from the series, juxtaposed in a deliberate order in league with the conventions of music videos, combined with cheesy music that has not been referenced in the program (for example Enya's "Only Time" [2000], Elton John and LeAnn Rimes's "Written in the Stars" [1999], and Madonna's "Crazy for You" [1985]).

Musical genres and specific songs carry cultural connotations, and it is in the application of these songs to sampled images from *Buffy* that new meanings are explicitly indicated. For Henry Jenkins, media fans are "consumers who also produce, readers who also write, spectators who also participate."[3] Rather than focus on the acts of consumption, reading, and visual spectatorship, I argue here that the production of these fan videos—which work in several ways to "slash" the text by drawing on hidden themes, elements, or genres—are produced by fans who are also listeners and who have paid attention to the ways in which sound in the *Buffy* text is not only integral to the production of textual meanings but can be reproduced, reconfigured, replaced, or remixed in order to provide new meanings. I will discuss how *Buffy* works as an intermedial text before considering the ways in which breaching and remixing its intermedia foundations opens it up to meanings that make room for the cheese.

Remixing the Text: *Buffy the Vampire Slayer* and Fan Music Videos as Intermedia

There has been some considerable debate in recent years, emerging particularly through discussions on digital media technologies, on how to view and differentiate multimedia, new media and intermedia.[4] While some writers—including Dick Higgins, who coined the term—prefer to view intermedia as "that sort of text

---

[3] Henry Jenkins, "'Strangers No More, We Sing': Filking and the Social Construction of the Science Fiction Fan Community," in Lisa Lewis (ed.) *The Adoring Audience* (New York, 1992), p. 208.

[4] W.J.T. Mitchell, *Iconology: Image, Text, Ideology* (Chicago, 1986); Mette Ramsgard Thomsen, "Positioning Intermedia: Intermedia and Mixed Reality," *Convergence: The Journal of Research into New Media Technologies* 8/4 (2002), pp. 37–45.

which falls between media,"[5] others link it more strongly with the different senses activated in joint spectatorship, listening and reading, particularly with various ways in which visual and audio components are combined to form a text. Where a pedestrian perception of mixed-media or multimedia make clear the separate sense-based elements, intermedia represents a unique interdependence and interconnection between visual and sound elements, particularly in terms of the ways in which a text masquerades with a framed-off unity and narrative coherence. In this sense, a text is to be seen not as a new product emerging through a combination of material perceived by two different senses—which would be to imply an originary purity of the two forms or components and the potential for their splicing or separation—but as an organic production which is engaged with by audiences in terms of sensory complexity, fusion, and construction across the audio and the visual. In other words, an intermedial text is only intermedial in its considerable reliance on more than one sense to provide the signifiers available to the reader to be activated as meaning.

Whether or not the concept of intermedia is easily applicable to contemporary television and for debating the transformative promises of new digital media is a discussion too broad to engage with here. However, I would suggest that there is a significant tradition in which television is viewed not merely as the mixing bowl of two sensory ingredients, but as a form which has always relied on the audio and the visual as fused. Indeed, as Raymond Williams pointed out, contrary to much popular imagination and critique, the television has greater affinity with the sound-radio than with cinema. For Williams, the visual inefficiency of the (pre-digital) television set and the broadcast nature of television dissemination as it was modeled on the radio provide a stronger relationship with the audio component than does cinema, which continues to emulate theater and which has a history of production prior to the technological reproducibility of sound.[6] The fact that much analysis of television narrative continues to work either with the visual or with the dialogue as the visual supplement stems importantly from the development of theories within cinema and film studies, rather than through the separate evolution and expansion of a television studies subdiscipline until much more recently. Rather than preserving the concept of intermedia for the engagement with interactive, digital texts, it is important then to allow it to be applied to previous texts, forms, and genres which depend significantly on the productive fusion of different sensory perceptions—the history of the television form indicating this fusion and begging a return to the complex intermedial nature of its production and dissemination in analysis.

It is through the intermedial experience of the televisual text that narrative meaning in *Buffy* and *Angel* can be conveyed, disseminated and activated from the perspective of the audience member. More than just a watcher or viewer, the

---

[5] Dick Higgins, "Intermedia," *Leonardo* 34/1 (2001), p. 52.

[6] Raymond Williams, "The Technology and the Society," in Tony Bennett (ed.) *Popular Fiction: Technology, Ideology, Production, Reading* (London, 1990), p. 22.

audience member *engages* with the text as an organic fusion of different sense components in order to read the narrative. As a television narrative, *Buffy* is best located in what Reeves et al. refer to as a shift from TV I to TV II, a shift from modern to postmodern structures as they govern the television narrative form.[7] This shift in television production has allowed more complex and fluid play with the structure of a series, such that the series's reliance on episodic closure through recuperation as a repetitive process is sidelined in favor of complex narratives which stretch across episodes, and play with the styles and conventions of the episodic series. Given the multi-year arcs and the rich complexity of the text, it is particularly valuable to consider the ways in which sound and music (both overt and incidental) operate as inseparable elements that drive the *Buffy* narrative.

As S. Renee Dechert points out, the episode "The Body" (5.16), as an episode without music, works within the narrative to open the story of Joyce's death to a depth and range of meanings: "there is no score to tell the audience how to feel; in the same way, Buffy and her friends struggle to understand."[8] The absence of an incidental score and the heightened focus on the common sounds of the everyday is inseparable from the meanings conveyed—or lack of them, in the case of death—in the program, and works to highlight the intermedial nature of television by showing up the ways in which television normativity informs particular expectations *of* the audience. Likewise, the presence of music-making as a central motif in the series is not to be viewed as an added bonus, a good set of tracks to obtain a broader audience demographic or a spin-off consumable to sell as a CD. Rather, music-making is inseparable from plot, narrative, and visuals. Oz, as a musician, is central to much of the plot in seasons 2–4, and it is both his role as musician and the music itself which drives the significant plot line in which he encounters questions about his identity as both musician and werewolf, his desires, and his relationship with Willow.[9] As important as his look, the ways in which his body is seen to move onscreen, its stances and its styles interweave through the sounds of the show. For example, in the episode "Bewitched, Bothered and Bewildered" (2.16), Willow points to his onstage appearance—"Oz has his cool hair today!"—over the significatory lyrics of Four Star Mary's "Pain"— "You can never understand me/unless you've seen those tears"—as well as the specific sounds of the setting, the aggressive guitarwork of the band, the half-muffled half-shouted background noises and speech of the setting in the Bronze. All of these work together to invoke a particular set of meanings about the sort

---

[7] Jimmie L. Reeves, Mark C. Rodgers and Michael Epstein, "Rewriting Popularity: The Cult *Files*," in David Lavery, Angela Hague, and Marla Cartwright (eds) *Deny All Knowledge: Reading the X-Files* (London, 1996), p. 26.

[8] S. Renee Dechert, "'My Boyfriend's in the Band!' *Buffy* and the Rhetoric of Music," in Rhonda V. Wilcox and David Lavery (eds) *Fighting the Forces: What's at Stake in Buffy the Vampire Slayer* (Lanham, MD, 2002), p. 220.

[9] See Janet K. Halfyard, "Love, Death, Curses and Reverses (in F minor): Music, Gender, and Identity in *Buffy the Vampire Slayer*," *Slayage* 4 (2001).

of relationship Willow and Oz have and, indeed, also the relationships of Xander and Buffy—both of which are central to that episode's plot. It is not something which can be indicated in dialogue except perhaps in a lengthy explanatory scene, something *Buffy* avoids. Rather, it is through the music and lyrics of the soundtrack, the masculinity and desire connoted by the guitarwork and the lyrics, and the significations of an alternative popular music genre that the alternative desire between a potential witch and a werewolf are conveyed.

The point here is that no one element of sound or visual can be separated from the narrative, which moves forward through the interconnections between both in all televisual texts and, in the case of *Buffy*, is carefully and often explicitly constructed. Sound as a disseminator of meaning through incidental effects, music, and other material is, as Cindy Patton points out, something which can be differentiated from dialogue or codes-in-speech. The latter should be considered the "exceptional case of sound: the case in which a sound is produced in a witnessed real time, and in which the witness acts as if the moment of production is equivalent to the sounds being produced."[10] For Patton, alternative sound is equally available for the performative act of conveying a meaning or signification; and indeed the cry, the intonation, the punch, the slam, the splatter, the audible signifiers of pain, or that which replicates emotion—such as particular forms of music—can be seen in *Buffy* as productive means by which meaning is conveyed within the context of the other forms of meaning-making in an audiovisual system of television production. Furthermore, this is to suggest that the dialogue as the prime location of textual meaning is a view which cannot be held so securely in relation to an intermedial text, and that in reproducing sequences of *Buffy* in different audio contexts—such as in the replacement of dialogue with music or other types of sound—is to reconfigure the intermedial structure but not necessarily to reduce the ability of the reconfigured text to provide the signifiers necessary for making meaning.

The *Buffy* amateur music video productions work in some respects to "release" the visuals: firstly from their narrative sequence which provides a set of nodes for the structure of meaning over temporality—their location in a before and after; secondly, and more importantly, from the intermedial ways in which sound operates with visuals to provide and convey the meaning. It is important to understand the structure of these amateur music videos not as the overlay of sound on an existing text, nor as some sort of perversion of the visual that splits it from the sound with which it was professionally produced and subsequently broadcast while adding in its place the amateur choice of an alternative sound text. The original sound of the textual production replicates real time in both dialogue and background, incidental sound effects, but there is no necessary logic indicating this to be a "real" text in opposition to the amateur music video production. Indeed, as Patton has pointed out, a number of pornography productions in the 1970s and 1980s played with sound, often repeating a single sound loop of the guttural noises of sex without

---

[10] Cindy Patton, "How to Do Things With Sound," *Cultural Studies*, 13/3 (1999), p. 473.

any necessary congruence with the visual action—and indeed the sound was often created by other than the visual porn actors.[11] Under analysis, the soundtrack can be considered as another set of meanings, a separate text by which the sounds represent the memories and recollections of the vocalists' own sexual experiences, but, in terms of the textuality of the pornographic film, these sounds are inseparable elements of an intermedial experience for its audience. Nevertheless, a tradition does therefore exist in which footage is released from the actual or fictional real time of sound, such as dialogue, and repackaged with an alternative audio track, reconfiguring the intermedia experience and thereby reconfiguring the potential meanings and significations of the text.

How the meaning of the text changes in remixing the audiovisual components is seen particularly in one amateur music video example: *With or Without You: A Buffy/Spike Video*.[12] This music video draws on 29 scenes or segments selected from the original broadcast program, ranging from the second to the sixth season of *Buffy the Vampire Slayer*. These scenes, out of narrative sequence, are set against U2's track "With or Without You," from the album *The Joshua Tree* (1987).[13] The individual scenes come to signify not the connotations within the original narrative—much of which depends on the temporal location of the scene across a significantly large, multi-year narrative arc—but on the visual as fused with the soundtrack. Three scenes demonstrate not only the ways in which narrative meaning is altered or repositioned temporally but how the entire scene works to build a completely different intermedial text.

The segment 17 in this video is a seven-second extract from the episode "Intervention" (5.18). Having been captured by the demon goddess Glory, who is seeking the whereabouts of the Key (disguised as Buffy's "new" sister Dawn), Spike has gone against his own self-preservation and accepted torture in order to keep the identity of the Key secret. Dressed as the Buffybot, Buffy comes to Spike's crypt to trick him into confirming that nothing about Dawn has been revealed.[14] In gratitude and comradeship, Buffy leans in to kiss him, and as she pulls away Spike's face betrays his astonishment that he has been engaging with the real Buffy. This significant scene is, in my own reading, one in which affection in *Buffy* is indicated through the politics of agency, the self-improvement and search for redemption of the characters whose moral valency falls into grey areas, and the interdependence of those committed together to fight injustice. However, within the context of the music video, the appearance of the scene follows

---

[11] Ibid., p. 475.

[12] Louloucn, *With or Without You: A Buffy/Spike Video* (2001), accessed 12 December 2003 via peer-to-peer file-sharing download. Also available at http://www.youtube.com/watch?v=olxQMBu7zlo.

[13] The 1987 Grammy Winner for Album of the Year and Best Rock Performance by a Duo or Group.

[14] The Buffybot was built to Spike's specifications by Warren Meers, and up to this point Spike has been using it as both sex-slave and paramour.

several in which an approach to affection has been made and culminates in the observable reaction of rejection and uncertainty. Placed where it is, it indicates a peak moment in the narrative of romantic love "found" between Buffy and Spike across the entire four minutes and forty-nine seconds of the clip. Extracted from its temporal location in the *Buffy* narrative, the reading of the scene as one in which Buffy theatrically performs herself as a robot is only possible by those familiar enough with the original broadcast narrative to place it. More importantly, in the fusion with the track "With or Without You" this scene conveys its meaning as a consummate moment of passion between Spike and the real Buffy. U2's hit 1987 song maintains a pounding bass-line on a repetitive tonic–dominant–submediant riff that, in intermedial terms as fusion between lyric and bass, connotes a drive towards a potentially unfulfillable desire. The lyric "My hands are tied/My body bruised" works neatly with the visual image, in which a battered Spike is shown affection from a lover who has, perhaps, been the indirect cause of his abuse. The fact that the track has also returned to its first theme, its verse, is significant in drawing out this scene as one of climax and ascendancy. In its remixed form—without dialogue or the accompanying incidental effects—the scene has no relationship with the narrative from which it was initially drawn. Rather, through its intermedial relationship with the song, it is a pretence of romantic love and affection that would not work or be activated in the context of its first intermedial presentation in the broadcast series itself.

In segment 28, we have an extract from the episode "After Life" (6.3), in which Buffy has just confessed to Spike that she was brought back from heaven, not hell, and that she is now in pain knowing the bliss that she has lost. Her actual words during this scene are as follows:

> Buffy: Wherever I ... was ... I was happy. At peace. I knew that everyone I cared about was all right. I knew it. Time ... didn't mean anything ... nothing had form ... but I was still me, you know? And I was warm ... and I was loved ... and I was finished. Complete. I don't understand about theology or dimensions, or ... any of it, really ... but I think I was in heaven. And now I'm not. [Almost tearful] I was torn out of there. Pulled out ... by my friends. Everything here is ... hard, and bright, and violent. Everything I feel, everything I touch ... this is Hell. Just getting through the next moment, and the one after that ... knowing what I've lost.

Buffy has confessed this to Spike who, as the undead, she views as best positioned to make intelligible her experience of that which she encountered in the beyond of the temporal lifecycle of birth-to-death that characterizes humans but neither her resurrected self nor vampires. In the overall narrative arc that centers on Buffy's death, resurrection, and recuperation from the trauma of rebirth and readjustment to life on a hellish earth, this scene is of great significance in being the first revelation to the viewer that Buffy has not spent the previous 147 days in a hell dimension. In the context of its re-presentation in the music video, it denotes the continuing play in the previous few scenes of conjoint affection and separation, the "with" and "without you." In segment 27 against the words "with or without you", Buffy is seen to approach Spike in a clichéd representation of a descent down stairs to the waiting man. Segment 28 thereby gives the walk away to the saddened romantic male lead, impressing upon the reader through the juxtaposition of the song and the footage the idea that this scene is Buffy's departure—whether symbolic or real—from a relationship or, at least, a potential one. Love unrequited or love lost, but love nevertheless.

Segment 23 provides perhaps the most compelling indication of the ways in which the application of a musical text to an intermedial text works to breach the intermedia of the text and provide a new one with highly divergent meanings. The change of audio context alters both the narrative function and the significations of this scene. In the episode "Family" (5.6) the original scene of a fight between Buffy and Spike is built with both a powerful visual momentum and some strong fighting sound effects (kicks, punches, wall-smashes, reverb) along with an orchestral score which replicates some of the more intense and emotional fight-scenes encountered both previously and later on in the *Buffy* series. Furthermore, the intensity of the scene as an intermedial text connotes grandeur quite specifically—a grandeur necessary to the subsequent revelation that it was not a real fight between Buffy and Spike but a sexual fantasy playing in Spike's mind while he has sex with Harmony. Once the visuality of the scene breaches its originary intermedial relationship with the effects and the grand score, we have a set of significations that work within Frank Kermode's assertion of a cultural taste for closure in his *The Sense of an Ending*.[15] The temporal location of this moment following segments 21 (Spike stops Buffy dancing) and 22 (Spike and Buffy kiss passionately) provides the connotation of the troubled relationship, the intensity of slippage between anger-pain and passion-affection. Juxtaposed against the vocal intonations of this climactic moment in the song, we have a carefully worked-out sequence in which a narrative story is told as one which cannot in fact be found in the text with its original score, as it lacked dialogue during these three scenes in their original broadcast in three episodes across two seasons.

Utilizing Text and Genre: Slash, Filk and Remixed Intermedia

In an interview with *The Onion*, Whedon points out that he designed *Buffy* to be an emotional experience, he "wanted people to internalize it, and make up fantasies where they were in the story, to take it home with them, for it to exist beyond the TV show."[16] He has also suggested that relationships on the show should be

---

[15] Frank Kermode, *The Sense of an Ending: Studies in the Theory of Fiction* (London, 1967).

[16] Tasha Robinson, "Joss Whedon," *The Onion*, 37 (2001), accessed 12 December 2003 at http://www.theonionavclub.com/avclub3731/avfeature_3731.html.

treated by audience members with a "Bring Your Own Subtext" principle.[17] Such descriptions are not different from the idea of slash fiction, which began in the late 1960s with fiction written from a feminist viewpoint that propounded an intimate, homosexual, or homoerotic relationship between Captain Kirk and his First Officer Spock in the original series of *Star Trek*. According to Constance Penley, K/S (Kirk-Spock) fiction is the result of the recognition of a usually homosexual erotic subtext "or at least one that could easily be *made* to be there."[18] Slash fiction reads a subtextual sexual undercurrent in a program and centers it in a subsequent new work that retains its intertextual links with the original text and contributes to a fan artworld. Not dissimilarly, there has been some considerable slash fiction based on *Buffy*. Buffy-Faith and Spike-Angel slash fiction and artwork are the most predominant, and often feature on private fan websites, linked to fan message boards and available by email alerts. These are written in the tradition of K/S slash, and draw on the subtle subtextual representations that indicate the slippage between homosociality and homosexual desire of these characters—an art form which makes an important queer theoretical statement on the fluidity of sexual and sensual desire and the point that no matter how prominent a heterosexual orientation is given in a text, its characters are never exempt from being witnessed as non-stereotypically queer.[19]

The music videos I am examining here are not slash in the term's original usage. These videos do not bring out an alternative sexual undercurrent, but are the creation of a cheesy romantic-styled text in the borrowed design of a popular music video. It is the romance that is the undercurrent in the original text, made central in the videoclip and working effectively to reduce an element of the *Buffy* text to a limited narrative of love-and-coupledom. I will return to the politics of this new form of slash below, but what must be stated here is that the narrative works only through the reconfiguration of the intermedia of audio and visual in order to create a new text with subsequent new potential meanings. In that sense, this differs considerably from slash as a written prose form of reworking the text; at the same time they are more than just another form of fan art appreciation or celebration of the original text, because they do indeed attempt to reconfigure the text to provide it with new meanings that are either submerged or unavailable in its original reception. For Saxey, *Buffy* slash draws out not what is submerged in the text nor makes a purely radical reading of the text, but focuses on that which in her terms is "thrown out" of the text: "themes dwelt on in the middle of episodes or plot lines,

---

[17] Roz Kaveney, "'She Saved the World. A Lot': An Introduction to the Themes and Structures of *Buffy* and *Angel*," in Roz Kaveney (ed.) *Reading the Vampire Slayer: An Unofficial Critical Companion to Buffy and Angel* (London/New York, 2001), p. 10.

[18] Constance Penley, *Nasa/Trek: Popular Science and Sex in America* (London/New York, 1997), pp. 101–102.

[19] Judith Butler, *Excitable Speech: A Politics of the Performative* (New York/London, 1997), p. 107.

which are then abandoned or overcome as part of the plot dynamic."[20] These are the possibilities, as readings, generated by the middle of narratives, which closure cannot tie up.[21] This, then, is not to see the production of music videos as slashing *Buffy* relationships or read them "otherwise" as a form of textual poaching, as Henry Jenkins puts it.[22] Rather than being seen as parasitic upon an original text,[23] or as the scavenging of both *Buffy* and popular songs to be sewn together to bring subtextual relationships to the fore, these new texts are formed within the notion of reconfiguration as renewal, working with the postmodern spirit of the *Buffy* phenomenon. Such digital remixing fosters Whedon's desire for "bringing your own subtext" as the active, productive realisation of *Buffy* audiencehood.

In contrast, *Star Trek* music videos seek not so much to rework the text by reconfiguring its intermedia, but function as an appreciation or confirmation of other slash readings of the text. Since at least the 1980s and the advent of the video recorder, fans have taken footage from television texts and edited them to construct their own videos through the reordering of that footage to articulate new or celebratory meanings.[24] Penley has identified several K/S slash music videos that are produced by the juxtaposition of meaningful scenes and segments drawn from fans' own private collections of *Star Trek* episodes.[25] Interestingly, advice given at a workshop on how to put together a K/S slash video suggested the fan examine "the video material without sound—the sound will confuse you."[26] The production of the *Buffy* music videos operates within the same utilization of the visual and the style of song, albeit with a more sophisticated and semiprofessional level of editing made available through newer interactive technologies such as Macromedia Flash and other programs facilitating the multimedia reconfiguring of audio, photographic footage, and animation. Initially, the digital technology used to sample the visuals and juxtapose them with a song was sophisticated and required a much greater level of expertise than was needed to make an edited dub through two video cassette recorders; likewise, some skill was required to share these through peer-to-peer (P2P) file-sharing systems online. More recently, the advent of YouTube in 2005 has seen the broader emergence of what Lawrence Lessig refers to as a Remix Culture—"a rich, diverse outpouring of creativity based on creativity"[27]—where such playful development of music videos

---

[20] Esther Saxey, "Staking a Claim: the Series and its Slash Fan-Fiction," in Kaveney (ed.), *Reading the Vampire Slayer*, p. 199.

[21] Ibid., p. 207.

[22] Jenkins, "Strangers No More," p. 216.

[23] Penley, *Nasa/Trek*, p. 106.

[24] Jenkins, "Strangers No More," p. 212.

[25] Penley, *Nasa/Trek*, p. 114.

[26] Ibid.

[27] Lawerence Lessig, "Remixing Culture: An Interview with Lawrence Lessig by Richard Koman," *O'Reilly Policy DevCentre* (2005), accessed 12 June 2008 at http://www.oreillynet.com/pub/a/policy/2005/02/24/lessig.html.

sampling different texts is not only easily created and shared but becomes the manner in which new audiences engage with texts. While the democratization of professional audiovisual production skill has enabled the widespread emergence of fan music videos, they do continue the slash tradition of indicating their own amateur origins. This is seen particularly in the title screens and closing credits, which explicitly utilize the signifiers of slash such as "A Buffy/Spike Video," or indicate the poaching mentality within fan art production in phrases such as "Clips taken from 'Buffy the Vampire Slayer' (Joss Whedon). They don't belong to me, I just borrowed them for a while."[28]

Rather than understanding them as a multimedia form of "pseudo"-slash focusing on the normative-romantic rather than the hidden homoerotic, these music videos might also be considered a form of "filking": that is, the making of songs and other musical forms about, or around, or from the perspective of fictional characters drawn from a television series. According to Henry Jenkins, filking is best understood as "a vehicle for extending or commenting upon preexisting texts; it may be a way of taking textual materials and pulling to the surface characters or concerns which have been marginalized."[29] Filking is generally created for and practiced within the cultural form of the convention and is a joint activity among a number of fans deliberately crossing a range of fan interests. Filk songs as performed and participated in at conventions are either trial-runs of new work or songs which have circulated within the fan community for some time. What makes the production of these videos a form of filking is not that they are expected to be joined in with, sung together in real time along with the played sound and footage by fans in communities. Rather, it is filk by virtue of the songs' appeal to the popular imaginary. Each of the tracks in the music videos have clearly been chosen as particular favorites of the music videos' authors, or as having some culturally held understanding drawn from their reception within popular culture. Certainly, tracks like U2's "With or Without You" and Madonna's "Crazy for You" are instantly recognizable as mainstream, mass-circulation, chart-making songs, recalled from past hearings, from repetitive broadcast on radio, in shops and cars and pubs.

Perhaps the most interesting way in which these music videos can be understood as a hybrid form of the slash art production and the recorded filk-sing is in their crossing over of the fan subculture and the popular mainstream. These songs are popular in the sense that they have been disseminated to a broad audience; and in their addition to the reconfigured intermedia of the music videos, they work differently from the *Star Trek* slash videos, partly in going beyond the K/S slash clips' use as a celebration of visual confirmation of preexisting slash, partly through the very different form of romantic cheese that they offer, and partly through their recombining of the popular visual with the even more popular song to create significantly diverse meanings. Presented as a multimedia recording, they

---

[28] Louloucn, *With or Without You*.
[29] Jenkins, "Strangers No More," pp. 215–16.

are beyond the real time of filking, yet work to evoke several of the same elements of emotion and shared experience.

The Tara and Willow montage, *Crazy For You* made by GaBs_HoPe,[30] operates in the same way as louloucn's *With or Without You* through the reconfiguration of the text with re-sequenced visual segments drawn from seasons 4 and 5, defined through Madonna's popular hit. As a markedly cheesy, romantic popular song, it serves to re-signify the individual visual scenes without their original dialogue and incidental sound from the *Buffy* text. As a combined form of slash-filk, this 3'36" sequence differs both from the fan video re-sequences identified by Jenkins and the slash-appreciation clips described by Penley. Rather than working through a radical reading of the text, it operates by drawing on an existing lesbian relationship in the primary text. Given the sheer scarcity of overt or explicit representations on television of homosexuality and homoeroticism, this is perhaps to be considered a new departure for fan art forms in general—it is now possible to write or create a homoerotic fan text based on an explicit homoeroticism in the original, using the style of slash production in such a way that in fact fails to slash the primary text.

Unlike the *With or Without You* videoclip, which drew out a relationship that had been fantasized, emerging but certainly not fully declared at the time at which the clip was produced (drawing on the series material from season 5 and the first third of season 6), this music video works to celebrate the Willow-Tara relationship, not least through the popularity of Madonna's "Crazy for You." This was released with the 1985 film *Vision Quest* and distributed on the film soundtrack and as European 7" and 12" singles the same year, was re-released as a single in 1991, and appeared on both the Madonna compilation albums *Immaculate Collection* (1990) and *Something to Remember* (1995), arguably inserting the song into the popular imaginary of both 1980s and 1990s youth and adult audiences. In configuring this text through such a notably cheesy popular song, the images extracted from the series form much less of a narrative than the other video clips, but serve to enhance a sort of "pre-recorded" filk—the connotations of the song's lyrics and simple melody being themselves representative of Willow and Tara's relationship. In this case, the visuals serve more to enhance the celebratory aspect of the text; they are the supplement rather than the primary element in this intermedia production. Effectively, drawing the song "Crazy for You" into the intermedial experience of the Willow-Tara relationship makes it a song we all filk-sing in commemoration of the relationship, filk being not purely a personal expression but a communal contribution to fan culture. The title phrase "Crazy for You" might thereby be less a statement the characters make to each other and more a statement we make in our appreciation and adoration of them. At the same time, it is a node by which the mainstream commercial and popular becomes a point of potential identification between the fan-world and the world of the broad popular audience, including the Madonna fan audience (who of course may or may

---

[30] GaBs_HoPe, *Crazy for You* (2001), accessed 12 December 2003 via peer-to-peer file-sharing download. Also available as *Willow Tara – Crazy for You* at http://www.youtube.com/watch?v=36qrXcjnGEs.

not agree with the song's use in this context). The traditions of both filk and song in general have been about bridging gaps between various audiences and, in this sense, the work might certainly be considered more in league with filking than with slash that relies on visuality and sound.

Digital Networking and *Buffy* Intermedia as Process and Flow

New interactive technologies have been utilized both to bring about new means of creating amateur and slash fan music videos by increasing the potential for sampling digital works for intermedial reconfiguration and to allow new, networked means of distributing such production. Where digital networking and convergence allow greater access to the tools that give a professional gloss to an amateur work, the risk exists that a star system will develop,[31] as well as the possibility of commodification of the more professional texts. However, resistance to professionalization by defying the appeal of the music video genre and style does indeed occur. The 2001 music video *Only Time* (credited to onlytime.8m.com) is of a professional standard of multimedia production, yet differs strongly from the conventions of the video clip, as well as the other *Buffy* fan productions, in its refusal to juxtapose segmented extracts of moving footage from the show against an external audio track.[32] Rather, the production utilizes both still shots from the broadcast series and a large number of publicity photographs, some of which are of the actors (Sarah Michelle Gellar and James Marsters) disconnected from their roles. These have been interspersed with printed quotations from the dialogue, as well as textual commentary, giving more the effect of a silent film than a popular music video. This indicates a continued commitment in fan art production to the juggling of both professional and deliberately amateurish standards in order to maintain a certain distance from professionalized gloss.

New technologies allowing transformation of the text and the making available of new meanings through intermedial play are equally important to the effects of new forms of distribution. Amateur music videos using footage from *Buffy* and recorded songs from other sources have been circulating on the internet since around 2000, with most of my examples drawn from 2001. Amateur music videos based on *Buffy* are available occasionally from websites, but are to be found circulating more frequently through P2P networks that allow access to another's personal hard drive without using a central server, and more recently on YouTube. The legitimacy of these methods of exchange and distribution is yet to be fully tested, given the scandal around Napster and other mp3 P2P distribution circuits, and the question of copyright over fan production and utilization of televisual extracts is one which has not yet been, and hopefully will not be, broadly put to the legal test.

---

[31] Jenkins, "Strangers No More," p. 231.

[32] Also available as *Buffy and Spike – Only Time* at http://www.youtube.com/watch?v=RfMLi4US-ZA.

The shift of fan art production, and particularly *Buffy* slash fiction, onto the internet has been discussed at length by Esther Saxey, who makes the point that where once a fan had to attend a conference, be part of a tight-knit group of fellow fans, or use a fanzine catalogue in order to access a zine, one can now access "a hundred sites in an afternoon through links pages, web rings and search engines."[33] This has had the effect of popularizing slash production and disseminating it more widely and frequently to an audience who are not deliberately seeking slash artwork: one can stumble on it while searching for other information on the program. Technologies associated with music distribution on the internet are, as Steve Jones points out, technologies both of *geography* that transmit across distances and of *audience* that allow a form of interactivity as co-participation in the creation of narratives.[34] This suggests considerable consequences not only for how fan art production is distributed, but for the ways in which it is put together (in digital forms), for the ways in which it is accessed, and—in the broader schema of intertextuality—for the ways in which the program itself as a meta-text finds a space or cyberspace in which to exist as flow and as process. These music videos are, of course, now available through the speed allowed by current network distribution, and surpass the idea of fan art production as produced-and-distributed physical copies.

Conceptualizing fan art as intermedia-edited "flow" from the original text is also orchestrated by new technologies. Where once slash, filking, and other fan productions were to be considered in Jenkins's terms as poaching, pilfering, and scavenging, it is perhaps more appropriate now to view the reconfiguration of the *Buffy* intermedial experience as the flow-on effect of a text received by particular sorts of audiences and actively, technologically reconceptualized through emerging participatory user-audience remixing. Where particular *Buffy* music videos are pulled together by drawing on previously digitally sampled extracts from the program, particularly those sampled in an mpeg format, the juxtaposition of these texts against particular songs—found, borrowed, or bought in digital mp3 format and accessed across networks—allows us to see and hear the original text as just one stage in a process by which it evolves through its engagement with an audience equipped to play with its intermedial form.

Recuperating the Normative in the *Buffy* Slash Text

Intended much more as a coda than a conclusion, I want to write briefly of the politics of utilizing the slash form, filking, and the music video as a means of making room for the cheese. While much of the narrative of *Buffy* revolves around the attempt to have relationships, it is also explicitly a text which seeks to problematize the perceived teenage social need for romantic relationships,

---

[33] Saxey, "Staking a Claim," pp. 188–9.
[34] Steve Jones, "Music That Moves: Popular Music, Distribution and Network Technologies," *Cultural Studies*, 16/2 (2002), p. 214.

making it quite distinct from other television drama and series of the same period. This opens up several questions as to how we should politically view these music videos as additions to the encompassing knowledge around *Buffy*. In *Buffy* the statement underlying the narrative development of relationships is that normative, heterosexual coupling is not only difficult to achieve and maintain but borders on the unworkable. Buffy's mother, Joyce, is a divorced single mother. Although Giles has had lovers including Jenny Calendar and Olivia—and in slash-terms there is certainly enough material in the program to find a marginal statement suggesting that he and his rival Ethan Rayne were one-time lovers of some sort— he both begins and ends the seven-year narrative as a man married to his work and responsibilities, less under a work ethic than an ethic of care and communitarian spirit. Buffy has had four romantic partners (Angel, Scott, Riley, and Spike) and a fifth, short-lived sexual encounter (Parker Abrams), and in all cases what has proven workable has been the avoidance of the romantic cliché.[35] Her relationship with Spike—as it develops throughout the sixth season and in the latter part of the seventh after he has acquired a soul—clearly indicates she finds greater comfort in something less well defined in narrow, stereotyped terms: a relationship that is built on a sadomasochistic set of pleasures as well as a (later) comradely respect defies the normative cliché of the patriarchal heteronormative stereotype. Likewise, Xander and Anya find a certain mutual respect when their relationship becomes more a sexual one than a cliché of the young, engaged couple. In fact, the only relationship that is broadly defined in terms of the figure of coupledom is Willow and Tara's—non-normative itself by virtue of their gender.

The largest statement opposed to narrow and cheesy definitions of romantic coupledom is made in the episode "Something Blue" (4.9) in which Willow has cast a spell that has gone awry, leaving the currently mortal enemies Buffy and Spike wanting to marry and obsessing over all the trappings of marriage and romantically coupled life. As farce, Buffy is later forced to explain away her behavior to Riley by denouncing cheesy romance and girlhood wedding desires, and the final lines suggest the awful absurdity that she had planned to have Bette Midler's "Wind Beneath My Wings" for the first wedding dance. As she retorts uncertainly, "that was the spell," indicating both the ease of slippage into the cultural imperatives of cheesy romance and the rejection of same in the show itself. In the final episode of the seventh series ("Chosen" [7.22]), it is Buffy herself who articulates the ways in which romantic, cheesy coupledom is not something easily achieved and should not be taken as a means for the development of a self-identity through a narrow definition of relationship and relationship behavior. In a humorous speech to her former lover Angel, she utilizes Buffy-speak to make clear the reasons why she

---

[35] The main exception is Riley, who demonstrated that away from Buffy and Sunnydale he was able to forge a workable, romantic relationship leading to marital bliss. How his own narrative proceeds is, of course, a matter for the extratextual sphere and, indeed, perhaps for a fan music videoclip of his own.

feels her identity is not yet complete enough to return to a relationship with him in the foreseeable future:

> Buffy: I always figured there was something wrong with me, because I couldn't make it work. Maybe I'm not supposed to.
> Angel: Because you're the Slayer?
> Buffy: Because ... okay, I'm cookie dough. I'm not done baking. I'm not finished becoming whoever the hell it is I'm going to turn out to be. I make it through this, and the next thing, and the next thing, and maybe one day I turn around and realize I'm ready. I'm cookies. And then, you know, if I want someone to eat ... or ... enjoy warm, delicious cookie-me, then that's fine. That'll be then. When I'm done [...] It'll be a long time coming. Years, if ever.

An argument is available, then, to suggest that the orientation of the series is one which attempts to find alternatives beyond romantic coupledom while articulating the ways in which a cultural imperative continues to push younger people to view it as the only means by which to acquire and stabilize self-identity. As Saxey puts it: "the slavish respecting of closure—the actual pairings of the show, the declared motives of the characters—is not what the show's structure encourages."[36] This is an orientation that is politically powerful, located in a postmodern, anarchic set of ethics which seeks to destabilize the normative in favor of the imaginable, the unimaginable, and the transformative. Importantly, the selection of songs in *Buffy* soundtracks indicates an avoidance of the cheesy romantic and the pushing aside of normative desire through the use of songs that deal less with such romantic intent, whether fulfilled or not.

However, from a cultural studies perspective ultimate meaning is not located in a text but produced only in its reception.[37] For Bennett, it is the "reading formation" which governs the reception, "the set of intersecting discourses which productively activate a given body of texts and the relations between them in a specific way."[38] In this case, the discursive formation is the widespread cultural imperative of heteronormative coupledom that broadly governs the available ways in which to think about identity, selfhood, gender, home, lifecycles, lifestyles, friendship, and belonging. What is interesting here, then, is that in utilizing common cultural narratives of romantic coupledom and partnership in the production of these music videos, the reader is reading against the grain of the text,[39] but only in such a way that accepts a dominant cultural reading in opposition to the minority and alternative concepts disseminated in the text.

---

[36] Saxey, "Staking a Claim," p. 192.

[37] Tony Bennett, "Texts, Readers, Reading Formations," *Literature and History*, 9/2 (1983), p. 218.

[38] Ibid., p. 216.

[39] John Fiske, *Understanding Popular Culture* (London, 1989), p. 181.

This is not altogether uncommon in *Buffy* fan discourse. Arguments on the discussion boards on fan websites such as Buffyworld.com indicate some heated factionalization between those fans who adhered to a strongly held belief or wish that Buffy would eventually and properly get together with either Angel or Spike. These fans were known by others as the "shippers" (relationshippers) and were categorized Bangels (Buffy/Angel shippers) and Spuffies (Spike/Buffy shippers)—a fascinating example of fans emulating the propensity of *Buffy* characters for making up or self-consciously evolving new descriptive terms. Characters from both *Buffy* and *Angel* are now being pseudo-slashed along such lines, including a Fred/Willow—or Frillow—shipper slash motif. Where these new terms are significant is in the multiple plays on words: "shipper" as a term is known to connote not only relationship but worship (of the relationship), and shipping lines indicates a fan community subset traveling through the waves of the Buffyverse together. The naming involved in such fan production in fact takes the signification of slash to a new level: beyond slash. Rather than referencing a slash work in the original-style K/S, the creation of new terms such as Spuffy and Bangel seems to feed the cultural narratives of normative coupledom to the extent that "two become one." Indeed, many fans commenting from shipper perspectives refer to the coupled phenomenon in the duo-as-singular, hence "Spuffy is hot, sexy, and in love, god I miss those kids" and "Go Frillow it's your birthday."[40]

There is certainly room for an argument that this form of reception-production is a perversion of the spirit of fan art production and particularly slash and filk, both of which made strong radical readings not merely "against the grain" of what is explicit in a text,[41] but against the normative. Can the production of multimedia and intermedia video clips be both slash and a restoration of the normative romantic couple, whether or not that normativity is produced through hetero- or homosexual coupling? Should such productions be viewed negatively for their attempt to insert the normative into what has always been a text seeking to transgress, transform, and subvert the model, the measure, the average, and the mediocre? Certainly it is through drawing on songs such as Enya's "Only Time," Shakira's "Whenever, Wherever," Sheryl Crow's "I Shall Believe," or Elton John and LeAnn Rimes's "Written in the Stars"—all of which can be categorized together as cheesy in terms of *Buffy's* own musical acquisition—that such productions are much less slash and perhaps indicate most of all the importance of both incidental music and dialogue to the political imperatives around coupledom and romance on the show. Personal interests and experiences of individual fans are, of course, necessary counterparts to the interpretive and reconfigurative functions of all fan production.

Although I would not want to suggest here that there can be any one, definable motivation for the production of these music videos—for certainly what impels a fan to produce such a text is multiple, diverse, and located in a broad network of conventions, behaviors, and desires, it would nevertheless seem that a significant

---

[40] Posts to forums in Buffyworld.com are no longer accessible.
[41] Jenkins, "Strangers No More," p. 226.

motivation for the reconfiguring of the text by transforming its intermedia with new, external material is that it is one of the more efficient ways in which to achieve the sorts of relationship statements that the show itself sidelines, denies, or outrightly rejects. Naturally, there is no reason to suggest that such motives are necessarily conscious or explicit, because much fan cultural production exists not only as a vehicle for commenting on the primary text but also "as a means of building and maintaining solidarity within the fan community."[42] What this highlights, if nothing else, is the importance of audio in both the program and the fan artwork in the production and transformation of meaning.

---

[42] Ibid., p. 213.

Chapter 9
"You're Just a Girl!" Punk Rock Feminism and the New Hero in *Buffy the Vampire Slayer*

Renée T. Coulombe

Riot Grrrl, as a media phenomenon, was short-lived.[1] In 1992, news of a new underground feminist movement hit the mainstream media suddenly and then, just as suddenly, all but disappeared. One can surmise that popular culture's antennae were particularly attuned to news on the feminist front at that historic moment: the emergence of Riot Grrrl to the mainstream closely followed the publication of Susan Faludi's groundbreaking and polemical *Backlash: The Undeclared War on American Women*, and Naomi Wolf's *The Beauty Myth* in 1991. That same year, the Anita Hill sexual harassment hearings enflamed feminist passions, which contributed to 1992's election year being labeled "the year of the woman." News of the demise of feminism, a movement long declared dead by mainstream media in the wake of 1980s cultural retrenchment, would appear to have been exaggerated. Scholars and cultural critics soon associated this movement as a youth subculture of the new "Third Wave" of feminism, well under way by the early 1990s.[2] And while the Third Wave of feminism is far broader, Riot Grrrl became a popular media face.

Also during 1992, Joss Whedon's movie, *Buffy the Vampire Slayer*, opened with little critical acclaim. The film, starring Kristy Swanson as the eponymous Buffy, portrayed a contemporary blonde "valley girl" caught unawares by her inherited destiny: to kill vampires and save the world. While the movie was by no means a hit by industry standards, in its theme of female conquering hero it

---

[1] An earlier version of this paper was given at the conference on Feminist Theory in Music (7), at Bowling Green State University, Bowling Green, Ohio in July 2003. I would like to thank the many attendees of the session who contributed helpful feedback and Eric Peterson, who provided much editorial assistance. Understanding that Riot Grrrl still exists as a subculture, albeit much diminished, I have nonetheless chosen to refer to it here in the past tense. This is mostly for convenience, as many mainstream publications use the past tense when referring to Riot Grrrl and the movement is considerably smaller since the 1990s.

[2] Rebecca Walker, "Becoming the Third Wave," *Ms*, January/February (1992), pp. 39–41.

presaged several TV hits that for many defined the feminist 1990s, most notably *Xena: Warrior Princess* (1995–2001) and the *Buffy* series. These two are often cited together as contemporary icons of warrior women and the culmination of several decades of modern feminism.³ But while *Buffy* is often cited as an example of "young" feminism, Riot Grrrl characteristics, both in the auditory and visual construction of the series and characters, have not been documented, despite Riot Grrrl being the only identifiable youth movement in modern feminism.

In this article, I will discuss how Riot Grrrl initially manifested as a movement, what values it promoted, and how the movement was portrayed in the mainstream media. As there are excellent examples of contemporary scholarship which document Riot Grrrl, the discussion of its characteristics, aesthetics, and values will be limited to those areas relevant to the analysis of *Buffy*.⁴ This will necessitate some unfortunate simplification, as Riot Grrrl is a complex and diverse movement with no one philosophical centre. I will attempt to ameliorate the simplification with references to more complete documents.

It should be said from the outset that there are no overt references to the Riot Grrrl movement in the series: there does not need to be. The series takes advantage of the popular cultural references (musical and otherwise) of Riot Grrrl to help situate *Buffy*'s title character within the pop-culture landscape as a girl who fights back, and in the 1990s this alone associates her with Riot Grrrl. In many ways, locating Buffy within a specific youth subculture *by name* would disrupt her character's position as the centre of her own youth subculture with her peers Willow, Xander, Cordelia, Angel, and, to a certain extent, Giles. So as not to compete with this basic identification, the Riot Grrrl references are more subtle, implicit, and strategically employed in the source and non-source music, the narrative arc, and the visual language of the series.

I begin with a brief history and discussion of the Riot Grrrl movement, including a look at the mainstream media's relationship to Riot Grrrl—at what "stories" were being told about the movement and riot grrrls themselves in the mainstream press. This discussion will determine which values of Riot Grrrl were transmitted widely in the mainstream: in other words, what things came to signify "Riot Grrrl," whether or not they are rooted in actual Riot Grrrl experience. I then analyze the function of Riot Grrrl in *Buffy* at these two levels: those values of Riot

---

³ See Sherryl Vint, "'Killing us Softly?' A Feminist Search for the 'Real' Buffy," *Slayage* 5 (2002); Frances H. Early, "Staking her Claim: Buffy the Vampire Slayer as Transgressive Woman Warrior," *Journal of Popular Culture*, 35/3 (2001), pp. 11–37; and Frances Early and Kathleen Kennedy (eds), *Athena's Daughter's: Television's New Women Warriors* (Syracuse, 2003) for examples linking Xena and Buffy in feminist critique.

⁴ For summarized interviews and documenting of Riot Grrrl values, see Caroline Kaltefleiter, *Revolution Girl Style Now: Trebled Reflexivity and the Riot Grrrl Network* (PhD thesis, Ohio University, 1995); Angela Johnson, "Start a Fucking Riot," *Off Our Backs*, 23/5 (1993), pp. 6–10; Jessica Rosenberg and Gitana Garofalo, "Riot Grrrl: Revolutions from Within," *Signs*, 23/3 (1998), pp. 809–841.

Grrrl feminism that are present in the series, and values erroneously associated with Riot Grrrl feminism in the media that are present. This dual analysis reveals layers of Third Wave feminist thought and experience deployed throughout the musical and visual world of *Buffy*, speaking powerfully to the diverse audience of the series.

Riot Grrrl 101

Caroline Kaltefleiter clearly delineates many important themes of the Riot Grrrl movement. She notes: "the Riot Grrrl network is a feminist subcultural scene made popular by the emergence of alternative Punk rock girl groups."[5] She goes on to label the movement a "postmodern feminist group" which attempts to "disrupt ideologies of femininity through counter-representation" and remarks on their "linguistic jujitsu" in recuperating words like "girl" that had taken on derogatory connotations in contemporary speech. Like other authors, Kaltefleiter notes that "Grrrls accessorize their bodies with black magic markers, printing … in your face words like 'rape,' 'guilt,' or 'slut.' That they fus[e] a discourse of femininity into a collage of Mod-Hippie-Skinhead-Punk codes and styles[;]" and that Riot Grrrl "reaches into the realism of political strategizing, (re)inserting a self-definition of girl Punkness through fanzine publication, community-oriented activism, and musical celebration."[6]

The term Riot Grrrl, coined by Bikini Kill singer and feminist activist Kathleen Hanna, attempts to recapture girlhood as an extremely positive experience:

> Grrrl … is a spontaneous young-feminist reclamation of the word "girl."… "Grrrl" puts the growl back in our pussycat throats. "Grrrl" is intended to recall the naughty, confident and curious ten-year-olds we were before the society made it clear it was time to stop being loud.[7]

From the early 1990s when the Riot Grrrl subculture emerged, riot grrrls re-envisioned feminism, restoring the power of the word "girl" and placing the empowering of girls center stage. They did so by producing alternative, home-published fanzines (zines), and independent music recordings; wearing ironic, gender-challenging, or extremely "girly" fashions; and using whatever technology was available to do so. Their association with cutting edge technologies—particularly through web-based zines, grrrl-oriented chatrooms, and message boards—placed Riot Grrrl firmly within the emergent technology-oriented youth subcultures with strong punk associations.

---

[5] Caroline Kaltefleiter, *Revolution Girl-Style Now*, p. 9.
[6] Ibid., pp. 9–17.
[7] Laurel Gilbert and Crystal Kile, *Surfergrrrls: Look Ethel! An Internet Guide for Us* (Seattle, 1996), p. 5.

Riot Grrrl was seen by many as more radicalized than the second wave of liberal feminism it followed, mostly because of the confrontational style of its members. Riot Grrrl feminists learned from radical direct-action groups such as ACT UP, Queer Nation, and the Lesbian Avengers, and shared many young members with them. They gravitated toward their bodies (and by extension, fashion) as a primary locus of protest, as they had been indoctrinated from childhood to see their bodies as being "for public consumption." Their use of the body to display a verbal message plays upon their "looked-at-ness" to draw attention to their own bodies as sites for social struggle. This reflected a deep level of visual media engagement on the part of this particular youth subculture, even though that culture took as its central focus the overlapping webs of oppression around issues such as race, class, gender, size, and sexual orientation that were (and are) promulgated in the media.

Riot Grrrl adopted a late capitalist, postmodern association to text, an association made possible by the second wave feminism of the 1970s.[8] Scrawling words on the flesh also brought together language and the body in Riot Grrrl feminism. But if 1970s' feminism had used political speech for change (in insisting, for instance, on being called women rather than girls), Riot Grrrl feminists turned this on its head, recouping the word "girl" and placing everyday speech at the center of the movement. This centrality of words to Riot Grrrl appeared repeatedly in the production of zines, filled with grrrls' uncensored writings and images.[9] These zines varied dramatically in style and context, and reflected a tremendous variety of experience and interests. They are often visually striking: collaged and chaotic. The texts found in zines are equally diverse in style and content, incorporating stream of consciousness, manifestos, diary entries, poetry, scholarly essays, song lyrics, and so on. They are often unedited, sometimes contradictory from page to page, and frequently painfully personal. Zines were designed to reflect a multitude of voices, fostering uncensored expression for all of girls' experiences including taboo subjects like abuse, discrimination, and despair.

Grrrls saw technology as an important tool of "the revolution" and quickly moved online with the advent of the internet: web sites for riot grrrls provided a useful media outlet, but also a virtual gathering site and forum. This can be viewed as evidence of a larger concern: riot grrrls wanted girls to assume the means of production and becoming familiar with all sorts of technologies, from designing web sites to amplifying guitars, was central. Early punks used Riot Grrrl concerts, conventions, and meetings to encourage girls to play instruments, form their own bands, and play their own music.[10]

---

[8] See Kaltefleiter, *Revolution Girl Style Now*, and Rosenberg and Garofalo, "Riot Grrrl."

[9] For a sampling see Tristan Taormino and Karen Green (eds), *A Girl's Guide to Taking Over the World: Writings from the Girl Zine Revolution* (New York, 1997).

[10] See Kaltefleiter, *Revolution Girl Style Now* for extensive interviews with riot grrrls reflecting a diversity of Riot Grrrl interests.

Indeed, a central locus for protest in Riot Grrrl was music. Growing out of the punk music scenes in communities such as Washington, DC and Olympia, WA, Riot Grrrl began with all-girl bands like Bikini Kill, Bratmobile and Team Dresch. They wrote music that confronted many societal ills toward girls: violence, rape, incest, teen pregnancy, girl-girl violence and competition, issues of access to technology, and material/economic resources. Their fans, the earliest riot grrrls, embraced punk values of "Do It Yourself," and assumed punk's marginalized stance *vis-à-vis* mainstream culture. Grrrls came together around music to create alternative families and support structures, ones that can reflect the difficulties in being a girl in a culture with overlapping layers of discrimination.

Unlike previous feminist movements that had produced media-savvy critics and mainstream publishing dynamos, the members of this new loose affiliation went underground almost immediately upon surfacing to avoid the media onslaught. While grrrls wanted girls to have a voice, they did not want the media to carry that voice. Tired of seeing feminists misread by a patriarchal media system, the young women of Riot Grrrl simply chose to opt out of the media circus. The most visible proponents of Riot Grrrl, the musicians, stopped doing interviews, and chapter meetings became closed. This rejection of mainstream media meant that ultimately Riot Grrrl's impact on the greater society was limited and most that remains in the mainstream is appropriation and packaging of Riot Grrrl messages stripped of their greater context.[11]

The media's interest in Riot Grrrl must surely have been, in some part, self-interest. Recapturing the "girl" has synergies with market research in a youth-oriented society. Corporate America was right to believe in Riot Grrrl marketing potential: as a youth-centered subculture, riot grrrls were mostly young (under 25), educated women and girls with access to new technologies[12] that allowed them control over the means of production of their cultural materials.

It was noted as early as 1993 that Riot Grrrl was being co-opted and neutralized as a counterculture for commercial gain.[13] By 1995–96, the death of Riot Grrrl was being proclaimed in the media,[14] but even before that pro-Grrrl media writers lamented that "today, the only traces of Riot Grrrl-dom outside its insular core are cutesy mutations of its once ironic fashions in perky teen magazines."[15] This

---

[11] See Kristen Schilt, "A Little Too Ironic: The Appropriation and Packaging of Riot Grrrl Politics by Mainstream Female Musicians," *Popular Music and Society*, 26/1 (2003), pp. 5–16.

[12] Ednie Kaeh Garrison discusses Riot Grrrl and late capitalism extremely well in "US Feminism-Grrrl Style! Youth (Sub)Cultures and the Technologics of the Third Wave," *Feminist Studies*, 26/1 (2000), pp. 141–70.

[13] Ann Japenga, "Grunge 'R' Us: Exploiting, Co-opting and Neutralizing the Counterculture," *Los Angeles Times Magazine*, 14 November 1993, p. 26.

[14] Schilt, "A Little Too Ironic," p. 9.

[15] Lorraine Ali, "The Grrrls Fight Back: Girl-Rock Tour is Also a Lesson in Self-Defense," *Los Angeles Times*, 27 July 1995, F1.

brief emergence, however, was enough to establish Riot Grrrl as both a cultural force and a media stereotype. Soon young, punkish women with short, often dyed hair, in combat boots, baby-doll clothes, and accessories (or Fluffiana)[16] began turning up in television and movies aimed at the teenage market. These girls were sometimes angry or confrontational, or portrayed as hackers or computer geeks, but their models were clearly drawn from Riot Grrrl.

Every Girl is a Riot Grrrl

Created by the child of a feminist mother, and a student of feminist and gender theory, Joss Whedon's series displays many of the values of 1970s feminism[17] but does so employing a musical and visual language often associated with Riot Grrrl feminism. As a representative text, the series calls upon the symbolic value of associations teens have with music, fashion, and pop culture to situate the main characters as marginalized teens, despite their economic, geographic, and racial association with the majority. Musically, *Buffy* draws from flavors of punk and alternative music by mostly unknown and independent artists. This is in keeping, in part, with *Buffy*'s specific genre precedents: gothic novels, teen horror flicks, superhero comics, martial arts films, and teen-angst comedies. But *Buffy*'s heavy leaning on the hardcore end of alternative music is surely not coincidental: punk and alternative music were strongly associated with the image of Riot Grrrl in the mainstream media.[18]

One striking element in the source music of the series, much of which emanates from the Bronze, is the plethora of female voices contained therein. While the non-source music of the series is often by all-male artists (with some notable exceptions like Sarah McLachlan and Alison Krauss), many of the bands that provide source music—the artists who perform at the Bronze—are fronted by women. The bands encompass diverse styles and genres, from Cibo Matto and Velvet Chain, to Splendid, Aimee Mann, and Michelle Branch: so many female artists in a club is unusual.[19] In "Smashed" (6.9), Willow and her newly de-ratted

---

[16] "Fluffy" girly fashions worn with an ironic stance to recapture and recuperate girlhood through fashion choices and the mixing of "gendered" clothing, like dresses with leather jackets and combat boots. See Kaltefleiter, *Revolution Girl Style Now*.

[17] See Early, "Staking her Claim."

[18] Sadly, the feature film of *Buffy* was too early to display Riot Grrrl musical aesthetics, and had a far more mainstream pop music score. However, Kristy Swanson *does* vanquish her vampire in Riot Grrrl garb: frilly prom dress, white doc martens, and a black leather jacket, which closely ressembles Buffy's outfit in season 1's final confrontation with the Master.

[19] As a female performer in a band I can attest that, in the rock and jazz venues I frequent and perform in, there are never many women in the lineup. This is particularly true of smaller clubs, especially in communities smaller than Los Angeles, like the fictional Sunnydale.

friend Amy make a series of changes at the Bronze, including changing the grungy male band Virgil into the perky female Halo Friendlies in a move which visually encompasses many aims of the Riot Grrrls movement with stunning immediacy.

While female vocalists are certainly a start, Riot Grrrl values would favor bands made up entirely of women, performing songs by women, at venues in which girls are safe and welcomed. These are distinctions, however, often lost in the translation to the wider culture. The fact remains that many bands performing at the Bronze feature female vocalists, and this itself was an early media association with Riot Grrrl, linking artists like Alanis Morissette (who did not play an instrument), or Fiona Apple (who did) with the Riot Grrrl movement in rock.[20] Highlighting performances by bands like Cibo Matto, a multi-racial group fronted by two female musicians, both proficient with music technology and one of whom produces their work, goes far in reinforcing the Riot Grrrl subtext in the source music.

At least one female vocalist also appears, if only briefly, as a character: Veruca's visual presentation, with shaggy hair and tattoos, certainly owes much to Riot Grrrl images.[21] Her wolf growl even references the gutteral "grrrl" of Riot Grrrl. Her band, Shy, has a female bass player, whose stage persona was also in keeping with Riot Grrrl norms (dress and boots), and is perhaps even a sly reference to Hole's popular and outspoken bass player, Melissa Auf Der Mar (although her "playing" is much less convincing).

So many female voices in the source and non-source music creates a diverse "cloud" of women's voices that extends from the music to the narrative, a point I will return to. This cloud of female voices portrays the feminist backdrop of the story convincingly. Buffy is aurally contextualized as part of a (feminist) matrilineage, a status outlined in the voiceover narrative of the opening sequence at the start of the series: "she alone will stand against the vampires."[22]

Less obvious feminist music (and pop culture) references continue in the series in the number of Lilith Fair artist references scattered liberally throughout

---

[20] See Schilt, "A Little Too Ironic," *passim*.

[21] While Nikki Stafford notes in her episode summary that Paige Moss overacts consistently and annoyingly (including her terrible lip-synching), I must wonder if this is in some ways another nod at Riot Grrrl feminism which suffered, like earlier feminist movements, from the perception that feminists were too serious and had no sense of humor. While this is a subtle distinction, the series has evinced such a love of minute and significant detail, it would not be surprising. See Nikki Stafford, *Bite Me! The Unofficial Guide to Buffy the Vampire Slayer* (Toronto, 2007), p. 221.

[22] Buffy is outraged when she discovers that the Slayer was originally created by men who infused the original Slayer with the essence of a demon—there is a clear rape metaphor in the visual sequence in "Get it Done" (7.15). The Slayer's legacy is reclaimed for feminism and girl power when she subverts the male intentions for what a Slayer should be (isolated and exceptional as a woman with power) and decides to "call" all the potential Slayers simultaneously in the final episode [Ed].

the source and non-source music of the series.[23] Be it Sarah McLachlan's "Full of Grace," heard as Buffy leaves town in "Becoming, Part 2" (2.22), K's Choice on stage during "Doppelgangland" (3.16), or the Luscious Jackson video ("Ladyfingers," from *Electric Honey* [1999]) in "Beer Bad" (4.5), those "in the know" will catch these references. This is in keeping with real Riot Grrrl experience: when meetings went underground to avoid the media onslaught, Grrrl meetings became difficult to find. As with many youth subcultures, there is a gate-keeping aspect of Riot Grrrl, its borders policed by the members themselves. Subtle feminist musical references like this perpetuate the "in the know" aesthetic associated with Riot Grrrl.

While no actual Riot Grrrl band appears on the series, the multitude of lesser-known artists approximates the stereotype evinced in the media, which alone is enough to reference the movement to the young audience of the series. The use of music by lesser-known artists in *Buffy* served several purposes. First, it lent a certain "DIY street cred" both for the teens and older viewers who had, by the series's 1997 beginnings, already made the association between youth feminism and punk rock for almost a decade. Use of many little-known artists references the insular world of marginalized teen subcultures, especially punk, which is a music easily produced by alienated youth with little musical training. Because Buffy as a character is already the ultimate "DIY-er" (for example, her exclamation "I have to save the world! Again!" in "Becoming, Part 2" [2.22]), the do-it-yourself flavor of the music is enough to cement the association. To portray Buffy as angry young warrior woman, the musical stereotypes of alternative/punk rock with female singers or musicians surrounding her are enough to situate her with the audience as a kind of Riot Grrrl. In other words, Buffy's place as warrior necessitates that she be situated both as marginalized teen and angry girl—and both are most easily located in the musical margins associated with Riot Grrrl.

Action Girl

The title music, associated strongly with the main character, often looms large in the battle music in action and horror genres.[24] *Buffy*'s title theme by Nerf Herder is introduced with stereotypical horror signifiers, most notably the wolf howl and organ chords which lead in, but the rest is pure rock, with a strong alternative/punk flavor. The pipe organ is interrupted, not by the scream of a damsel in distress, but

---

[23] Lilith Fair, organized by Sarah McLachlan, toured for several years in the late 1990s with dozens of female artists on several stages. This was interpreted by many in the press at the time as further evidence of women's "arrival" as major forces in rock.

[24] See Janet K. Halfyard, "Love, Death, Curses and Reverses (in F minor): Music, Gender, and Identity in *Buffy the Vampire Slayer* and *Angel*," *Slayage* 4 (2001) for a discussion of the theme music. She talks about the relationship between youth subculture and music in the opening paragraphs of this version of her essay.

by the scream of a powerful, distorted electric guitar and rolling drum break. The theme, in typical rock chorus-and-bridge form, borrows heavily from surfer/skater punk. The punk feel is cemented in the final return of the main theme, this time with melody. Thus, the title theme places Buffy musically the way a teenager does: at once associating specific styles of music with various groups or cliques. Here, Buffy is firmly in the indie, or Riot Grrrl, camp, while the surfer elements place her more specifically in California.

But while many action genres incorporate the title music into the fight scenes, here Buffy's title theme never plays as she fights. The title theme, while accompanied in the opening credits with intense fight scenes and images from the series, is only once heard in its original form in the non-source music of the series. Therefore, it cannot be that in the title theme we are being told who Buffy is as a warrior. Instead we are told who she is as a teen. Through the Riot Grrrl association with punk rock, we identify her with an angry girl subculture, useful for defining her character.

So, while Buffy is so often identified with her warrior persona in the media, the fact that this theme is missing from the underscore's fight music of the series is interesting—and not in keeping with that other butt-kicking warrior-woman, Xena.[25] Frequently, Buffy fights with light underscoring, bearing no relation to the title theme, and establishing little musical "character" in the fighting. This is unusual for any action genre but especially here, in that the battle with monsters in the series is so much a part of the metaphorical message of the show, where vampires stand in for a host of adolescent terrors and realities. It is interesting that the fight scenes are not more clearly musically marked as the basis of Buffy's heroism. That they are so often marked with words instead, in the form of Buffy's much-remarked puns and quips, situates the battle along feminist rather than masculinist heroic models.[26] The battle here is as much one of words as of actions, with the ability to frame the struggle one of Buffy's core powers.

The one exception is "Prophecy Girl" (1.12), where the title music does enter the narrative in its original form. It is set up as the underscore music for the climactic battle of the first season which, at the time it was filmed, might have been the last episode of the series. In this episode, Buffy learns of a prophecy foretelling her death in a battle with the Master, an ancient vampire intent on starting the apocalypse. Along with many other episodes in the first season, there are strongly sexual overtones: the white-clad virginal Buffy goes up against the primeval leather-clad evil. At first learning of her impending death (ironically scheduled for Prom night), she tries to quit, then escape. But as the forces of darkness close in on

---

[25] The title theme of *Xena: Warrior Princess* is the theme used during almost every one of Xena's fights.

[26] See Karen Eileen Overbey and Lahney Preston-Matto, "Staking in Tongues: Speech Act as Weapon in *Buffy*," in Rhonda V. Wilcox and David Lavery (eds) *Fighting the Forces: What's at Stake in Buffy the Vampire Slayer* (Lanham, MD, 2002), pp. 73–84 for a discussion on the importance of language in *Buffy*.

her family and friends, she knows she is the only one who can halt the destruction and must face her destiny. She dons her prom gown, grabs a crossbow, and sets out to save the world again, this time hoping to, at best, "take him with me." However, she is defeated: he bites into her neck, she faints; he dumps her face down into the groundwater and rises triumphant from his underground prison. But even in death all is not lost. Xander (with Angel) comes along just in time to revive her with CPR. Buffy, realizing she has at once fulfilled and defied the prophesy, sets out to face the Master once more.

It is in this moment, for the first and last time in the series, that we hear the title theme as underscore music for the action. While we may expect, from the filmic and television precedents, that this climactic battle will feature Buffy fighting to her title theme music, this does not actually happen. The title theme begins during a cut-away scene of the apocalypse underway at the school library, where vampires are attempting to break in, and hell is succeeding in breaking out. As Willow, Giles, and Jenny Calendar struggle valiantly, Cordelia finally screams "somebody help me," which cues the opening guitar distortion "scream" from the title theme. We cut to Buffy, considerably "punked up" by her encounter with the Master, eyes now rimmed black with smudged mascara, in dirty satin dress and shoes, striding purposefully toward the final confrontation. It is perhaps the most potently stereotypic "hero" moment in the entire series.[27]

But then something interesting happens: the theme cuts out, literally at the first punch that is dealt. This abrupt cut is at once startling and unexpected: it is sobering. It also makes it indisputable: the power of Buffy's title theme, in all its driving punk rock glory, plays to signify *her* battle, an internal one—her ascendance to power over herself. It does not glorify her physical prowess. She has faced what is to her the scariest thing in the world and yet has risen to fight again. It is, then, not in Buffy's winning but in losing the initial battle with the Master that we become aware of her internal ascendance to the status of hero, for that internal ascendance happens before the first punch of the final confrontation is thrown. This is precisely the moment when Buffy is most like a riot grrrl —not a moment of external battle, but of internal transformation, for at the heart of Riot Grrrl is not clothes or music or zines but the scream that refuses to be silenced. Buffy is not a made a hero by battle through violence, however justified, but by taking the power to live, to survive, and not allowing her female identity to be compromised in the process.

---

[27] Interestingly this moment is highlighted by Nikki Stafford in her "Nitpicks" for the episode: "Buffy charging toward the library with her theme music playing has got to be the single cheesiest moment on *Buffy* ever" (Stafford, *Bite Me!*, p. 146).

Buffy and Fluffiana

After punk/alternative music, the most obvious signifiers of Riot Grrrl involve fashion and technology-based media. The character of Willow evinces the clearest Riot Grrrl characteristics amongst the main characters of the series.[28] Her status as the computer geek, scholar, and eventually powerful witch means she is often second only to Buffy herself in usefulness in the campaigns against evil. Her association with Wiccan magic[29] and, from season four onward, lesbianism, references earlier 1970s feminist tropes that continued to some extent in the Riot Grrrl movement. Willow becomes, in many ways, the series's poster-child for Third Wave youth feminism, flavored strongly with earlier feminist ideals. Her familiarity with technology is clearly an allusion to Riot Grrrl, particularly her status as hacker, a role strongly linked to Riot Grrrl in the press.[30] This techno-savvy, taken together with her fashion sense, clearly denotes Riot Grrrl. Her fashion choices were marked through much of the series with a penchant toward "cutsey," with accessories like fuzzy flower backpacks and barrettes.

As Willow's character evolved, particularly in the move to college, she moved along these fashion lines to embrace hip alternative fashions but retained a strong girlish streak. Through most of the series she was ambivalent, and sometimes achingly self-aware, of her cutesy fashion sense. She breaks down, for instance, in the episode "The Body" (5.16) over her lack of sensible sweaters to wear in light of Joyce Summer's death.[31] In season 4, when confronted with Veruca's confident, sexy, and in some ways more traditionally punk/Riot Grrrl garb in "Wild at Heart" (4.6) she wonders aloud why Buffy didn't warn her that her shirt "looks like a freaked-out birthday cake." To which a puzzled Buffy responds "I thought that was the point." That Willow's fashion choices lie at the heart of so many jokes—including Cordelia's withering first comment about the "softer side of Sears" in "Welcome to the Hellmouth" (1.1)—tends to forefront her fashion choices as a

---

[28] Jenny Calendar, as a thirty-something computer teacher, also displays Third Wave feminist traits: she is comfortable with technology, especially the internet, which she uses for her own subcultural pursuits amongst the techno-pagans. While she would have been older than most riot grrrls, it would be easy to include her amongst the Riot Grrrl characters of the show, but her association is principally with the "adults" (i.e. Giles) rather than the youth subculture of Buffy and her peers.

[29] For an excellent discussion of the Wiccan relationship to pop culture and *Buffy*, see J. Lawton Winslade, "Teen Witches, Wiccans and 'Wanna-Blessed Be's': Pop-Culture Magic in *Buffy the Vampire Slayer*," *Slayage* 1 (2001).

[30] See Dennis Romero, "A New Force Lurks Amid the Cyber Shadows," *Los Angeles Times*, 1 December 1995, E1, E6.

[31] This is an episode in which many characters reveal their core insecurities. Willow's ambivalence over her personal experience is a powerful feminist moment, in that the first concern she has at Joyce Summer's death is over how to present herself as "serious" and "adult" and realizing she does not associate her clothing with those qualities.

significant key to her character. That she voices insecurities about these choices adds weight to their significance in her mind, and their importance in connecting her to the fluffiana of Riot Grrrl.

Like those of other characters, Willow's fashion trajectory closely follows her character development—an important arc through the series, culminating in the painful ending of season 6. She transforms herself from an overachieving, disempowered, passive teen girl to a strong, complex, and sometimes dark adult. She provides a kind of counterpoint to Buffy's power in the series and pursues many of the traditional paths to personal power encouraged by modern feminism. These include her pursuit of proficiency in academia, embrace of emergent technologies, and exploration of Wiccan magic, associated with modes of female power and knowing popularized in modern feminism. In the series, where societal monsters become real, Willow develops powerful tools through research, technology, and witchcraft, tools applied repeatedly to the conquest of demons and vampires—even gods. If we transpose the character of Willow outward into the "real world" we can easily imagine her applying these tools to smash global capitalism, save the environment, or fight for human rights—in other words, she would be a Riot Grrrl, whether she so identified or not.

Revolutions from Within

Because the monsters in the series operate at the level of metaphor, they are often frighteningly close to the monsters faced by teenaged girls and "called out" in Riot Grrrl music and text.[32] One example, Ted, Buffy's potential stepfather in season 2, is particularly chilling. His wholesome family-values personal style covers a depraved, serial-killing mysoginist. The fact that, as scholars have noted, so many of the adults in the series are unaware of the presence of monsters echoes deeply in Riot Grrrl-documented experience. Many riot grrrls were drawn to concerts, zines, and other Grrrl-events for the opportunity to talk about their personal experiences with domestic violence, incest, rape—often at the hands of adults in their lives. Riot grrrls understand, as do Buffy and her peers, that the police are not equipped or able to protect them from the crimes they most often (and least publicly) face in their own homes and schools. Buffy's reality seems to separate her from her peers (other than the Scoobies) and adults. Susan Owen notes that "she longs for safety and stability—to be like 'other girls'."[33] These are sentiments expressed frequently in zines and personal narratives of girls who became riot grrrls because their experience in facing rape, incest, or violence left them feeling completely alone.

---

[32] Rhonda V. Wilcox, "Who Died and Made Her the Boss?: Patterns of Mortality in *Buffy*," in Wilcox and Lavery (eds) *Fighting the Forces*, pp. 3–18.

[33] Susan, A. Owen, "Vampires, Postmodernity, Postfeminism: *Buffy the Vampire Slayer*," *Journal of Popular Film and Television*, 27/2 (1999), p. 25.

In many ways the narrative itself evinces Riot Grrrl values in that it is girl-centered and complex, and in that it returns so often to themes of power and connectedness. The masculinist model usually serves up heroes who work alone, in effect trading peer relationships, especially intimate ones, for heroic status. The original Riot Grrrl mantra, "girl power", however corrupted by its association with the Spice Girls, reveals power to be at the heart of Grrrl feminism. Buffy's most important struggle, to realize her personal power and remain connected and interdependent, defines riot grrrls. They are, after all, trying to grow up as powerful and connected feminist women in a society that tends to eat its young. Buffy does not always win this struggle, and in the series this failure has also been accompanied by significant source music.

Cibo Matto's performance in "When She Was Bad" (2.1) is a particularly good example of Buffy's power being portrayed musically, this time in the source music for a scene. It is interesting, too, in that it is a scene in which Buffy uses her power for evil, not good. The importance of the performance is highlighted in the episode in several ways that set it apart from other performances in the series. Cibo Matto's appearance is mentioned several times before they are seen on stage, in an important conversation between Buffy, Xander, and Willow early in the episode. We see a huge Cibo Matto banner at the entrance to the Bronze, and the first cut to the interior of the club is a middle-depth angled shot on the lead singer, Miho Hatori. The camera slowly revolves around her, and she functions as the center of gravity in the shot, seeming to hold the camera on her. The camera returns repeatedly to Hatori and Yuko Honda, Cibo Matto's female musicians, highlighting the connection between their femininity, performance, and power.

"Sugar Water" is the second song we hear in the scene, and it opens with Hatori speaking lines over Honda's ethereal keyboard chords to a seemingly rapt (read: silent) audience. Hatori's voice fills the Bronze. This aural and visual image of power sets the stage well for Buffy, whose entrance steps are timed to the band's rhythms just as they shift into the sexy "slow-ride" back beat of the song. As the camera pans up Buffy's body, attired in platform heels and slinky dress, a looped vocal sample of an angelic soprano inserts itself at the front of the mix. Cibo Matto's power has been located in their performance as they dominate the scene at the Bronze, and with this synchronization of her entrance to the beat, this power is extended to Buffy and located at the outset with her body and movement.[34] She then uses the power of her sexuality (and Xander's attraction to her) to hurt everyone. She cruelly announces to Angel that she has "moved on ... to the living," then seduces Xander onto the dance floor (in front of the pining Willow), only to slap him down as well.

The circular movement of the camera gives the viewer the sense of disorientation, as if one is spinning, drowning. As Buffy and Xander move on to the dance floor, the medium shot here shows Buffy and Miho Hatori at the center.

---

[34] See Elyce Rae Helford, "My Emotions Give me Power: The Containment of Girls' Anger in *Buffy*," in Wilcox and Lavery (eds) *Fighting the Forces*, pp. 18–34.

But as the camera revolves around the dance floor, this time we lose Hatori in the shot, and the power-center of the scene shifts to Buffy. The drowning feeling invoked by the camera movement now can be associated with Xander, who is letting himself drown in Buffy.

The song, "Sugar Water," with its references to the voice and images of sensory sweetness, slyly references "sugar and spice" as Buffy uses her sexuality and "sweetness" to seduce Xander. She becomes sugar water, and the image of wetness, combined with the swirling camera work and sensual movements of Buffy and Hatori, heighten the feeling of drowning in female sexual power. The song contains a host of other fantasy references: black cats, riding on a camel, buildings turning into coconut trees little by little, and especially "a woman in the moon … singing to the earth" which directly references mythic images of female power. Buffy leads Xander onto the floor as Hatori sings "a black cat crosses my path." Buffy here is clearly the black cat, with all its implied mystery, beauty, and danger. The references confirm that Xander's fantasy appears to be coming true—but the black cat reference returns, and Buffy coos: "Xander. Did I ever thank you for saving my life? [Xander: No] Don't you wish I would?" Then she turns and leaves.

The playful "La La La" refrain follows Buffy's triumphant exit, as if communicating her girlish delight in this new-found power. Just as earlier in the episode, when Alison Krauss's song "It Doesn't Matter" aurally represented Buffy's inner turmoil and depression, Cibo Matto steps up to aurally embody her flirtation with the abuse of power. "Sugar Water" is perfect in this scene as it provides powerful female performers, slow-grind grooves and, with its lyrics, populates the landscape of the scene with female-associated metaphors and meaning.

This episode is also exemplary, with regard to Riot Grrrl aesthetics, in its narrative arc. Having to negotiate with her demons—or, as Xander says as he watches Buffy's climactic fight, "[work] out her issues"—to remain connected to herself and her family of choice while remaining powerful is a good example of Riot Grrrl values in the popular media. The series has a complex outlook on morality, often seeing many shades of gray, understanding that teen girls face complex realities and have few truly safe places to inhabit. This complex reality extends to the webs of oppression that riot grrrls see oppressing them and many other communities. Riot Grrrl, as a loose affiliation of grrrls, never fell into the earlier feminist trap of working on feminist issues to the exclusion of race, sexuality, size, age, economic deprivation, and so on. Buffy is constructed as one of the few heroes who must stay open to complexity, accounting for shifting alliances, realities, and emotional ties.

The relationship of the *Buffy* series to Riot Grrrl feminism is complicated by a media perception of Riot Grrrl that is not always in keeping with the lived experience of actual riot grrrls. Any discussion of Riot Grrrl aesthetics must take into account both what Riot Grrrl actually is and what Riot Grrrl has been said to be in the media, as both might be at play in varying degrees. This is particularly true for Joss Whedon and the writers of *Buffy*, who might not have had access to actual riot grrrls or zines and only had the mainstream media as a source of information.

While it is reasonable from his own statements to expect that Whedon's series would evince 1970s feminist values but deploy Third Wave feminist (Riot Grrrl) signifiers to keep the characters less anachronistic, what is surprising is how close the series often is to lived (and documented) Riot Grrrl experience. The plethora of female voices in the source and non-source music, and the centrality of music and musical performance to the emotional life of the central characters, owes much to Riot Grrrl rock, where performers tried to mirror girls' experience and empower them musically.

Buffy's control of the narrative—and the girl-centeredness of the series—is in keeping with the Riot Grrrl zines, meetings, and web sites that provided a place for girls to control their own narrative. The strong distinction between metaphorical violence (against vampires and demons), and actual violence (physical or emotional) in the series means that issues like rape, domestic violence—even the pain of a guy turning into someone else after sex—keeps the narrative real to lived grrrl experience. Her emotional connectedness means that while Buffy's power as girl and hero may be captured in her strong punk theme music you will not catch her fighting accompanied by the strains of electric guitar. Her real battles are internal, and thus music is central in the series to telling that internal story. The plethora of female voices that hover like clouds in the music of the series evinces the strong connection between girl liberation and music.

This is not to say that there are not glaring areas in which the series is not true to Riot Grrrl feminism. The show reinforces dominant cultural notions about the centrality of being white, thin, middle-class, eurocentric, and educated in television narratives, and this is certainly not in keeping with Riot Grrrl values.[35] We never get to see Bikini Kill, or L7 or Tribe-8 at the Bronze—a move that would certainly have caused a stir in Sunnydale. In the series we might get a character who is Wiccan, lesbian, techno-savvy, and Jewish, but she's still white, thin, and attractive. These departures are unfortunate, as they detract from what the show is able to accurately portray: while girl power may be a wonderful and laudable concept, it is not so easy in practice. It is too easy to shut down, disconnect, and lose the enormous power of interdependence. In this regard Buffy captures the struggle of all grrrls: to grow up a strong, centered woman in a dangerous world that is often out to get you. Like riot grrrls everywhere, the creators of *Buffy* know too that this struggle is helped along considerably by some really great tunes.

---

[35] There are many articles that deal with these aspects, including: Dominic Alessio, "'Things are Different Now'?: A Postcolonial Analysis of *Buffy the Vampire Slayer*," *The European Legacy*, 6/6 (2001), pp. 731–40; Anne Millard Daugherty, "Just a Girl: Buffy as Icon," in Roz Kaveney (ed.), *Reading the Vampire Slayer: An Unofficial Critical Companion to Buffy and Angel* (London/New York, 2002), pp. 148–65; Lynne Edwards, "Slaying in Black and White: Kendra as Tragic Mulatta in *Buffy*," in Wilcox and Lavery (eds) *Fighting the Forces*, pp. 85–97.

Chapter 10
Punks, Geeks, and Goths:
Buffy the Vampire Slayer as a Study of Popular Music Demographics on American Commercial Television

Kathryn Hill

Joss Whedon, creator of the cult television series *Buffy the Vampire Slayer* (1997–2003), describes his show as "a pop culture blender" the aim of which is to "talk about everything."[1] As journalist Annalee Newitz notes: "*Buffy*'s strength has been the show's ability to reflect the obsessions of pop culture around it."[2] Every episode of *Buffy* abounds with pop culture references. As a result this tale of life on the Hellmouth, a metaphor for the volatile teenage years, is a reflection of more social issues than the show itself could hope to address formally: alcohol and drug abuse, gang violence, homework and SATs, peer pressures, self-esteem and sexual double-standards.

The use of pre-existing popular music is an integral part of the story process and acts as a commentary on many such social issues. As Shumway notes, "such commentary is one of the major ways popular songs have been used" ever since Mike Nichols opened *The Graduate* (1967) to Simon and Garfunkel's "The Sound of Silence."[3] What is perhaps unique about *Buffy* is that this popular music is mainly of the alternative/independent variety and plays an important role in establishing the show's sense of alternative/independent credibility. To quote S. Renee Dechert: "[the] music works to reinforce the communal identity between the program, *Buffy*, and its fans, all of whom exist on the fringe of mainstream

---

[1] Edward Gross, *Vampires and Slayers: Interviews with Joss Whedon*, pdf edition 1 (2004), p. 41, accessed 19 January 2004 at http://www.vampiresandslayers.com (no longer available).

[2] Annalee Newitz, "Buffy Rides Again: Why Originality Gets you Nowhere on TV," *San Francisco Bay Guardian Online*, 6 August 2002, accessed 6 August 2003 at http://www.sfbg.com/36/22/art_buffy.html.

[3] David R. Shumway, "Rock'n'Roll Sound Tracks and the Production of Nostalgia," *Cinema Journal*, 38/2 (1999), p. 37.

network television."⁴ If fringe is to be understood as the opposite of mainstream and mainstream equates to commercial availability, then the alternative/independent music played on *Buffy* could not be more fringe. At the time of airing, it was not easy to find out what bands were featured on the show: no information was offered from the official *Buffy* webpages at the Warner Bros. Network (WB) or United Paramount Network (UPN). Fans were best served by Leslie Remencus's fansite *The Buffy and Angel Music Pages*, which was online from August 1997 to October 2003 but is no longer available.⁵ As Dechert notes:

> In doing this, the clear message is that *Buffy*, unlike other WB shows, is an independent program, with the same ethos as an independent record label, more interested in art than advertising. Unlike, say *Dawson's Creek*, *Buffy* is not selling out. It suggests that *Buffy* viewers are smarter than the "*Creek*ers," people who must be told what they have just seen in an overt promotional strategy.⁶

Simon Frith asserts that rock music "rests on an ideology of the *peer group* ... [It is] about difference and what distinguishes us from people with other tastes."⁷ This type of approach can be used to assess the meaning of the alternative/independent soundtrack to *Buffy*.

In terms of the market domination of American television by the four big networks, Fox Television, NBC, CBS, and ABC, a certain fringe mentality also defines *Buffy*'s two homes on network television, the fledgling WB (1997–2001) and UPN (2001–2003). As Whedon once remarked, "believe me, the WB is a tiny, tiny microphone,"⁸ but this small network also presented him with a unique opportunity:

> Part of my extraordinary luck was to get into American television during this one bubble, where it was expanding ... The little networks were coming up and they needed an identity and there was room for a guy like me to step in and do what he wanted. That started the year I started *Buffy*.⁹

---

⁴ S. Renee Dechert, "'My Boyfriend's in the Band!' *Buffy* and the Rhetoric of Music," in Rhonda V. Wilcox and David Lavery (eds) *Fighting the Forces: What's at Stake in Buffy the Vampire Slayer* (Lanham, MD, 2002), p. 219.

⁵ Other fan sites such as *Buffyworld* (www.buffyworld.com) and *Buffy vs Angel* (www.buffy-vs-angel.com) continue to offer episode guides to the music of the shows.

⁶ Dechert, "My Boyfriend's in the Band!", p. 224.

⁷ Simon Frith, "Making Sense of Video," *Music for Pleasure: Essays in the Sociology of Pop* (Canbridge, 1988), p. 213.

⁸ Joss Whedon, "Buffy the Vampire Slayer: Television with a Bite," *Buffy the Vampire Slayer Season Six DVD Collection* (Twentieth Century Fox, 2003).

⁹ James Dyer, "Joss Whedon—About Buffy/Serenity/Wonder Woman," *Empire Online*, 26 October 2005, reproduced at *Dollhouse, Firefly & Serenity, Angel, Buffy: news,*

By 1997, the WB was actively pursuing "new programming that went after young white viewers."¹⁰ With *Buffy*, the WB aimed to reach the 18–35 demographic. It is no coincidence that the soundtrack for *Buffy* reflects the musical tastes of an important subgroup within this target demographic. People who listen to alternative/independent music, the play-list of American college radio, tend to be young, white, college-educated, and middle-class.

In addition to using alternative/independent music to symbolize a recent vibrant youth culture, *Buffy*'s soundtrack represents this target demographic in its references to various, mainly American, white music subgenres: "geek" music of the post-slackers, female empowerment of the Riot Grrrls and Girl Power music, Goth and heavy metal subcultures, white appropriation of black genres such as rap and hip-hop, are all explored.¹¹ This chapter discusses the ways popular music is used in *Buffy* to reflect a postmodern image of society, that is the social values of its target demographic—young, middle-class America—as portrayed by WB and UPN. This will raise contradictory issues. Whedon saw *Buffy* as a text in which "many things feed into art which are beyond the artist's conscious control—not only his personal unconscious ... but the cultural assumptions of his society."¹² The following therefore raises questions as to whether the popular music referenced in this program, of a type known for "skewering [sic] TV viewer expectations,"¹³ provides a reflection or critique of those values.

An Alternative Youth Culture: "As far as I know there's very little Celine Dion and *Buffy* fan overlap"

In an online interview for the BBC, executive story editor for *Buffy*, Doug Petrie, remarked "as far as I know there's very little Celine Dion and *Buffy* fan overlap. That Venn diagram just doesn't intersect."¹⁴ Fans of *Buffy* know this Celine Dion

---

photos, videos, interviews and more..., accessed 25 August 2008 at http://www.whedon.info/Joss-Whedon-About-Buffy-Serenity.html.

¹⁰ James Poniewozik, "How the 'Buffy' Coup Could Change TV," *Time*, 23 April 2001, accessed 16 June 2006 at http://www.time.com/time/columnist/poniewozik/article/0,9565,107337,00.html.

¹¹ The aesthetics of Riot Grrrl culture and music are the focus of Renée Coulombe's chapter in this volume and so are not explicitly discussed here.

¹² Robin Wood, "The Incoherent Text: Narrative in the 70s," in *Hollywood from Vietnam to Reagan... And Beyond* (New York, 2003), p. 42.

¹³ Victor D. Infante, "She Saved the World a Lot," *Orange County Weekly*, 22 May 2003, accessed 28 August 2008 at http://www.ocweekly.com/culture/tv/she-saved-the-world-a-lot/16019/.

¹⁴ Rob Francis, "BBC – Cult – Buffy – Doug Petrie, Buffy producer's guide to season four – Living Conditions" (2001), *BBC*, accessed 5 April 2006 at http://www.bbc.co.uk/cult/buffy/interviews/doug/index.shtml.

reference concerns the musical tastes of Buffy's college roommate at the start of season 4, Kathy Newman. Kathy is the roommate from hell and it comes as no surprise to Buffy when she turns out to be a demon. As Dechert points out, who else but a demon would exhibit such an appalling lack of taste:

> We know instantly, as she hangs up her Celine Dion poster while perkily predicting the year will be "Superfun!" that this is not a typical coed. And our worst fears are confirmed ... when Kathy plays Cher's "Do You Believe in Love" [sic.] repeatedly. Who but a monster could endure that? As Willow moves into Buffy's room ... she brings with her a poster for the much cooler Dingoes Ate My Baby. The Dingoes may be unknown, but they sure beat a battery of primped and padded VH1 divas.[15]

That Kathy is a demon is an in-joke for *Buffy* fans.[16] Her tastes in pop music represent those of the more conservative mainstream audience to whom *Buffy* was not primarily expected or intended to appeal. In contrast, Willow's identification with the fictitious independent band Dingoes Ate My Baby, whose music is supplied by Los Angeles band Four Star Mary, shows that her musical tastes run to the quirkier, perhaps more discerning alternative and independent edges of popular music, a taste implicitly shared by both the producers and the fans of the show.

The first wave of independent music labels started in the late 1970s and early 1980s. Labels such as Epitaph, SST, and Twin/Tone were proactive in documenting the sudden upsurge in do-it-yourself punk-rock bands with strong regional followings. During his college days Whedon's own musical taste included the punk/pop of two Minneapolis bands, the Replacements (released on Twin/Tone) and Hüsker Dü (SST).[17] It is likely the soundtrack to Whedon's college days provided the inspiration for *Buffy*'s resident Sunnydale indie bands such as Four Star Mary, Splendid, Sprung Monkey, and Velvet Chain. As Leslie Remencus comments: "I think of the indie music as a character on *Buffy*. The music adds another dimension of the show that reinforces Joss Whedon's dark, irreverent humor and edgy dialogue. The music, like the show, is independent, stylish, and eclectic."[18]

---

[15] Dechert, "My Boyfriend's in the Band!", p. 221.

[16] The use of songs by Celine Dion or Cher by *Buffy* vidders (fans that edit clips from TV shows to make their own music videos) suggests audience reception may be more varied than that imagined by the show's producers. See the chapter by Rob Cover in this volume. [Ed.]

[17] For Whedon's comments concerning the Replacements and Hüsker Dü see online posting "joss says" (3 December 1998) *The Bronze VIP Posting Board Archives*, accessed 5 July 2003 at http://www.cise.ufl.edu/cgi-bin/cgiwrap/hsiao/buffy/get-archive?date=19981203.

[18] Leslie Remencus, "Re: buffy lyrics," email to the author, 22 April 2003.

Compared to the target audience for mainstream programming, *Buffy*'s fan base was comparatively small but the academic interest it inspired shows this fan base can also be intelligent. Jeanine Basinger, chairwoman of the film department at Wesleyan College where she taught Whedon as an undergraduate, notes that "if you have a small, loyal audience of a high level of intelligence across age groups, you have a cult hit, and that influences the culture."[19] The popular music used on *Buffy* occupies a similar position. Many of the independent artists such as Aberdeen, Azure Ray, the Breeders, Brian Jonestown Massacre, Jonatha Brooke, Lori Carson, Cibo Matto, the Devics, Fonda, Lotion, Man of the Year, Aimee Mann, Splendid, Sprung Monkey, that dog, or Yo La Tengo, may receive critical praise but tend to miss out on the large-scale public success of mainstream performers such as Cher or Celine Dion. However, like the show they are happy to cater for their own small, loyal fan bases.

Buffy's music supervisor, John C. King, used a wide range of sources for popular music but made the effort to find independent artists for the show. From the outset, *Buffy*'s producers let it be known they wanted to use indie artists and were encouraging submissions. Rob Grad of Superfine, whose song "Already Met You" featured in the first-season episode "Teacher's Pet" (1.4), as well as the 1999 soundtrack album,[20] offers this insight into his personal involvement with *Buffy*:

> In 1996 and 1997 I was renting a room in the house of a music attorney in Los Angeles ... She came home one day saying she had heard that a new show was looking for indie bands and wanted to submit us ... Superfine had released a 7" vinyl single on a label called Fish of Death Records and so she sent it to John King for us.[21]

In addition, King would scout the local talent in and around Hollywood and Los Angeles. According to King one of the most memorable bands to perform live on *Buffy*, the Devics, were discovered this way.[22] The dark bluesy sound of the Devics's song "Key", from their album *If You Forget Me*, rereleased on their own private label Splinter in 2004, provides the perfect soundtrack for serial killers in love, Spike and Drusilla, as they dance together at the Bronze in "Crush" (5.14). David Klotz of local Los Angeles independent band Fonda—whose songs are heard in two episodes "Where the Wild Things Are" (4.18) and "All the Way" (6.6)—offers another typical tale: "Fonda got used in the show 'cause I was a friend of John's.

---

[19] In Lisa Rosen, "R.I.P. Buffy: You Drove a Stake through Convention," *Los Angeles Times*, 20 May 2003, accessed 17 August 2008 at http://articles.latimes.com/2003/may/20/entertainment/et-rosen20.

[20] *Buffy the Vampire Slayer: The Album* was released in October 1999 by TVT Records.

[21] Rob Grad, "Re: Buffy and indie music," email to the author, 14 October 2003.

[22] John C. King, "Hello Razorbacks, John King here, welcoming you to Radio Sunnydale!" *Buffy the Vampire Slayer: Radio Sunnydale* (Virgin, 2003), CD notes.

John came to see Fonda play live with one of the guys from Four Star Mary a long time ago and I kept in touch with him." According to Klotz, "John King had really good sense of finding cool, new bands ... but he also knew what Joss would like too."[23] Knowing what Whedon wanted, other personnel associated with *Buffy* also scouted local indie talent. According to Lisa Black, guitarist for Bellylove, Marti Noxon recommended them to Whedon, which led to this female duo performing their song "Back to Freedom" live at the Bronze in "Anne" (4.1).[24] The melancholic sound of this song—from Bellylove's eponymously named first album released on their own label Badboykitty—conveys the worry Buffy's friends, Willow and Xander, feel when Buffy runs away from home. Colleen Duffy's song "Faith in Love"—from 2003 album *Queen of Pain*, released by Duffy on her own label Lucky Bluebird—plays while Harmony cajoles Spike into bed in "The Harsh Light of Day" (4.3). Duffy, who performs solo as Devil Doll, was recommended to King by her personal friend, independent music fan and actor on *Buffy* Seth Green.[25]

On one level, using local Los Angeles artists was a financial consideration. As King states: "We established early on, because we were a nobody show and we were usually denied [music] licences, that we would go to the local music scene and use unsigned artists."[26] Despite the benefit of such financial considerations Whedon's decision to use independent artists was also ideological. Rob Grad makes some interesting observations on this issue: "I remember when we first got approached ... they told us that they were going to use new bands as an integral part of the show. It was part of how they were going to sell the show. Pretty forward thinking at the time, actually."[27] King comments further on Whedon's independent musical tastes and ideals in his sleeve notes to *Radio Sunnydale*, the CD album released shortly after the series's conclusion:

> I think it's important to point out that one of the most notable "musical" attributes of *Buffy the Vampire Slayer* was Joss Whedon's willingness to allow independent and/or unsigned artists to have their music heard and performed in an area where they would not otherwise have had a chance. *Buffy* found a way to give the independent artists a fair shot and it seems that the viewers themselves found it refreshing to discover independent artists they had never heard of before, and were moved enough by the music to investigate those artists further. It was good for the show and great for the artists.[28]

---

[23] David Klotz, "Re: music on Buffy," email to the author, 22 October 2003. Klotz was *Buffy*'s music editor in season 7 and has worked extensively as a music editor for television since then, including working again with Whedon on *Firefly*.

[24] Lisa Black, "Re: buffy music for book," email to the author, 11 October 2003.

[25] Duffy, "Re: buffy music for book," email to the author, 23 October 2003.

[26] Joanne Ostrow, "WB Shows an Entrée for Unsung Musicians," *Denver Post*, 18 August 2000, H2.

[27] Grad, "Re: Buffy and indie music."

[28] King, "Hello Razorbacks."

Despite such noble intentions, complicated distribution deals and company mergers make it increasingly difficult to discern true independent labels. Many examples can be found in relation to alternative music used on *Buffy*, such as former Pixie Kim Deal's bluesy Riot Grrrl-inspired band, the Breeders. Signed to the independent label 4AD, the Breeders recorded their own live grunge version of the *Buffy* theme for the single *Son of Three* (2002). According to King, Deal then rang and asked if they could appear on *Buffy*, an event that took him by surprise: "I stuttered for a moment ... trying to get over the fact I was actually talking to 'the' Kim Deal, à la The Pixies."[29] As a result the Breeders appear live in the episode "Him" (7.4) performing two songs from their 2002 album *Title TK*, with their version of the *Buffy* theme subsequently featuring on *Radio Sunnydale*.

However, the independence of the labels associated with *Buffy*'s music is not always as clear cut as it might first appear. 4AD is still an independent label but is distributed by the record label Reprise, which is in turn owned by Warner Brothers. As Holly Kruse notes:

> you may choose to buy the latest record by the Breeders instead of Color Me Badd's platinum album—but both CDs are put out by Warner ... Defining yourself in opposition to mainstream music merely means that Warner can sell you the Throwing Muses instead of Madonna.[30]

Bands such as Aberdeen, the Breeders, Cibo Matto, and Sprung Monkey may have the alternative credibility *Buffy*'s producers were looking for, but these acts also have licensing arrangements with the WB television network's parent company, Warner Bros. Such licensing may have been an important factor in keeping down production costs when selecting artists to performed live on the show—perfectly understandable considering *Buffy* and the network's limited budget.

The use of local independent bands on *Buffy* creates a distinct Californian sound. As John Aberdeen notes, Whedon and King favor "jangly guitars, girl singers, nice melodies,"[31] a post-grunge sound evoking sunny Californian pop but without the Britpop influence and with just a hint of the best American alternative music. A good example is defunct Los Angeles-based indie-pop quartet, that dog, whose song "Never Say Never" from their 1997 album *Retreat from Sun* is heard as Buffy dances at a fraternity party in "The Initiative" (4.7). The term "pop" describes this indie scene's emphasis on melody and strong song structure, which nevertheless strives to avoid any association with Top 40 pop or the dark grunge sound that, alongside industrial/nü-metal rap, is released as alternative music by the major labels.

---

[29] King, "Hello Razorbacks."

[30] Holly Kruse, "Subcultural Identity in Alternative Music Culture," *Popular Music*, 12/1 (1993), p. 34.

[31] John Aberdeen, "aberdeen in the buff," email to the author, 13 October 2003.

Californian indie-pop and related genres associated with independent music are often used in *Buffy* to convey the vibrancy and individualism of a confident youth culture. For example, Australian band Splendid's live performances at the Bronze of their quirky "twee pop" Belle and Sebastian-like songs "Charge" in "I Only Have Eyes For You" (2.19) and "You and Me" in "The Freshman" (4.1) create an appropriate atmosphere for a melancholy Buffy.[32] Equally unique are songs by quirky Santa Barbara punk-pop band, Nerf Herder, featured in the episodes "Who Are You?" (4.16) and "Empty Places" (7.19). Nerf Herder, the band who wrote the *Buffy* title theme, are released on San Francisco independent label Honest Don's, a label known for fast post-Ramones punk with an emphasis on comedic popular culture references.

As well as Nerf Herder, Honest Don's catalogue includes former riot grrrl Kim Shattuck's the Muffs,[33] also heard in the *Buffy* episode "The Freshman." Whedon's own taste in Riot Grrrl, a taste acknowledged by *Buffy*'s creator on many occasions—"lots of earthy girl-rock, because I'm me"[34]—is well represented. For example, the raucous garage rock of California pop-punk band, Third Grade Teacher, complete with female screams, provides the perfect soundtrack for high-jinks as college students throw toilet paper into the trees in the Halloween episode "Fear Itself" (4.4). This band is released on California-based label Pinch Hit Records, an independent label known for its discerning mix of original music in many genres including the Californian indie sound. Similarly the track "How She Died" by Canadian alternative pop band Treble Charger, used in the episode "Halloween" (2.6), conveys a positive pop-punk feel as it accompanies Willow's awakening of self-confidence. This track is prominent as, in the leather miniskirt Buffy picked out for her, an unusually sexy Willow walks across the street in front Oz's van. Oz, symbol of indie coolness on *Buffy*, is instantly enchanted: "Who IS that girl?" he asks.

The infamous independent band Brian Jonestown Massacre, a band known for its references to the psychedelic rhythm and blues of the Rolling Stones, is heard at the start of the third-season episode "Faith, Hope and Trick" (3.3). Apart from one album release on TVT, Brian Jonestown Massacre is released on the California-based indie label Bomp.[35] The instrumental electric 12-string guitar

---

[32] Angie Hart of Splendid subsequently co-wrote the song "Blue" with Whedon, which she performs live at the start of "Conversations with Dead People" (7.7), while her ex-husband, and also Splendid band-member, Jesse Tobias helped Christophe Beck arrange Whedon's songs for the musical episode "Once More with Feeling" (6.7).

[33] A Muffs poster can be seen inside Oz's van in "Graduation Day, Part 2" (3.22) as the students pack the explosives Buffy will subsequently use to destroy the mayor and Sunnydale High.

[34] Mike Russell, "The CulturePulp Q&A with Joss Whedon," *CulturePulp: Writings and Comics by Mike Russell*, 25 September 2005, accessed 14 December 2005 at http://homepage.mac.com/merussell/iblog/B835531044/C1592678312/E20050916182427/.

[35] Bomp's catalogue features an eclectic mix of genres from British invasion to college, female vocal, hardcore, indie, metal, new wave, powerpop, and psychedelia.

sound opening of their song "Going to Hell" evokes emotional reminiscences of the liberated 1960s, specifically the Rickenbacker sound associated with the Byrds and the Beatles. Its use in "Faith, Hope and Trick" therefore provides the perfect soundtrack for the Scoobies' first day as high school seniors:

> Willow: I'm giddy
> Oz: Oh, I like you giddy. Always have.
> Willow: It's the freedom! As Seniors, we can go off-campus now for lunch. It's no longer cutting. It's legal! Heck, it's expected! Wow, it's, uh, also a big step forward, a Senior moment, one that has to be savored.

In *Buffy* there are many references to earlier genres of alternative music, from Spike's preference for the Ramones in "Into the Woods" (5.10)[36] and Sid Vicious in "Lover's Walk" (3.8) to Giles's taste for 1960s counterculture icons: witness his acoustic renditions of The Who's "Behind Blue Eyes" in the episode "Where the Wild Things Are" (4.18) and Lynyrd Skynyrd's "Free Bird" in "Yoko Factor" (4.20); his listening to David Bowie's "Memory of a Free Concert" in "The Freshman," or "Tales of Brave Ulysses" by Cream in both "Band Candy" (3.6) and "The Body" (5.16); or his joke about being a founding member of Pink Floyd in "Hush" (4.10). There are also generational links that can be identified. Spike's favorite 1970s punk bands were the inspiration for the 1980s alternative punk scene in America that provided the soundtrack to Whedon's own college days. In "The Harsh Light of Day" (4.3) *Buffy*'s rock connoisseurs, Giles and Oz, jointly acknowledge the seminal influence upon contemporary alternative music of the Velvet Underground:

> Oz: Okay, I'm either borrowing all your albums or I'm moving in.
> Giles: Oz, there are more important things than records right now.
> [Oz holds up the album "Loaded" by the Velvet Underground.]
> Giles: Yes, well, I suppose an argument could be made…

From Oz's appreciation of the Velvet Underground and Radiohead in "New Moon Rising" (4.19), to Willow and Tara's identification with the Indigo Girls in "Conversations with Dead People" (7.7), an important subtext in *Buffy* is how alternative music defines the non-conformism and individualities of the central characters.

---

[36] A poster of the album *Acid Eaters* (released December 1993), perhaps significantly The Ramones' cover album of garage and psychedelic rock classics from the 1960s, can be seen in various second- and third-season episodes (for example, in "I Only Have Eyes For You" (2.19) in the school hall it is seen on its side as Buffy says to Xander "Something weird is going on." Xander: "Isn't that our school motto?").

Losers, Geek-Rock and Scruffy Nerf Herders

A cornerstone of *Buffy* is its self-deprecating "geek" humor, a humor laced with witty pop culture references. When Buffy loses her strength in "Helpless" (3.12) Xander, referencing *Superman*, observes: "Maybe we're on the wrong track with the spells, curses and whammies. Maybe what we should be looking for is something like Slayer kryptonite." Similarly in "Two to Go" (6.21) Andrew says "we've got seconds before Darth Rosenberg grinds us all into Jawa-burgers and not one of you has the midichlorians to stop her," alluding to *Star Wars*. Xander and Andrew are geeks or nerds. To appreciate such "geeky" popular culture references on *Buffy* implies one is in possession of an inverted form of hip or coolness. Lynne Edwards notes that *Buffy* is "getting into an area of cool nerdiness, and I think kids who didn't necessarily see themselves in television programming are starting to see themselves in [this] show."[37] When it comes to the general public's awareness of colloquial teen-speak and its associated geek factor, as Adams notes, perhaps no other recent source has been more influential than *Buffy the Vampire Slayer*.[38]

The idea of the geek in popular culture is inextricably linked to an important theme explored on *Buffy*, namely the roles open to young white males in contemporary society. As Lorna Jowett notes, in *Buffy* "masculinity remains binary: either old, macho and monstrous, or new, weak and 'feminized' ... Masculinity is in crisis because it cannot transform or grow up."[39] In 1992, Everett True, journalist for the British rock paper *Melody Maker*, asked Thurston Moore of New York band Sonic Youth: "Do you think men can be revolutionary in rock music any more?" to which Moore jokingly replied "if they wear pyjamas."[40] In other words, in the era of grunge, young males can only make an anarchic statement within rock music if, like Kurt Cobain, they explore alternative forms of expression that sidestep or send up the clichés of male patriarchy.[41] Denied the traditional masculine

---

[37] Lynne Edwards, quoted in Andy Walton, "Bye-bye, Buffy: Cult Hit Rides into its Last Sunset," *CNN.com*, 19 May 2003, accessed 14 July 2003 at http://www.cnn.com/2003/SHOWBIZ/TV/05/19/buffy.finale/.

[38] Michael Adams, *Slayer Slang: A Buffy the Vampire Slayer Lexicon* (Oxford/New York, 2003), p. 30.

[39] Lorna Jowett, "Masculinity, Monstrosity and Behaviour Modification in Buffy the Vampire Slayer," *Foundations*, 84 (2002), p. 71.

[40] Everett True, *Live Through This: American Rock Music in the Nineties* (London, 2001), p. 223.

[41] For academic literature on the feminization of rock music see Matthew Bannister, *White Boys, White Noise: Masculinities and 1980s Indie Guitar Rock* (Aldershot, 2006); Jeremy Gilbert, "White Light/White Heat: *Jouissance* beyond Gender in the Velvet Underground," in Andrew Blake (ed.) *Living Through Pop* (London/New York, 1999), pp. 31–48; Tony Grajeda, "The 'Feminization' of Rock," in Roger Beebe, Denise Fulbrook, and Ben Saunders (eds), *Rock Over the Edge: Transformations in Popular Music Culture* (Durham, NC, 2002), pp. 233–54; Fred Pfeil, *White Guys: Studies in Postmodern*

narratives previously associated with rock'n'roll—for example, the archetype of lone bluesman or working-class hero—punk-pop bands find inspiration in their youth, celebrating their own immaturity with the same pop culture references and nerdy wordplays that are the cornerstones of *Buffy*'s celebration of geeky male adolescence.[42]

When it comes to ironic references to geek culture in the current music scene the perfect fit for *Buffy* is local Californian band Nerf Herder. Nerf Herder play fast punk pop, also called "skatepunk," in the style of blink 182, Greenday and Weezer, characterized by short tracks that combine "power-pop melodies and chord changes with speedy punk tempos and loud guitars."[43] Featuring their own distinct blend of punk and humorous pop culture references, perhaps the term geek-rock would be more appropriate for Nerf Herder: certainly, Alyson Hannigan, understanding the geek quality to the story line, knew they could supply the perfect theme song, and she therefore directed Whedon to them. As Whedon describes events:

> We had a composer do a credit sequence for us, a song rather, it didn't really work out and so we went to a few unknown rock bands to see what they could come up with. Alyson Hannigan turned me on to Nerf Herder and … they won the prize. They did a great job.[44]

Nerf Herder's theme for *Buffy* is a defiantly up-tempo punk-pop tune and, like *Buffy*, their songs are generally "littered with more pop-culture references than a Quentin Tarantino flick."[45] Even their name is a geeky in-joke, coming from a line in *The Empire Strikes Back* (1981).

As the first band to be heard (if not seen) on *Buffy*, it is fitting that, with the final apocalypse approaching, Nerf Herder are the last band to play live at the Bronze in the episode "Empty Places" (7.19). That circularity is obliquely noted by Kennedy and Dawn on the dance floor: Kennedy asks "So what kind of band plays during

---

Domination and Difference (Cambridge, MA, 1995); Simon Reynolds and Joy Press, *The Sex Revolts: Gender, Rebellion and Rock'n'Roll* (London, 1995).

[42] While the use of punk-pop styles of music on *Buffy* reinforces a celebration of adolescent immaturity, it can apply to the geek girls as much as the boys. One thinks of the Riot Grrrl/skatepunk band, the Halo Friendlies, accompanying Willow's slide into irresponsible "dark magics" in "Smashed" (6.9), or Willow drowning her sorrows following her break-up with Oz to blink 182's "All the small things" in "Something Blue" (4.9).

[43] "Genre: Punk-Pop," *All Music Guide*, n.d., accessed 16 November 2006 at http://www.allmusic.com/cg/amg.dll?p=amg&sql=77:2928.

[44] Joss Whedon, "Welcome to the Hellmouth" audio commentary, *Buffy the Vampire Slayer: Season One, Collector's Edition* (Twentieth Century Fox Home Entertainment, 1997).

[45] Julio Diaz, "Nerf Herder: *How to Meet Girls*," [Album review], *Ink19* (2000), accessed 6 January 2003 at http://www.ink19.com/issues_F/00_04/wet_ink/music_no/nerf_herder.shtml. See also Janet K. Halfyard's chapter in this volume for a discussion of the intertextual references in the theme tune.

an apocalypse?" Dawn replies "I think this band might actually be one of the signs." It is also appropriate that on a program that questions traditional patriarchal roles, and also celebrates popular geek culture, the song Nerf Herder play here is "Mr Spock." In the Buffyverse, traditional heroic male behavior—represented by Captain Kirk's no-nonsense use of macho physical force—has been usurped by a female superhero, with the insipid name "Buffy." What heroic roles are left for a red-blooded male, or geek for that matter? Nerf Herder do not see Mr Spock's cold green-blooded logic as a valid alternative: "You don't want a boyfriend, what you want is Mr Spock/... You want something better than me."

The above has shown how alternative and geek musical subgenres are used in *Buffy* to reflect the alternative identity of its audience demographic. The following will now turn to those music subgenres with much less positive social associations.

Goths and Vampires

The 1999 *Buffy the Vampire Slayer* soundtrack album included popular music featured in the first three years of *Buffy*, including Los Angeles band Velvet Chain's haunting melody "Strong," performed by them in the episode "Never Kill a Boy on the First Date" (1.5). The featured lyrics include the lines "You're so strong ... you would starve for me ... suffer for me." In an interview for this album, lead singer Erika Amato had this to say about the music featured on *Buffy*:

> I think the Buffy sound can be described as dark, yet melodic. I think all the bands they've used on the show share a certain dark quality combined with pop sensibility, whether it be a harder-edged sound like Nerf Herder or something odd and eclectic like Cibo Matto. The sound really complements the writing tone, which combines a rather dark subject matter with humour.[46]

Goth music is characterized by the exploration of dark, often sexual, and sometimes violent themes. The first pivotal expression of this dark genre in popular music is the Cure's 1981 album *Faith*, where Robert Smith's lyrics to songs such as "Doubt" establish a dark area to be explored by subsequent Goth bands. The popular music used in *Buffy* often conveys a similar feel. For example, in "The Harvest" (1.2), the slow-motion sequence in which the vampire Darla and her gang arrive at the Bronze for a night of murder and mayhem is evocatively accompanied by the Dashboard Prophet's "Ballad for Dead Friends." This may be rock but its slow pace contains an element of gothic menace. Similarly, the music to Four Star Mary's "Violent" heard in "Band Candy" (3.6) is rock, but Tad

---

[46] Cynthia Boris, "Music to Slay By," *Buffy the Vampire Slayer Magazine* [Australia], 1 (2000), p. 4.

Looney's lyrics, with their references to slaying, darkened fields and blood, are essentially gothic in their imagery.

Much of the music used in *Buffy* illustrates how the darkness associated with Goth has come to permeate what is ostensibly more mainstream music in the pop/rock genres. Another example of such dark rock is the song "Cure" by Los Angeles band Darling Violetta. Darling Violetta performed this song in the episode "Faith, Hope and Trick" as Faith dances with a vampire. Apart from being responsible for the haunting opening theme for the *Angel* series—a piece of music Jymm Thomas describes as a cross between "dark superhero and cello-rock"[47]—Darling Violetta is not strictly a Goth band, and considering how much *Buffy* "exudes the kind of ambient dark sarcasm you find everywhere in pop culture these days,"[48] it is surprising how little true Goth music is used in the series. An exception is the song "Virgin State of Mind" by Swedish band K's Choice. The song does not feature on any K's Choice albums, suggesting it may have been specifically written for *Buffy*. Starting with a recording of children playing in a schoolyard, the wavering sound of a synthesizer/harmonium emerges evoking a mix of childhood memories and psychedelia, perhaps conjuring associations with the Beatles's "Strawberry Fields." Appearing first in 1960s psychedelia, long sustained tones were to become synonymous with Goth following the Velvet Underground singer Nico's use of the harmonium on solo projects such as her 1968 album *The Marble Index*. Over the top of this introduction to "Virgin State of Mind" a deep female voice emerges singing a wordless melodic line, now also a defining stylistic feature of Goth music. Used to accompany Willow's evil doppelgänger as she arrives at the Bronze in the episode "Doppelgangland" (3.16), the darkly surreal lyrics of "Virgin State of Mind" ("There's a key where my wonderful mouth used to be") suggest this androgynous, murderous vampire may be a dark reflection of gentle, insecure Willow's own nature.

Buffy's fans identify with this dark sensibility central to the show. In 2003, "vidders" (fans who create their own music videos) tended to favor current bands who combine nü-metal with a Goth feel—Evanescence and their hit "Bring Me to Life" was a favorite.[49] However, while fans are free to associate the personal angst of the main characters with this kind of music, the way Goth and heavy-metal-related genres are used on *Buffy* appears to be tempered by commercial media policy. This could reflect the fact that Goth, along with heavy metal and rap, are forms of popular music that generate negative public opinion or "moral panic." Whedon's script "Lie to Me" (2.7) presents a stereotypical media depiction of Goth subculture. Broadcast less than eighteen months before the Columbine

---

[47] Lisa Kohles, "The Music of Angels," *The 11th Hour web magazine*, 6 (1999), accessed 15 June 2006 at http://www.the11thhour.com/archives/111999/features/darlingvioletta2.html.

[48] Newitz, "Buffy Rides Again."

[49] An advertisement for Evanescence's single "Bring Me to Life" appeared in the *Buffy the Vampire Slayer Magazine* [Australia], 48 (2003), p. 9.

shooting, this is the only *Buffy* episode featuring authentic 1980s Goth music, the use of which, in the context of the story, is a clever exploration of moral panic themes. Ford, a former friend of Buffy's from Los Angeles, has come to Sunnydale to finish high school. It is subsequently revealed that he is dying of a brain tumor and has really come to Sunnydale in order to save himself. His plan is to start a (Goth) club and then give the members and, if possible, the Slayer herself to Spike in exchange for immortal life as a vampire. Ford tricks the club patrons into believing they too will be "blessed," made into vampires.

The Goth music chosen for this episode incorporates the type of Goth themes that inspire moral panic. For the first scene, set in the wannabe vampire club, the music is vintage English Goth: "Neverland (a fragment)" from the Sisters of Mercy's pivotal 1987 album *Floodland*, is a song about the impulse to self-destructiveness, someone throwing their life away.[50] In a later scene when Angel, Willow, and Xander visit the club a second time, the soundtrack uses "Reptile" from the album *Guilt by Association* (1992) by English metal-Goth band The Creaming Jesus. This features the same booming drums and bass with intermittent guitar screeches and low droning vocals that characterize the earlier Sisters of Mercy track. This time the lyrics allude more closely to vampirism with their references to heightened senses and hunger: "The one hungry life/My life with the other/She starts to smile/She smells like a lover." In terms of moral panic and the idea that dark alternative musics might be potentially harmful, the lyric "this hungry life" suggests a link between vampiric hunger and anorexia. Commenting on the challenge of maintaining his own acute thinness while filming *Buffy*, James Marsters points to the psychological aspects of dieting embodied in the role of Spike, who he describes as "a metaphor for hunger—psychological and sexual."[51] Likewise, anorexic female vampires are the theme of the song "Transylvanian Concubine" by Goth cello trio Rasputina to which Drusilla dances to in "Surprise" (2.13).

The appeal of the Goth cult as portrayed in this episode is that in becoming one of the Undead one can forget all the pain, responsibilities, and problems associated with encroaching adulthood. As Ford says to one of the club patrons, "we'll get to do the two things every American teen should have the chance to do. Die young—and stay pretty." Ford's own inevitable slow death from cancer is a metaphorical

---

[50] According to Remencus's *Buffy and Angel Music Pages* this song was only used for the initial broadcast as copyright was not obtained for repeat broadcasts, cable, or recorded media such as video or DVD. The music to this scene was therefore re-scored by resident *Buffy* musicians Sean Murray and Shawn Clement. The new song, "Blood of a Stranger," features dark booming drums, intermittent piano tinkles, and a dirge-like female voice repeating the same indecipherable words—in other words it sounds almost identical to "Neverland (a fragment)," suggesting how easy it is to recreate the classic Goth sound.

[51] James Marsters, "Cries and Whispers," *Hollywood Reporter*, 374/42, 20 August 2002, p. 20, accessed 26 August 2008 at http://www.morethanspike.com/index.php?page=6;cat=1;p=3;art=98.

representation of what these adolescents fear about adulthood: getting old and ugly, and eventually dying. This prospect is what motivates Ford and what he uses to justify his actions. Whedon depicts Goths as naïve, gullible teenagers, susceptible to any cult promising them a new life. As Ford tells Buffy: "These people are sheep. They want to be vampires 'cause they're lonely, or miserable, or bored."

The idea that Goths are naïve cult members brainwashed by propaganda is illustrated by the welcome Willow, Xander, and Angel receive from Chantarelle as they arrive at the club: "We welcome anyone who's interested in the Lonely Ones … they who walk with the night are not interested in harming anyone. They're separate from humanity, and must carry the burden of immortality. They are creatures above us. Exalted." Realizing this is an infantile romantic fantasy, Angel responds angrily and later explains the reasons for his disgust to his companions:

> Angel: These people don't know anything about vampires. What they are, how they live, how they dress…
> [The moment he says that a club member walks by in THE EXACT SAME OUTFIT that Angel is wearing. Angel looks sheepish for a moment as Xander and Willow eye him sardonically.][52]

Angel's trademark long black coat brings to mind the "Trenchcoat Mafia" referred to by news reports describing the Columbine shooters.[53] His criticisms of the Goth club members suggest how the news media is itself unable to appraise the Goth subculture beyond the "moral panic" stereotyping discussed above, a stereotyping that in *Buffy* at times, as in most television, identifies good and bad characters with simplified associations including specific music genres.

Heavy Metal Demons

As well as Goth various other forms of dark subgenres within popular music are used on *Buffy*: the grunge of Californian band Far ("The Pack" [1.6]) and the Goth/industrial techno of Curve ("Bad Girls" [3.14]); the industrial noise/nü-metal of Static-X ("Bargaining, Part 1" [6.1]); and the 1980s heavy punk-metal sounds of the Misfits ("Villains" [6.20]). Arguably, in relation to the use of such music subgenres on *Buffy* Whedon never planned to be topical, but in making the central metaphor "high school is hell" he created a television show that resonated with American society beyond what he initially intended. Over the last twenty years,

---

[52] Joss Whedon, "Lie to Me," *Buffy the Vampire Slayer: The Script Book, Season Two* (New York, 2001), vol. 2, p. 32.

[53] See Ann Powers, "The Stresses of Youth, the Strains of Its Music," *New York Times*, 25 April 1999, D18; Brett Pulley, "Students on the Fringe Found a Way to Stand Out," *New York Times*, 21 April 1999, A17; and Todd S. Purdum, "Goth Genres, Fringe Rock and Germany," *The New York Times*, 22 April 1999, A28.

many of the darker themes of heavy metal music and its related subgenres all reflect topics explored regularly on the show.[54] In view of the moral panic prevalent in American popular culture during *Buffy*'s lifetime on commercial television, it is a testament to the intelligent script writing, with its subtle combining of humor and metaphor, that *Buffy* dared to go to some of the places it did.

This is clearly illustrated in the episode "Gingerbread" (3.11), which explores how blanket censorship denies a problem and ultimately helps propagate it by closing avenues for discussion. Two young children are found murdered with occult symbols drawn on their hands. According to Moynihan and Søderlind, there are recorded cases in both America and Norway of groups of teenagers, motivated by heavy metal music and satanic literature associated with heavy metal subcultures, committing acts of murder and leaving such marks on their victims.[55] Up to this point on *Buffy* such violence is only associated with demons and vampires. The radical notion that human beings could commit such atrocities is discussed in the following exchange between Buffy and Giles:

> Giles: I wonder if we're looking for a "thing." The use of a symbol on a victim, it suggests ritual murder, an occult sacrifice by a group.
> Buffy: A group of ... human beings. Someone with a soul did this?

At the end of this episode it is discovered there were no murdered children: the bodies were a mirage created by a demon that feeds on the fear and turmoil it creates within a community. Initially it achieves just that as, horrified by the murder of innocent children, Buffy's mother forms a citizen action group MOO (Mothers Opposed to the Occult). Joyce's formation of MOO brings to mind the problematic good intentions of Tipper Gore, wife of US senator Al Gore, who in 1985 formed the PMRC (Parents' Music Resource Center). The PMRC had considerable success in "persuading state legislatures to censor certain types of music, chiefly rap and heavy metal."[56] One of its achievements was the requirement that CDs containing certain types of material must display the label "Parental Advisory: Explicit Lyrics" to enable parents to censor their adolescent children's listening habits.[57] Blanket censorship initiated by well-meaning but naïve citizen

---

[54] As Michael Ventura notes: "Drugs, alcohol and gangs are conspicuously absent from Buffy's high school, but it's clear that these are Hell Mouth's vomitus. Demons are the gangs. The surreal transformations in gullible kids victimized by demons—that's your brain on drugs" ("Warrior Women," *Psychology Today*, 31/6 (1998), p. 59).

[55] See Michael Moynihan and Didrick Søderlind, *Lords of Chaos: The Bloody Rise of the Satanic Metal Under-Ground* (Venice, CA, 1998), pp. 267–300.

[56] Robert Walser, *Running with the Devil: Power, Gender, and Madness in Heavy Metal Music* (Middletown, CT, 1993), p. 138.

[57] A poster of this Parental Advisory sticker is often seen in Dawn's bedroom. Perhaps to avoid such labeling the 1999 *Buffy the Vampire Slayer* soundtrack omits the lyrics "do not fuck with me" from the Four Star Mary track "Pain (Slayer Mix)."

groups can cause more harm than good, as explored in "Gingerbread" when Joyce delivers a motivational speech that identifies her own daughter and her daughter's best friend as part of the problem:

> Joyce: This is not a good town. How many of us have lost someone who just— disappeared, or got skinned, or suffered "neck rupture"? And how many of us have been too afraid to speak out? I was supposed to lead us in a moment of silence. But silence is this town's disease. For too long, it's been plagued by unnatural evils. It's not our town anymore. It belongs to the monsters, to the witches and Slayers.

In associating her daughter with the evil she fights, Joyce is unwittingly censoring those who are acknowledging and confronting the problem. In order to avoid any further threat by "satanic influences" she arranges for all of Giles's reference books to be confiscated from the school library, making it impossible for Buffy, her Watcher or her friends to research the demon they are dealing with. This depiction of blanket censorship resonates with contemporaneous events in America. The previous year, the assistant principal of Michigan's Zeeland High School, Gretchen Plewe, suspended a student for wearing a T-shirt emblazoned with the logo of nü-metal/rap band Korn. Offended by profanity in Korn's lyrics, Plewe stated: "Korn is indecent, vulgar, obscene, and intends to be insulting. It is no different than a person wearing a middle finger on their shirt."[58] This may be a valid comment, but Plewe's position might have been tempered if she had been aware of the underlying social issues (for example, homophobia, abuse, and bullying) that the confrontational language of Jonathan Davis's lyrics was addressing.

Following the deaths at Columbine in April 1999, the American government started taking a closer interest in the influence of the media on adolescents. In a desire to find immediate answers, blame was placed upon clear targets like Marilyn Manson[59] and *Buffy*. As US Senator Joseph Liebermann stated in May 1999: "It is just plain irresponsible and immoral to be marketing violence to teenagers by doing such things as including teen TV stars in ultraviolent movies or featuring them in such violent programs such as *Buffy, the Vampire Slayer*."[60] As Goode et al. observe, "moral panics require the existence of an identifiable deviant group or "folk devil" who functions as the centerpiece and scapegoat for public fears."[61] *Buffy* is an easy target because, as McConnell observes, in an

---

[58] Dick Porter, *Rapcore: The Nu-Metal Rap Fusion* (London, 2003), p. 91.

[59] See Gary Burns, "Marilyn Manson and the Apt Pupils of Littleton," *Popular Music and Society*, 23/3 (1999), pp. 3–8; and Robert Wright, "'I'd Sell You Suicide': Pop Music and Moral Panic in the Age of Marilyn Manson," *Popular Music*, 19/3 (2000), pp. 365–85.

[60] Paige Albiniak, "Washington Demands," *Broadcasting and Cable*, 129/21 (1999), p. 23.

[61] Erich Goode and Nachman Ben-Yehua, *Moral Panics: The Social Construction of Deviance* (Oxford, 1994), p. 73, quoted in John Lynxwiler and David Gay, "Moral

environment of moral panic a society will respond to the public presentation of such themes with censorship:

> *Buffy the Vampire Slayer* is a fiction that re-entrenches the myth of high school as hell: Columbine both happened because, and proves that, *Buffy*'s central tenet is not fiction, and so the show forces one of those fears unacknowledged by conventional culture into the face of that culture, which simply reacted to repress it.[62]

Despite the liberal position ultimately endorsed in many *Buffy* episodes such as "Gingerbread," the use of heavy metal and other darker musical subgenres on the show usually confirms rather than challenges moral-panic stereotypes: heavy-metal and its related subgenres, such as death metal, grindcore and rap/nü-metal, are almost exclusively associated with demons, implying their soulless, violent nature. For example, in "Bargaining, Part 1," the industrial sound of Static-X's track "Permanence" from their 2001 album *Machine* provides the background diegetic soundtrack for a demon biker bar. In keeping with the demon bikers' extreme tattoos and body piercing, the music is dehumanized in its rigid jack-hammer guitars and distorted, demon-like vocals. The message to the viewer is clear: no well-adjusted human listens to such music.

When normal teenagers do listen to such music it has serious psychological repercussions. For example, "Bad Girls" shows Buffy being drawn to her own dark side by Faith, and one element of this involves them dancing at the Bronze. The relentlessly abrasive techno track in this scene is "Chinese Burn" by English alternative electronica band, Curve. The amplified distortion, manic beat, strobe lighting, and the sight of Buffy and Faith dancing with abandon bring to mind moral-panic descriptions of acid house music and the associated rave scene in the 1980s by the British press and academia, in which teenagers attending raves were viewed as at risk of losing control and committing dangerous acts on themselves and others.[63] In "Bad Girls" this moral-panic cliché is utilized as both Slayers depart the Bronze in a euphoric state to patrol for vampires. Upon realizing they don't have any weapons, Faith easily convinces Buffy to break into a sporting goods store, indoctrinating her into Faith's simplistic code of "take, want, have." The implication is that Buffy's judgment has been corrupted not only by Faith but

---

Boundaries and Deviant Music: Public Attitudes towards Heavy Metal and Rap," *Deviant Behavior: An Interdisciplinary Journal*, 21 (2000), p. 80.

[62] Kathleen McConnell, "Chaos at the Mouth of Hell: Why Columbine High School Massacre had Repercussions for Buffy the Vampire Slayer," *Gothic Studies*, 2/1 (2000), p. 128.

[63] See for example Jacqueline Merchant and Robert McDonald, "Youth and the Rave Culture, Ecstasy and Health," *Youth and Policy*, 45 (1994), pp. 16–38; Deborah Lupton, *Risk and Sociocultural Theory: New Directions and Perspectives* (London, 1999); and Matthew Collin with John Godfrey, *Altered State: The Story of Ecstasy Culture and Acid House*, 2nd edition (London, 1998).

also by the loud techno music and associated strobe lighting accompanying the previous scene.

Unlike most American television, *Buffy* does at other times challenge such stereotypes. For example, Whedon's own beliefs as expressed in *Buffy* share many similarities with ideas explored in heavy metal music. In interviews Whedon often describes himself as an atheist and yet, according to Noxon "his work is full of yearning for belief ... the whole show ping pongs between the darkest night of the soul and this whole yearning for belief."[64] This is an important issue that Whedon himself acknowledges: "I'm a very hard-line, angry atheist. Yet I am fascinated by the concept of devotion. And I want to explore that."[65]

A link between the search for meaning and social dislocation is addressed in *Buffy* in the first-season episode "The Pack." Xander and Sunnydale High's resident gang of tough kids are possessed by hyena spirits, causing the group to descend into animalistic pack behavior, committing random acts of violence. The music providing the soundtrack as they walk in the school grounds explores those themes of religious disillusionment that Noxon alludes to above. "Job"s Eyes" (Far, 1996) evokes the nü-metal sound of Korn and The Deftones, with lyrics that are also thematically linked to the lyrics of the song "Mark of Cain" (1988) by Glenn Danzig, a seminal influence on the aforementioned nü-metal bands. Like "Mark of Cain", "Job's Eyes" is a song about being deserted by God. In a film-music strategy not often used in *Buffy*, the words of the song are foregrounded as the camera focuses on Xander's face, specifically lending him a darkness and disillusionment never previously associated with this character. Xander has always aspired to be the class clown but his new acceptance by the gang of hippest kids at school has given him a new cool status amongst his peers—but at what price? One could argue the song has been chosen for its ambience, but the theme of disillusionment reveals a thematic link between Whedon's own views and current themes of social and religious disillusionment in heavy metal music.

White Appropriation of Black Music

There are no black music genres featured on *Buffy*. The only black voice heard —other than Hinton Battle's in "Once More, with Feeling" (6.7)—is that of the English singer of the electronica fusion band Morcheeba, Skye Edwards, in "Passion" (2.17). This could suggest the desire of both television networks, the WB and UPN, to aim for a white, middle-class, American audience. Kent Ono argues that this lack of black representation on *Buffy* reflects a problem endemic

---

[64] Mary O'Connell, "Buffyworld: Marti Noxon Interview with Mary O'Connell," *CBC Radio*, 17 January 2003, accessed 25 April 2003 at http://www.cbc.ca/ideas/features/buffy.

[65] Emily Nussbaum, "Must See Metaphysics," *New York Times*, 22 September 2002, F56.

to American television in general: "*Buffy* ultimately *privileges* an antiseptic white culture and takes part in TV's overall habit of marginalizing people of color and other marginalized groups."[66] Ono's comments are interesting in view of the original programming demographic of both these networks. According to Poniewozik, when UPN and the WB

> first went on the air in the mid-1990s, they followed a similar path, blazed by Fox in the 1980s: They started with a schedule heavy on African-American stars, built an instant following among minority audiences, then largely spurned them with new programming that went after young white viewers.[67]

This still does not explain the total lack of black music on *Buffy*: after all, young, white, middle-class Americans like black music genres. As UPN's entertainment president Dawn Ostroff noted in early 2003: "When you look at statistics about who buys rap and hip-hop music among adults 18–34, 70 percent of the music is bought by Caucasians."[68] In *Buffy*'s unaired pilot, Whedon clearly seeks to reflect this by shooting a scene using hip-hop/reggae trio Da Bush Babees, which was excised from the televised first episode, "Welcome to the Hellmouth" (1.1). Both the pilot and televised first episode feature a scene in which two girls, one of whom is black, are discussing the new girl, Buffy. The black girl opens her locker and the body of a dead boy, who was murdered in the show's teaser, falls onto her. In the pilot this girl's screams blend into the next scene in which the viewer is confronted with a ghetto blaster blaring out the lyrics "sometimes I get so wild" from Da Bush Babees's 1994 track "Pon De Attack." The viewer's perspective moves from the ghetto blaster to Xander, running to catch up with the new girl, Buffy. In the foreground is a group of white male students in dark glasses making hand signs to each other, grooving to the music, as the lyrics say "check out the new style." Xander, carrying a skateboard to assign him to the geek skatepunk demographic, explains Sunnydale High's student cliques: "Those guys be the 'Housers.' They'd be genuine hardcore gangsters 'cept for the upper-class white-guy stigma. Total wannabes but they're okay." Xander establishes here that white kids like black music because it fulfils their fantasy to be "genuine hardcore gangsters" and Whedon clearly saw this as a relevant aspect of white teenage culture, an important reference to popular music culture that was removed from the broadcasted version.

---

[66] Kent A. Ono, "To Be a Vampire on *Buffy the Vampire Slayer*: Race and ('Other') Socially Marginalizing Positions on Horror TV," in Elyce Rae Helford (ed.) *Fantasy Girls: Gender in the New Universe of Science Fiction and Fantasy Television* (Lanham, MD, 2000), p. 164.

[67] Poniewozik, "How the 'Buffy' Coup Could Change TV."

[68] A.J. Frutkin, "Generation Next," *Mediaweek*, 3 February 2003, accessed 18 August 2008 at http://www.allbusiness.com/services/business-services-miscellaneous-business/4826412-1.html.

The reason there is no black music in *Buffy* can be explained by the potential problems this scene may have presented for the network: the girl's screams blending into the rap could have been construed by some viewers as suggesting a link between rap and high-school violence. When *Buffy* went on air in 1997, five years after the race riots surrounding the arrest of Rodney King in Los Angeles, the networks were still careful to avoid anything that could trigger race-related problems. Comments made in 2000 by WB's executive producer, George Snyder, support this interpretation. Snyder recalls Whedon originally wanted the role of Cordelia to be played by a black actress:

> One of the stumbling blocks there was the way we knew Joss anticipated the relationships shifting and changing ... there was some concern at the network at the time that interracial relationships would be problematic ... Joss said "I can't have restraints on how I mix and match the dynamics. That's part of the fun of the show, that Willow is in love with Xander, Xander is in love with Buffy, Cordelia can't stand any of them, yet finds herself drawn to Xander." Joss decided it wasn't worth fighting that fight at that particular time.[69]

This might explain why no popular music is ever used in *Buffy* to establish non-white characters including Kendra, Mr Trick and Robin Wood. As black people depicted within a white, middle-class, suburban environment on commercial television, they are required to remain marginalized by the network's fears of potential moral panic.

When *Buffy* came off air in 2003, white and African American programming on American television remained separate. A rap version of the Who's "My Generation," the anthem of working-class London teenagers in the mid-1960s, was used to advertise the WB's 2001 Fall season. In a montage sequence, attractive young stars from all the WB shows—*Angel, Charmed, Dawson's Creek,* and *Felicity*—are presented grooving to the rap "talkin' 'bout my generation," encouraging audience identification—but the use of rap music made the lack of a single non-white actor in this WB promotional video only more conspicuous.

Conclusion

This study of the uses of popular music in *Buffy* reveals it to be a text with multiple layers of meaning often communicating contradictory information. *Buffy* was designed to "reflect the obsessions of pop culture around it"[70] and, as Ken Tucker notes, it "became that rare kind of TV programming: a show ... in which episodes

---

[69] "Buffy: The Beginning 'Cordelia'," *SFX Special Edition*, December (2000), accessed 8 February 2003 at http://www.dumb-inc.nz/delusions/articles/btvs23.html (no longer available).

[70] Newitz, "Buffy Rides Again."

began adding up to a rich, expansive mythology that could accommodate any comment Whedon and company wanted to make on contemporary culture."[71] In providing commentary and subtext on the show's plot lines and characterizations, popular music became an integral part of this rich mythology. Various subgenres of music are used in *Buffy* from alternate/independent pop, skate punk of geeks/post-slackers, "girl power," and Riot Grrrl music, to Goth, grunge rock, and heavy metal. The various ways such subgenres within popular music are used in *Buffy* reflect not only the originality and alternative position of the show's creator and principal writer, Joss Whedon, but also "moral panics" and the resulting conservative policies of American commercial television. *Buffy* grew beyond Whedon's original intentions into a multifaceted reflection of American popular culture, a complex site of contradictions within which the social meaning of popular music can be read and interpreted in many ways.

---

[71] In Adams, *Slayer Slang*, p. 5. Tucker is a television critic for *Entertainment Weekly* who frequently called *Buffy* the best show on television.

PART III
Making Music: *Buffy*, the Musical

Chapter 11
Not "The Same Arrangement": Breaking Utopian Promises in the *Buffy* Musical[1]

Diana Sandars and Rhonda V. Wilcox

> "Every single night, the same arrangement …"
> (Buffy's first words in "Once More, with Feeling.")

Introduction

The opening titles of early episodes of *Buffy the Vampire Slayer* proclaim that "she alone will fight the vampires, the demons, and the forces of darkness." However, the promise of solo heroics declared by this standard opening voiceover is consistently undercut by the series's emphasis on communal values and group co-operation. The tension between the mythic allusion of this voiceover and the narrative's telos forms the basis of the sixth season's central enigma. Buffy is brought back to life through Willow's use of witchcraft, with the help of Xander, Tara, and Anya. Willow and the Scoobies think that they have valiantly rescued Buffy from a hell dimension, creating and believing their own mythology that they are Buffy's saviors. However, behind this *Sleeping Beauty* fairytale lies the reality that they have dragged Buffy out of heaven. In "Once More, with Feeling," a magical, demon-invoking spell forces characters to sing their true feelings. Jamie Clarke argues that "music as utopian and therefore demonic interferes [with] and distracts from the day-to-day experience of living, suffering … Indeed the significance of the episode within the series is to drag Buffy back from heaven/utopia and into the real world of struggle and slaying."[2] Through the fantasy structures of pop song and the Hollywood musical, "Once More, with Feeling" (6.7) unsettles this mythology and the myths the Scoobies carry about their individual journeys and personal relationships. When Buffy sings that she is "going through the motions" in the opening musical number, she adds "I can't even see if this is really me." This personal dilemma becomes a theme for all of the Scooby gang in this episode.

---

[1] Elements of this chapter were previously published in Chapter 12 of Rhonda V. Wilcox, *Why Buffy Matters: The Art of Buffy the Vampire Slayer* (IB Tauris 2005). Used by permission.

[2] Jamie Clarke, "Affective Entertainment in 'Once More with Feeling': A Manifesto for Fandom," *Refractory*, 2 (2003), accessed 12 August 2008 at http://blogs.arts.unimelb.edu.au/refractory/2003/03/18/affective-entertainment-in-once-more-with-feeling-a-manifesto-for-fandom-jamie-clarke/.

As major characters struggle into their adulthood, "Once More, with Feeling" depicts the difficulty of balance between the individual and the community—"understand we'll go hand in hand, but we'll walk alone in fear," they sing in the finale—just as it depicts the interplay between solo and harmony, duet, or group. Differing performance styles including solos, duets, and ensemble numbers complement the use of varying musical genres to define the relationships within the Scooby gang. Through the musical's inversion of the usually realist narrative, Tara, Giles, and Spike (as marginalized or overlooked characters) are granted narrative control via the powerful emotional medium of song. The shared style of their performance numbers aligns these characters through a reconsideration of their roles as "watchers." Comparably, Anya and Xander voice what has been previously silenced. These voices articulate the potential for self-destruction inherent in the Scoobies' key relationships and signal the impending radical changes the group will undergo. Through a narrative structured by song, "Once More, with Feeling" deconstructs the myths created by the classical Hollywood musical and some readings of the Buffyverse. Myths surrounding fairytale, the heterosexual coupling of the musical, and the romantic myths of pop songs are inverted to reveal the delusions the Scoobies have constructed about themselves and their relationships. Simon Frith suggests that "different pop forms ... engage their listeners in different narratives of desire."[3] The deconstruction of the musical's myths of desire is enacted across a range of music genres, reflecting the multiplicity and complexity of desires with which each Scooby member struggles. Like Stephen Sondheim and others who echo him,[4] Whedon sings a different sort of song in "Once More, with Feeling"; and he does so in part by very purposefully playing off the patterns of the Hollywood past.

Straining at Textual Bounds

Anahid Kassabian has theorized that for visual texts with composed scores, such as the film musical, "the boundary between unconscious and conscious processes is permeable."[5] The very fact that "Once More, with Feeling" was originally broadcast for 68 minutes—breaking from the series's normal 60-minute time slot in a fashion almost unprecedented for narrative television (as opposed, for example, to televized sporting events)—meant that the audience was unusually conscious of its straining

---

[3] Simon Frith, "Why Do Songs Have Words?" *Music For Pleasure: Essays in the Sociology of Pop* (Cambridge, 1988), p. 121.

[4] In the DVD audio commentary for "Bargaining, Parts 1 and 2," Marti Noxon says that Whedon "kind of made a big announcement at the end of season five that he was going away for a while just to chill out and, you know, become Sondheim in his own way which, scarily, he did." Marti Noxon, "Bargaining, Parts 1 and 2" audio commentary, *The Chosen Collection* (2005).

[5] Anahid Kassabian, *Hearing Film: Tracking Identification in Contemporary Hollywood Film Music* (New York, 2001), p. 88.

at textual bounds. The episode was also the only *Buffy* shot in widescreen;[6] and pre-broadcast extratextual information furthermore meant that faithful viewers of the series in a sense cooperated in the break with the standard format, thus entering the viewing experience with a heightened consciousness of form.

The balance between textual immersion and distance is key to Jane Feuer's discussion of the Hollywood musical. Feuer argues that "the Hollywood musical as a genre perceives the gap between producer and consumer, the breakdown of community designated by the very distinction between performer and audience, as a form of cinematic original sin."[7] She notes that the pretence of spontaneity is a standard technique to induce immersion and identification. Furthermore, many musicals—such as "backstage musicals"—include an internal audience to cue us emotionally and to bridge that breakdown: we are offered a "doubled or split identification of both stars and internal audience."[8] For those films for which there is no diegetic performance, no play-within-a-play, Feuer argues that "proscenium or stage-like arenas are often created" so that, for example, Judy Garland is framed in windows in *Meet Me in St Louis* (1944).[9] In other words, the distance between performer and audience is created only to be collapsed, for the pleasure of being overcome. Along the way, Feuer notes that techniques of apparently distancing the viewer from the fiction—such as the use of direct address by a performer—can, in fact, be used to give quite the opposite effect depending on the context, providing the spectator with a direct emotional address and subsequent engagement.

Feuer argues that in the classical Hollywood musical more than one mode of address is employed. The mode of address of the musical numbers normally provides a closer level of identification as the film audience is performed to directly, encouraging the spectatorial position of being a participant in live entertainment rather than an outside observer.[10] This feature of the classical Hollywood musical and its divergent modes of address and audience identification is stylistically and thematically adopted by "Once More, with Feeling." As the characters balance the drive toward their individual searches with communal caring and purpose, the audience balances textual consciousness with emotional immersion. Feuer further notes that "one may argue that direct address is inherently subversive or radical. It is not."[11] Even in sophisticated Hollywood musicals, she contends, there is a process of distancing or "demystification and remystification[.] ... The narrative gets sutured back together again for the final bow."[12] Accordingly we would like to offer her ideas as critical background in part to make clear the originality and effectiveness of what UPN called the *Buffy* Musical.

---

[6] Thanks to Vanessa Knights for noting this.
[7] Jane Feuer, *The Hollywood Musical*, 2nd ed. (London, 1993), p. 3.
[8] Ibid., pp. 26–7; p. 29.
[9] Ibid., pp. 23–4.
[10] Ibid., p. 29.
[11] Ibid., p. 39.
[12] Ibid., pp. 43–4.

Buffy has always used sound, music, and musical references very consciously. Janet Halfyard has analyzed at length the theme tune's play with traditional genre and gender tropes (as well as the interrelationship with the theme song of the *Angel* series).[13] As with many other categories of knowledge, the *Buffy* writers assume of the audience a familiarity with and ability to reference Hollywood musicals. In season 2's "The Dark Age" (2.8), after Jenny Calendar has emotionally withdrawn from Rupert Giles because of an encounter with a demon from his Ripper past, she says that she is fine: "I mean I'm not running around, wind in my hair, the hills are alive with the sound of music fine, but I'm coping." His later unhappy translation of this for Buffy is the brief, sad, but humorously inexplicit report that "the hills are not alive." The characters in the Buffyverse do not live in the emotional world of *The Sound of Music* (1965); its Nazis are eminently more escapable than the vampires and demons which incarnate the evil that permeates Buffy's world.

Not only allusion to the world of music but music itself—and sound—are delicately employed in the series. In "The Body" (5.16), as many of us have noted, there is no non-diegetic music.[14] At a particularly poignant moment when, coming to terms with her mother's death, Buffy stands with her face in the sun looking out over the threshold of her back door, she hears the sounds of life proceeding: children's voices, the distant rush of the ocean, a horn playing scales. The rise and fall of the notes is faintly irregular and inexpert: it suggests someone making an effort, someone learning and—as the scales continue—the idea of life persisting. As Kassabian says, there is an "attention continuum," with some music, particularly vocalized music, more consciously notable, whereas some instrumental music or other sounds may be barely noted at all.[15] But the sounds in this scene in "The Body" cooperate to create a finely tuned emotional and thematic effect of the experience of loss and the poignancy of life's persistence.

The emotional effect of the diegetic use of Cream's "Tales of Great Ulysses" (1967) in "Forever" (5.17) depends on, among other things, its being doubly allusive. When Giles and Joyce listen to this song in "Band Candy" (3.6), in which they magically lose their inhibitions and return to an exaggeratedly emotional (teenage) state, its connection to the 1960s allows the song to signify Giles's Ripper persona. We also see that for this encounter Joyce is going to be sharing his music and emulating his attitude, rather than the reverse: thus the first level of the allusion. In "Forever," Giles plays the music again after Joyce's funeral, and it serves as an emotional connection to the past and a reward to faithful viewers, the recognition of the musical reference allowing a consciousness of involvement with the series's fictional world.

---

[13] Janet K. Halfyard, "Love, Death, Curses and Reverses (in F minor): Music, Gender and Identity in *Buffy the Vampire Slayer* and *Angel*," *Slayage* 4 (2001). See also chapter 1 of this volume.

[14] See, for example, Rhonda Wilcox, *Why Buffy Matters: The Art of Buffy the Vampire Slayer* (London, 2005), pp. 42–3, 180–90, as well as chapters 4, 5, and 6 in this volume.

[15] Kassabian, *Hearing Film*, pp. 52–3.

A very different effect is created by Giles's own song in his dream sequence of the fourth season finale "Restless" (4.22). Giles repeats Willow's focus on performance in dream—her dream dealing with acting, his with singing—as he performs a song in the Bronze with Xander, Willow, and other Bronze patrons listening. But the song is at the same time a declaration of information—operatic in function, though not in style—as Giles ponders aloud the mystery of their dream danger. As Halfyard says:

> Effectively, this song manages to be both diegetic and non-diegetic simultaneously. Although Giles does clearly know he is singing, he and everyone else fail to perceive what is clear to us, the audience, namely that the song itself is abnormal, the usual rules of musical diegesis having been suspended by the dream-state.[16]

While Giles's playing "Tales of Brave Ulysses" serves to bind viewers to the characters' world, awareness of the nature of Giles's dream song, in contrast, separates viewers from characters, though this may serve to indicate a failure in perception on the part of the character and does not necessarily indicate a separation of viewer from identification with the text.

Throughout the series, then, there is a precisely effective use of music and sound; and these particular examples illustrate some of the possibilities of emotional immersion and distance. By the time of the sixth season, Whedon and company could draw on considerable expertise in these techniques as well as in the use of narrative, language, and visuals. Michael Dunne argues that "['Once More, with Feeling's'] self-conscious separation of 'natural' diegesis and 'unnatural' musical production numbers would seem to fulfill Bertolt Brecht's program for denaturalizing art."[17] Of the standard "fused" production, Dunne notes that Brecht complains, with imagaic prescience, that "Witchcraft of this sort must of course be fought against."[18] And in "Once More, with Feeling" we share in fighting the spell.

The musical numbers in "Once More, with Feeling" forcefully develop the characters, their relationships, and the narrative arc in season 6 primarily by capitalizing on the power and resonance words gain when songwriters put words to music.[19] From the opening number, the power of song is contrasted with the dynamic of the performer-audience relationship to articulate the growing disparity between subject and audience, the theme of this episode: there needs to be someone

---

[16] Janet K. Halfyard, "Singing Their Hearts Out: the Problem of Performance in *Buffy the Vampire Slayer* and *Angel*," *Slayage* 17 (2005), 34.

[17] Michael Dunne, *American Film Musical Themes and Forms* (Jefferson, NC, 2004), p. 181.

[18] Bertolt Brecht, "The Modern Theatre is the Epic Theatre" (1930) in Dunne, *American Film Musical*, p. 181.

[19] Frith, "Why Do Songs Have Words?" pp. 120–21.

to listen. The dilemma of being heard is emphasized by the dichotomies between the lyric and spoken word, and the divisions between characters and spectator. Until the final number, in many cases the spectator is positioned as the only one prepared to listen.

The episode proper begins with distancing, demystification, through various avenues, many of them allusive. The *Buffy* theme tune, as Halfyard has noted, normally starts with instrumentation recalling horror movies and shifts to rock instruments, thus indicating the series's genre and gender-bending take on horror, with the rock music associated with the feminist hero Buffy.[20] For "Once More, with Feeling," instead of a rock arrangement, there is an orchestral arrangement of the theme with instrumentation and rhythm recalling 1950s and 1960s television. The visuals add to the effect: the names—series title, characters, actors, and creator—are presented in cartoon red lettering, and the faces (not including Whedon's) are presented in cartoon outline, in sepia colors.[21] After the commercial break, the screen again shows cartoon red lettering with the episode title.[22] For the first several moments of the action on screen, we hear an orchestral overture and are given glimpses of the characters without, however, hearing any dialogue; furthermore, their motions are correlated with the rhythm of the music. All of this goes towards creating distance—the conscious realization that we are watching a special episode, which is balanced for many of us against an emotional investment of many years' standing. And this pull of distancing *versus* emotional identification can be seen in the group dynamics of the characters as well.

"Once More, with Feeling" employs the musical's key formal structure of song and dance to convey character and narrative information more succinctly and profoundly than is possible through the series's usual narrative structure which, within its own fictional world's rules, is realist. While the parodic excess of many of the musical performances in this episode is a source of humor, these musical production numbers represent an ambivalence towards the utopian expression of the classical Hollywood musical. The classical Hollywood musical's impetus for the spontaneous eruption into song and dance is typically the result of being overwhelmed by positive feelings of love and exuberance for life. Antithetically, the musical numbers in this episode are generally defined by the mundane, suggesting these numbers are a dragging-up of the repressed—that which dares not be

---

[20] Halfyard, "Love, Death, Curses and Reverses."

[21] These images reflect the artwork created for the episode poster, DVD, CD, and script book by comic-book legend Adam Hughes.

[22] Incidentally, for Keith Topping, the episode title is an allusion to Joan Armatrading's "Love and Affection" (*Slayer: The Next Generation: An Unofficial and Unauthorised Guide to Season Six of Buffy the Vampire Slayer* (London, 2003), p. 71), while for Michael Dunne it is a reference to the title of a "1960 Stanley Donen film starring Yul Brynner and Kay Kendall and the Broadway play on which it was based, with all the aura of musical show business common to both" (*American Film Musical*, p. 11). It is also a line from Sweet's final song and a phrase common in musical rehearsals.

articulated rather than that which is so joyous that no words could possibly contain it.[23] In this episode, the fantasy structures of the Hollywood musical operate as the formal equivalent of witchcraft, creating a distorted reality that, like a transparency spell, enables the truth to be revealed in a ritualistic performative manner.

Jane Feuer further notes of song in Hollywood musical that "in becoming song, language is in a sense transfigured, lifted up into a higher, more expressive realm."[24] Song is accorded primacy of place in the construction of this episode, effectively compartmentalizing it as a series of vignettes designed to investigate the disintegrating Scooby relationships. These songs inform the image and the narrative through song's emotive fluxes of the aural; it "engulfs one in the fantasy terrain of its own imagined social space."[25] As such, it constructs what Philip Brophy terms "'vertical narration', where everything is told … 'all at once'."[26] The use of various music genres in "Once More, with Feeling" reflects "music's ability to cross and *confuse* cinematic and cultural codes in their construction of sound 'narratives',"[27] and creates a complex emotionally governed social landscape. The device of "Once More, with Feeling"—having the characters magically forced to sing their true feelings—works like a soliloquy, in that we can be assured we will hear interior truth for that character: "as spectators we are drawn to identify not with the characters themselves but with their emotions, which are signalled pre-eminently by music which can offer us emotional experience directly."[28] This magical assurance of emotional truth counterbalances the high consciousness of textuality in the episode.

---

[23] This is a common trait amongst post-classical Hollywood musicals, especially evident in Bob Fosse's work, notably *Cabaret* (1972), as well as *The Rocky Horror Picture Show* (1975) and more recently *Hedwig and the Angry Inch* (2001). The primary difference between these latter musicals and "Once More, with Feeling" is the articulation of the socially repressed subjects of queer sexuality and identity and the individually repressed issues of personal discontent. Many thanks to Vanessa Knights for highlighting this point and to Tommy DeFrantz for opening the question.

[24] Cited in Heather Laing, "Emotion by Numbers: Music, Song and the Musical," in Bill Marshall and Robynn Stilwell (eds), *Musicals: Hollywood and Beyond* (Exeter/Portland, OR, 2000), p. 5.

[25] Philip Brophy, "*Magnolia*: The Power of Song," *Real Time*, 36/7 (2000), accessed 25 August 2008 at http://www.philipbrophy.com/projects/cnsncs/Magnolia.html.

[26] Ibid.

[27] Frith, "Why Do Songs Have Words?" p. 133, our italics.

[28] Ibid., p. 136. This alternative level of emotional engagement and character knowledge or identification that is elicited from the alternative mode of the musical—this difference between being sung to or listening to characters talk—is further layered by the range of the actors' singing abilities from professional to novice. Amber Benson and Anthony Stewart Head's abilities are reflected in the lyrical complexity of their numbers and the poignant emotions their more professional performances are able to elicit. In contrast, Gellar's thinner, plaintive voice threatens to diminish the emotional effect of her performances. Many thanks to Vanessa Knights for this observation.

"Does Anybody Notice? Does Anybody Even Care?"[29] The Spell of Song

In "Once More, with Feeling" the intimate access provided by the musical numbers provides a greater impetus for the audience to identify with the Scoobies at a time when they are at their most vulnerable and emotionally isolated, stylistically amplifying their individual feelings of turmoil and the fragmentation of their relationships, a pivotal point in the story arc for the season. This fragmentation can be seen in the first group number. The "I've Got a Theory/Bunnies/We're Together" number is structured with various solo vocals as different characters express different theories to explain the magical compulsion to sing—from Giles's spot-on but self-dismissed "dancing demon" to Anya's bunnies—culminating in Buffy's solo question "What can't we face if we're together?" which is then reiterated in choral unison by the Scoobies. The singers look into each other's eyes as they sing, then conclude by turning to face in the same direction—as if towards the edge of a stage—though not directly into the camera. The superficial vocal and visual togetherness, however, is undercut lyrically by Buffy's theory that "it doesn't matter"; and though she then seems to say we do not need to care because we can be confident of success, she also adds that, since these are "the same old trips, why should we care?"—a question that Giles hears clearly, if the others do not.

Who is listening in this episode is prioritized as much as who is singing. This grants the audience a greater degree of character access and narrative privilege than is otherwise afforded through *Buffy*'s conventional narrative structure. Buffy, Dawn, Giles, Spike, and Tara all perform musical numbers that are defined as "introspective performances" where "a sole character performs to no coded audience," unheard by the other characters in the diegesis.[30] This song coding locates the audience in an intimately informed position unavailable to the characters in the diegesis. This classical Hollywood musical convention is further reconfigured through the ensemble performances and Anya and Xander's duet, as although they perform with and to each other, their fears prevent them from truly hearing the message of their lyrics.

The diegesis commences with Buffy's so-called "I Want" song, "Going Through the Motions," which, similar to the later "Walk Through the Fire," is in essence a solo performance but is layered with ensemble production pieces.[31]

---

[29] This is the title of Dawn's musical foreshortened number.

[30] Jacques Schultz, "Categories of Song," *Journal of Popular Film and Television*, 8/1 (1980), p. 24.

[31] The "I want song" is identified as Alan Menken's pivotal song composition device in the contemporary Disney animated feature films. This song identifies the main protagonist's desire which itself is the source of these films' narrative trajectory. Attainment of these desires facilitates the narrative closure of these films. This "Ashman-Menken musical formula is described in Disney production circles as the 'I Want' number." Laura Sells, "'Where Do the Mermaids Stand?' Voice and Body in *The Little Mermaid*," in Elizabeth

Buffy makes it clear that she feels cut off from that sense of connection; in fact, she feels cut off from life—and what she wants is to reconnect. The adult nature of her emotional problem is emphasized by contrast with the fact that this number is what Whedon calls "wicked Disney."[32] Disney animated feature films are founded on fairytale, myths, and legends for the narrative's vehicle, employing the power of myth to mask "contradiction and then, as ideology, act as a charter for understanding and policy."[33] In the classical period, Disney used his re-inscription of the fairytale to capitalize on "American innocence and utopianism to reinforce the social and political status quo."[34] In contrast, "Once More, with Feeling" uses its Disney-stylized "I want" songs to disrupt the status quo by signalling the end of the deceptions that define the Scoobies's lives. Buffy dances with monsters rather than cute little mice, tea cups, or sea creatures, and instead of closing her song in a *Little Mermaid*-style spray of hair and foam, she is framed in a spray of vampire dust[35]—the ashes of the dead cheerfully crossing musical comedy with horror. It is appropriate that Buffy is at first singing solo, only heard by the monsters—though they occasionally provide harmonious interjections. The Handsome Young Man she rescues—with his Disney-like flowing white shirt and shining blond hair, by all appearances the romantic hero—is so far from interesting her that he does not even merit formal rejection, merely the one word "whatever" before she turns away from him.

Buffy's romantic indifference in her solo "I want" song contrasts to the passionate excess expressed through Tara and Spike's "I want" songs. These perpetuate the gender-bending use of music in the theme titles and grant their sexual expressions an acceptability not afforded by the realist narrative structures. Tara's representation as Willow's ideal lover is constructed through Tara's first solo number, where the intimacy of sexually implicit images that accompany the sexual metaphors of Tara's lyrics and the objective narrational mode, in contrast to the visual direct address of the musical, locate the spectator as a voyeur in Tara's

---

Bell, Lynda Haas, and Laura Sells (eds), *From Mouse to Mermaid: The Politics of Film, Gender and Culture* (Bloomington, IN, 1995), p. 178.

[32] Mary Kaye Schilling, "Vamping It Up," *Entertainment Weekly*, 9 November 2001, pp. 18–19. Though it might be seen as having some elements in common with the opening number of *Beauty and the Beast* (1991)—in itself a variant on the usual Disney because of the heroine Belle's unhappiness with small-town anti-intellectuals—Buffy's number certainly goes counter to the usual Disney number. Jack Zipes suggests that "Disney identified so closely with the fairy tales he appropriated that it is no wonder his name virtually became synonymous with the genre of the fairy tale." See Jack Zipes, "Breaking the Disney Spell," in Bell et al. (eds), *From Mouse to Mermaid*, p. 28.

[33] Stephen. M. Fjellman, *Vinyl Leaves: Walt Disney World and America* (Boulder, CO, 1992), p. 259.

[34] Zipes, "Breaking the Disney Spell," pp. 21–2.

[35] See Whedon's comments on this moment in Joss Whedon and Paul Ruditis, *Buffy the Vampire Slayer: "Once More with Feeling," The Script Book*, ed. Micol Ostow (New York, 2002), p. 76.

performance. This situates Tara as the instigator of an unsettling public display of private desire. In addition to employing the emotively personal power of pop, this ballad ("Under Your Spell"), also inverts the dominant heterosexual conventions of female pop music, particularly through its allusion to Kate Bush's video for "Wuthering Heights" (1977).[36] Accompanied by back-up dancers, she becomes the solo star of her own musical number. In the musical finale, this choreography is mimicked by Buffy, which aligns Tara and Buffy in the powerful roles of lead vocalists. Tara's pop ballad is thus poised to be the 'breakaway pop hit" that Anya so desperately desires for herself.

The public rendering of Tara's highly intimate and private message for Willow in this number further attains its powerful impact through Tara's explicit articulation of her desire. Tara's love and esteem for Willow had previously only been expressed through furtive gazes and mumbled words. When Willow points out that boys are checking Tara out, Tara replies that what they see in Tara is Willow. This defines the main way Tara has been constructed for us since her introduction to *Buffy*, as an extension of Willow, a signifier of Willow's sexuality, Willow's humanity, and Willow's evolving authoritative personality. The conventions of the musical in "Once More, with Feeling" provide Tara with the ability to function as a character in her own right: the musical's performance conventions that subvert the realist narrative permit Tara a voice and position of authority otherwise denied to her. Tara's polished and defining voice juxtaposed with Willow's almost absent singing voice further restructures our identification with Tara and her relationship with Willow. Through her song we hear Tara speak freely and commandingly.

Ironically, Tara's song is partially the product of the thought manipulation Willow has perpetrated on her, erasing Tara's knowledge that their relationship is fraught with problems. This manipulation informs the structure of this number, as Tara dances and sings her love of Willow whilst Willow watches. The persuasive power of rhythm and melody is presented as a powerful tool rhetorically to affect emotion and thus to influence thought. The myth of a perfect romantic love evoked through the pop ballad structure is signified by the irony of lyrics "I'm under your spell," the metaphor that Tara uses to celebrate their love. Tara's performance enacts Willow's reflective identity—the Tara that Willow needs her to be and will use magic to maintain. However, because she adopts song as her form of communication we are able to hear Tara: through song she is guaranteed that the audience is listening. With Amber Benson's vocals, the romantic costumes, and the idyllic setting of the song Tara's voice is for once far up on the "attention

---

[36] In the same way that Theresa Jill Buckland suggests of Bush's video, dance is employed in Tara's song "as an expressive tool to underline the emotional state of the ... heroine." See Buckland with Elizabeth Stewart, "Dance and Music Video," in Stephanie Jordan and Dave Allen (eds), *Parallel Lines: Media Representations of Dance* (London, 1993), p. 57. Tara's tumultuous relationship with Willow evokes the gothic romance of Cathy and Heathcliff, especially in Willow's reaction to Tara's death, which evokes that of Heathcliff to Cathy's.

continuum." Thus the structure and presentation of Tara's number simultaneously presents her at her most empowered but most beguiled: Tara's is the voice we hear, but Tara is under Willow's spell.

Spike's love song, "Rest in Peace," visually and aurally complements Tara's love song and similarly legitimates a desire which up to this point in the series has been depicted as awkward and embarrassing. "Rest in Peace" is structured as an introspective solo performance where Spike sings to Buffy, rendering her mute and reactive; the same position occupied by Willow in Tara's number. Song therefore affords Spike a controlling position of annunciation, which (similar to Tara) he is denied in *Buffy*'s conventional narrative. The structuring of these two musical numbers according to similar visual and aural conventions aligns Tara's relationship with Willow with that of Spike and Buffy, establishing a previously unemphasized connection between these Scooby-partner characters.

The night setting in the graveyard represents a binary opposition to Tara's sunny park setting and evokes iconographic elements from Billy Idol's later videos: Spike's disruption of a funeral at night, the scaring of the guests, overturning of the chairs and riding the coffin reference elements of Idol's "White Wedding" video (1982). Consequently, Spike's declaration of his love is issued as an edict in a punkish rock ballad, contrasting with the poetic style of Tara's pop love song for Willow. The anti-authoritarian ideologies of punk rock are also established through Spike's striking resemblance to Billy Idol, which is confirmed in a later episode of *Buffy*.[37]

As expectations of the classical Hollywood musical are subverted in "Once More, with Feeling," so too are those set up by the rock and pop music conventions and the lyrical content of the songs themselves. The truths conveyed by these songs are, by the end of the episode, dismantled. Rather than being "left in peace" Spike unites with Buffy at the closure of the narrative and instead of being made "complete," Tara realizes that she must leave her relationship for fear that this poetic love will destroy her.

Other parallels can be seen in the problematic relationship of Giles and Buffy, made clear in his solo "Standing," in which he expresses his concern that she will never achieve independence unless he leaves her. Although the lyrics of the song suggest that Giles is voicing his fears about their relationship directly to Buffy, the staging of the performance is coded through the conventions of an introspective performance, as Buffy remains oblivious to his song: at his solo's end, she asks "did you say something?" This lack of communication is visually emphasized through the composite image that locates Buffy's training movements in an overlayed filmic space to that of the singing Giles. Giles's ponderous movements match the despair articulated in his lyrics and function as a ghostly contrast to Buffy's hyperkinetic gymnastic movements displayed in slow motion to fit the tempo of Giles's song. The desynchronization of Buffy's movements with Giles's

---

[37] In "Sleeper" (7.8), it is posited by Buffy that Billy Idol stole his look from Spike and not vice versa.

song (requiring slow-motion display in order to be synchronized) suggests the gulf in their relationship and future expectations, enhancing the lyrical intent of Giles's song. This disparity and Buffy's obliviousness to Giles's performance aligns Giles with Spike, as both characters experience a state of turmoil and longing in their relationships with Buffy after her resurrection. When Spike sings "Rest in Peace," Buffy rolls her eyes but at least she listens. Similarly, when Tara sings, Willow listens; but how much Buffy or Willow understands is another question.

Songs of Desire and Isolation

"Once More, with Feeling" subverts the classical Hollywood musical's reliance on the duet to emphasize the themes of isolation and desperation resulting from not listening and not being heard. In the classical Hollywood musical, "the duet is the musical's center of gravity, its method of summarizing in a single scene the film's entire structure."[38] Instead of conveying the desirability of the romantic couple's compatibility, the duet is reconfigured as a source of hopelessness and self-destruction in Tara and Giles's and Spike and Buffy's duets, and parodic excess in Xander and Anya's duet. In contrast to Rick Altman's argument that in the supradiegetic moments of musicals "the music creates a utopian space in which all singers and dancers achieve a unity unimaginable in the now superseded world of temporal, psychological causality,"[39] in "Once More, with Feeling" the emergence of the supradiegetic duets is the result of black magic and coded as an infliction. This provides another level through which the conventions of the Hollywood musical are prevented from "going through the motions." A separation between audience and characters occurs through this structure as *Buffy* fans often find joy and comedy in the musical numbers, unlike the characters, who, for the most part, experience these musical moments as a source of pain or affliction. As a result, although the supradiegesis is employed to reveal the essence of things in *Buffy*, it is not a utopian space which is created, but one defined by anxiety, deception, and disunity.

The fragility of the love within pop songs is conveyed through the rescripting of Tara's lyrics in her duet with Giles, after she discovers that Willow has been manipulating her through magic. In his work on meaning and the listening subject, Sean Cubitt suggests that listening is a more persuasive, realistic, and intimate sense than vision, and that an awareness of difference and identity is carried in the singing voice.[40] This provides music with its emotive power for identification. In the first shared musical number, "I've Got a Theory/Bunnies/Together," Willow

---

[38] Rick Altman, *The American Film Musical* (Bloomington, IN, 1987), p. 37.
[39] Ibid, p. 69.
[40] Sean Cubitt, "'Maybellene': Meaning and the Listening Subject," in Richard Middleton (ed.), *Reading Pop: Approaches to Textual Analysis in Popular Music* (Oxford, 2000), pp. 148, 155.

and Giles are aligned when they sit next to each other and prophesy that "it could get serious before it's past." This is typical of their positions as wise and sensible leaders; however, as this episode progresses, it is Tara who becomes aligned with Giles, as both Tara and Giles realize their diminished status and destructive relationships.[41] The melody stays the same but the lyrics change, so that the intensity with which Tara sang that Willow "make[s] me complete" is transferred to the new lyrics, when Tara declares that by staying with Willow "there will be nothing left of me." Tara and Giles's chorus is "Believe me/I don't want to go/And it'll grieve me/'Cause I love you so." Tara's duet aligns her with Giles whilst also queerly inverting the classical Hollywood use of the duet—as in Tara's case it signifies the end of an idyllic queer romance.

Rick Altman theorizes that "pairing off is the natural impulse of the musical, whether it be in the presentation of the plot, the splitting of the screen, the choreography of the dance, or even the repetition of a melody."[42] He further clarifies that in the musical, "the duet serves the important function of crystallizing the couple's attitudes and emotions."[43] However, Buffy and Spike's duet represents another inversion of the film musical's heterosexual courtship myth and perhaps the ultimate parody of the musical's narrative conventions as their subsequent sadomasochistic relationship will further subvert the romance of the musical. Buffy and Spike's relationship results in part from the merging of their outcast status, sanctioned neither by society nor by the Scooby gang; and the intermeshing of their two songs sets up their kiss as the product of conflicting and self-centered desires. The composition of their duet, defined by Spike's punk-rocker and Buffy's pop-ballad musical styles, reflects the discordance of their relationship and the undercutting of the courtship myth.[44] They do not, like Xander and Anya, share a chorus, melody, or even the same lines. Consequently, we understand from Spike and Buffy's duet how they feel about themselves but not how they feel about a relationship with each other.

Spike and Buffy's duet and kiss results from the final big production number, which depicts the Scoobies drifting away from each other and Spike and Buffy walking out on all of them. With Spike and Buffy's kiss the heartache and the loss of love for all begins. The finale of the musical in this episode, therefore, cannot simply be a metaphor for lasting romance and compatibility. Instead, this echoing, complex moment engenders the disintegration of the Scoobies' relationships, as it creates the opening for Buffy and Spike's relationship and the destruction to come.

---

[41] In the next episode, "Tabula Rasa" (6.8), this alignment is continued through the scene of Tara and Giles separately leaving to the accompaniment of the Michelle Branch track "Goodbye To You."

[42] Altman, *The American Film Musical*, p. 32

[43] Ibid., p. 37.

[44] Earlier, in the episode "Crush" (5.14), Spike unsuccessfully tries to court Buffy by taking her on a stakeout to the accompaniment of the Ramones.

The Horror of the Musical's Courtship Myth

In contrast to the other aurally dominated performances, the emotional excess of Anya and Xander's performance exceeds the song-governed aural level to be equally connoted through their visually synchronized, highly choreographed dance number. Their performance is a pastiche of Fred Astaire and Ginger Rogers's production numbers, which represented a significant shift in American song-writing conventions: "Astaire and Rogers moved as effortlessly from talking to singing as they did from walking to dancing, and lyricists could write for them in a more thoroughly natural style."[45] The degree of naturalness was relative to earlier performances. Adapted for the diegetic realm of *Buffy*, it is the relative artificiality of this musical style and its metaphor for musical's heterosexual courtship myth which is on display. Anya and Xander's integrated aural and visual spectacular performance style of the classical Hollywood musical is reserved for this number, the opening number, the minor pieces performed by extras in the streets, especially the chimney sweep pastiche of *Mary Poppins* (1964) and the finale. However, their choreographed performance is clearly distinct from the usual choreographed, Chinese-inspired *Buffy* action sequences and their musical adaptation in Buffy's opening musical number. Anya and Xander's relationship and its imminent sanctification through marriage enacts the heterosexual courtship myth of the classical Hollywood musical, imbuing this couple with their most socially inclusory status. This performance style in itself sets Anya and Xander apart from the other Scoobies, who in their emotional moments echo the emotions and music videos of pop or rock stars.

The setting in their art deco apartment, Xander's silk pyjamas, Anya's fluffy slippers and shorty pyjamas and their synchronized tap dance style reference the Astaire-Rogers trademarks that, in addition to identifying these performers, symbolize "a way of life, a mediation between the way a character sees the world and the way the world sees the character."[46] Although the synchronized dancing of Xander and Anya likens them to Astaire and Rogers, the lyric of their song deconstructs the romantic myth. Their ironically titled number, "I'll Never Tell," is perhaps most clearly modeled on traditional Hollywood couples dances: Anya calls it a "retro pastiche" and not only the setting of their apartment, as Whedon points out,[47] but also the clothing they wear evokes the 1930s—as costume designer Bergstrom confirms it was intended to do.[48]

---

[45] Philip Furia, "Something to Sing About: America's Greatest Lyricists," *American Scholar*, 66/3 (1997), p. 385. See also Amy Bauer's chapter in this volume for further discussion of Astaire and Rogers in relation to this episode.

[46] Gerald Mast, *Can't Help Singin: The American Musical on Stage and Screen* (Woodstock, NY, 1987), p. 142.

[47] Whedon and Ruditis, *The Script Book*, p. 77.

[48] Ibid., p. 74.

Alluding to the dance performances of Astaire and Rogers supports Fiske and Hartley's contention that "dance in a typical entertainment programme ... [manages] the tensions inherent in our social structure and activity."[49] The underlying ideological appeal of the Astaire-Rogers musicals is their enactment of the Cinderella fable, "that class differences are merely superficial ones of appearance and behaviour."[50] Adapted by Anya and Xander, class difference is exchanged for species difference (she is an ex-demon) and the shared desire for a place of acceptance and belonging of two differently defined social misfits. The perseverance of this myth is reflected through the requirement of both music and dance to enact its deconstruction, unlike pop song's romantic myth that can be unsettled with only a phrase change.

This musical number reinforces Douglas Kellner's contention that through television, as through so many other avenues across the centuries, "comedy and satire have often been effective means of social criticism and enlightenment."[51] The use of direct address could be interpreted as bringing the audience into their humorous complaints (to receive Xander's mugging unhappiness over Anya's cheese, we must locate ourselves in the back of their refrigerator), and they invite identification by long-term viewers with intratextual references such as Anya's complaint that "his penis got diseases from the Chumash tribe," referring to "Pangs" (4.8). They exhibit a seemingly chipper reflexivity, such as Xander's irritation at Anya's vocal interruption: "This is my verse, hello!" At the end of the number, they fall together laughing in a typical musical comedy closing suggestive of the supposed spontaneity of their performance, intentionally mirroring the end of the "Good Morning" number in *Singin' in the Rain* (1952).[52] Anya and Xander's duet wavers from love, acceptance, and commitment, to fear, criticism, and complaints. The words of their song, delivered comically, pastiche what Furia describes as the "thorny phrases" Ira Gershwin used in the songs he wrote for Fred Astaire, especially, "Let's Call the Whole Thing Off."[53] "I'll Never Tell" expresses Anya and Xander's apprehensions about their relationship and dissatisfactions with each other but always returns to the refrain, promising "I'll never tell"—a phrase which fails to recoup the love in their relationship or suggest that these problems can be contained by this simple solution.

The unity conveyed by Anya and Xander's synchronized movements, completed by falling onto a sofa and laughing at the end of their song, suggests that they are perfectly matched and, like the couples in Hollywood musicals, their compatibility means they will work out their problems and unite happily ever after. This relationship of the visual performance juxtaposed to the intent of the

---

[49] John Fiske and John Hartley, *Reading Television* (London, 1978), p. 127.
[50] Ibid.
[51] Douglas Kellner, "TV, Ideology, and Emancipatory Popular Culture," in Horace Newcomb (ed.), *Television: The Critical View* (New York, Oxford, 1987), p. 487.
[52] Whedon and Ruditis, *The Script Book*, p. 59.
[53] Furia, "Something to Sing About," p. 389.

lyrics remodels the juxaposition established in Tara's pop love song. The bedroom scene in Tara's performance of "Under Your Spell" is so explicitly intimate that for some it may invoke parody. In contrast the visual dance images of "I'll Never Tell" connote an intimacy and synchronicity between Anya and Xander that their lyrics seek to dispel. However, the cut from their musical number to the following scene where Xander and Anya walk down the street separated by Giles, undermines this visual, choreographed assuredness and instead reaffirms the self-deception of their performance.

Their dance operates as a contemporary reconfiguration of the dancers and performances on the television series *Come Dancing* discussed by Fiske and Hartley. Similar to these dancers, Anya and Xander are "using a form of behavioural irony by appearing to act as … [something they are not, using] formalizations of the dances traditionally performed in ordinary social life."[54] They talk over each other when they disparately describe their musical number as "a nightmare, a plague" and the horror that it was a "retro pastiche" rather than "breakaway pop hit."[55] This use of "retro" song and dance effectively highlights the couple's ideological separation from the rest of the Scoobies, whose own identity issues are reflected through musical performances from far more contemporary musical subcultures. Anya and Xander's number recodes the Hollywood musical's usually positive emotional impetus for the spontaneous eruption into song and dance. Consequently, the ideologies surrounding heterosexual courtship conveyed by these musicals is equally suggested to be socially inadequate, a social veneer used to mask complexity and disintegration.

The street scene subsequent to "I'll Never Tell" is marked by their physical separation and loss of any synchronicity previously displayed in speech, outlook and movements. This effectively dismantles the social coherence and harmony of their musical number. Instead of the joy of barrier-breaking for the characters and those who identify with them, we are given a sense of loss of control. Their musical number expresses the reason for the later demise of their relationship. At the end of the musical, we find that Xander, the least magical of the Scoobies, has invoked the demon of the dance—because, as he says, addressing Anya, "I wanted to be sure we'd work out. Get a happy ending." Even by the end of this episode, with Anya and Xander barely looking at each other, the musical comedy ending is in doubt; and by the end of the season we have seen Xander jilt Anya at the altar and Anya return to being a vengeance demon (as she foreshadows in "Once More, with Feeling" when she sings, "There's wedding and betrayal").

Thomas Schatz suggests that "the musical celebrates the resolution of its inherent cultural conflicts—which are generally couched in terms of American

---

[54] Fiske and Hartley, *Reading Television*, pp. 130–31.

[55] Fiske and Hartley suggest that "the ritual of dance is not a form of psychotherapy for the individual, for what it offers is effective for him only in so far as it binds him into his subculture." Ibid., p. 139.

courtship—by projecting the moment of romantic fulfilment into eternity."[56] Andrew Sarris further suggests that this romantic myth holds greater currency "in the nineties than it did in the forties."[57] In the classical Hollywood musical, the successful coupling is achieved through a romantic fallacy dependent on "reconciling terms previously seen as mutually exclusive ... reducing an unsatisfactory paradox to a more workable configuration, a concordance of opposites."[58] The narrative trajectory of "Once More, with Feeling" seemingly supports this romantic ideology. However, the supradiegetic moments do not revel in the fantasy of utopian love and romance as in the Hollywood musical; instead they reveal the myth of heterosexual courtship to be a fallacy based on a deceptive image which masks deeply held anxieties and resentment. Therefore, when the musical's danced duet is adapted for television, the promise never to tell negates the promise to live happily ever after. The pastiche of Anya and Xander's number informs the dance finale of the episode constructed around the disintegration of the group because of the disintegrating couples and the formation of the destructive coupling of Buffy and Spike.

Deconstructing the Classical Hollywood Musical Utopian Ending

Towards the end of the episode, "Walk Through the Fire" operates like the "Tonight" number in Sondheim and Bernstein's *West Side Story* (1961),[59] cutting from character to character in different locations as they sing first separately, then in interwoven parts, just as they move together physically as well. But "Walk Through the Fire," in the Christophe Beck/Jesse Tobias arrangement, begins with the same guitar notes that open Simon and Garfunkel's "The Sound of Silence," that ultimate ode to the failure to communicate. Michael Dunne praises "I've Got a Theory," saying "the song sets all of the characters in motion and even predicts the ultimate resolution because Buffy does need the help of others to stand up to Sweet in the end."[60] However, as Buffy and her friends seem to move towards each other in "Walk Through the Fire," they are not simply singing of the traditional idea of going through difficulty for each other, walking through fire for each other; they end the song by singing that they will "let it burn." And, in fact, in the following number, "Something to Sing About," they do almost let Buffy burn: they are so shocked by her announcement that they have pulled her out of heaven that they do

---

[56] Thomas Schatz, *Old Hollywood/New Hollywood: Ritual, Art and Industry* (Ann Arbor, MI, 1983), p. 125.

[57] Andrew Sarris, *You Ain't Heard Nothin' Yet: The American Talking Film History and Memory 1927–1949* (Oxford/New York, 1998), p. 61.

[58] Altman, *The American Film Musical*, p. 27.

[59] Joss Whedon, "Once More with Feeling" audio commentary, *Buffy the Vampire Slayer Season Six DVD Collection* (2003).

[60] Dunne, *American Film Musical*, p. 180.

nothing as she begins to spontaneously combust, to dance herself to death. It is the late-arriving Spike (presumably the most flammable among them) who stops her, not the group acting together (although Giles has earlier asked Tara and Anya to act as her "back-up"). It should also be noted that when Buffy uses direct address to the audience in "Something to Sing About"—looking at the camera and singing "and you can sing along"—she is inviting the audience to share not the traditional musical wish-fulfilment, but her sense of lonely despair.

The formal conventions of a television series and the unsatisfactory paradox of Spike and Buffy's union both undermine the validity of the film musical's ending. Thomas Schatz argues that, in the classical Hollywood musical, "it is precisely because of the musical finale and its ritualistic function of celebrating romantic love and American courtship rites that we do not speculate beyond the film's closing moments."[61] In contrast, the closing production number, "Where Do We Go from Here?" brings the larger group together physically on the floor of the Bronze, which has become the stage of the small screen; but the number undercuts that togetherness in a variety of ways. While in "I've Got a Theory," the Scoobies sing directly to each other, in "Where Do We Go," they start the song scattered about the stage, facing different directions; only Buffy and Spike are facing each other, and they seem hardly to dare to glance at each other. Similarly, Xander and Anya look at each other only briefly, and the others do not make any eye contact. Costumer Cynthia Bergstrom notes that "throughout the episode there was a very subtle color coding going on. I had picked various colors for each character."[62] At one point in "Where Do We Go from Here?" the eight characters—an octave—stand in a line literally displaying all the colors of the rainbow. The rainbow could suggest joining in variety, or simply difference, but the interrelationships are even more specific: Willow and Tara are in complementary colors, violet and yellow; Xander and Anya are in similarly complementary orangey brown and grayish blue; Spike and Buffy are dressed in the same colors of black and red. The separation of colors could, of course, indicate the separation of the characters—or, in Buffy and Spike's case, the joining that would soon come. The color coding is perhaps most clearly apparent at the part of the production number which displays the tension between individual and group: all the characters stand in a diagonal line, clasping hands in a heavy-handed, mechanical fashion in time to the music, one after another, and then at once flinging apart from each other. The accompanying lyrics for this movement in the visual are "Understand we'll go hand in hand, but we'll walk alone in fear"—not "We'll walk alone in fear, but understand we'll go hand in hand"—and it hardly takes a rhetorical expert to note the difference in the emphasis.

"Once More, with Feeling" demonstrates that working in community is not a simple or easy thing. Its narrative, visual, musical, and dance structures challenge, without finally rejecting, this important Buffyverse value. Both the demon's

---

[61] Schatz, *Old Hollywood/New Hollywood*, p. 158.
[62] Whedon and Ruditis, *The Script Book*, p. 74.

closing song and the Scoobies' final number question their community. Michael Wood asserts that in music "as in literature you take journeys, and (if you're lucky) you come home. But home, every time, is different because of your journey."[63] The Scoobies' community is different because of their musical journey. This episode thus questions the standard Hollywood musical value of the concluding reintegration into the community, so important a part of the Hollywood musical romance; and this questioning finds repeated support in the episode's various methods of demystification.

Conclusion

"Once More, with Feeling" strains at emotional and textual boundaries as it rewrites *Buffy*'s and the classical Hollywood musical's balance between textual consciousness and emotional immersion. Undercutting the Hollywood musical's cheery conclusion, and reconfiguring its founding premise, the musical episode of *Buffy* even prevents the very form itself from "going through the motions." It is the classical Hollywood musical's ideologies that are ultimately rejected. "Once More, with Feeling" makes this explicit through its formal structure.

Contrary to the classical Hollywood musical, this episode provides the foundations for the disintegration of relationships: the musical numbers announce the deterioration of romance. When the musical's style and ideology is mapped onto an episode of this horror-fantasy television series, the fantasy structures of the musical are reconfigured to no longer suggest utopian transcendence and optimism, but the horror of the mundane and the loss of joyful romantic closure. By emphasizing these utopian romantic expectations, the series's later tragedies of romance become all the more pronounced. For those who view the episode as a standalone event (as has often happened, sometimes with movie-theater screenings), the balance is changed: audiences respond with ebullient pleasure; but in these situations the narrative structure has been changed by the episode's extraction from the series.

The demon Sweet (who undermines saccharine romance), has been invoked by Xander to get "a happy ending" but in the end, Sweet (actor Hinton Battle, the consummate representative of Broadway) sings: "There's not a one/Who can say this ended well/All those secrets you've been concealing/Say you're happy now/Once more, with feeling." As that great popular entertainer Dickens long ago suggested, "false pretences" can lead metaphorically to spontaneous combustion.[64] Xander's secret invocation of Sweet for the sake of his own happy ending is just one of the many deceptions that tear at both the community and individual happiness.

---

[63] Michael Wood, "Blue in Green," *The Antioch Review*, 57/3 (1999), p. 302. Wood is speaking in particular about jazz here, but his comments are equally applicable to all musical idioms.

[64] Charles Dickens, *Bleak House* [1853] (Harmondsworth, 1971), p. 511.

"Some characters just die combusting," as Sweet says, apparently those who were holding in so much that the final release is overpowering—a few unnamed souls, though Buffy is almost among them. "The curtains close with a kiss, God knows," the Scoobies sing just before Buffy and Spike's closing embrace. The narrative, for some, is re-sutured with this kiss. But in the moment that we see the happy ending, we are lyrically reminded that we are seeing a "happy ending," a "closing kiss": we balance between immersion and distance. For some of us, the balance is lost: in this long-term television narrative, the musical's vertical narration, its supposed ability to tell everything at once, is shadowed by our knowledge of what lies ahead. None of the Scoobies dies in this episode; however, all of them will suffer. The emotional self-combustion that threatens them throughout the last years of the series is adumbrated in the slow burn of "Once More, with Feeling." And the Hollywood musical itself may be smoldering, too.

Chapter 12
"Give Me Something to Sing About": Intertextuality and the Audience in "Once More, with Feeling"

Amy Bauer

> "I love all musicals."
> (Joss Whedon, audio commentary to
> "Once More, with Feeling.")

Critics hailed "Once More, with Feeling" (6.7) as a brilliant example of the television musical. Its musical numbers flow from the narrative, yet prove integral to the seven-year arc of the series, and its eclectic but unified score was written expressly for the talents of a cast (mostly) new to the genre. Notably, its book, score, and concept all sprang from one mind, that of the Buffyverse's primary architect, Joss Whedon.

Although untrained in musical composition, Whedon's affection for and knowledge of the American musical are everywhere evident, even if we did not have John Kenneth Muir's admission that he is a "virtual encyclopedia of musical film history."[1] Analogous to the combined cinematic genres—from horror to religious epic—that mark *Buffy the Vampire Slayer* and *Angel*, "Once More, with Feeling" alludes to Sondheim and Loesser alongside the sardonic charm of 1940s music, 1950s swing jazz, 1970s arena rock, 1980s power ballads, and 1990s soft-rock confessionals, all within a lean, swift-moving structure that performs the dramatic functions of the classic American musical.

Much has already been written regarding the novelty, influence, and intertextual richness of the *Buffy* musical.[2] My contribution to that literature analyzes the musical structure of the songs themselves and places it in a dialogic relationship to the sources they summon. Such intertextual richness acknowledges fans' devotion to and knowledge of both the show's history and cultural references to the

---

[1] John Kenneth Muir, *Singing a New Tune: The Rebirth of the Modern Film Musical, from Evita to De-Lovely and Beyond* (New York, 2005), p. 10.

[2] See, for example, essays in the bibliography by Richard S. Albright, Jamie Clarke, and Jeffrey R. Middents, as well as conference papers by William Donaruma, Cynthia Masson, and Todd Williams. It is also discussed by Rhonda Wilcox in *Why Buffy Matters: the Art of Buffy the Vampire Slayer* (London, 2005), pp. 191–205, and the other chapters in Part III of this volume.

American musical. The harmonic and rhythmic structure of songs, in conjunction with dance, book, and stage direction, self-reflexively evokes distinct musical eras, held up as paradigms for the situation of characters in the fictional world of Sunnydale. Whedon's own commentaries suggest that "Once More, with Feeling" functions as a critique of the genre and its history on both small and large screen. In this it reflects the fears and desires of "genre fans" everywhere, as it conflates the utopian fantasy of the musical with the dystopian fantasy of the Buffyverse.[3] Whedon acknowledges and incorporates those fears within the narrative as ironic asides, juxtapositions, and musical jokes that ease our entry into the episode. The conflation of two fantasy worlds—the musical and the fantasy/sci-fi show—generates a greater truth, to the surprise of both the characters "on stage" and those of us in the audience.

To this end, I analyze the songs and their contexts in a (rough) parallel to the history of the American stage and screen musical. Numbers are grouped by style and intratextual reference, followed by summary remarks on the musical as a whole and how it functions within the history of the series.

Swing Time

> I believe all film in the history of cinema aspires to be Fred Astaire. I think he is the single greatest phenomenon in the history of film. The airiness, the transcendence, the delight, the absolute authority ... He was built to dance.[4]

I'll Never Tell

The most self-consciously historical number of "Once More, with Feeling" is Anya and Xander's self-described "retro pastiche" dance number in the key of C, "I'll Never Tell," in the style of a classic Astaire-partnered comedy dance (a staple of his films with Ginger Rogers in the 1930s). The jazzy chords that slide down chromatically in the bass signal the typical vamp intro to a tune straight out of the Great American Songbook. But by actually beginning the tune with the indecisive vamp in B♭ (arriving in the middle of a cadence that never achieves closure) Whedon heightens the ambivalence of Anya and Xander's emotions toward their approaching wedding.

---

[3] On the musical as utopian fantasy, see Paul Filmer, Val Rimmer, and Dave Walsh, "'Oklahoma!': Ideology and Politics in the Vernacular Tradition of the American Musical," *Popular Music*, 18/3 (1999), pp. 381–95. A discussion of the history of the term "genre" as it connotes current sci-fi and fantasy texts in general is found in Matthew Surridge, "Comics and Codes: Biography as Genre (a Reply to 'Based on a True Story')," *The Comics Journal*, September (1999), accessed 1 May 2008 at http://www.tcj.com/3_online/b_surridge_092299.html.

[4] Joss Whedon quoted in Muir, *Singing a New Tune*, p. 27.

"I'll Never Tell" is composed as a standard: as opposed to the rock-influenced numbers that precede it, its harmony remains in a jazz-influenced traditional style. Anya and Xander trade unstable verses that never reach the tonic (the home chord), hitting the chord a half-step above the dominant chord instead, to force a traditional if witty modulation to the key of G. In this way, A♭ (as ♭VI) becomes the tritone substitute for the secondary dominant as they enter the chorus, as shown in Figure 12.1.[5] As Anya and Xander consistently "miss" the tonic, despite their best intentions, so they have missed one another's true fears, and their engagement will never find closure in marriage.

Figure 12.1   Tritone substitution in "I'll Never Tell"

The overtones of a later era of Broadway surface as the leads trade bars, and the battling chorus moves into a quickstep swing rhythm in 4/4. The *No, No, Nanette* (1925) styling of the music includes the strong two-beat feel and the Charleston rhythm that closes every four bars, while the accompanying lyrical ripostes recall the clever banter by Dorothy Field or Ira Gershwin that characterized the Astaire-Rogers duets in the films *Swing Time* (1936) and *Shall We Dance* (1937).

---

[5]   I use both Roman numeral and pop chord analytic symbols, with major and minor triads differentiated by upper- and lower-case letters respectively. All musical examples are based on the published sheet music in Joss Whedon and Paul Ruditis, *Buffy the Vampire Slayer, 'Once More, With Feeling': The Script Book*, ed. Micol Ostow (New York, 2002). Lyrics refer to those published in Whedon and Ruditis, as well as the CD notes to *Buffy the Vampire Slayer: "Once More, with Feeling"* (Rounder Records, 2002).

Both music and lyrics betray an ironic distance: the closed high-hat and stomp rhythm of the chorus—slowed and stylized to allow the leads to interact—evokes an earlier era than that of the "hip" lyrics. Yet the frank dialogue is not out of place in the pre-Hays Code 1920s atmosphere evoked by the music ("His penis got diseases from a Chumash tribe" is an intratextual reference to an event in the episode "Pangs" [4.8]). The specific reference is to the genteel comedic banter enjoyed by the post-code Fred and Ginger: where Fred sang "You like vanilla and I like vanella,"[6] Xander sings "She eats these skeezy cheeses that I can't describe"; where Ginger complained that Fred was "no insults and all morals," Anya complains that "When things get rough he just hides behind his Buffy."

The double-time wordless dance bridge that follows serves the same function that dance did in those classic 1930s musicals: where words fail, feet take over, and Anya and Xander are re-united in movement. The irony continues unabated, however, as they swing dance to a late-1960s mocking funk vamp, a coded sign of the "swinging sixties" that segues into their warm reunion. Here both language and music reflect an earlier era, while a dark hint of what will come later in the sixth season enters in the chorus ("I read this tale, there's wedding then betrayal"). The climax of the number, with Anya and Xander singing in unison "We could really raise the beam in making marriage a hell" perfectly unites *Buffy*'s supernatural premise with the legacy of the partner dance and the very ordinary fears of the mortal fan contemplating a defining stage of adulthood, a staple of the show from the beginning.

The final verse plays with the rhythm as both lyrics and music (with a temporary resolution of the continually evaded cadence) resolve the song's internal tensions. Yet those tensions resurface and come to a peak in the coda, to delay the climactic dominant (D^7) with a sly reference to A♭ in "thank God, I'll never tell" as the pair strike one more evocative pose and topple back into the sofa "laughing, in classic post-musical number style." Here Anya and Xander reference a very specific scene in *Shall We Dance*, where Fred and Ginger strike one last "balletic" pose before toppling into the grass at the close of "Let's Call the Whole Thing Off." As Anya and Xander were uncomfortable mounting a classic partner dance—complete with overhead angled shot—so Astaire and Rogers were uncharacteristically awkward on roller skates, with their clumsiness operating as an ironic backdrop to the sophisticated rhymes of Ira Gershwin's lyrics.

As the only stable couple in "Once More, with Feeling,"[7] Xander and Anya's extended battle serves the same purpose as do the partner dances of Astaire and Rogers, which "choreograph their sexual relation in terms of comparability and

---

[6] Ira Gershwin, lyrics, "Let's Call the Whole Thing Off" (1937).

[7] An online analysis by Rowan gives as astute analysis of the three couples in "Let's Face the Music and Dance: Couples in 'OMwF,'" *Tabula Rasa—Love. Redemption. Spike.* (2001), accessed 2 May 2008 at http://www.btvs-tabularasa.net/essays/FaceTheMusic.html.

partnership without losing its romance and erotic charge."⁸ The viewer experiences a rich portrait of the couple in a relatively brief time: Anya was a man-hating demon reformed by Xander's love, while Xander is a "regular guy" both smitten with and somewhat troubled by his mate.

The props that serve as reflections of their "ordinary life" reflect the magical role of props in famous scenes such as "Make 'em Laugh" from *Singin' in the Rain* (1952), in which Donald O'Connor dodges a sound stage full of everyday hazards. By overcoming them and taming his surroundings, he opens up the physical and virtual space of the musical number (a metaphor highlighted when O'Connor confuses the canvas wall of the set with an actual wall at the dance's climax). The Sunnydale Press newspaper advertising the musical mayhem, the refrigerator, and the kitchen table are all players in "I'll Never Tell," and through them the viewer realizes the extent of the town's transformation. As Sutton described the meaning of props in the musical,

> This transmutation of objects, of the quotidian, is achieved by sheer force of imagination in the protagonists. Objects and settings from the everyday world of the surrounding plot (the "real" world) are given a new meaning by their use within the number (the idealized world).⁹

At the end of Anya and Xander's dance we smash cut to them walking with Giles through Sunnydale. At this point, our protagonists have not given all that much thought to their impulsive need to sing and dance away their innermost fears and hopes. Anya, ever the cultural critic, worries aloud over why her and Xander's number was a "retro pastiche," while Xander, the most anxious of the Scoobies, proclaims it "a nightmare, a plague … it's like a nightmare about a plague." Giles confirms their fears by noting that, indeed, a musical immolation occurred, although in his self-effacing fashion he dryly notes "I just saw the one—I managed to examine the body while the police were taking witness arias." Their self-analysis cuts deeper as all three are, in fact, still very much within the "retro pastiche," as street cleaners synchronously dance and a young woman (played by co-executive producer Marti Noxon) pleads her case with a traffic cop.

What You Feel

We caught a glimpse of the musical demon Sweet—played by Broadway star Hinton Battle—at the close of Act I, at the point where the musical spell that has infected Sunnydale took a turn toward the dark side. Upon the spontaneous combustion of a man who literally danced himself to death, Sweet intones "That's

---

⁸ Steven Cohan, "Feminizing the Song and Dance Man," in Steven Cohan (ed.), *Hollywood Musicals: The Film Reader* (New York, 2002), p. 93.

⁹ Martin Sutton, "Patterns of Meaning in the Musical," in Rick Altman (ed.), *Genre: The Musical* (London, 1981), p. 190.

entertainment!". This directly references *The Band Wagon* (1953) as well as a 1974 collection of favorite musical clips that defined and classified the American film musical for later generations. The numbers in *That's Entertainment!* allow the stars of the American film musical to live forever; but the dance to death is Sweet's distillation of the musical "plague," the finale for which he sits patiently through love songs, dancing dry-cleaner patrons and witness arias. As we prepare for his official entrance, the hapless Dawn is kidnapped just as she breaks into song, only to awaken splayed out on a pool table in the Bronze. Dawn's number is thus transformed into an elegant, Cyd Charisse-like dance number as she negotiates the space of the Bronze with Sweet's puppet-masked henchmen.[10]

Darkly coded, minor-key orchestral background music leads up to Sweet's entrance during Dawn's ballet.[11] As Dawn feints with the puppet minions, strings sigh over *pizzicato* cellos, an ominous oboe melody, and a diminished run in harp and bell chimes, orchestration that alludes to the cinematic reveal of a villain's dark plans in fantastic films from the 1980s onward (for example, in Danny Elfman's scores for Tim Burton such as the entrance of Catwoman in *Batman Returns*, 1992, or the "Evil Eye" scene in *Sleepy Hollow*, 1999). Yet at Sweet's entrance the music is pared down to a jazz trio with a distinctly laid-back shuffle rhythm. Whedon notes that Dawn's confrontation with Sweet "brings her to a sexualized place."[12] Likewise the fantasy scoring gives way to jazz and blues with its cinematic connotations of seduction. Whedon also mentions that he had stairs added to the Bronze set so that Sweet could descend onto the stage gradually in a scene that recalls Astaire's use of steps on the shipboard set of "Slap That Bass," also from *Shall We Dance*,[13] the lyrics of which also echo the sentiments of Sweet's song.

As we might expect from Sweet's modified zoot suit and his soft-shoe entrance, "What You Feel" is a jazz swing tune with blues inflections. The "cool" vibe of the demon is coded by his dress and the particulars of his tune: its cyclic structure, blues appropriations, and the gently rocking, double plagal cadence that marks the last four bars of the refrain: g minor–C–g minor–F–g minor (i–IV–i–♭VII–i). Figure 12.2 gives an overview of the structure: upper-case letters are assigned to each repetition of the refrain: all *A* sections begin on the tonic, while *B* sections

---

[10] Dawn's ballet with the masked henchman reminds Jamie Clarke of the rape scene in Stanley Kubrick's *A Clockwork Orange* (1971), "that similarly demonised the musical by being accompanied by a rendition of 'Singin' in the Rain'." Jamie Clarke, "Affective Entertainment In 'Once More, with Feeling': A Manifesto for Fandom," *Refractory*, 2 (2003), accessed 1 May 2008 at http://blogs.arts.unimelb.edu.au/refractory/2003/03/18/affective-entertainment-in-once-more-with-feeling-a-manifesto-for-fandom-jamie-clarke/.

[11] Whedon reveals that he asked Beck for "something like Peter and the Wolf." Joss Whedon, "Once More, with Feeling" audio commentary, *Buffy the Vampire Slayer: Season Six DVD Collection* (2003).

[12] Ibid.

[13] Ibid.

begin on the supertonic.[14] Although the audience never hears his name ("I got a hundred" he later tells Buffy), we will call him "Sweet".[15] Whether intentional irony or not, "sweet" was the term for the saccharine, pre-composed vocal and orchestrally enhanced jazz pioneered by Paul Whiteman and marketed to a predominantly white audience through the 1920s and 1930s.[16]

Figure 12.2   Phrase structure of "What you Feel"

>A: a a' b a"
>Why'd you run away? ...

>A: a a' b a"
>I'm the heart of swing ...

>A': a''' a''' a a'
>'Cause I know what you feel, girl ...

>B: b a" b' b"
>All those hearts lay open, that must sting ...

>A": a''' a''' b b (harmonic syncopation)
>'Cause I know what you feel, girl ...

>Tag: b''' a"
>I bought Nero his very first fiddle ... That's what it's all about!

Sweet approaches Dawn, and reveals to her and the audience why he has arrived in Sunnydale in the first (*A*) chorus. The second chorus details the nature of the particular musical curse he inflicts, leading Dawn to the (spoken) interjection "So, you're, like, a good demon? Bringin' the fun in?" Once again, props define the diegetic space and delineate characters in lieu of verbal exposition. Dawn and the minions journey off the pool table and around the Bronze to define Sweet's lair and the space that will later serve as a showdown between Buffy and the demon. Sweet towers over Dawn, who slides across the floor submissively as he enters in a low-angle shot. Yet his descent mirrors the ambiguity voiced in the first two refrains: an angel might descend, metaphorically, from some moral height, but

---

[14]   Lower-case letters indicate four-bar phrases and are assigned by harmonic function (a phrases begin on the tonic, while b phrases begin on a pre-dominant), to reveal each a phrase as a microcosm of the whole. The lyrics quoted indicate only the beginning of the relevant verse, not the complete lyric associated with that phrase.

[15]   Whedon and Ruditis, *The Script Book*, p. 16.

[16]   Lewis A. Erenberg, *Swingin' the Dream: Big Band Jazz and the Rebirth of American Culture* (Chicago, 1998), p. 11.

we expect a "bad" demon to ascend from hell. Later Sweet ascends the stairs, as did Jack Buchanan playing the tyrannical but cowed director Jeffrey Cordova in the backstage version of *Faust* that illuminated the larger romantic drama of *The Band Wagon*.

The third chorus suggests the dark side of Sweet's reign, while the second (*B*) chorus confirms it: by causing people to sing and dance their most intimate and intense emotions, "that energy/Starts to come on way too strong." The result is pain and the occasional self-immolation, the Faustian bargain or "penalty/When life is but a song." We leave the stability of the tonic in favor of the unstable Neapolitan (♭II) harmony when Sweet sings "You brought me down and doomed this town." Yet, despite his power, Sweet never professes factual, empirical knowledge of the world. His repeated claims that "I know what you feel, girl" sum up his character. Sweet is an empathic demon who unleashes his emotional knowledge in that popular dramatic form that enshrines heightened emotion as its *raison d'être*: the musical. He has existed for centuries; his brief visit to Sunnydale comes not coincidentally at a point in Buffy's journey in which everyone in her orbit bears difficult and painful passions that need release. Whedon explains why Sweet is later allowed a mysterious exit: "He is the musical, incarnate, and he's all around us, and that's where we put him."[17]

That Sweet is a "professional" music demon is marked, as Jeffrey Middents notes, by Hinton Battle's superior singing and dancing skills.[18] Middents feels that the singular nature of Battle's performance dangerously recalls those Golden Era musicals that confined African-American performers to one walk-on performance per film. Casting Sweet as African-American may be an ironic reference to earlier codes, but there is no doubt that Battle's skills, in conjunction with the jazz idiom, slick dress, and casual speech mark him as profoundly hip. The fascination of white culture with the masculine attributes of the African–American musician entails harmful ethical assumptions. Yet, as Ingrid Monson notes, the notion of "hipness" relies as much on discipline, dignity, and social consciousness as it does on transgressive or socially marginal behavior.[19] Sweet is not only the sole professional entertainer in Sunnydale; he is the only character comfortable with who and what he is, with nothing to hide from the world. Hence his comfort with one key and one style: Sweet has the only number with a clearly defined, unambiguous cadential closure. As Middents notes, he has the upper hand throughout the episode, and leaves of his own accord. When "What You Feel" is reprised, Sweet delivers the episode's title as an ironic aside, as "All those secrets you've been concealing" succeeded in bringing hell on earth.

---

[17] Whedon, "Once More, with Feeling" audio commentary.

[18] Jeffrey R. Middents, "A Sweet Vamp: Critiquing the Treatment of Race in *Buffy* and the American Musical Once More (with Feeling)," *Slayage* 17 (2005): 19.

[19] Ingrid Monson, "The Problem with White Hipness: Race, Gender, and Cultural Conceptions in Jazz Historical Discourse," *Journal of the American Musicological Society*, 48/3 (1995), p. 422.

That's Entertainment

> Vincente Minnelli is the beginning and the end of musical directors. I think that's exemplified in the number in *Brigadoon*'s "Waiting for My Dearie," which I could watch four hundred times. He could do more with a very little bit of movement in a very small room, than [other] people could do with a stadium.[20]

Under Your Spell

The central love song of "Once More, with Feeling" was shot in an "old-fashioned" long take,[21] as Tara professes not only her love to Willow but her belief that Willow's love has renewed her. Tara's lyrics reflect the larger-than-life fantasy projection that the "show of love," as Dennis Giles puts it, will abolish difference and result in a larger unity.[22] The diegetic staging of "Under Your Spell" literalizes the magic implied by the show of love in all musicals as the two witches transform their surroundings, moving from the idealized nature of a beautiful park to the intimate space of their bedroom, accompanied by dancing girls and pixie dust as metaphors for infatuation, and using levitation as a transparent metaphor for sexual union.

The structure of this scene and its carefully choreographed spaces recall Vincente Minnelli's staging of *Brigadoon* (1954), where magic was manifest in the shift from one place to another. In both musicals the experience of enchantment momentarily expands from a select group to admit outsiders: inhabitants of Brigadoon encounter visiting hunters, and Xander's invocation subsumes the whole of Sunnydale under its spell. Because "Under Your Spell" interrupts the Scooby gang's search for the musical menace behind this curse, it appears to halt the plot at this point; it thus hearkens back to the tension in classic MGM musicals of "a shifting and volatile dialectic between integrative and nonintegrative elements," or story versus spectacle.[23]

Yet, as did many of the romantic numbers in MGM musicals from *Meet Me in St Louis* (1944) to *Gigi* (1958), "Under Your Spell" has several functions that are crucial to the story. On the surface, innocent, trusting Tara is positioned at one end of a continuum, and her later break with the duplicitous Willow maintains a classic parallelism characteristic to musicals as a genre. As Tara and Willow delight in the joy of expressing their deepest emotions in song and dance—only to later become disillusioned and shocked by the result—so will the larger narrative unfold, as ever greater secrets emerge in song, and ever more desperate events unfold on Sunnydale's stage. In an even larger sense, this scene, like many others, hints at

---

[20] Whedon in Muir, *Singing a New Tune*, p. 51.
[21] Whedon, "Once More, with Feeling," audio commentary.
[22] Dennis Giles, "Show-making," in Altman (ed.), *Genre: The Musical*, p. 86.
[23] Martin Rubin, *Showstoppers: Busby Berkeley and the Tradition of Spectacle* (New York, 1993), p. 12.

events to come in the Buffyverse, when a large chunk of California will be under the spell of Dark Willow.

Tara's ballad answers the need for an unabashed love song; its purity of tone and intent highlights the pain of betrayal and loss when later reprised. Written in D major, the opening tonic-dominant chords promise a simple upbeat pop song, yet come to rest with a deceptive cadence on a subdominant ninth chord to reveal dark undercurrents as Tara details her earlier, unhappy life.

The first verse ends on an extended half cadence, while the chorus begins deceptively on the submediant (b minor). Tara's declaration combines "rock" Mixolydian with major: moving between parallel modes allows her to express her intensely amorous feelings with not one but two dominants, as subsequent phrases move through the A major dominant chord to cadence on C (♭VII).[24] She remains essentially on the dominant of B major during the bridge, before returning to D and another half cadence on A, the open musical structure expressive of her desire (see Figure 12.3).

Figure 12.3   Analytical reduction of verse, chorus, and bridge of "Under your Spell"

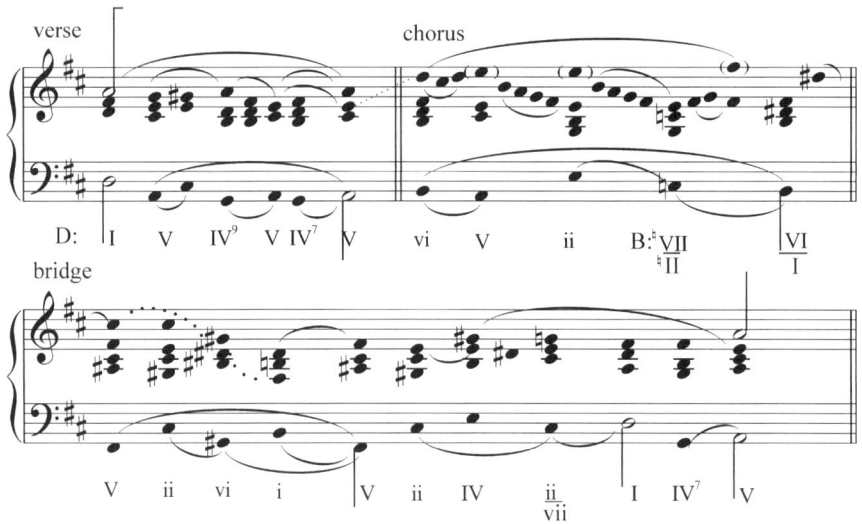

[24] The majority of contemporary rock songs have a modal basis in Mixolydian or Aeolian; both these and other so-called church modes serve as genre markers which became more important after the 1960s as pop genres fragmented into numerous subgenres. See especially Robert Walser's *Running With the Devil: Power, Genre, and Madness in Heavy Metal Music* (Middleton, CT, 1993), and Allan Moore's two articles, "Patterns of Harmony," *Popular Music*, 11/1 (1992), pp. 73–106, and "The So-called 'Flatted Seventh' in Rock," *Popular Music*, 14/2 (1995), pp. 185–201.

The verse never returns. Instead, a final chorus incorporates the bridge, its telescoped form signaling Willow and Tara's consummation. The filmic convention of an abrupt cut—so that the number never closes—signals the pleasurable excess of Tara and Willow's love, the "show of love" their number represents, and the capacity of the musical to contain this excess.

Rest in Peace

The second love song of "Once More, with Feeling" belongs to Spike, the vampire torn between his violent nature and his affection for Buffy and her sister. In a shot that rhymes with the opening to "Under Your Spell," the camera enters Spike's crypt with a generous pan, modeled on the first widescreen movies.[25] Given his inner battle, Spike gets a suitably conflicted ballad that forms a mirrored pair with "Under Your Spell." Tara expresses contentment while outside in the sun and open air; as her passion grows more intense, the pair retires to a bedroom and a mutual expression of love. Spike, hurt and angry, repudiates Buffy's scorn in his underground crypt. As his irritation finds release the two move to an outdoor cemetery but end the number with an accidental embrace in an open grave that repulses Buffy and leads her to flee.

Both intimate in the verse and brash in the chorus, "Rest in Peace," juxtaposes expressions of self-pity with fierce protest. It is constructed differently from either "Under Your Spell" or the retro numbers of Anya, Xander, and Sweet. Rather than four-bar phrases with closure, both verse and chorus of Spike's ballad are based on a circular chord progression composed of one- and two-bar harmonic modules. Its harmonic language remains resolutely modal (E Mixolydian) and elliptical, allowing the harmony to follow Spike's mercurial mood without taking the listener out of the tonal and emotional context. "Rest in Peace" frustrates cadential release by remaining Mixolydian, moving habitually to D and A (♭VII and IV) in a plagal motion repeated in the key of G (♭III).

The forward thrust of the song relies on rhythm, meter, and tempo: a harmonic rhythm of one chord per bar is associated with stability, two chords with motion, and four chords with closure. Spike does not find harmonic release until the climactic bridge, where an abrupt pivot through b minor takes him to the key of C♯ major (VI, enharmonically written as D♭ in the sheet music). Only in this guitar-unfriendly key will Spike reach a "real" dominant in the form of G♯, before a deceptive cadence returns him to the E Mixolydian of the chorus (the transition from C♯ back to E is shown in an analytical reduction in Figure 12.4).

---

[25] Whedon cites *Brigadoon, West Side Story, Les Girls* and *It's Always Fair Weather* in his audio commentary to the episode.

Figure 12.4   Transition from C♯ to E in "Rest in Peace"

Chris McDonald calls such a progression modal subversion, identifying it with the practices of guitar-oriented alternative rock musicians of the 1990s.[26] Thus the shift to C♯ in the bridge reveals Spike's true feelings, as well as his true Otherness, as neither monster nor man, neither sentimental crooner nor hardcore punk. The progression that ends both verse and chorus signals closure primarily as a descending bass line, one that slides down anticlimactically to the tonic (G–F♯–E). This "anti-cadence" projects Spike's world-weary outlook and implies that he must wait to find true closure.

The mainstream rock style evoked in the chorus strikes a balance between Spike's association with both punk rock/cultural rebellion and sentimental fare (such as his peculiar attachment to daytime soap opera and the mundane conviviality of pub crawling). Loyal viewers will recognize allusions to Spike's long history of romantic suffering in the lyrics, which feature anaphora ("Let me rest … Let me get … Let me take …"), ironic metaphor ("since I'm only dead to you") and relentless rhyming in the climactic bridge ("… possessed … breast … guessed … chest … unimpressed"), all nods to his human past as a failed Victorian poet.

While Spike's persona is of recent vintage, the role of an unrequited lover with a highly ambivalent relationship to the object of his affection has been a staple of the classic musical since Laurey's dream in *Oklahoma!* (1943). Spike will leave behind the person he was, as Fred Astaire's cinematic hoofer left behind his former self to forge a new professional and personal union with Cyd Charisse at the close of *The Band Wagon*. The show of love enacted by Tara and Willow mirrors the show of love between the reluctant but passionate lovers Buffy and Spike, who will close the musical in a new relationship not only with one another but with their world.

---

[26] Chris McDonald, "Exploring Modal Subversions in Alternative Music," *Popular Music*, 19/3 (2000), pp. 360–63.

Comedy Tonight

> [My influences] were the old guys: Bock and Harnick, Frank Loesser; these were really big with me… Sondheim is, of course, the God of all things.[27]

I've Got a Theory/Bunnies/We're Together

The first ensemble piece, and the one that introduces the central conflict that drives the plot, is "I've Got a Theory/Bunnies/We're Together," sung by the Scooby gang as they gather in The Magic Box. Although "Theory" lies firmly in the musical comedy tradition,[28] its opening changes (A–G–f♯ minor–E) occur over a repeating "lament" descent in the bass (A–G–F♯–E), whose cyclic structure—and long-standing association with dread and romantic longing—suggest the complications to follow.

Each phrase expresses a theory on the surface (regarding the narrative's central conflict), as well as a theory regarding the characters and their relationship, coded through word choice, vocal contour, and rhythmic cadence. Giles states the truth (as a demon *does* cause all the mayhem), yet, in his typical, self-effacing manner, withdraws this insight. Willow reveals her characteristic optimism and prodigious memory in reaching back to season one ("Nightmares" [1.10]) for a possible solution ("some kid is dreamin'"). Reflecting the static situation, each phrase of the bassline returns to the beginning without resolution, structuring the verse as a question and answer. Characteristically, Xander interrupts the return to the beginning, subverting the formula with a Gilbert and Sullivan-like line of patter ("Which is ridiculous 'cause/witches they were persecuted Wicca good and love the earth and women power, and/I'll be over here.")

Xander's stoptime sets up Anya's break with the tune altogether: despite Tara's attempts to continue, she begins her own number, a heavy-metal diatribe against her sworn nemeses. "Bunnies" signals heavy-metal in timbre, dynamics, and mode, shifting to open guitar voicings on E (chord V of A),[29] and reversing the bassline with an ascent that emphasizes the didactic dominant-tonic cadence (Anya is quite sure that bunnies are evil). "Bunnies" is staged as a laser light show with appropriate histrionics as Anya screams "bunnies!" before an amusing *volte-face* pivot on G major for "Or maybe midgets."

As in the classic integrated musical, Anya's anthem serves as more than comic relief; it reveals Emma Caulfield as capable of great wit and emotional range. Anya has served as a bellwether of the Scoobies's emotional state since her reversion from vengeance demon to human. Thus, as the gang witness her outburst, their

---

[27] Whedon, "Once More, with Feeling," audio commentary.
[28] Ibid.
[29] We actually hear power chords that suggest D Dorian, the prototypical heavy metal mode. See Walser's discussion in *Running With the Devil*, pp. 46–51.

fears lock them into a repeating harmonic-emotional cycle of "what if?" that always ends on the dominant.

After "Bunnies" the two-beat feel of "Theory" returns, but the bassline continues to rise rather than fall, and a modulation from A to B major cues Buffy's disconsolate entrance. "We're Together" upsets the periodic four-bar motion from the tonic with a modulation to e minor prepared by the earlier shift to B major (chord V of E). The musical arrangement also shifts from orchestral scoring to 1970s soft-rock instrumentation, an appropriate accompaniment to hackneyed sentiments praising community ("What can't we face if we're together?") that mask our heroine's apathy and despair. Buffy's phrases don't follow the Baroque logic of "Theory" or the modal progression of "Bunnies," but begin and end with (chromatic) third relations: e minor–C and G–e minor. Just as her progression never cadences, so her question is never answered, requiring Anya's mini-reprise "except for bunnies" to close the number on an ironic note.

Unhappily Ever After

When Buffy peeks outside to see if all of Sunnydale really is "alive with music," she witnesses a classic production number, with a satirical twist: co-executive producer David Fury leads a dancing chorus of dry cleaning clients in "They Got the Mustard Out!" This nod to the musical past opens up the narrative present, as the insular and self-involved gang is thrust into something much larger than itself. As character revelations cause serious personal complications, so the community expression of joy in consumption will enact a price.

A musical like "Once More, with Feeling" would have been unthinkable before the split between the commercial Broadway musical and the art musical that occurred after Sondheim and Bernstein's *West Side Story* (1957). Like Whedon's musical, Sondheim's works combine modernist elements with "a thorough absorption and self-conscious utilization of the past."[30] Sondheim is famous for maintaining a high level of craftsmanship while deconstructing "happily ever after,"[31] a central theme in *Buffy the Vampire Slayer* and *Angel* as series. In a typical Sondheim musical, vernacular song enters the drama as "diegetic song," which—in contrast to the integrated book musical—creates a greater unity between verbal and musical elements. In Stephen Banfield's words, "the recognition of musical and lyric style [in diegetic song] actually becomes an issue in the plot ... [and] it takes on a heavily symbolic role."[32]

---

[30] Geoffrey Block, "The Broadway Canon from Show Boat to West Side Story and the European Operatic Ideal," *Journal of Musicology*, 11 (1993), pp. 541–2.

[31] David Walsh and Len Platt, *Musical Theater and American Culture* (Westport, CT, 2003), p. 134.

[32] Stephen Banfield, *Sondheim's Broadway Musicals* (Ann Arbor, 1993), pp. 184–6.

This is certainly the case with the wry asides peppered throughout "Once More, with Feeling"; Anya's self-conscious designation of her duet with Xander as retro pastiche, and her inquiry as to whether Spike's song was a "breakaway pop hit, or more of a book number," suggest that she perceives a larger form to the whole. Janet Halfyard problematizes this question, constructing a category of songs that are non-diegetic "whilst they are being sung" but which are perceived retrospectively as diegetic.[33] I agree with Richard S. Albright, who unequivocally states "there is no secondary diegesis, no separate world of the performance."[34] Not only is there no "backstage musical," but all that once was non-diegetic— emotional cues, background scoring and orchestral hits—is absorbed into the fabric of Sunnydale life, as revealed early in Act I when Giles quips "that would explain the huge backing orchestra I couldn't see and the synchronized dancing from the room service chaps."

Those caught up in the show are too busy disgorging their innermost feelings in song and dance to analyze the experience *in media res*. But Halfyard divines that "Once More, with Feeling" is not about the show—the threat of this week's villain—itself. As in painfully self-reflexive works such as Sondheim's *Company* (1970), in which characters comment upon their songs, and *Into the Woods* (1987), in which characters deconstruct the fables in which they're trapped, "Once More, with Feeling" is about the Scooby gang's reflection on their fate. And it is this self-reflexivity, rather than musical style, that links Whedon to Sondheim.

As Walsh and Platt note, Sondheim's musicals remain ethical to the core and are concerned throughout with establishing significant values through compromise. There is thus a political element to the Sondheim musical but not, they decide, a Brechtian one, as Sondheim always places character before politics.[35] Similarly, Whedon has refused every urge to reduce his work to a simple political message.[36] The complexity of "Once More, with Feeling" and what ultimately makes it such a satisfying "show" is the unpretentious yet profound nature of each character's reflexivity. Our heroes' concern reflects *Buffy*'s long history, in which no good thing or favorable event comes without cost. Although it is "all kind of romantic" to Dawn, most characters recognize the arrival of an all-singing, all-dancing musical spectacular as a sign that their repressed emotions, secrets, and fears have exceeded the bounds of drama as genre. They react with verbal and musical wit to their quandary, historicizing their predicament overtly (citing past events) and covertly (through the substance of each number). "Once More, with Feeling" thus

---

[33] Janet K. Halfyard, "Singing Their Hearts Out: The Problem of Performance in *Buffy the Vampire Slayer* and *Angel*," *Slayage* 17 (2005), 37.

[34] Richard S. Albright, "[B]reakaway pop hit or ... book number?: 'Once More, with Feeling' and Genre," *Slayage* 17 (2005), 10.

[35] Walsh and Platt, *Musical Theater and American Culture*, p. 145.

[36] Rhonda Wilcox discusses this in "'There Will Never Be a "Very Special" *Buffy*': Buffy and the Monsters of Teen Life," *Journal of Popular Film and Television*, 27/2 (1999), pp. 16–23.

references the history of the book musical, up to the point that it became self-aware and "conceptual" (from *West Side Story* to *Company*).

Part of Your World

> I think the greatest musicals—with the exception of *South Park*—that have come out of the American cinema in the last ten or twenty years have all been Disney musicals.[37]

Going Through the Motions

In interviews and commentary, Whedon has reiterated how Buffy's first number was inspired by the heroine's "I want" scenes that open recent Disney musicals like *The Little Mermaid* (1989) and *Beauty and the Beast* (1991).[38] This homage includes a strong female lead expressing pent-up emotion, simple but effective symbolism (Buffy staking a vampire while singing the word "heart"), and the climax.[39]

The "I want" number has a long history, from (*No, No*) Nanette's "I Want to Be Happy" to Golden Age female protagonists such as Annie Oakley (*Annie Get Your Gun*), Nellie Forbush (*South Pacific*) and the Marias of *The Sound of Music* and *West Side Story*. In the context of the American musical, a vampire Slayer cutting a wide swath through a hoard of undead is a novel take on both the "I want" number and the feminist heroine. Yet the central irony of "Going Through the Motions" rests on the revelation that Buffy has lost the fierce emotions that defined her power ("What's My Line, Part 2" [2.10]). The Greek chorus of demons has a Freudian bent, referencing Buffy's characteristic witty banter with her prey while dissecting her mental state. Although we are not formally introduced to the latest crisis in Sunnydale until "I've Got a Theory," Buffy drolly telegraphs the plot through her trademark puns (emphasis mine): "Every single night, the same *arrangement*. … I've been making *shows* of trading blows. … I've been *going through the motions. Walking through the part…*"

The orchestral overture opens on an F major six-four chord, an unstable dominant that should resolve to C, but moves down to an $E\flat^{7sus}$ chord instead, implying a resolution to $A\flat$. The opening chords serve as chromatic embellishments of E Mixolydian (a foretaste of Spike's ballad), as the nostalgic Technicolor titles give way to a prosaic scene of the housemates' morning rituals. But Buffy's concerns rise above the everyday, as signaled by her ascent back to F via a third progression (E–$A\flat$), and a dominant (C^{7sus}), that decisively announces her solo.

---

[37] Whedon in Muir, *Singing a New Tune*, p. 76.

[38] Whedon, "Once More, with Feeling" audio commentary. Whedon discusses this number specifically in relation to Ariel's "Part of Your World" in *The Little Mermaid* in Whedon and Ruditis, *The Script Book*, p. 76.

[39] Whedon in Muir, *Singing a New Tune*, p. 281.

The gist of the opening progression (shared by the Jam's "Absolute Beginners" among other upbeat 1980s songs) moves through ♭VII to the minor dominant, but the bass F–E♭–D–C is the same "lament" progression that underpins "I've Got a Theory."[40] As in Spike's plaint, Buffy's Mixolydian mode exploits the emotional contrast between major tonic and minor dominant. She hits the wrong dominant—G major—on "nothing here is right," followed by a her failed attempt to tonicize d (the relative minor) that enters the chorus with a deceptive cadence to symbolizes her loss of drive (as shown in an analytical reduction of the first verse and chorus in Figure 12.5).

Figure 12.5   Analytical reduction of first verse and chorus of "Going Through the Motions"

---

[40] A truncated form of this descending line appears in the solo lament of Spike, and in his duet with Buffy ("Walk Through the Fire"); it returns as Buffy reveals her deepest secret in the denouement of "Something to Sing About."

When the bridge finally reaches d minor, it rocks back and forth between d minor and G major, mired in plagal relations (I–IV) as Buffy cries "Will I stay this way forever? Sleepwalk through my life's endeavor." She rebuffs a buff a grateful victim only to rest on a crucial E♭ major chord—the 'plagal' dominant (♭VII) in F and the Neapolitan (♭II). As our hero dusts a vampire and kills a goat demon by turns, E♭ blossoms into a major seventh chord on "heart" and "owww." As a transient key center between F Mixolydian and d minor, E♭ represents the freedom of slaying, a freedom that no longer grounds the Slayer. In her final climactic phrase, Buffy returns to the tonic F, as her minor dominant on "be" (c minor) slowly mutates into major over a pedal F; reaching toward cadential closure but not achieving it as the dust swirls around her in the coda.

Something to Sing About

"Something to Sing About" is the fourth act companion piece to Buffy's opening number. It announces C Mixolydian, the missing "dominant" from "Going Through the Motions," and the key of hope in the final number, "Where Do We Go From Here?" Here Buffy faces Sweet's challenge and bluntly demands he give her "something to sing about." She drops her red coat (in what Whedon terms "a low-budget TV version of Cyd Charisse's classic *Bandwagon*" scene) to reveal no less than the "meaning of this show."[41] Buffy's emotional climax comes not when she is saved from a fiery death, but immediately afterward when, emotionally and physically exhausted, she reveals her darkest secret to the friends who raised her from the dead. With its major tonic and minor dominant, the key of this number parallels "Rest in Peace" as well, although here Buffy finds release at the end of each phrase on a full half cadence.

Irregular seven-bar phrases in the verse support the deeply ironic tone of "It's all right if some things come out wrong /We'll sing a happy song and you can sing along," before moving to a double-time feel (two chords per bar) in the chorus, the *B* section of a modified Rondo form: *ABABCBC*. During the *B* section, the implied 2/4 meter shifts to an implied 7/16 (7/8) then 3/8 (6/8) (as seen in Figure 12.6), as Buffy's lyrics grow ever more reflexive and sardonic ("Wishes can come true ...") and the harmony gets more tense (adding a ninth to the minor dominant). Buffy's frantic dance, accompanied by asymmetrical phrasing and a cyclical C–g minor vamp (I-v) leave us unsure of how or when her number might end.

But the double-time section also provides a sharp contrast when the verse returns to a broader 4/4 feel and a direct modulation up to D Mixolydian. In terms of genre, Buffy's call to "give me something to sing about" here becomes not only anthemic but hymn-like, with a slowed harmonic rhythm and choral backing, before a double-time turnaround vamp on e minor–b minor as the verse repeats.

---

[41] Whedon, "Once More, with Feeling" audio commentary.

Figure 12.6   Meter shifts in "Something to Sing About"

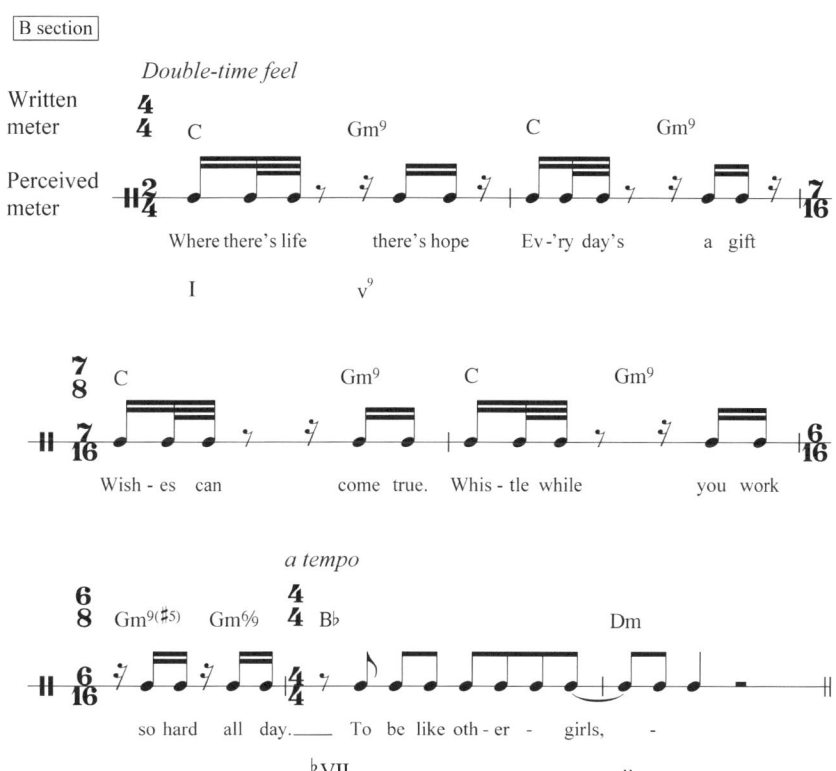

Buffy's emotional turmoil is reflected in the constant change of genre (rock ballad to punk polka to hymn) as well as meter; dance rhythms give way to a flexible 12/8 in the *C* section in b minor, with another repeated plagal motion. The diminished chord that merely embellished Buffy's "hymn" (C–C^{dim}–A under a chorus of "Ah") here appears on the tonic B, to render more acerbic her momentous revelation: she was pulled out of heaven, and now she feels as though she's in a living hell. At this point Spike alone steps up to save Buffy from self-immolation, taking over her despondent plaint (in a return of the *C* section), during which he repeats the b minor–B^{dim} slide three times on "living." Spike's reply energizes "Something to Sing About"; he transforms Buffy's B from failed tonic to leading-tone into C major, the key of hope, and the chord of emotional and tonal closure to Buffy's original F major.

What a Feeling

> The musical montage has become such a staple of film and TV that scripts must be thirty pages long by now: "He walks down the street. Cue oldie." Whether it's modern pop or a bunch of standards … it's just a really boring video. If they would just dance to pass the time while they're walking sadly down the street, they would do us all a favor.[42]

Standing

At the conclusion of Sweet and Dawn's number in the Bronze we immediately cut to the third and "saddest"[43] solo ballad in "Once More, with Feeling," given to Anthony Stewart Head, the one cast member with prior experience in stage musicals (most notably a West End performance of *Rocky Horror Picture Show*). Giles's isolation and yearning is heightened by his separation from Buffy in this scene; she moves at a slower pace in a "training montage," as she self-reflexively predicts, "from an eighties movie." "Well, if we hear any inspiration power chords we'll just lie down until they go away" he counters. But rather than *Rocky*-style, over-produced rock bombast, Giles breaks into a number whose stark intimacy—a quiet beginning on acoustic guitar—contrasts starkly with the dancing and singing spectacular of "What You Feel."

Giles's brief but powerful ballad is modeled on a singer/songwriter lament with contrasting stanzas, in an *AABAB* form. "Standing" begins in the key of F, quickly subverted as an F♯^{dim} chord on "ready" (and "pretending") tonicizes G. This clever harmonic feint relates forward and back: the F–g minor (♭VII–i) that embellished Sweet's number becomes the foundation of "Standing" (see Figure 12.7), while the disorienting shift from Buffy's tonic F to Sweet's G expresses Giles' anguish over his decision to leave Sunnydale.

The key of G represents "the world outside"; as soon as Giles mentions Buffy again he is back in F major. Giles attempt to reach G falls time and again back to F as he describes Buffy's emotional stasis. He reaches the major dominant when he declares "I know I said that I'd be standing by your side," yet words fail him (the phrase ends with "but I …"). The *A* section repeats before the climax brings a confusion of key centers; C major ("take you by the hand") followed by F Mixolydian. The song closes with the *B* section, leaving the form open, with a melancholy close on c minor–G ("standing in the way") that mirrors Buffy's cry of "be alive" from "Going Through the Motions."

"Standing" is immediately brought into conjunction with the reprise of "Under Your Spell," as Tara realizes she has been manipulated and literally put under a spell by her lover. As Tara comes to the heartbreaking realization that she must leave Willow, Giles joins her in the key of B major with "believe," on its

---

[42] Whedon in Muir, *Singing a New Tune*, p. 276.
[43] Whedon, "Once More, with Feeling" audio commentary.

Figure 12.7   Ending of "What You Feel" compared to the opening of "Standing"

bright dominant, F♯, and the duo shift from minor to major to express their grief in unison. Yet the modal shift to major cannot by itself contain their emotion, and the reprise moves to the dominant key. Tara and Giles sing their laments in counterpoint, coming together on "wish I could stay" over c♯ minor (the minor dominant). The open-ended progressions in the first incarnations of "Under Your Spell" and "Standing" come to a close here with the plagal progression A–E, with E major transformed into a signifier of loss and shattered hopes.

Walk Through the Fire

The ironic juxtaposition of genre and function continues with Buffy's training scene. Just as "Standing" is an understated lament rather than an angry rock screed, so Buffy's workout is a melancholy dance rather than a training montage from a 1980s movie. Although not without self-reflexive humor (Giles's throwing knives at Buffy while simultaneously singing about protecting her is an "ironic turnaround" that is "a staple of the Buffy universe"),[44] this scene parodies neither the underdog machismo of "Footloose" (*Footloose*, 1984), nor the female

[44]   Ibid.

empowerment enacted by "Flashdance ... What a Feeling" (*Flashdance*, 1983). Buffy's buff detachment represents a Pyrrhic victory over the grave, revealing her emotionally more dead than alive. Her alienation from Watcher, friends, and family prefigures her further isolation as she marches off to save Dawn alone in "Walk Through the Fire."

Co-executive producer David Fury lists "Walk Through the Fire" as his favorite number: "I think that was one of the most sophisticated numbers, musically and lyrically. Having all of the characters sing in it—obviously it was patterned after a sort of 'Tonight' number from *West Side Story*."[45] "Walk" marks the return of a full verse-chorus form, as well as the union of every character (save Dawn) as they converge on the Bronze for the showdown with Sweet. Its soft introduction, in which first piano, harp, and then strings emerge from silence, reaches back to the d minor bridge of "Going Through the Motion," over a somber pedal D that recalls both the end of that number (where "alive" rang out over a four-bar pedal F) and the inarticulate sigh that ended Giles's stanzas (an open D–A fifth with added E). "Walk Through the Fire" marries soft rock to the function of a dirge, as its opening verse alludes to the lament bass heard earlier (D–C–B♭). The verse references both Phrygian and Dorian modes, the shifting chord qualities matching the antithesis expressed by the lyrics (see Figure 12.8).

Figure 12.8   Phrygian and Dorian modes in "Walk Through the Fire"

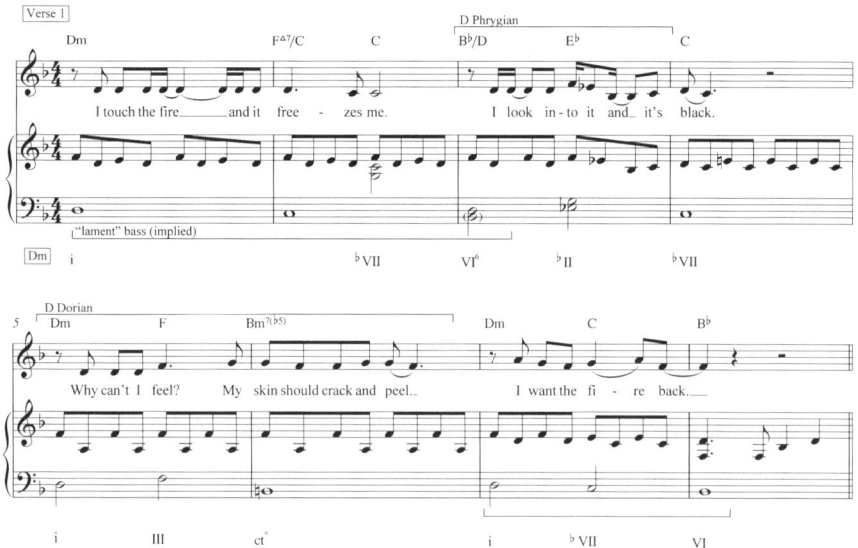

---

[45]   Quoted in Whedon and Ruditis, *The Script Book*, p. 79.

The verse moves from E♭ (♭II) to C (♭VII) through a B^{ø7} that forecasts the stinging revelation on B^{dim} yet to come in "Something to Sing About." In the third verse Spike joins Buffy, a burst of anger accompanying his own B^{ø7} ("I'm free if that bitch dies"), with a droll reversal that reflects the return to d♮ minor ("I'd better help her out"). Yet when the chorus enters in an anthemic F major, "Walk Through the Fire" is revealed as a mirror image of "Going Through the Motions." In the opening number Buffy came out fighting in F, but admitted her ennui and exhaustion in the d minor bridge, while in "Fire" she begins by confessing her emotional frigidity in d minor, only to resolve "Walk through the fire" with a defiant I–V–IV progression in F.[46]

Giles, Xander, and Anya join on the bridge, which prolongs B♭ (the subdominant), freezing the progression while the Scoobies voice their apprehension by turns. The vocal counterpoint in the fourth verse reflects the emotional counterpoint of the scene. Though separate and isolated, each line follows the same chord progression, just as all of the characters travel to the same destination. In the final verse, three contrapuntal lines accommodate five juxtaposed expressive modes: Buffy's indifference, Sweet's glee, Tara's despair, Spike's schizophrenia ("No I'll save her; then I'll kill her!"), Giles's anxiety, and Willow's ironic aside ("I think this line's mostly filler"). The final chorus moves to a deceptive cadence on D♭ (♭VI), as the note A that accompanied "walk," "fire" and "where else" slips to A♭ for three repetitions of "burn" that melt into F as the vocals fade and an ominous d minor returns as Buffy arrives at the Bronze.

Where Do We Go From Here?

Numbers such as "Walk Through the Fire" and "Something to Sing About" owe their choreography and editing to contemporary film and video, but their musical style is indebted to those recent, pop-influenced Broadway and West End productions of the 1980s and 1990s termed the megamusical. Platt and Walsh identify the soft-rock style of the megamusical with the glorification of spectacle over substance (for instance, the arrival of the helicopter in *Miss Saigon*), and an attendant simplification of music and narrative to meet the demands of international syndication.[47] At the opposite pole stand pop-rock musicals such as the Who's *Tommy* (1993) and Jonathan Larsen's *Rent* (1996),[48] whose specific focus and original music set them in a class apart. *Rent* proves an especially constructive comparison as it celebrates community in the context of social otherness, a

---

[46] Although a common rock progression, its treatment here recalls "Seasons of Love" from the musical *Rent*, discussed below.

[47] Walsh and Platt, *Musical Theater and American Culture*, pp. 157–64.

[48] Whedon lists *Rent* as one of his influences. See Whedon and Ruditis, *The Script Book*, p. 63.

bohemian life that "represents both individuality *and* community in a social world where difference ... stands at the centre."[49]

The characters in *Rent* find meaning through aestheticizing life; as they try to bridge their downtown sensibility with an uptown market without selling out, they find that paying the rent metaphorically takes their souls. In a similar sense Buffy and her friends are marginalized by practicing magic and hunting demons; their attempts to save the world certainly run the risk of death, but—as in the world of *Rent*—losing one's soul seems a far greater price to pay. In both its formal model (Puccini's *La Bohème*) and emotional scope, *Rent* is operatic, creating a world in which pop, jazz, and country styles speak equally to the characters' plights.[50] The cast's final assertion that there's "No day like today" leaves them in a quandary not unlike that of the Scooby gang. Yet "Once More, with Feeling" lacks *Rent*'s celebratory atmosphere and romanticizing of everyday life. Having just saved the world—or at least, Sunnydale—yet again, Buffy and her friends find the resolution of their personal dilemmas a far more daunting task, a theme celebrated in outstanding episodes from "Becoming, Part II" (2.22) to "The Body" (5.16).

The final number picks up right where "Something to Sing About" left off, but opens as a moderate shuffle in a bright C major. "Where Do We Go From Here?" may be the final chorus or "big group sing," as Spike puts it, but it marks a strikingly ambivalent end to an intense and cathartic journey. A relaxed, archetypically tonal progression begins the song (I–ii–vi–I–V–vi^{sus}), and each eight-bar phrase closes with a deceptive cadence on a minor, to project the open-ended sentiment of the title in the first chorus of 32 bars (a double period structured as *aa'ba'aa'ba'*, where each letter represents a four-bar segment).

The second chorus modulates up to D major, paralleling "Something to Sing About." But unlike the earlier number, "Where Do We Go From Here?" remains in D, growing brighter and more tonally defined with a steady alternation of tonic D and dominant A, as the chorus sings "When does 'The End' appear?/When do the trumpets cheer?" This question is never answered directly, although I would argue that it is indirectly, by the music. As the group slides up in the final cadence (closing unexpectedly in B major), their communal strength redeems the piquant diminished chord that earlier expressed Buffy's anguish: B diminished finally becomes B major, and "Once More, with Feeling" closes 180 degrees from where it began, on the opposite side of the Scoobies's tonal and emotional universe, a full tritone away from the F of the introduction.

The musical structure of "Once More, with Feeling" thus ends on an ironic reversal that, in its abstract beauty, serves as a synecdoche for the network of ironies throughout the show. Indeed, its complex discursive context offers a model

---

[49] Walsh and Platt, *Musical Theater and American Culture*, p. 152.

[50] Eric Salzman, "From Stage to Page: Music-Theater in Print," *Theater*, 32/1 (2002), pp. 65–6.

for the relational, inclusive, and differential nature of irony,[51] for it lampoons those stylistic genres that span the musical's history even as it revels in their power to express what lies beyond mere language.

It seems disingenuous to bring up irony and the American musical without mentioning this episode's allusion to camp as a cultural signifying practice associated especially with MGM musicals.[52] For instance Anya, the castrating man-eater turned domestic goddess, becomes a diva in "Bunnies," while her fiancé exhibits a typical American heterosexual male's anxiety about dancing and revealing emotion (a correlation that forms the crux of the plot). Yet whatever camp sensibility operates in *Buffy* is subtle and double-edged, inextricably bound up with its self-reflexive ability to mock its own conventions as well as those of the genres to which it alludes.[53] Thus the ease with which the series adapted to a musical format, one that included singing scofflaws, dancing dry-cleaning patrons and a "Six hundred pound Chorago demon making like Yma Sumac." As Whedon admits, "Buffy is so sophomoric, romantic, colorful, tense, sexual ... I think half the episodes feel like they're about to burst into song anyway ... So to say a demon has come in who causes musicals makes perfect sense in that world."[54]

Music has always held a central role in the Buffyverse,[55] taking as its premise the long-standing tradition of Hollywood and nineteenth-century opera that music does not lie.[56] "Once More, with Feeling" not only acknowledges the ethical nature of music but also asserts that candor as its *raison d'être*; indeed, the multiple plot lines of season six cannot move forward without the liberating if ugly truth of its performance. In staking its claim to candor, the musical honors its fans, who already associate musical performance on *Buffy* with questions of authenticity and sincerity.[57] Whedon treats his audience as equals, celebrating his nostalgic love for the idealistic charms of the musical while admitting, with sardonic asides, that his discursive community is far too knowing to accept

---

[51] See Linda Hutcheon, *Irony's Edge: The Theory and Politics of Irony* (New York/London, 1994), pp. 58, 64.

[52] See Steven Cohen's detailed study *Incongruous Entertainment: Camp, Cultural Value, and the MGM Musical* (Durham, NC, 2005).

[53] Roz Kaveney calls the show's reflexivity "almost obsessional" in "She Saves the World. A Lot," in Roz Kaveney (ed.), *Reading the Vampire Slayer: An Unofficial Critical Companion to Buffy and Angel* (London, 2001), p. 11.

[54] Muir, *Singing a New Tune*, p. 282.

[55] S. Renee Dechert writes: "Indeed, [music] functions as a form of rhetorical discourse every bit as important as the lines characters speak." "'My Boyfriend's in the Band!': Buffy and the Rhetoric of Music," in Rhonda V. Wilcox and David Lavery (eds) *Fighting the Forces: What's at Stake in Buffy the Vampire Slayer* (Lanham, MD, 2002), p. 219.

[56] Carolyn Abbate, *Unsung Voices: Opera and Musical Narrative in the Nineteenth Century* (Princeton, NJ, 1991), p. 156.

[57] Halfyard explores this at some length in "Singing Their Hearts Out."

such "entertainment" at face value. So to say a demon has arrived who causes musicals makes perfect sense to the *Buffy* fan, who knows that there may be closure without victory, and a kiss without a happy ending, but—in the end—there is always "something to sing about."

Chapter 13
Rock, Television, Paper, Musicals, Scissors: *Buffy*, *The Simpsons*, and Parody

Paul Attinello

Rock smashes scissors: that's easy enough, any child can see it. Scissors cut paper: again, entirely intuitive. But that paper smothers rock—that is not realistic, not intuitive. It is a fantastic innovation that creates a symmetrical structure as it links the first two relationships into a formal—and playable—tripartite game; but it is also a move that teaches children some rather unexpected things which might be useful for them to learn: that conflicts are complicated, strengths are various, and that ultimately the bigger, stronger opponent is not always the winner.

Television comedies, stage musicals, and movie musicals all have a long history of borrowing from and influencing each other.[1] However, at the beginning of the twenty-first century, no one can sensibly expect those genres even to pretend to a peaceful coexistence—not only economic support and audience attention, but also relative levels of cultural respect, cultural prestige, and even commonly available cultural capital have become irreparably unevenly divided among them.

Television shows that have made use of both kinds of musicals—especially *Buffy the Vampire Slayer* (1997–2003), *The Simpsons* (1989–), and its several imitators including *South Park* (1997–) and *Family Guy* (1999–)—reflect some of the complex alliances and hostilities that connect television, stage, and film. The latter shows are useful "controls" in analyzing *Buffy*, as they make a regular and more simply structured practice of deflating the world of song and dance, ripping apart its conventions and values, as well as all the things that can be read into them—everything from sentiment to emotional outbursts to gender stereotypes to the Grand Finale.

This discussion can be compared to Lawrence Kramer's playful cultural excavation of the media battle between opera and film, where he shows how the Marx Brothers' *A Night at the Opera* (1935) dramatizes that battle—one that film is destined to win.[2] However, if film smashes stage, and television cuts musicals, music is itself a secret trump card that completes the circle, enabling

---

[1] A version of this paper was presented to the Department of Music at the University of Liverpool in December 2006, at the invitation of Anahid Kassabian and Freya Jarman-Ivens. Thanks also to Robynn Stilwell for her helpful advice.

[2] Lawrence Kramer, "Glottis Envy: The Marx Brothers' *A Night at the Opera*," in *Musical Meaning: Toward a Critical History* (Berkeley, 2002), pp. 133–44.

the musical to frequently win out over other media when it is introduced in any combination with them.

The Kramer article is thus my direct precedent; but another part of my experience is a source for my polemical stance. There have been several studies published about television and musicals, and many about film and musicals;[3] most, especially the more recent, take an easily postmodern approach to the value systems involved—intertextuality, the polymorphous nature of genres, the flexible borrowing of cultural capital. However, from some points of view, the borrowing is not balanced—the playing field is not even, and the collaborators are by no means equally engaged in the free and friendly play of signifiers. As someone who used to perform in stage musicals, I am always aware of the weaker cultural, artistic, and economic position of the live, performed musical in the late twentieth and early twenty-first centuries. It is not controversial to assert that the world of the musical has devolved from its Golden Age status to one where smaller, often cult audiences, a loss of a cultural centrality and a common idiom, and a frequently insecure dependence on *outré* experiments and borrowings from more successful media have become the norm.[4]

Which is not to say, of course, that the musical is moribund: it is a running, if slightly grim, joke in the West End, on Broadway, and in regional theaters to say either that the musical is dead, or alternatively that it is *not* dead, and then to get into a pointless and circular argument about it all, using proofs based on a handful of dramatic but isolated examples, especially shows that do not seem to have engendered successful imitators—shows that may be successful or unsuccessful, but that seem to represent generic dead ends. Well, of course, the musical is *not* dead, and will not be dead any decade soon—any more than opera, or classical music, or jazz are about to fade from existence. In fact, over the past few years the reconfigured audiences that connect through globalized and virtualized networks have helped to stabilize the cultural position of the musical as much as they have those other relatively peripheral genres. But the musical, ever since the long and

---

[3] On television and musicals, see Robynn Stilwell, "It May Look Like a Living Room… : The Musical Number and the Sitcom," *Echo*, 5/1 (2003) accessed 25 August 2008 at http://www.echo.ucla.edu/volume5-issue1/stilwell/index.html; and Diana Sandars, "It's More Than Just Another Silly Love Song: *Ally McBeal* brings the Hollywood Musical to Television," in Elwood Watson (ed.), *Searching the Soul of Ally McBeal: Critical Essays* (Jefferson, NC/London, 2006), pp. 203–223). Many studies of musicals have tangled with the differences between stage and screen, but of particular interest are Rick Altman (ed.), *Genre: The Musical* (London, 1981); and Richard Dyer, *Only Entertainment* (London, 1992).

[4] I have talked more about the contemporary position of the musical in Paul Attinello, "chemical bodies," *Radical Musicology*, 2 (2007), accessed 25 August 2008 at http://www.radical-musicology.org.uk/2007/Attinello.htm; and Paul Attinello, "The Universe will Tell You What It Needs: Being, Time, Sondheim," in Steven Baur, Raymond Knapp, and Jacqueline Warwick (eds) *Musicological Identities: Essays in Honor of Susan McClary* (Aldershot, 2008), pp. 77–91.

rocky disintegration of Golden Age certainties that took place between *West Side Story* in 1957 and *Hair* in 1968, suffers not only from being less economically successful, but also less prestigious—as Miller explains, it is a guilty, in fact almost an embarrassing, pleasure.[5]

What I am talking about, therefore, is the power play between various media and genres: and also about the quiet secret embedded in the more obvious aspects of that power play—that not only does rock crush scissors and scissors cut paper; but that, unexpectedly, but very satisfyingly for those of us who are musicians or stage performers, paper can stop rock dead in its tracks.

I want to distinguish parts of this discussion from the otherwise interesting writing on musicals and television, including not only Stilwell and Sandars but also Dyer and Miller—not because I think they are wrong, but only because they are working at the problem from a different angle. If we are going to talk about contemporary television and the musical from the point of view of the latter, we need to be willing to leave that never-never land where the musical still seems healthy and certain of its identity; and also to pull the discussion of intertextuality and referentiality away from optimistic interpretations of postmodernism, and admit to the uneasy conflicts that structure the twenty-first-century musical.

Stilwell speaks of the common roots of the musical and the sitcom (and, by extension, all television, even a "dramedy" like *Buffy*). She points out the changing relationship between them, suggesting an early period of shared tropes and personnel through the mid-1960s, followed by a middle period up to the mid-1980s, at which point the musical's presence and cultural power is definitely on the wane.[6] I want instead to look at a third, "late" period, our own extended cultural present since the late 1980s, during which time the musical has returned to television—but with an altered, less assertive, more dependent status.

The "musical" that I want to speak about is one rooted in the stage and also in the "stagey"; although references to the film musical are often present (because, like most contemporary consumers, the creators of all the various media have probably seen far more filmed than staged musicals), I believe that the strongest derision and the greatest surprise at any given success is aimed at the musical's stage identity, not at its evolution into the film musical. This is a somewhat blurred distinction, especially after decades of mutual generic imitation.[7]

---

[5] D. A. Miller, *Place for Us: Essay on the Broadway Musical* (Cambridge, MA, 1998). Miller's take on the musical as related to being gay is not really about queer culture as such, but is embedded in an older oppression—the gayness of being beaten up at recess; which is perhaps an appropriate metaphor for the contemporary musical among its media peers.

[6] Stilwell, "It May Look Like a Living Room."

[7] Not to mention a great deal of cross-borrowing: the *New York Times* published a discussion of this (Charles Isherwood, "Singing! Dancing! Adapting! Stumbling!" *New York Times*, 6 August 2008, accessed 25 August 2008 at http://www.nytimes.

The stage transformations that have become not only necessary but also dangerously expensive for the megamusical are often just mechanical attempts at imitating gestures which are absurdly easy for film or television; while the film/television universe's restless search for innovation has resulted in a range of imitations of stage technology, where a traditional cut is replaced by the illusion of shifting sets and actors. However, generations accustomed to the polish of edited camera work are increasingly unwilling to put up with the glitches of the live stage, just as CD consumers have become incapable of ignoring mistakes in live performance; the loss to both audiences is, of course, the embodied reality of the live performer on stage.

As for my television examples, they cut through at least two contemporary and already hybridized genres. Although I would privilege *Buffy* as unusual and not entirely centered in any television genre, it does have several familiar roots: the increased number and popularity of science fiction and fantasy shows in the wake of a computerized culture that respects futurity, nerdiness, and imagination, and that has also greatly improved technology for the recreation of fantastic imagery; the innovation of *Babylon 5* (1994–98), which brought the long-term structures typical of "future-history" writing into television; and the emotional/familial context of the semicomic "serial drama."

The contemporary animated satire, although it has several different visual roots, has a clearer and more datable identity as a television genre. The success of *The Simpsons* resulted in a number of series, including *Family Guy*, *South Park*, *Beavis and Butthead* (1993–99), *King of the Hill* (1997–), *Drawn Together* (2004–), and a variety of others culminating in the distribution company Adult Swim (2001–); what they have in common are not only animation, permanent situations, and a wide range of satirical objects, but also an especially edgy, cynical quality of satire—we are all by now accustomed to the association of non-realistic, sometimes primitive animation with dark, surreal, and nihilistic humor, an association that would have seemed quite strange before the 1990s.

To draw all these together: musicals, television, film, and the popular stage are alike in belonging to popular culture, rather than to an older elite culture. But popular versus elite was a modernist dichotomy: it is not so important any more, and now we face somewhat different divisions and hostilities. The various segments, genres, and relics of popular culture are (or were) designed for different generations, different audiences; but perhaps it is enough to note that the large-scale quasi-Oedipal battle between popular and elite culture has now returned in a domesticated version, a less metaphorically Oedipal battle, between the tastes of the parents and those of the children.

---

com/2008/08/10/theater/10ishe.html) which treated the problem as almost new—which it most certainly is not.

The Simpsons and the Threat of Musicals

The multileveled, protean satires that make up the long history of *The Simpsons* may seem practically infinite in the range of topics, ideas, and objects. Certainly the show is characterized by invention as much as by critique—but that invention means that almost all the show's basic principles (fathers are stupid, families are dysfunctional, corporations are inept, etc.) have been overturned at one time or another for the purposes of endless surprise and comedy. The range of ways that musicals and their tropes have been used on the show is wide, but most examples proceed from the same assumption: that musicals are not only ridiculous, but also pernicious.

This is different from the way most other musics are treated—mainstream popular styles (including music by Michael Jackson or Barry White) are positioned variously, but usually with familiarity and implicitly shared affection; and less popular vernaculars (jazz, country) are given a more distant respect, combined with a patronizing amusement at their peripheral cultural status.[8] But musicals, ah, musicals: on *The Simpsons*, they are often grotesque, alien, even dangerous.

Why would this be? Mistrusting musicals is not new, or even unusual—many musicals are, after all, associated with a sentimental, conformist past. This includes not only the well-made shows of the Golden Age, but also revivals with their indelible nostalgia, and shows that try to blend countercultural rock, jazz, or blues into an ultimately traditional mix. The necessarily formulaic nature of musicals, as well as the economic pressure to create something new but at the same time make it sufficiently familiar to appeal to a varied audience, tends to force even normally innovative forms and genres to resemble each other. One cannot, after all, sing the rock in *Rent* as one would sing "real" rock, or the audience will not understand the words; and even the interpolation of ballet into a dance number needs to be brief and full of popular references in order to take the limitations of a non-specialist audience into account. Thus, the endless, sometimes subtle but usually less so, reenactment of an earlier, supposedly simpler time ends up becoming a scapegoat for an older, darker, but more fluidly defined culture: false sentimentality and concealed problems are shown to be oppressive, as merely letting a smile be your umbrella.

We can consider some of the musical parodies in *The Simpsons*. The first, "A Streetcar named Marge" (S4.2), involves Marge in a musical that never should have been written—a show based on *A Streetcar Named Desire*, where the surreal tragedy of the original turns into a loony circus of misplaced technologies. Later that season, an extended parody of the famous patter song from *The Music Man* (1962) manipulates Springfield into splurging on a monorail ("Marge vs. the Monorail" [S4.12]), and Krusty sings a self-pitying "Send in the Clowns" to benefit his own

---

[8] Michael Jackson is central to "Stark Raving Dad" (S3.1); Barry White to "Whacking Day" (S4.20); jazz is central to "Moaning Lisa" (S1.6); and country to "Colonel Homer" (S3.20).

collapsing career in "Krusty Gets Cancelled" (S4.22). More malign parodies appear in seasons 5 and 6: an acid-trip version of the New York montage from *On The Town* (1949) seduces Bart and Milhouse into eating themselves sick in "Boy-Scoutz N the Hood" (S5.8); the theme from *A Chorus Line* (1975) gives the hideously eviscerated family a grotesquely inappropriate finale for the Halloween episode "Treehouse of Horror V" (S6.6); and Mr Burns imitates *Beauty and the Beast* (1991) to celebrate his sartorial massacre of endangered animals in "Two Dozen and One Greyhounds" (S6.20).

Later episodes use musicals less often, but on a larger scale: the inept *Planet of the Apes* show in "A Fish called Selma" (S7.19) that gives the closeted Troy McClure a new career; the burlesque extravaganza that distracts Springfield from destroying its whorehouse in "Bart After Dark" (S8.5); and the sudden appearance of the ensemble "Kids" from *Bye, Bye, Birdie* to resolve an apparently impossible intergenerational conflict in "Wild Barts Can't Be Broken" (S10.11) all use musical finales as blinds for the manipulative concealment of unpalatable truths. There are also entire episodes designed around musicals—the *Mary Poppins* parody of "Simpsoncalifragilisticexpiala(Annoyed Grunt)cious" (S8.13) with its dark and even violent disruptions of the saccharine original; or the flaunted fakery of linking a clip show with segments of *All Singing, All Dancing* in the episode of the same name (S9.11). Finally, in recent years, extended pastiches of *Evita* ("The President Wore Pearls" [S15.3]) and *My Fair Lady* ("My Fair Laddy" [S17.12]) have dictated the artificial and ultimately unsuccessful transformations of Lisa and Groundskeeper Willie.

These latter episodes may be following a line of development that is not unique to *The Simpsons*, but which might instead be embedded in a wholesale shift in the relationship of sitcoms and musicals. According to Stilwell,

> In most sitcoms of the 1980s and 1990s, the musical number's function migrated from the gag as narrative disruption to the gag as generic disruption. Neale and Eaton argue that audience recognition of the play with generic conventions is often indispensable to the functioning of comedy narrative ... After such a long absence [i.e. the absence of the musical from television in the 1970s and early 1980s], the presence of a musical number in the narrative confines of a familiar genre like the sitcom transgresses genre boundaries in a way that provokes comedy, giving lie to Eaton's assertion that "... whilst comedy can be directed against anything, it cannot be analytical of anything" ... For do we not, on some level, have to analyze the conventions in order to recognize their transgressions?[9]

She later continues, in a brief comment on *The Simpsons* itself:

---

[9] Stilwell, "It May Look Like a Living Room," 58, citing Mick Eaton, "Laughter in the Dark," *Screen*, 22/2 (1981), pp. 22–5 and Steve Neale, "Psychoanalysis and Comedy," *Screen*, 22/2 (1981), pp. 19–21.

> In ... overtly satirical shows like *The Simpsons* ... the musical number falls somewhere between a Brechtian distancing and sheer surface play. *The Simpsons'* musical numbers may be parodies ("Springfield, Springfield" rather than "New York, New York," including the misplaced accentuation inherent in the transposition) or pastiches, but they tend to be framed like classical musical numbers.[10]

Ultimately, although *The Simpsons* and *South Park* revel in musicals, they also distrust them. For instance, in *The Simpsons'* burlesque house episode, "Bart After Dark," a spectacular musical number stops the angry mob—but not by appealing to anything at all sensible, merely by getting them excited by a simplistic chain of metaphors. This is merely a matter of bamboozling the public, and certainly not giving them anything more conscious or authentic than the mob violence attitudes they were experiencing before. Part of this is about cultural context: the classic "normative" Golden Age musical is associated with an optimistic view of America, the modern world, and so on—and often a repressively homogenous one, despite the gestures of certain musicals (*Show Boat*, *South Pacific*, *Fiddler on the Roof*) towards inclusiveness. Ultimately, for a certain generation, they are associated with a *bad* history, a history of suburbs and homogeneity. But, of course, the problem is bigger than that. After all...

Music Lies

All these episodes start from the assumption that musicals—with all their passionate sentimentality and rhythmically energetic manipulation of the listener—lie: if you are so stupid as to believe what they say, you deserve whatever happens to you. One of the bluntest statements occurs when Homer, furious that a rented videotape of *Paint Your Wagon* (1969) has singing instead of shooting, ejects the tape into a trashcan and bellows, "Singing is the lowest form of communication!" ("All Singing, All Dancing" [S9.11]).

After all, music *does* lie: singing about love or happiness creates vividly colored, powerfully manipulative cultural/psychological spaces that often ignore or cover up many of the negative or fragmented aspects of those experiences. Even singing about grief or loneliness makes those emotions seem more searching, more productive, and more sensual than they usually are: depression, anomie, and inappropriate behaviors are excluded as unsingable (and certainly undanceable). Music lies all the time: it takes us to a world where things are what we think we ought to want them to be.

However, many of *The Simpsons'* musical segments, though they may start in attack mode, do not end there. I would claim that one reason for the show's long life is its frequent tempering of cynicism with acceptance and even sentimentality.

---

[10] Stilwell, "It May Look Like a Living Room," 61.

This interface of harsh critique with forgiveness and understanding appeared even before the show was created, in Matt Groening's cartoons published as far back as 1984. Despite their nihilistic titles (including *Love is Hell*, *How to Go to Hell*, and *Huge Book of Hell*), these cartoons frequently exhibit uncertainty as to whether a father's abusive ineptitude and a wife's furious nagging are malevolent or merely pitiable and have a tendency to view dysfunctional behavior as merely the acting-out of victims. It also seems plausible that Groening, despite not being sole author of *The Simpsons*, has explored and exhibited his own mellowing attitudes in the show, including an increasing willingness to view authority (especially fathers) as not all bad.

Although many of *The Simpsons*' musical episodes do start out trying to attack and subvert the calculated effects of the music and theater, those effects frequently overwhelm the plot and win over the characters, their apparent emotions, and even the ends of stories—and often to everyone's benefit. For example, in "A Streetcar Named Marge," a cheesy and wildly misguided rewrite of the Tennessee Williams play is the vehicle for a satire of numerous elements—the pretensions of amateur theater, the narcissism of an obsessive director, the sexual cluelessness of suburbanites, absurdly inappropriate lyrics, ludicrous miscasting, and desperately overblown staging. However, the end of this segment resolves a fairly serious fight between Homer and Marge, caused when she decides that his inattentive lack of respect has become unforgivable. Music trumps all, as it ultimately resolves the needs of the story, as well as the inner and unacknowledged needs of the characters—the character identification conveyed by the show overcomes Homer's unconsciousness of his own insensitivity, and explains to him what Marge cannot.

Interlude: Cardboard Cutouts

Of course, *The Simpsons* is not the entire world of television; it is not even the entire world of animated satire. It is impossible to refer to television's use of musicals without mentioning *South Park* (including, if you will allow me a small expansion of this discussion, the film of the same name (1999), which is different chiefly in being longer and more architecturally structured). In the context of parody, the important difference between *The Simpsons* and *South Park* is the latter's crueler, more sophomoric, more two-dimensional emotional world. Despite similar attempts at innovative and wide-ranging satire, *South Park* rarely allows its characters or the objects of its derision to win, to develop, or to experience undamaged emotions.

One episode of *South Park* is particularly similar to *The Simpsons*' "Streetcar"— "Helen Keller: The Musical" (SP4.14), where the class makes a show out of Gibson's popular drama *The Miracle Worker* (1959). A director is brought in whose credentials consist of singing in a dinner theater production of *Les Misérables* (1985)—already a satiric deflation, as *Les Misérables* was not yet available for amateur performance, and in any case would be ridiculous in the pathetic confines of dinner theater. He constantly reminds us of his melodramatic roots by speaking in a recitative that resembles the musical rhetoric of that show. The misfit turkey at the center of the plot is drawn as a parody of the similarly pathetic Christmas tree that is central to the 1965 perennial *A Charlie Brown Christmas*; unlike that *Peanuts* special, however, in this case the misfit is repeatedly compared to the preening thoroughbred turkey brought in by the director, an object of resentment and rage that will ultimately lose out to the misfit "underdog."

The musical numbers are made ridiculous by being inappropriate and/or overdone. The show opens with an offensively blunt "Helen Keller, Helen Keller, blind as a bat;/She can't hear or speak—what's up with that?"; and the climactic moment, when Helen Keller recognizes the link between the word "water" and the thing it describes, is drowned in an absurd surfeit of water effects all over the stage. Such exaggerated writing and staging ruins the impact of the original because it subverts the play's naturalistic moments, not only with the unrealistic formal technologies of the musical but also through didactic manipulation of the audience that tells them how to respond. From the point of view of the proponents of naturalistic theater (and of television, and film), there seems to be no difference between these two techniques.

South Park usually upsets or elides moments of emotional completion such as the one found at the end of the "Streetcar" episode. However, these moments do occasionally appear in such episodes as "Mr Hankey's Christmas Classics" (SP3.15) and the parody-of-a-parody, "Kenny Dies" (SP5.13), as well as in various scenes in the feature film. There are a few moments where the unavoidable emotional authenticity of the music skews the satirical bent towards the sentimental, creating brief moments of positive emotion in the general atmosphere of deflation—something that becomes dangerous for the show's basic principles, which is probably why musical finales are almost always followed by a short, downbeat spoken scene that banishes any generated emotional capital.

An example of animated television's use of the musical that sometimes follows a different path is the frequently cancelled and revived *Family Guy*,[11] which shows more sympathy for and engagement with the musical stage than most television programs. The biggest difference between *Family Guy* and these other shows is that its creator is younger, which raises some doubts about my thesis—perhaps the period of heavy conflict between musicals and television is historically specific at both ends, and it is already fading away in the early twenty-first century. If a younger, more generically polymorphous generation is going to approach the world of media in a post-postmodern, increasingly non-hierarchical way, the time of conflict may be passing. However, most recent shows do not seem to have yet reached this point.

---

[11] *Family Guy* was cancelled in 2001, revived and then cancelled again in 2002 before being revived in 2005 thanks to evidence of its popularity in DVD sales.

Once More: *Buffy the Vampire Slayer*

The subtlest and most emotionally generous of all these shows articulates this pattern in the most definite terms. *Buffy the Vampire Slayer* reached its now famous musical episode during its darkest year, season 6, as a number of story lines reached crisis points, most of which were based on deception: Willow and Tara's magically elided argument over the misuse of magic, Dawn's shoplifting, Xander and Anya's ambivalence about their impending marriage, and above all Buffy's attempts to conceal her misery at being restored to life a second time.

The episode starts its exploration of musicals as a genre satire; the "overture" derives its humor from a choreographic combination of camera shots, movement, and exaggeratedly symbolic mime, all timed to a smooth wash of orchestral music that recalls the technical sophistication and emotional innocence of an early 1960s film musical. The shift in style at the first song indicates that each number will refer to different models and eras out of chronology.[12] This is needed to reflect a variety of elements: the plot (a demon is magically causing the people of Sunnyvale to sing and dance, and he is clearly uninterested whether the result is any kind of consistent *Gesamtkunstwerk*); the skills of the performers (which are varied, ranging from one nearly professional voice down to a refusal to sing a solo at all); the characters (with stylistic/generic emotions and characters often matched); and the entire game of turning an episode of a long-running serial into a musical.[13] This first number is characterized by Joss Whedon, auteur of *Buffy* and composer/lyricist of the musical episode, as a parody of the song sung by a Disney heroine in trouble; the number is filmic in its interlocking details and comic rhymes.[14]

The first few numbers emphasize the unnatural, pseudo-dramatic properties of the musical: after Buffy's solo, the ensemble's mutual realization of what is going on is fragmented, pointing to its own artificiality—interpolated chunks of rock opera (Anya, expressing her irrational fear of bunnies in a verse that could have been sung by Tina Turner in *Tommy*) and the most artistically self-conscious of Technicolor musicals ("They Got The Mustard Out")[15] make even Buffy's dip into

---

[12] The same is true, in a more exaggerated manner, of the film *South Park: Bigger, Longer and Uncut* (1999).

[13] Similarly fragmented approaches characterize the musical episodes of *Xena: Warrior Princess* (1995–2001), "The Bitter Suite" (X3.12) and "Lyre, Lyre, Hearts on Fire" (X5.10) among others.

[14] Joss Whedon, "Once More, with Feeling" audio commentary, *Buffy the Vampire Slayer: Season Six DVD Collection* (2003). Although the pastiche may chiefly be of Disney, Whedon's idolization of Sondheim and his imitations of Sondheim's complex moods and techniques start out the show in this space of irony—but an irony that is unlike the master's, as most of Sondheim's work (with the exception of *A Funny Thing Happened on the Way to the Forum*) does not attack musical conventions themselves.

[15] This brief passage can also be compared with Björk's video "It's Oh So Quiet" (1995), a somewhat more affectionate but still patronizing look at 1960s movie musicals,

apparent honesty ("hey, I've died twice") seem as self-serving as any late-1970s soft-rock solo musical.[16]

At this point it looks as if, although the characters may have to work to defeat whatever forces are causing them to engage in this nonsense, their medium—television—has already beaten the musical itself. Musicals are old-fashioned, artificial, silly, and based on a rhetoric of fraudulently overblown emotion and conformity that associates them with an archaic world imagined to contain the values associated with parents of characters, as well as those of its supposedly teenaged viewers. And, in fact, the random hijacking of different period styles is made unimportant, implying that although there may be change across the eras of the musical, there is never any progress.

The next solo—Tara's "Under Your Spell"—will offer one of several intermediate stages between artifice and "sincerity" (that is, the naturalism the actors normally employ, and also the authenticity of feeling that the characters want from themselves and each other). Beautifully and straightforwardly sung, this song is perhaps the furthest from any traditional show style, as its poetic/erotic girl stuff is of a piece with the kind of "womyn's music" that would not be out of place at Lilith Fair. It is also filled with references to the loneliness of the young lesbian ("I was the only one there") and her transformation to the happy lover, tied to the appropriate natural/pagan imagery. The third-related harmonies and guitar-style voice-leading establish a perfectly constructed authenticity, a style where every artful detail mimics an emotional artlessness. The situation is also ambivalent: Tara believes what she is saying, but we know she has been ensorcelled into that belief—we are in fact watching a reversal of the normal structures of naturalism and artifice, one that traps the character in an impossible and unreal position. The ambivalence is taken further when the song modulates up and adds backing voices; when it is truncated by Xander's lewd interruption of the women's magic/orgasmic love, Tara is prevented from reaching the tonic, suggesting that she won't leave this unreal fantasy until later in the episode. When she sings "something just isn't right/I'm under your spell," she intends to be affectionately metaphorical; but, as in the Sondheim songs that Whedon is imitating, her words reveal the bitter truth.

The next stage is Anya and Xander's knowing, ironical duet, a clear reference to the kind of early 1960s musical that tried to keep pace with social change but could not help foregrounding its own camp, anachronistic nature (such as *How to Succeed in Business Without Really Trying* [1961] or *Promises, Promises* [1968]). But truth is leaking out all over the place, and the worries that will later see their relationship destroyed in unexpected misery are already undermining this supposedly "fun" scene. After it is over, their frantic consultation with Giles zigzags across tropes of sincerity and artifice—Giles's mention of "witness arias" and the peculiarly

---

which shows that whatever the dynamics between the "cooler" genres, they can all afford to make fun of musicals.

[16] For example, the mawkish *I'm Getting My Act Together and Taking it On the Road* (1978).

comic theatrical vignettes taking place behind the main characters emphasize the increasingly chaotic results of this unreal musical world's invasion of the natural one. In addition, Anya's fear that the duet was just a "retro pastiche" (which, of course, it was) traps her in anxieties about being contemporary, being cool, which is the paramount fear that the musical evokes for more trendy media.

Spike's solo steps further into the problem of authenticity by enacting a rough-edged male rock'n'roll persona, associated with feelings whose sincerity is indicated by a masculine inability to express them. Although the elaborately athletic choreography and conveniently placed bystanders puncture this authenticity, his anger and frustration add to the emotional conflicts that each musical number is both organizing and releasing. The style chosen for Spike clearly fits his abilities, but it also emphasizes the central problem, as this kind of masculine statement of resentment has long been presented as the ultimate in "authentic" popular music, just as rock contrasts to the campy world of the musical. As various plot crises come to a head at the end of Act 2 and throughout Act 3—Dawn is kidnapped in a Cyd Charisse ballet, the demon shows his hand, Tara realizes she has been duped, Giles decides he must leave Sunnydale—artifice and sincerity, in musical styles and in staged emotions, collapse into an apparently inextricable tangle. It becomes clear on the one hand that even tap-dancing can kill, and on the other that the "real" long-term relationships enacted by the characters might actually collapse and end, destroyed by the increasingly unbearable weight of too many revelations.

Towards the end of the episode, although the demon is gone and the spell must thus be over, one last (perhaps completely sincere, because non-magical) finale is sung. Spike and Buffy abandon this finale, which is still too artificially constricted for their mutual anger and frustration, to trade a few phrases of bluntly naturalistic dialogue; but music catches them up again, trapping them in a final kiss that is both the apex of stagey artifice and at the same time exactly what their naturalistic characters desire. Although Act 4 is not entirely successful—the climax is perhaps too drawn out, the explanations and resolutions somewhat anti-climactic—the message is nevertheless clear: that the power of music has triumphed over not only those we are watching as characters and as performers but the entire world of naturalistic television narrative.[17] Because *Buffy* is not a sitcom but a drama where the general dramatic situation does change—and changes drastically—the

---

[17] Joss Whedon's miniature musical satire written during the 2008 US writers' strike, *Dr Horrible's Sing-Along Blog* (briefly but no longer available at http://www.drhorrible.com), has an ending that is markedly better constructed and performed. However, this ending is intensely problematic in terms of emotion and expectation: the tragedy of the heroine's death, and the resultant psychotic loss of affect by Dr Horrible himself, is both difficult to accept and hard to construct in terms of the traditional musical—which is one justification for the brutal removal of the musical accompaniment under the last two words. In fact, it is hard to believe that this is really the end of this story—perhaps Whedon will say more in time.

limitations to the television sitcom musical noted by Stilwell do not apply.[18] Within the confines of the series, all the truths have emerged, the characters have been forced into admitting their real feelings, and the episode moves the whole into a radically changed narrative space.

The Truth

The general consensus seems to be that musicals have always, already, sold us short. Their sentimentality and artifice have kept us from really experiencing fear, anger, passion—indeed, reality: in fact they *must* have kept us from experiencing all those things because they are too structured, too patterned, to be believed.

However, musicals consist, in large part, of music, and music may be a technology for creating emotions without guaranteeing their authenticity; but it is also a technology for discovering and amplifying emotions that we may find more authentic than any cynical, cool, in-control stance. It may *force* us to feel, but it also *allows* us to feel and to express things not normally allowed in the prosaic dullness of everyday communications. This ambiguity recreates the love/hate polarities aimed at music, which are embedded in the Marx Brothers film that caused Kramer to write his paper, and which in turn led to this one. But perhaps we should reverse our position and claim that anything so formal, so elaborately structured, *must* be, in a way, true.

One of the most ridiculous scenes ever enacted by late comedienne Gilda Radner—in which her weepy teenage nerd character Lisa Loopnerm plays, sings, and explains her way through a ludicrously bad performance of the ultra-nostalgic "The Way We Were"—ends up being a powerful emotional experience, perhaps one more powerful than any authentic performance would be.[19] The audience is virtually tricked into sympathizing with, and then identifying with, this pathetic loser, and they end up weeping with her in unabashed sentimentality. Music does lead us into unacceptable, but also unavoidable, emotional truths: what initially seems to be a falsification of gesture, of emotion, of identity, ends up becoming the only thing that is real.

And so, as your hand forms into a fist, then the first two fingers open out and away from each other, and then your entire hand flattens, you may come to realize that it is true: film beats opera; and television does, undeniably, beat musicals.

But as for music: music beats—well, everything…

---

[18] Stilwell, "It May Look Like a Living Room," 15–16.
[19] Gilda Radner, *Live from New York* (Warner Brothers Records, 1979).

Afterword

Anahid Kassabian

Buffy the Vampire Slayer (1997–2003) was an extraordinary moment in the history of television. Pitched to a concatenation of audiences generally ignored by producers and programmers—indie kids, vampire fans, and pop culture critics—it made a virtue of trading in practices generally eschewed by television writers—multiple, constant, and demanding intertextual references; complex and anti-realist narrative strategies; and creative and challenging uses of music and sound. Small wonder, then, that it has occasioned conferences, publications, and even its own peer-reviewed journal.

The current volume, however, is not only a major contribution to academic Buffydom. It is also a major contribution to the study of music and television. The study of television music is, to put it as generously as possible, in its infancy. In their 2002 introduction to *Popular Music*'s special issue on television, Keith Negus and John Street suggest that "music has played a part in organising our experience of television, whilst television has, in turn, played a key role in organising our experience of a range of musical genres."[1] Across this volume, genuinely new insights are offered that prove Negus and Street's point.

For example, there are two essays, Stevens and Bloustien, that substantially discuss and even theorize silence, which is rarely even mentioned in the various literatures on music and moving images. Bloustien appealingly finds a point of intersection with Derrida's thinking on the "demonic," a pre-Platonic state that seductively offers complete surrender. Or, for another example, Kathryn Hill's study of the place of unsigned bands in the articulation of the Buffyverse countervenes received wisdom about the placement of songs in youth-oriented TV series. The choice to use unsigned bands simultaneously validated the indie credentials of the show and saved the producers lots of money—a very different set of decisions than, for example, those of *Dawson's Creek* or *The OC*.

One more example will perhaps suffice. The three essays on "Once More with Feeling," the stunning musical episode in season six, collectively both offer and demand a reappraisal of thinking on both film and television musicals. When it was first aired, I took it to my students in an introductory course on popular music studies, and they used it as a springboard to discuss every major theoretical point the course had addressed. It is, to my mind, an important touchstone in television history, and absolutely unmatched by any other musical attempt, of which there

---

[1] Keith Negus and John Street, "Introduction to 'Music and Television' special issue," *Popular Music*, 21/3 (2002), p. 248.

have been surprisingly many. The chapters discuss parody (Attinello), genre (Bauer), and heteronormativity (Sandars and Wilcox), together taking stock of the musical in the twenty-first century in a way that scholarship on single films such as *Moulin Rouge* or *Dancer in the Dark* has simply not been able to do.

These are not just examples of solid scholarship. Rather they, like many essays in this volume, demand a rethinking of the little we believe we know about TV music. When I was writing my PhD thesis on film music in the late 1980s, Claudia Gorbman's book *Unheard Melodies* appeared, and I thought the topic had been treated and was done. There have been at least half a dozen important single-authored works and another half dozen collections since, and now a handful of journals. I was, thankfully, wrong, and the field is thriving.

But it's like that when there's little or no scholarship in an area. (Negus and Street describe their apprehensions for the journal issue along these lines in their introduction.) In its thirteen essays, *Music, Sound, and Silence in* Buffy the Vampire Slayer opens many new directions for television music scholarship, and the essays offer important models for how and where to begin.

Let us simply hope, then, that its readers accept the challenge it offers.

Bibliography

Abbate, Carolyn, *Unsung Voices: Opera and Musical Narrative in the Nineteenth Century* (Princeton: Princeton University Press, 1991).

Adams, Michael, *Slayer Slang: A Buffy the Vampire Slayer Lexicon* (Oxford/New York: Oxford University Press, 2003).

Adorno, Theodor W., *Essays on Music*, ed. Richard Leppert (Los Angeles: University of California Press, 2002).

Affron, Charles, *Cinema and Sentiment* (Chicago: University of Chicago Press, 1982).

Albright, Richard S., "'[B]reakaway pop hit or … book number?': 'Once More, with Feeling' and Genre," *Slayage: The Online International Journal of Buffy Studies*, 17 (2005), accessed 18 August 2008 at http://www.slayageonline.com/essays/slayage17/albright.htm.

Alessio, Dominic, "'Things are Different Now'?: A Postcolonial Analysis of *Buffy the Vampire Slayer*," *The European Legacy*, 6/6 (2001): 731–40.

Allanbrook, Wye Jamison, *Rhythmic Gesture in Mozart: Le nozze di Figaro and Don Giovanni* (Chicago/London: University of Chicago Press, 1983).

Altman, Rick (ed.), *Genre: The Musical* (London: Routledge, 1981).

——, *The American Film Musical* (Bloomington, IN: Indiana University Press, 1987).

Attali, Jacques, *Noise: The Political Economy of Music* (Manchester: Manchester University Press, 1985).

Attinello, Paul, "chemical bodies," *Radical Musicology*, 2 (2008), accessed 25 August 2008 at http://www.radical-musicology.org.uk/2007/Attinello.htm.

——, "The Universe Will Tell You What It Needs: Being, Time, Sondheim," in Steven Baur, Raymond Knapp, and Jacqueline Warwick (eds), *Musicological Identities: Essays in Honor of Susan McClary* (Aldershot: Ashgate, 2008).

Ayers, Sheli, "Virile Magic: Bataille, Baudelaire, Ballard," *Speed: Electronic Journal of Science and Re-Enchantment*, 1/2 (2001), accessed 18 August 2008 at http://proxy.arts.uci.edu/~nideffer/_SPEED_/1.2/ayers.html.

Baddeley, Alan, *Working Memory* (New York: Oxford University Press, 1986).

Bakhtin, Mikhail, *Rabelais and His World*, trans. Helene Iswolsky (Cambridge, MA: MIT Press, 1968).

Banfield, Stephen, *Sondheim's Broadway Musicals* (Ann Arbor: University of Michigan Press, 1993).

Bannister, Matthew, *White Boys, White Noise: Masculinities and 1980s Indie Guitar Rock* (Aldershot: Ashgate, 2006).

Barthes, Roland, *The Pleasure of the Text*, trans. Richard Miller (New York: Hill and Wang, 1975).

Bataille, Georges, *Visions of Excess: Selected Writings, 1927–39 (Theory and History of Literature)* (Minneapolis: University of Minnesota Press, 1985).

Beebe, Roger, Ben Saunders, and Denise Fulbrook (eds), *Rock over the Edge: Transformations in Popular Music Culture* (Durham, NC: Duke University Press, 2002).

Bell, Elizabeth, Lynda Haas, and Laura Sells (eds), *From Mouse to Mermaid: The Politics of Film, Gender and Culture* (Bloomington: Indiana University Press, 1995).

Belsey, Catherine, *Critical Practice* (London: Methuen, 1980).

Benjamin, Walter, *Reflections: Essays, Aphorisms, Autobiographical Writings*, ed. Peter Demetz (New York: Schocken Books, 1986).

Bennett, Andy, *Popular Music and Youth Culture: Music, Identity and Place* (London: Macmillan, 2000).

Bennett, Tony, "Texts, Readers, Reading Formations," *Literature and History*, 9/2 (1983): 214–27.

Block, Geoffrey, "The Broadway Canon from *Show Boat* to *West Side Story* and the European Operatic Ideal," *Journal of Musicology*, 11/4 (1993): 525–44.

Bloustien, Gerry, "Fans with a Lot at Stake: Serious Play and Mimesis in *Buffy the Vampire Slayer*," *European Journal of Cultural Studies*, 5/4 (2002): 427–51.

——, *Girl Making: A Cross-Cultural Ethnography on the Processes of Growing up Female* (New York: Berghahn Books, 2003).

Bosma, Hannah, "Male and Female Voices in Computer Music," *Proceedings of the International Computer Music Conference 1995* (San Francisco: International Computer Music Association, 1995).

Bourdieu, Pierre, *Distinction: A Social Critique of the Judgement of Taste*, trans. Richard Nice (Cambridge, MA: Harvard University Press, 1986).

——, *The Field of Cultural Production*, trans. Randal Johnson (New York: Columbia University Press, 1993).

Bradney, Anthony, "Choosing Laws, Choosing Families: Images of Law, Love and Authority in *BtVS*," *Web Journal of Current Legal Issues*, 2 (2003), accessed 17 October 2003 at http://webjcli.ncl.ac.uk/2003/issue2/bradney2.html.

Bremer, Carolyn, "Duality and Completeness: An Analysis of the *Xena: Warrior Princess* Theme Music," *Whoosh!*, 20 (1998), accessed 27 January 2003 at http://www.whoosh.org/issue20/bremer1.html.

Brophy, Philip, "*Magnolia*: The Power of Song," *Real Time*, 36/7 (2000), accessed 25 August 2008 at http://www.philipbrophy.com/projects/cnsncs/Magnolia.html.

Brown, Julie, "*Ally McBeal*'s Postmodern Soundtrack," *Journal of the Royal Musical Association*, 126 (2001): 275–303.

Brown, Royal, S., *Overtones and Undertones: Reading Film Music* (Berkeley: University of California Press, 1994).

Buckland, Theresa Jill with Elizabeth Stewart, "Dance and Music Video," in Stephanie Jordan and Dave Allen (eds), *Parallel Lines: Media Representations of Dance* (London: John Libbey, 1993).

"Buffy the Vampire Slayer Theme Tab," *Tabcrawler*, accessed 2 April 2006 at http://tabcrawler.com/search.php?show=viewfileandid=501377andletter=nandartist=nerf+herderandtabname=buffy+the+vampire+slayer+theme+tabandtabtype=guitar+tab.

Burns, Gary, "Marilyn Manson and the Apt Pupils of Littleton," *Popular Music and Society*, 23/3 (1999): 3–8.

Busse, Kristina and Karen Hellekson (eds), *Fanfiction and Fan Communities in the Age of the Internet: New Essays* (New York: McFarland, 2006).

Butler, Judith, *Excitable Speech: A Politics of the Performative* (New York/London: Routledge, 1997).

Cage, John, *Silence: Lectures and Writings* (London: Marion Boyars, 1987).

Caillois, Roger, "Mimicry and Legendary Psychasthenia," trans. J. Shepley, *October*, 31 (1984): 17–32.

de Certeau, Michel, "The Place from Which One Deals with Culture," trans. Tom Conley, in Luce Giard (ed.), *Cultural in the Plural* (Minneapolis: University of Minnesota Press, 1997).

Chion, Michel, *Audio-Vision: Sound on Screen*, ed. and trans. Claudia Gorbman (New York: Columbia University Press, 1994).

———, *The Voice in Cinema*, trans. Claudia Gorbman (New York: Columbia University Press, 1999).

Clarke, Jamie, "Affective Entertainment in 'Once More With Feeling': A Manifesto for Fandom," *Refractory*, 2 (2003), accessed 12 August 2008 at http://blogs.arts.unimelb.edu.au/refractory/2003/03/18/affective-entertainment-in-once-more-with-feeling-a-manifesto-for-fandom-jamie-clarke/.

Clover, Carol, *Men, Women and Chainsaws: Gender in the Modern Horror Film* (London: BFI, 1992).

Coates, Norma, "Music Television or Television Music? Pop Music on American Television as the Implementation of Contemporary Business Trends and Strategies," paper presented at the 12th Conference of IASPM, McGill University, Montreal, 3–7 July 2003.

Cohan, Steven, "Feminizing the Song and Dance Man," in Steven Cohan (ed.), *Hollywood Musicals: The Film Reader* (New York: Routledge, 2002).

———, *Incongruous Entertainment: Camp, Cultural Value, and the MGM Musical* (Durham, NC: Duke University Press, 2005).

Collin, Matthew with John Godfrey, *Altered State: The Story of Ecstasy Culture and Acid House*, 2nd edition (London: Serpent's Tail, 1998).

Collins, Jim, *Uncommon Cultures: Popular Culture and Post-Modernism* (New York/London, 1989)

Cox, Arnie, "The Mimetic Hypothesis and Embodied Musical Meaning," *Musicae Scientiae*, 5/2 (2001): 195–209.

———, "Hearing, Feeling, Grasping Gestures," in Elaine King and Anthony Gritten (eds), *Music and Gesture* (Aldershot: Ashgate, 2006).

Cubitt, Sean, "'Maybellene': Meaning and the Listening Subject," in Richard Middleton (ed.), *Reading Pop: Approaches to Textual Analysis in Popular Music* (Oxford: Oxford University Press, 2000).

Dahlhaus, Carl, *Richard Wagner's Music Dramas*, trans. Mary Whittall (Cambridge: Cambridge University Press, 1979).

Daney, Serge and Bill Krohn, "Les Cahiers du Cinéma 1968–1977: Interview with Serge Daney," trans. Bill Krohn, *The Thousand Eyes*, 2 (1977), accessed October 2002, at http://home.earthlink.net/~steevee/Daney_1977.html.

Daugherty, Anne Millard, "Just a Girl: Buffy as Icon," in Roz Kaveney (ed.), *Reading the Vampire Slayer: An Unofficial Critical Companion to Buffy and Angel* (London/New York: Tauris Parke, 2002).

Dechert, S. Renee, "'My Boyfriend's in the Band!' *Buffy* and the Rhetoric of Music," in Rhonda V. Wilcox and David Lavery (eds), *Fighting the Forces: What's at Stake in Buffy the Vampire Slayer* (Lanham, MD: Rowman and Littlefield, 2002).

Derrida, Jacques, *Writing and Difference*, trans. Alan Bass (London: Routledge, 1978).

——, *The Gift of Death* (Chicago: The University of Chicago Press, 1995).

Doherty, Thomas, *Teenagers and Teenpics: The Juvenilization of American Movies in the 1950s* (Philadelphia, PA: Temple University Press, 2002).

Donaruma, William, "'Once More With Feeling': the Hellmouth in Postmodern Heaven," paper presented at the *Slayage* Conference on *Buffy the Vampire Slayer*, Middle Tennessee State University, Nashville, Tennessee, 28–30 May 2004, archived at http://www.slayageonline.com/SCBtVS_Archive/Talks/Donaruma.pdf.

Donnelly, K. J., "Tracking British Television: Pop Music as Stock Soundtrack to the Small Screen," *Popular Music*, 21/3 (2002): 331–43.

Driscoll, Catherine, "Girl Culture, Revenge and Global Capitalism: Cybergirls, Riot Grrrls, Spice Girls," *Australian Feminist Studies*, 14/29 (1999): 173–93.

——, *Girls: Feminine Adolescence in Popular Culture and Cultural Theory* (New York: Columbia University Press, 2002).

Dunne, Michael, *American Film Musical Themes and Forms* (Jefferson, NC: McFarland, 2004).

Dyer, James, "Joss Whedon—About Buffy/Serenity/Wonder Woman," *Empire Online*, 26 October 2005, reproduced at *Dollhouse, Firefly & Serenity, Angel, Buffy: news, photos, videos, interviews and more…*, accessed 25 August 2008 at http://www.whedon.info/Joss-Whedon-About-Buffy-Serenity.html.

Dyer, Richard, *Only Entertainment* (London: Routledge, 1992).

Early, Frances H., "Staking her Claim: Buffy the Vampire Slayer as Transgressive Woman Warrior," *Journal of Popular Culture*, 35/3 (2001): 11–37.

—— and Kathleen Kennedy (eds), *Athena's Daughters: Television's New Women Warriors* (Syracuse, NY: Syracuse University Press, 2003).

Edwards, Lynne, "Slaying in Black and White: Kendra as Tragic Mulatta in *Buffy*," in Rhonda V. Wilcox and David Lavery (eds), *Fighting the Forces: What's at Stake in Buffy the Vampire Slayer* (Lanham, MD: Rowman and Littlefield, 2002).

Ellis, John, *Visible Fictions: Cinema, Television, Video* (London: Routledge and Kegan Paul, 1982).

——, "Broadcast TV as Sound and Image," in Leo Braudy and Marshall Cohen (eds), *Film Theory and Criticism*, 6th edition (Oxford: Oxford University Press, 2004).

Ellis, Markman, *The History of Gothic Fiction* (Edinburgh: Edinburgh University Press, 2000).

Erenberg, Lewis A., *Swingin' the Dream: Big Band Jazz and the Rebirth of American Culture* (Chicago: University of Chicago Press, 1998).

Feuer, Jane, *The Hollywood Musical*, 2nd edition (London: Palgrave Macmillan, 1993).

Filmer, Paul, Val Rimmer, and Dave Walsh, "*Oklahoma!*: Ideology and Politics in the Vernacular Tradition of the American Musical," *Popular Music*, 18/3 (1999): 381–95.

FilmForce, "An Interview with Joss Whedon," *IGN.com*, 23 June 2003, accessed 17 July 2003 at http://filmforce.ign.com/articles/425/425492p1.html.

Fiske, John, *Television Culture* (London: Routledge, 1987).

——, *Understanding Popular Culture* (London: Routledge, 1989).

—— and John Hartley, *Reading Television* (London: Routledge, 1978).

Fjellman, Stephen. M., *Vinyl Leaves: Walt Disney World and America* (Boulder, CO: Westview Press, 1992).

Francis, Rob, "BBC – Cult – Buffy – Doug Petrie, Buffy producer's guide to season four – Living Conditions," (2001), *BBC*, accessed 5 April 2006 at http://www.bbc.co.uk/cult/buffy/interviews/doug/index.shtml.

Freud, Sigmund, *Jokes and Their Relation to the Unconscious*, trans. James Strachey (New York: W. W. Norton and Company, 1963).

——, *Beyond the Pleasure Principle*, trans. James Strachey (New York: W. W. Norton and Company, 1991).

Frith, Simon, *Music for Pleasure: Essays in the Sociology of Pop* (Cambridge: Polity Press, 1988)

——, *Performing Rites* (Cambridge, MA: Harvard University Press, 1996).

——, "Music and Everyday Life," in Martin Clayton, Trevor Herbert, and Richard Middleton (eds), *The Cultural Study of Music: A Critical Introduction*. (New York: Routledge, 2003).

—— and Andrew Goodwin (eds), *On Record: Rock Pop and the Written Word* (London: Pantheon, 2000).

Furia, Philip, "Something to Sing About: America's Greatest Lyricists," *American Scholar*, 66/3 (1997): 379–95.

Garner, Ken, "'Would you Like to Hear Some Music?' Music in-and-out-of-control in the Films of Quentin Tarantino," in K. J. Donnelly (ed.), *Film Music: Critical Approaches* (Edinburgh: Edinburgh University Press, 2001).

Garrison, Ednie Kaeh, "US feminism-grrrl style! Youth (sub)cultures and the technologics of the third wave," *Feminist Studies*, 26/1 (2000): 141–70.

Gebauer, Gunter and Christopher Wulf, *Mimesis* (Berkeley: University of California Press, 1992).

Geraghty, Christine, *Women and Soap Opera: A Study of Prime-Time Soaps* (Cambridge: Polity Press, 1990).

Gilbert, Jeremy, "White Light/White Heat: *Jouissance* Beyond Gender in the Velvet Underground," in Andrew Blake (ed.), *Living Through Pop* (London/ New York: Routledge, 1999), pp. 31–48.

Gilbert, Laurel and Crystal Kile, *Surfergrrrls: Look Ethel! An Internet Guide for Us* (Seattle, WA: Seal Press, 1996).

Giles, Dennis, "Show-making," in Rick Altman (ed.), *Genre: The Musical* (London: Routledge, 1981).

Gokee, Rob, "Buffy the Vampire Slayer 3.06: Band Candy," *Resource Site for Chris[tophe] Beck@Blunt Instrument*, 19 June 2005, accessed 29 February 2008 at http://www.bluntinstrument.org.uk/beck/buffy/3-06/bandcandy.htm.

——, "Buffy the Vampire Slayer 3.13: The Zeppo," *Resource Site for Chris[tophe] Beck@Blunt Instrument*, 25 August 2005, accessed 30 June 2006 at http:// www.bluntinstrument.org.uk/beck/buffy/3-13/thezeppo.htm.

Golden, Christopher and Nancy Holder, *The Watcher's Guide* vol. 1 (New York: Pocket Books, 1998).

Goode, Erich and Nachman Ben-Yehua, *Moral Panics: The Social Construction of Deviance* (Oxford: Blackwell, 1994).

Gorbman, Claudia, *Unheard Melodies: Narrative Film Music* (Bloomington: Indiana University Press, 1987).

Grajeda, Tony, "The "Feminization" of Rock," in Roger Beebe, Ben Saunders, and Denise Fulbrook (eds), *Rock Over the Edge: Transformations in Popular Music Culture* (Durham, NC: Duke University Press, 2002).

Groening, Matt, *Love is Hell: A Cartoon Book* (Los Angeles: Life in Hell, 1984).

——, *How to Go to Hell: A Cartoon Book* (New York: HarperPerennial, 1991).

——, *Huge Book of Hell* (New York: Penguin Books, 1997).

Grossberg, Lawrence, "Reflections of a Disappointed Popular Music Scholar," in Roger Beebe, Ben Saunders, and Denise Fulbrook (eds), *Rock Over the Edge: Transformations in Popular Music Culture* (Durham, NC: Duke University Press, 2002), pp. 25–59.

Halfyard, Janet K., "Love, Death, Curses and Reverses (in F minor): Music, Gender and Identity in *Buffy the Vampire Slayer* and *Angel*," *Slayage: The Online International Journal of Buffy Studies*, 4 (2001), accessed 18 August 2008 at http://www.slayageonline.com/essays/slayage4/halfyard.htm.

——, "Singing Their Hearts Out: Performance, Sincerity and Musical Diegesis in *Buffy the Vampire Slayer* and *Angel*," paper presented at the "Blood, Text and Fears: Reading Around *Buffy the Vampire Slayer*" conference, University of East Anglia, Norwich, 19–20 October 2002.

——, "Singing Their Hearts Out: The Problem of Performance in *Buffy the Vampire Slayer* and *Angel*," *Slayage: The Online International Journal of Buffy Studies*, 17 (2005), accessed 18 August 2008 at http://www.slayageonline.com/essays/slayage17/Halfyard.htm.

——, "The Dark Avenger: Angel and the Cinematic Superhero," in Stacey Abbott (ed.), *Reading Angel* (New York: IB Tauris, 2005).

Halligan, Marion, "He Kindly Stopped for Me," *The Weekend Australian* [Review section], 19–20 August 2006: 9.

Handelman, Don, *Models and Mirrors: Towards an Anthropology of Public Events* (Cambridge: Cambridge University Press, 1990).

Hansen, Mark, *Embodying Technesis: Technology Beyond Writing* (Ann Arbor: University of Michigan Press, 2000).

Helford, Elyce Rae, "My Emotions Give me Power: The Containment of Girls' Anger in *Buffy*," in Rhonda V. Wilcox and David Lavery (eds), *Fighting the Forces: What's at Stake in Buffy the Vampire Slayer* (Lanham, MD: Rowman and Littlefield, 2002).

Higgins, Dick, "Intermedia," *Leonardo* 34/1 (2001): 52.

Hill, Kathryn, "Music, subtexts, and foreshadowing: the contextual role of 'source' music in *Buffy the Vampire Slayer*," paper presented at the *Slayage* Conference on *Buffy the Vampire Slayer*, Middle Tennessee State University, Nashville, Tennessee, 28–30 May 2004, archived at http://www.slayageonline.com/SCBtVS_Archive/Talks/KHill.pdf.

Hills, Matt, *Fan Cultures* (London: Routledge, 2002).

Holder, Nancy with Jeff Mariotte and Maryelizabeth Hart, *The Watcher's Guide* vol. 2 (New York: Pocket Books, 2000).

Howell, Amanda. "'If we hear any inspirational power chords …' Rock Music, Rock Culture on *Buffy the Vampire Slayer*," *Continuum: Journal of Media and Cultural Studies*, 18/3 (2004): 406–422.

Hullot-Kentor, Robert. *Things Beyond Resemblance: Collected Essays on Theodor W. Adorno* (New York: Columbia University Press, 2008).

Iacoboni, Marco, *Mirroring People: The New Science of How We Connect with Others* (New York: Farrar, Straus and Giroux, 2008).

Infante, Victor D., "She Saved the World a Lot," *Orange County Weekly*, 22 May 2003, accessed 28 August 2008 at http://www.ocweekly.com/culture/tv/she-saved-the-world-a-lot/16019/.

Isherwood, Charles, "Singing! Dancing! Adapting! Stumbling!" *New York Times*, 6 August 2008, accessed 25 August 2008 at http://www.nytimes.com/2008/08/10/theater/10ishe.html.

Jackson, Rosemary, *Fantasy: The Literature of Subversion* (London: Methuen, 1981).

Jacobs, Dorothy H., "A New Arcadia: Daytime Television Drama," *Journal of American Culture*, 6/3 (1983): 92–6.

Jameson, Fredric, "Postmodernism and Consumer Society," in E. Ann Kaplan (ed.), *Postmodernism and Its Discontents: Theories, Practices* (London/New York: Verso, 1988).

Jenkins, Henry, "'Strangers No More, We Sing': Filking and the Social Construction of the Science Fiction Fan Community," in Lisa Lewis (ed.), *The Adoring Audience* (New York: Routledge, 1992).

—— and John Tulloch, "Beyond the *Star Trek* Phenomenon: Reconceptualizing the Science Fiction Audience," in John Tulloch (ed.), *Science Fiction Audiences: Watching Star Trek and Dr Who* (London: Routledge, 1995).

Johnson, Angela, "Start a fucking riot," *Off Our Backs*, 23/5 (1993): 6–10.

Jones, Steve, "Music That Moves: Popular Music, Distribution and Network Technologies," *Cultural Studies*, 16/2 (2002): 213–32.

Jowett, Lorna, "Masculinity, Monstrosity and Behaviour Modification in *Buffy the Vampire Slayer*," *Foundations*, 84 (2002): 59–73.

Kalinak, Kathryn, *Settling the Score: Music and the Classical Hollywood Film* (Madison: University of Wisconsin Press, 1992).

Kaltefleiter, Caroline, *Revolution Girl Style Now: Trebled Reflexivity and the Riot Grrrl Network* (PhD thesis, Ohio University, 1995).

Kassabian, Anahid, *Hearing Film: Tracking Identifications in Contemporary Hollywood Film Music* (London: Routledge, 2001).

Kaveney, Roz (ed.), *Reading the Vampire Slayer: An Unofficial Critical Companion to Buffy and Angel* (London/New York: Tauris Parke, 2001).

——, "'She Saved the World. A Lot': An Introduction to the Themes and Structures of *Buffy* and *Angel*," in Roz Kaveney (ed.), *Reading the Vampire Slayer: An Unofficial Critical Companion to Buffy and Angel* (London/New York: Tauris Parke, 2001).

Kellner, Douglas, "TV, Ideology, and Emancipatory Popular Culture," in Horace Newcomb (ed.), *Television: The Critical View* (Oxford/New York: Oxford University Press, 1987).

Kermode, Frank, *The Sense of an Ending: Studies in the Theory of Fiction* (London: Oxford University Press, 1967).

King, Norman, "The Sound of Silents," in Richard Abel (ed.), *Silent Film* (London: Athlone Press, 1996).

Knights, Vanessa, "'Bay City Rollers. Now That's Music': Coolness, Crassness and Characterisation on *Buffy the Vampire Slayer*," paper presented at the Sonic Synergies: Creative Cultures Conference, University of South Australia, The Hawke Research Institute and IASPM Australia/New Zealand, 17–20 July 2003.

Koelsch, Stefan, Thomas Fritz, D. Yves, V. Cramon, Karsten Müller, and Angela D. Friederici, "Investigating Emotion with Music: An fMRI Study," *Human Brain Mapping*, 28/3 (2005): 239–50.

Kohles, Lisa, "The Music of Angels," *The 11th Hour web magazine*, 6 (1999), accessed 15 June 2006 at http://www.the11thhour.com/archives/111999/features/darlingvioletta2.html.

Kramer, Lawrence, *Musical Meaning: Toward a Critical History* (Berkeley: University of California Press, 2002).

Krimmer, Elizabeth and Shilpa Raval, "Digging the Undead: Death and Desire in *Buffy*," in Rhonda V. Wilcox and David Lavery (eds), *Fighting the Forces: What's at Stake in Buffy the Vampire Slayer* (Lanham, MD: Rowan and Littlefield, 2002).

Kromer, Kelly, "Silence as Symptom: A Psychoanalytic Reading of 'Hush'," *Slayage: The Online International Journal of Buffy Studies*, 19 (2006), accessed 18 August 2008 at http://www.slayageonline.com/essays/slayage19/Kromer.htm.

Kruse, Holly, "Subcultural Identity in Alternative Music Culture," *Popular Music*, 12/1 (1993): 34–41.

Laing, Heather, "Emotion by Numbers: Music, Song and the Musical," in Bill Marshall and Robynn Stilwell (eds), *Musicals: Hollywood and Beyond* (Exeter/Portland, OR: Intellect Books, 2000).

Larsen, Janet and Alan Baddeley, "Disruption of Verbal STM by Irrelevant Speech, Articulatory Suppression, and Manual Tapping: Do they Have a Common Source?" *The Quarterly Journal of Experimental Psychology A*, 56/8 (2003): 1249–68.

Lavery, David, "'Emotional Resonance and Rocket Launchers': Joss Whedon's Commentaries on the *Buffy the Vampire Slayer* DVDs," *Slayage: The Online International Journal of Buffy Studies*, 6 (2002), accessed 25 August 2008 at http://www.slayageonline.com/essays/slayage6/Lavery.htm.

——, Angela Hague, and Marla Cartwright (eds), *Deny All Knowledge: Reading the X-Files* (London: Faber, 1996).

Lerner, Neil, "Christophe Beck and Buffy's First Romances: Paradoxes of Musical Scoring in *Buffy the Vampire Slayer*," paper presented at the *Slayage* conference on *Buffy the Vampire Slayer*, Middle Tennessee State University, Nashville, Tennessee, 28–30 May 2004.

——, "The Buffy–Riley Leitmotif and Musical Evidence for the Romantic Conflation of Angel and Riley," paper presented at *SC3: Slayage* conference on the Whedonverse, Henderson State University, Arkadelphia, Arkansas, 5–8 June 2008.

Lessig, Lawrence, "Re-mixing Culture: An Interview with Lawrence Lessig by Richard Koman," *O'Reilly Policy DevCentre* (2005), accessed 12 June 2008 at http://www.oreillynet.com/pub/a/policy/2005/02/24/lessig.html.

Little, Tracy, "High School of Hell: Metaphor made Literal in *Buffy the Vampire Slayer*," in James B. South (ed.), *Buffy the Vampire Slayer and Philosophy: Fear and Trembling in Sunnydale* (Chicago: Open Court, 2003).

Lupton, Deborah, *Risk and Sociocultural Theory: New Directions and Perspectives* (London: Cambridge University Press, 1999).

Lynxwiler, John and David Gay, "Moral Boundaries and Deviant Music: Public Attitudes towards Heavy Metal and Rap," *Deviant Behavior: An Interdisciplinary Journal*, 21 (2000): 63–85.

McConnell, Kathleen, "Chaos at the Mouth of Hell: Why Columbine High School Massacre had Repercussions for *Buffy the Vampire Slayer*," *Gothic Studies*, 2/1 (2000): 119–35.

McDonald, Chris, "Exploring Modal Subversions in Alternative Music," *Popular Music*, 19/3 (2000): 355–63.

Macherey, Pierre, *A Theory of Literary Production* (London: Routledge, 1978).

Marsters, James, "Cries and Whispers," *Hollywood Reporter* 374/42, 20 August 2002, p. 20, accessed 6 December 2005 at http://www.morethanspike.com/index.php?page=6;cat=1;p=3;art=98.

Martin, Adrian, *Phantasms* (Ringwood: McPhee Gribble, 1994).

Masson, Cynthia, "'What Did You Sing About?': Acts of Questioning in 'Once More With Feeling'," paper presented at *SC2*: the *Slayage* Conference on the Whedonverses, Gordon College, Barnesville, Georgia, 26–28 May 2006, archived at http://slayageonline.com/SCW_Archive/Masson.pdf.

Mast, Gerald, *Can't Help Singin: The American Musical on Stage and Screen* (Woodstock, NY: Overlook Press, 1987).

Meltzoff, Andrew and Wolfgang Prinz, *The Imitative Mind: Development, Evolution, and Brain Bases* (Cambridge: Cambridge University Press, 2002).

Merchant, Jacqueline and Robert McDonald, "Youth and the Rave Culture, Ecstasy and Health," *Youth and Policy*, 45 (1994): 16–38.

Metz, Christian, "Aural Objects," in Leo Braudy and Marshall Cohen (eds), *Film Theory and Criticism*, 6th edition (Oxford: Oxford University Press, 2004).

Middents, Jeffrey, "A Sweet Vamp: Critiquing the Treatment of Race in *Buffy* and the American Musical Once More (with Feeling)," *Slayage: The Online International Journal of Buffy Studies*, 17 (2005), accessed 18 August 2008 at http://www.slayageonline.com/essays/slayage17/middents.htm.

Miller, D. A., *Place for Us: Essay on the Broadway Musical* (Cambridge, MA: Harvard University Press, 1998).

Millman, Joyce, "Dark Shadows," *salon.com*, 20 May 2002, accessed 20 June 2006 at http://dir.salon.com/story/ent/masterpiece/2002/05/20/dark_shadows/index.html.

Mitchell, W. J. T., *Iconology: Image, Text, Ideology* (Chicago: Chicago University Press, 1986).

Molnar-Szakacs, Istvan, and Katie Overy, "Music and Mirror Neurons: From Motion to 'E'motion," *Social Cognitive and Affective Neuroscience*, 1/3 (2006): 235–41.

Money, Mary Alice, "The Undemonization of Supporting Characters in *Buffy*," in Rhonda V. Wilcox and David Lavery (eds), *Fighting the Forces: What's at Stake in Buffy the Vampire Slayer* (Lanham, MD: Rowman and Littlefield, 2002).

Monson, Ingrid, "The Problem with White Hipness: Race, Gender, and Cultural Conceptions in Jazz Historical Discourse," *Journal of the American Musicological Society*, 48/3 (1995): 396–422.

Moore, Allan, "Patterns of Harmony," *Popular Music*, 11/1 (1992): 73–106.

——, "The So-called 'Flatted Seventh' in Rock," *Popular Music*, 14/2 (1995): 185–201.

Moynihan, Michael and Didrick Søderlind, *Lords of Chaos: The Bloody Rise of the Satanic Metal Under-Ground* (Venice, CA: Feral House, 1998).

Muir, John Kenneth, "Cult TV Friday Flashback #9: Buffy the Vampire Slayer: 'Once More With Feeling'," September (2005), accessed 26 June 2006 at http://reflectionsonfilmandtelevision.blogspot.com/2005/09/cult-tv-friday-flashback-9-buffy.html.

——, *Singing a New Tune: The Rebirth of the Modern Film Musical, from Evita to De-Lovely and Beyond* (New York: Applause, 2005).

Mundy, John, *Popular Music on Screen: From Hollywood Musical to Music Video* (Manchester: Manchester University Press, 1999).

Negus, Keith and John Street, "Introduction to 'Music and Television' special issue," *Popular Music*, 21/3 (2002): 245–8.

Nehamas, Alexander, "Serious Watching," in Ruth Lorand (ed.), *Television: Aesthetic Reflections* (Oxford/New York: Peter Lang, 2002).

Newitz, Annalee, "Buffy Rides Again: Why Originality Gets you Nowhere on TV," *San Francisco Bay Guardian Online*, 6 August 2002, accessed 6 August 2003 at http://www.sfbg.com/36/22/art_buffy.html.

Noxon, Marti, "Bargaining, Parts 1 and 2" audio commentary, *The Chosen Collection* (Twentieth Century Fox Home Entertainment, 2005).

O'Connell, Mary, "Buffyworld: Marti Noxon Interview with Mary O'Connell," *CBC Radio*, 17 January 2003, accessed 25 April 2003 at http://www.cbc.ca/ideas/features/buffy.

Ono, Kent A., "To Be a Vampire on *Buffy the Vampire Slayer*: Race and ('Other') Socially Marginalizing Positions on Horror TV," in Elyce Rae Helford (ed.), *Fantasy Girls: Gender in the New Universe of Science Fiction and Fantasy Television* (Lanham, MD: Rowman and Littlefield, 2000).

Ostrower, Chaya, *Humor as a Defense Mechanism in the Holocaust* (PhD thesis, Tel-Aviv University, 2000).

Overbey, Karen Eileen and Lahney Preston-Matto, "Staking in Tongues: Speech Act as Weapon in *Buffy*," in Rhonda V. Wilcox and David Lavery (eds), *Fighting the Forces: What's at Stake in Buffy the Vampire Slayer* (Lanham, MD: Rowan and Littlefield, 2002).

Owen, Susan, A., "Vampires, Postmodernity, Postfeminism: *Buffy the Vampire Slayer*," *Journal of Popular Film and Television*, 27/2 (1999): 24–31.

Pateman, Matthew, *The Aesthetics of Culture in Buffy the Vampire Slayer* (Jefferson, NC: McFarland, 2006).

Patton, Cindy, "How to Do Things With Sound," *Cultural Studies*, 13/3 (1999): 466–87.

Penley, Constance, *Nasa/Trek: Popular Science and Sex in America* (London/New York: Verso, 1997).

Pfeil, Fred, *White Guys: Studies in Postmodern Domination and Difference* (London: Verso, 1995).

Poniewozik, James, "How the 'Buffy' Coup Could Change TV," *Time*, 23 April 2001, accessed 16 June 2006 at http://www.time.com/time/columnist/poniewozik/article/0,9565,107337,00.html.

Porter, Dick, *Rapcore: the Nu-Metal Rap Fusion* (London: Plexus, 2003).

Reeves, Jimmie L., Mark C. Rodgers, and Michael Epstein, "Rewriting Popularity: The Cult *Files*," in David Lavery, Angela Hague, and Marla Cartwright (eds), *Deny All Knowledge: Reading the X-Files* (London: Faber, 1996).

Regev, Motti, "Producing Artistic Value: The Case of Rock Music," *The Sociological Quarterly*, 35/1 (1994): 85–102.

Reynolds, Richard, *Superheroes: A Modern Mythology* (London: B.T. Batsford, 1992).

Reynolds, Simon and Joy Press, *The Sex Revolts: Gender, Rebellion and Rock'n'Roll* (Cambridge, MA: Harvard University Press, 1995).

Robertson Wojcik, Pamela and Arthur Knight (eds), *Soundtrack Available: Essays on Film and Popular Music* (Durham, NC: Duke University Press, 2001).

Robinson, Tasha, "Joss Whedon," *The Onion*, 37 (2001), accessed 12 December 2003 at http://www.theonionavclub.com/avclub3731/avfeature_3731.html.

Romney, Jonathan and Adrian Wootton (eds), *Celluloid Jukebox: Popular Music and the Movies Since the 50s* (London: BFI Publishing, 1995).

Rosen, Lisa, "R.I.P. Buffy: You Drove a Stake through Convention," *Los Angeles Times*, 20 May 2003, accessed 17 August 2008 at http://articles.latimes.com/2003/may/20/entertainment/et-rosen20.

Rosenberg, Jessica and Gitana Garofalo, "Riot Grrrl: Revolutions from Within," *Signs*, 23/3 (1998): 809–841.

Rowan, "Let's Face the Music and Dance: Couples in 'OmwF'," *Tabula Rasa—Love. Redemption. Spike* (2001), accessed 2 May 2008 at http://www.btvstabularasa.net/essays/FaceTheMusic.html.

Rubin, Martin, *Showstoppers: Busby Berkeley and the Tradition of Spectacle* (New York: Columbia University Press, 1993).

Russell, Mike, "The CulturePulp Q&A with Joss Whedon," *CulturePulp: Writings and Comics by Mike Russell*, 25 September 2005, accessed 14 December 2005 at http://homepage.mac.com/merussell/iblog/B835531044/C1592678312/E20050916182427/.

Salzman, Eric, "From Stage to Page: Music-Theater in Print," *Theater*, 32/1 (2002): 63–71.

Sandars, Diana, "It's More Than Just Another Silly Love Song: *Ally McBeal* brings the Hollywood Musical to Television," in Elwood Watson (ed.), *Searching the Soul of Ally McBeal: Critical Essays* (Jefferson, NC/London: McFarland, 2006).

Sarris, Andrew, *You Ain't Heard Nothin' Yet: The American Talking Film History and Memory 1927–1949* (Oxford/New York: Oxford University Press, 1998).

Saxey, Esther, "Staking a Claim: The Series and its Slash Fan-Fiction," in Roz Kaveney (ed.), *Reading the Vampire Slayer: An Unofficial Critical Companion to Buffy and Angel* (London/New York: Tauris Parke, 2001).

Schatz, Thomas, *Old Hollywood/New Hollywood: Ritual, Art and Industry* (Ann Arbor, MI: UMI Research Press, 1983).

Schechner, Richard, *The Future of Ritual* (London: Routledge, 1993).

Schilling, Mary Kaye, "Vamping It Up," *Entertainment Weekly*, 9 November 2001.

Schilt, Kristen, "A Little Too Ironic: The Appropriation and Packaging of Riot Grrrl Politics by Mainstream Female Musicians," *Popular Music and Society*, 26/1 (2003): 5–16.

Schultz, Jacques, "Categories of Song," *Journal of Popular Film and Television*, 8/1 (1980): 15–25.

Scott, Kathryn Leigh (ed.), *The Dark Shadows Companion* (Universal City, CA: Pomegranate Press, 1990).

Sells, Laura, "'Where Do the Mermaids Stand?' Voice and Body in *The Little Mermaid*," in Elizabeth Bell, Lynda Haas, and Laura Sells (eds), *From Mouse to Mermaid: The Politics of Film, Gender and Culture* (Bloomington: Indiana University Press, 1995).

Shade, Patrick, "Screaming to be Heard: Reminders and Insights on Community and Communication in 'Hush'," *Slayage: The Online International Journal of Buffy Studies*, 21 (2006), accessed 18 August 2008 at http://www.slayageonline.com/essays/slayage21/Shade.htm.

Shaviro, Steven, *The Cinematic Body* (Minneapolis: University of Minnesota Press, 1993).

Shumway, David R., "Rock'n'Roll Sound Tracks and the Production of Nostalgia," *Cinema Journal*, 38/2 (1999): 36–51.

Silverman, Kaja, *The Acoustic Mirror: the Female Voice in Psychoanalysis and Cinema* (Bloomington: Indiana University Press, 1988).

Smith, Jeff, *The Sounds of Commerce* (New York: Columbia University Press, 1998).

South, James B. (ed.), *Buffy the Vampire Slayer and Philosophy: Fear and Trembling in Sunnydale* (Chicago: Open Court, 2003).

Stafford, Nikki, *Bite Me! The Unofficial Guide to Buffy the Vampire Slayer* (Toronto: ECW Press, 2007).

Stallybrass, Peter and Allon White, *The Politics and Poetics of Transgression* (Ithaca, NY: Cornell University Press, 1986).

Stilwell, Robynn, "'In the Air Tonight': Text, Intertextuality and the Construction of Meaning," *Popular Music and Society*, 19 (1996): 67–103.

——, "It May Look Like a Living Room…: the Musical Number and the Sitcom," *Echo*, 5/1 (2003), accessed 25 August 2008 at http://www.echo.ucla.edu/Volume5-Issue1/stilwell/stilwell.pdf.

Surridge, Matthew, "Comics and Codes: Biography as Genre (a Reply to 'Based on a True Story')," *The Comics Journal*, September (1999), accessed 1 May 2008 at http://www.tcj.com/3_online/b_surridge_092299.html.

Sutton, Martin, "Patterns of Meaning in the Musical," in Rick Altman (ed.), *Genre: The Musical* (London: Routledge, 1981).

Tagg, Philip, "An Anthropology of Stereotypes in TV Music?" *Swedish Musicological Journal* (1989): 19–42, accessed 12 August 2008 at http://tagg.org/articles/xpdfs/tvanthro.pdf.

——, "Music Analysis for 'Non-Musos': Popular Perception as a Basis for Understanding Musical Structure and Signification," paper presented at the Conference on Popular Music Analysis, University of Cardiff, Cardiff, 17 November 2001, accessed 18 August 2008 at http://www.tagg.org/articles/cardiff01.html.

—— and Bob Clarida, *Ten Little Title Tunes* (Lima, OH: MMMSP, 2003).

Taormino, Tristan and Karen Green (eds), *A Girl's Guide to Taking Over the World: Writings from the Girl Zine Revolution* (New York: St Martin's Press, 1997).

Taussig, Michael, *Mimesis and Alterity* (New York: Routledge, 1993).

Thomsen, Mette Ramsgard, "Positioning Intermedia: Intermedia and Mixed Reality," *Convergence: The Journal of Research into New Media Technologies*, 8/4 (2002): 37–45.

Thornton, Sarah, "The Logic of Subcultural Capital," in Sarah Thornton and Ken Gelder (eds), *The Subcultures Reader* (London: Routledge, 1997).

Tonkin, Boyd, "Entropy as Demon: Buffy in Southern California," in Roz Kaveney (ed.), *Reading the Vampire Slayer: An Unofficial Critical Companion to Buffy and Angel* (London/New York: Tauris Parke, 2001).

Topping, Keith, *The Totally Cool Unofficial Guide to Buffy* (London: Virgin, 1999).

——, *Slayer: The Next Generation: An Unofficial and Unauthorised Guide to Season Six of Buffy the Vampire Slayer* (London: Virgin Books, 2003).

True, Everett, *Live Through This: American Rock Music in the Nineties* (London: Virgin Books, 2001).

Ventura, Michael, "Warrior Women," *Psychology Today*, 31/6 (1998): 58–63.

Vint, Sherryl, "'Killing us Softly?' A Feminist Search for the 'Real' Buffy," *Slayage: The Online International Journal of Buffy Studies*, 5 (2002), accessed 26 August 2008 at http://www.slayageonline.com/essays/slayage5/vint.htm.

Wajnryb, Ruth, *The Silence: How Tragedy Shapes Talk* (Sydney: Allen and Unwin, 2001).

Walker, Rebecca, "Becoming the Third Wave," *Ms*, January/February (1992): 39–41.

Walser, Robert, *Running with the Devil: Power, Gender, and Madness in Heavy Metal Music* (Middletown, CT: Weslyan University Press, 1993)

Walsh, David and Len Platt, *Musical Theater and American Culture* (Westport, CT: Greenwood, 2003).

Walton, Andy, "Bye-bye, Buffy: Cult Hit Rides into its Last Sunset," *CNN.com*, 19 May 2003, accessed 14 July 2003 at http://www.cnn.com/2003/SHOWBIZ/TV/05/19/buffy.finale/.

Warner, Marina, *No Go the Bogeyman: Scaring, Lulling and Making Mock* (London: Chatto and Windus, 2000).

Weinstein, Deena, "Youth," in Bruce Horner and Thomas Swiss (eds), *Key Terms in Popular Music and Culture* (Oxford: Blackwell, 1999).

Whedon, Joss, "Welcome to the Hellmouth" audio commentary, *Buffy the Vampire Slayer: Season One Collector's Edition* (Twentieth Century Fox Home Entertainment, 2000).

——, "Lie to Me," *Buffy the Vampire Slayer: The Script Book, Season Two, Volume 2* (New York: Pocket Books, 2001).

——, "Once More, with Feeling" audio commentary, *Buffy the Vampire Slayer: Season Six DVD Collection* (Twentieth Century Fox Home Entertainment, 2003).

——, "Buffy the Vampire Slayer: Television with a Bite," *Buffy the Vampire Slayer Season Six DVD Collection* (Twentieth Century Fox Home Entertainment, 2003).

—— and Paul Ruditis, *Buffy the Vampire Slayer, "Once More, With Feeling," The Script Book*, ed. Micol Ostow (New York: Simon and Schuster, 2002).

Wilcox, Rhonda, "'There will never be "a Very Special" *Buffy*': Buffy and the Monsters of Teen Life," *Journal of Popular Film and Television*, 27/2 (1999): 16–23.

—— "Who Died and Made Her the Boss?: Patterns of Mortality in *Buffy*," in Rhonda V. Wilcox and David Lavery (eds), *Fighting the Forces: What's at Stake in Buffy the Vampire Slayer* (Lanham, MD: Rowman and Littlefield, 2002).

——, *Why Buffy Matters: The Art of Buffy the Vampire Slayer* (London: IB Tauris, 2005).

—— and David Lavery (eds), *Fighting the Forces: What's at Stake in Buffy the Vampire Slayer* (Lanham, MD: Rowman and Littlefield, 2002).

Williams, Raymond, "The Technology and the Society," in Tony Bennett (ed.), *Popular Fiction: Technology, Ideology, Production, Reading* (London: Routledge, 1990).

Williams, Todd, "The Threat to the Subject in 'Once More, with Feeling'," paper presented at the *Slayage* Conference on *Buffy the Vampire Slayer*, Middle Tennessee State University, Nashville, Tennessee, 28–30 May 2004, archived at http://www.slayageonline.com/SCBtVS_Archive/Talks/TWilliams.pdf.

Winslade, J. Lawton, "Teen Witches, Wiccans and 'Wanna-Blessed Be's': Pop-Culture Magic in *Buffy the Vampire Slayer*," *Slayage: The Online International Journal of Buffy Studies*, 1 (2001), accessed 26 August 2008 at http://www.slayageonline.com/essays/slayage1/winslade.htm.

Wood, Michael, "Blue in Green," *The Antioch Review*, 57/3 (1999): 296–305.

Wood, Robin, *Hollywood from Vietnam to Reagan ... And Beyond* (New York: Columbia University Press, 2003).

Wright, Robert, "'I'd Sell You Suicide': Pop Music and Moral Panic in the Age of Marilyn Manson," *Popular Music*, 19/3 (2000): 365–85.

Zipes, Jack, "Breaking the Disney Spell," in Elizabeth Bell, Lynda Haas, and Laura Sells (eds), *From Mouse to Mermaid: The Politics of Film, Gender and Culture* (Bloomington: Indiana University Press, 1995).

Index

Abbate, Carolyn, 233
Adam, 105
Adams, Michael, 81, 99, 174, 186
adolescence, 40, 94n9, 116–17, 120–21, 126, 157, 175, 179, 180, 181
Adorno, Theodor W., 117
affect, 11, 62–4, 79, 86, 88, 99
    musical, 7, 53, 62, 65, 67–8, 72–3, 75, 77–8, 198
Affron, Charles, 86
Albright, Richard S., 3, 209, 223
Alessio, Dominic, 163
Alias, 26–7
Allanbrook, Wye Jamison, 50
Ally McBeal, 5–6, 36
alternative music, xxi, 2, 4–5, 8–9, 36, 46, 49, 52–3, 55–6, 114, 116, 127–8, 130, 135, 151–7, 165–86
Altman, Rick, 200–201, 236
Amy, 122n24, 154–5
Andrew, 174
Angel, 58, 121, 158; *see also* Buffy; masculinity
    appearance, 10, 179
    and agency, 21, 28–30
    as Angelus, 39, 51, 57, 61–2, 74
    and music, 17–20, 62, 69; *see also Buffy the Vampire Slayer*'s music
    return from hell dimension, 39–40, 56–7, 70, 91
    and sex, 30, 70
    and Spike, 30, 61, 121–2, 139
Angel (TV show), xxiii, 3, 8n29, 10, 12, 177, 209
    theme tune, 15–20, 28, 30–31, 192
animation, 238, 242–3
Anya, 28, 49n7, 101–5, 107, 123, 145, 189–90, 198, 202–5
Astaire, Fred, 202–3, 210–12, 214, 220
Attali, Jacques, 91

audiences, xviii, xxi, 18, 35, 39, 133–4, 138–41, 144, 192, 200, 210, 233, 240, 243
    attention, xviii, 38, 79–80, 82, 85, 192, 235
    and cultural knowledge, xvi, 10, 34, 36, 74, 126, 190, 192
    demographics, xviii, xxii, 111–14, 134, 151, 156, 167, 169, 176, 183–4, 236, 239, 249
    expectations of, xviii, 7, 34–6, 89, 95, 134, 167
    internal, 106–7, 120, 161, 191, 193; *see also* Bronze, the
    and music, xxi, xxii, 6–8, 11, 37, 47, 62, 72, 74, 78, 85, 113–15, 121–3, 126, 142, 168, 170
    as privileged observers, 105–8, 191–92, 196, 203, 206; *see also* music and identification; fandom
Ayers, Sheli, 98

Babylon 5, 33, 238
Baddeley, Alan, 64
Bakhtin, Mikhail, 97
The Band Wagon, 214–16, 220, 226
Banfield, Stephen, 62
Barthes, Roland, 87
Basinger, Jeanine, 169
Bataille, Georges, 97–8
Battle, Hinton, 183, 207, 213, 216
Bay City Rollers, the, 2, 11
Beatles, the, xv, 173, 177
Beck, Christophe, xxii–xxiii, 6–7, 9, 36, 44–6, 51, 56, 59, 67–8, 72, 82, 95, 102, 172n32; *see also Buffy the Vampire Slayer*'s music
Bell, Elizabeth, 196–7
Belsey, Catherine, 41
Benjamin, Walter, 98

Bennett, Andy, 112
Bennett, Tony, 133, 146
Benson, Amber, 195n27, 198
Bernstein, Leonard, 205, 222
Bikini Kill, 151, 163
Block, Geoffrey, 222
Bloustien, Gerry, 7, 249
Bond, James, 10
Boreanaz, David, 30
Bosma, Hannah, 27
Bourdieu, Pierre, 120–21, 123–5
Bowie, David
   "Memory of a Free Festival", 2, 173
Bradney, Anthony, 21–2
Branch, Michelle, xxi, 5–6, 129, 154
Brecht, Bertolt, 193, 223, 241
Bremer, Carolyn, 29
Bronze, the, xxi, 5, 8–9, 15, 17, 38–9, 42, 45, 49, 65, 70, 75n18, 95, 107, 115–16, 118–20, 122, 124, 126–7, 134, 154–5, 161, 169, 175–6, 182, 193, 206, 214, 230
Brophy, Philip, 195
Brown, Julie, 5–6
Brown, Royal S., 34, 38–9
Buckland, Theresa Jill, 198
Buffy, 83, 88, 100, 102–4, 160, 170, 22
   as adult, 35, 113
   and Angel, 9, 17, 24–6, 36–7, 43–6, 49, 51–2, 56–7, 61, 67–71, 121, 131, 145–67, 157
   appearance, 24, 154, 157–8, 161
   and Cordelia, 49n7, 113
   and Dawn, 77, 88, 91n1, 104, 230
   death(s) of, 24, 62, 91, 107, 137, 158, 189, 226, 245
   and despair, 196–7, 206, 222, 224, 226, 230–32, 244
   and domesticity, 7, 100, 107, 113
   and Faith, 52, 58–9, 122, 139, 182–3
   as feminist, 155–7, 163, 224
   and gender, 18–22, 24–6, 85
   and Giles, 1, 25, 44, 57–8, 61, 100, 107, 118–19, 124n30, 180, 192, 199–200, 228
   as girl, 24–6, 149, 156–7, 163
   as hero and warrior, 21–6, 84–5, 156–8, 162, 174
   and Joyce, 2n3, 9, 86, 98, 103
   and language, 96, 99–100, 145–6, 157, 224
   and music, 1–2, 5, 8–9, 15, 24–5, 35, 36–7, 39–40, 43–4, 45–6, 60, 76, 113, 116, 122, 123, 127, 161–2, 168, 198, 224–7; *see also Buffy the Vampire Slayer*'s music;
   and power, 9, 23, 112, 155, 157, 161–3
   and Riley, 11, 69, 71–3, 101–2, 145
   and Riot Grrrl, 150, 154, 156, 158, 161–2
   and romance, 9, 36–7, 39–40, 42–4, 67–71, 145
   and the Scoobies, 9, 28–9, 57–8, 60, 103n45, 105, 189, 205–6, 230
   and the series theme tune, 16–17, 24–6, 157–8, 194
   as Slayer, 22, 37, 41, 52, 105–6, 113, 116, 155
   and Spike, 6, 8, 37, 43–4, 106–7, 130, 136–8, 145, 147, 199–201, 205–6, 208, 219–20
   as teenager, 39, 69, 112, 156, 157
   and Willow, 9, 58, 94, 104, 159, 160
   and Xander, 24, 41, 52, 135, 161–2, 185, 212
Buffy the Vampire Slayer (film), xxi, 33, 89, 92, 149
Buffy the Vampire Slayer (TV show)
   episodes
   "After Life", 137
   "All the Way", 169
   "Angel", 36
   "Anne", 9, 170
   "Bad Girls", 179, 182
   "Band candy", 2n3, 9, 11n36, 37, 94n9, 118–19, 173, 176, 192
   "Bargaining, Part 1", 179, 182
   "Beauty and the Beasts", 2n2, 118, 124
   "Becoming, Part 1", 45, 70
   "Becoming, Part 2", 70, 156, 232
   "Beer Bad", 118, 124, 127, 156
   "Bewitched, Bothers and Bewildered", 9, 10, 42, 61, 134
   "The Body", xxiii, 7, 34n3, 51, 75–6, 79, 82, 85–6, 93, 95, 101, 103, 134, 159, 173, 192, 232

"Buffy versus Dracula", 23
"Choices", 70
"Chosen", 8, 100, 145
"Conversations with Dead People", 95, 173
"Crush", 169, 201n43
"The Dark Age", 1, 25, 91, 129n38, 192
"Dead Man's Party", 9, 125
"Doppelgangland", 156
"Earshot", 123
"Empty Places", 126, 172
"Faith, Hope and Trick", 39, 172–3, 177
"Family", 138
"Fear Itself", 172
"First Date", 102
"Flooded", 7
"Fool for Love", 106
"Forever", 9, 192
"The Freshman", 95, 131, 172–3
"Get it Done", 155n22
"The Gift", 62, 76–8, 91, 95
"Gingerbread", 100, 102n42, 180–82
"Gone", 9
"Goodbye, Iowa", 105
"Graduation Day, Part 2", 70–71, 172n33
"Grave", 62
"Halloween", 172
"The Harsh Light of Day", 2, 95, 124, 170, 173
"The Harvest", 115–16, 176
"Helpless", 100, 174
"Him", 43, 171
"Hush", xxiii, 2, 7, 11, 51, 71, 79, 82–6, 88, 92n3, 93–5, 100–103, 173
"The 'I' in Team", 8
"I Only Have Eyes for You", 95, 122, 172
"The Initiative", 41, 171
"Innocence", 70
"Intervention", 136
"Into the Woods", 173
"Killed by Death", 102n42, 103
"The Killer in Me", 99
"Lessons", 100

"Lie to Me", 96, 177–8
"Living Conditions", 8, 9, 83, 131
"Lover's Walk", 120–21, 123, 173
"Never Kill a Boy on the First Date", 176
"A New Man", 94
"New Moon Rising", 173
"Nightmares", 36, 74n17, 221, 94, 105n48
"Normal Again", 95, 101
"Once More, with Feeling", xxiii, 3, 4, 7, 9, 11, 23, 50, 91, 100–101, 107, 123, 189–208, 209–34, 244–7, 249; *see also Buffy the Vampire Slayer*'s music
  and the American musical, 189–208, 222–4, 231, 233
  audience-character relationships, 190–91, 193–5, 196, 200, 204, 206, 210, 246
  and camp, 233, 245–6
  and dancing, 194, 197, 198, 202–6, 210–14, 222, 229, 233, 246
  and Disney, 197, 224, 244
  distancing techniques, 190–91, 193–4
  and duets, 190, 200–205, 210–13, 245–6
  as dystopian fantasy, 189, 194, 197, 200, 205–7, 210, 222–3, 245
  and ensemble singing, 190, 196, 221, 230–32
  "I want" songs, 196–7, 224
  and intertextuality, 209–10, 212
  and jazz, 209, 211, 214–16, 232
  and listening, 194, 196, 198, 200
  musical structures in, 210–11
  and revelations, 190, 195, 200, 205, 223, 226, 230, 233, 245, 245–7
  and singing, 189, 195–6, 199, 200, 206, 213, 222, 244
  and solo song, 190, 196–9, 217–20, 228, 244, 246
"Out of Sight, Out of Mind", 100
"The Pack", 122, 179, 183
"Pangs", 203, 212
"Passion", 61–2, 74–5

"Primeval", 103n45
"Prophecy Girl", 9, 24–5, 36–7, 45n2, 96, 100
"The Puppet Show", 8n29, 36, 94
"Restless", 6, 88n19, 94, 95, 101, 105–6, 131, 193
"Revelations", 37, 49, 56–60
"School Hard", 23
"Seeing Red", 76
"Selfless", 23
"Showtime", 95
"Sleeper", 129
"Smashed", 122, 154
"Some Assembly Required", 61, 94
"Something Blue", 8, 43–4, 145
"Storyteller", 100
"Superstar", 5, 10, 96n15, 105
"Surprise", xxiii, 36, 39–40, 49, 69, 178
"Tabula rasa", 5, 75, 129, 201n40
"Teacher's Pet", 8n29, 125, 169
"Ted", 160
"The Yoko Factor", 105, 128, 173
"The Zeppo", 43, 52–6, 57, 131
"Two to Go", 174
"Villains", 85, 179
"Welcome to the Hellmouth", 15–16, 21n12, 94, 100, 105, 112, 115–16, 124, 126, 159, 184
"What's my Line? Part 1", 25, 224
"What's my Line? Part 2", 25
"When She was Bad", 122, 128, 161
"Where the Wild Things Are", 169, 173
"Who Are You?", 122, 172
"Wild at Heart", 62, 66–7, 75, 124, 159
"The Wish", 49n7, 70
"The Witch", 100
Buffy the Vampire Slayer's music
academic research in, 3, 169, 249
appropriation of, 167, 183–5
"Buffy-Angel love theme", xxiii, 9, 24, 36–7, 39–40, 43, 45–6, 49–50, 67–71, 95, 97
"Buffy-Riley love theme", 9, 36, 69, 71–3, 77
and genre, xvii, 3, 10, 15–16, 21n15, 33–44, 79, 154, 209, 244
as instrumental underscore, xxii–xxiii, 3, 4, 5, 6, 24, 33, 36–40, 41, 43, 45–6, 49–60, 62, 66, 67–73, 76–8, 82, 85–6, 94–5, 102–3, 106–7, 112, 128, 131, 134, 157
live bands, xxi, 38–9, 45, 95, 116, 125, 127, 165–86
narrative, 1–3, 6, 11, 35–6, 51, 56–60, 76, 112–15, 122, 125, 130, 133–8, 155, 163, 185, 190, 209
musical performance in, 6, 107, 123–4, 126, 134, 154–5, 161–3, 189–208, 216, 244–5
musical strategy, 33, 36, 41, 44, 62, 146, 189, 249
"Once More, with Feeling" songs
"Going Through the Motions", 107, 189, 196, 224–5, 231
"I'll Never Tell", 108, 202–5, 210–13
"I've got a theory/ Bunnies/If We're Together", 196, 200–201, 205–6, 221–2, 224, 244
"Overture", 194
"Rest in Peace", 107, 199, 219–20
"Something to Sing About", 107–8, 205–6, 225n40, 226–7, 231–2
"Standing", 199, 228–9
"They Got the Mustard Out!", 222, 244
"Under Your Spell", 107, 198–9, 217–19, 228, 245
"Walk Through the Fire", 196, 205, 225n40, 230–31
"What You Feel", 213–15, 226
"Where Do We Go from Here" (Finale), 189–90, 198, 201, 206, 231
soundtrack and diegetic bands
Aberdeen, 169, 171
Aragon, Dave, 113
Average White Band, 10, 42
Azure Ray, 169
Bellylove, 170
Bif Naked, 95
Blink 182, 175
Breeders, the, xxi, 169, 171
Brian Jonestown Massacre, 169, 172
Brooke, Jonatha, 169

Carson, Lori, 169
Cibo Matto, 127, 129, 154–5, 161–2, 169, 171, 176
Curve, 179, 182
Darling Violetta, 17, 42, 177
Dashboard Prophets, the, 122, 176
Devics, the, 169
Devil Doll, 170
Every Bit of Nothing, 119
Far, 122, 179, 183
Flamingos, the, 122
Fonda, 169–70
Four Star Mary, 6, 9, 126, 131, 134, 168, 170, 176, 180n57
Halo Friendlies, 122n24, 155, 175n42
K's Choice, 156, 177
Lotion, 169
Luscious Jackson, 156
Man of the Year, 169
Misfits, the, 179
Muffs, the, 172
Nerf Herder, 15–17, 25, 95, 111–12, 114, 122–3, 156, 172, 174–5
Rasputina, 178
Shy (fictitious band), 127, 129, 155
Sisters of Mercy, the, 178
Splendid, 95, 154, 168, 169, 172
Sprung Monkey, 116, 168, 171
Static-X, 179, 182
Superfine, 169
that dog, 169, 171
THC, 127, 129
Third Eye Blind, 39
Third Grade Teacher, 172
Treble Charger, 172
Velvet Chain, 154, 168, 176
Virgil, 122n24, 155
Yo La Tengo, 169
soundtrack CDs, xxii, 3, 114–15, 169, 170–71, 176
theme tune, 15–20, 24–6, 31, 36, 40, 45, 95, 111–12, 156–8, 172, 175, 192, 194
unaired pilot, 184; *see also* popular music; classical music; opera; silence

Buffybot, 99, 136
Burns, Gary, 181
Burton, Tim, 102–3, 214
Butler, Judith, 139

Cage, John, xvii, 92
Caillois, Roger, 93
Calendar, Jenny, 1, 28, 48, 61–2, 74, 94, 145, 158, 159n28, 192
Caulfield, Emma, 221
de Certeau, Michel, 125
Chantarelle, 179
Charisse, Cyd, 214, 220, 226, 246
Charmed, 5, 6n23, 21–3, 27–9, 185
Chase, Cordelia; *see* Cordelia
cheese, 131–2, 139, 141–2, 144–7, 158n27, 203, 212, 242
Cher, 8–9, 131, 168, 169
Chion, Michel, 38, 80, 82, 85, 103
Clarida, Bob, 7, 18–19
Clarke, Jamie, 3, 189, 209, 214
classical music, 10, 46, 49, 51, 236; *see also* opera
Clement, Shawn, xxiii, 178n50
Cline, Patsy, 9
Clover, Carol, 112
Coates, Norma, 8
Cobert, Robert, 45–46, 48
Cohan, Steven, 213
Collins, Jim, 34, 47–8
Columbine High School shooting, 177–9, 181–2
comedy; *see* humor
Connor, 28
Cordelia, 8–10, 28–30, 42, 49n7, 52, 54–5, 60, 70, 99, 113, 120, 125–6, 150, 158–9, 185
The Craft, 22
Cream
 "Tales of Brave Ulysses", 2, 9, 118–19, 173, 192–3
Cubitt, Sean, 200
Curtis, Dan, 45n1, 47

Dahlhaus, Carl, 50
Daney, Serge, 86, 89
Danse Macabre; *see* Saint-Saens, Camille
Dark Angel, 26–7

Dark Shadows, 47–9
Darla, 21, 30, 112, 176
Darling Violetta, 17, 42
Daugherty, Anne Millard, 193
Dawn, 6, 28, 43, 77, 88, 91n1, 95, 104, 136, 175–6, 214–16, 246
Dawson's Creek, 166, 185, 249
death, 91–108
Dechert, S. Renee, 3, 5, 8, 15, 42, 65, 113, 118, 122, 125, 127, 129, 134, 165–6, 168, 233
demons, 1, 9, 25, 52, 83, 94, 100, 105, 155n22, 168, 180, 183, 189, 204, 244
Derrida, Jacques, 93, 96, 249
diegesis, musical
    ambiguity, 5–6, 42, 74–5, 193, 223
    diegetic music (source music), 5, 16, 65
    diegetic music (source music) in *Buffy*, 2–3, 5, 15, 38–9, 45, 65–6, 74, 95, 116, 154–6, 161–2, 182, 192; *see also Buffy the Vampire Slayer*'s music: sound track and diegetic bands; musical performance
    diegetic song, 217
    diegetic sound, 7, 38, 65, 74, 83–4, 86–8, 94–5, 104, 108, 114–15
    extra-diegetic music, 6, 40
    metadiegesis, 35, 95
    non-diegetic music (underscore) in *Buffy*, 5, 15, 36–8, 43, 62, 66, 85, 94–5, 106, 157; *see also Buffy the Vampire Slayer*'s music: instrumental scoring
    non-diegetic popular music in *Buffy*, 38–9, 43, 95, 104, 114, 154, 192
    supradiegesis, 200, 205
diegesis, narrative, xviii, 5, 41–2, 84–5, 107, 196, 202
digital technology, 140–41, 143–4, 151–3, 159
Dingoes Ate My Baby, 9, 119, 122, 125–6, 131, 168
Dion, Celine, 8, 9, 131, 167–8, 169
Doherty, Thomas, 114
Donaruma, William, 209
Donnelly, K. J., 5, 7, 75
Doyle, 28, 30
Dr Horrible's Sing-Along Blog, 246n17

Drusilla, 30, 121, 169, 178
Dunne, Michael, 193–4, 205
Dyer, James, 166
Dyer, Richard, 236–7

Early, Frances H., 150, 152
Edwards, Lynne, 163, 174
Elfman, Danny, 102–3, 214
Ellis, John, 79–80, 115
Ellis, Markman, 106
Encyclopedia of Buffy Studies, 4
Erenberg, Lewis A., 215
Ethan Rayne, 119, 145
ethics, 223, 233, 235; *see also* morality

Faith, 28, 30, 43, 52, 56–60, 122, 176, 182–3
Family Guy, 235, 243
fan fiction, 114, 129, 132, 139, 144–5, 147; *see also* songfic; filk song
fandom, xviii, 3–4, 6, 8, 10–11, 112–14, 116, 125–6, 128–30, 132, 139–42, 144, 147–8, 153, 160, 165, 168; *see also* audiences
    internet sites and communities, 10, 128, 139–41, 144, 147–8, 151–2, 163, 166
    zines, 144, 151–2, 160, 163
fantasy, 3, 33, 79, 102, 121, 162, 189, 195, 205, 207, 210, 214, 217, 238
feminism, 149–63, 194, 224
Feuer, Jane, 191, 195
filk song, 6, 141–5, 147
Filmer, Paul, 210
First Slayer, the, 105–7
First, the, 100, 106
Fiske, John, 5, 117, 146, 203–4
Fjellman, Stephen. M., 197
Flashdance, 230
Footloose, 229
Ford, 178–9
Forrest, 84
Fred, 28–9, 147
Freud, Sigmund, 93, 98, 101, 224
Frith, Simon, 91, 166, 190, 195
Furia, Philip, 202–3
Fury, David, 230

Garner, Ken, 75
Garofalo, Gitana, 150, 152
Garrison, Ednie Kaeh, 153
geeks, 52, 159, 167, 174–6
gender, 19–30, 79, 85, 102, 135, 49–163, 174, 216, 246
Gentlemen, the, 83–5, 102–3
Geraghty, Christine, xviii
Gershwin, Ira, 203, 211–12
Gilbert, Laurel, 151
Giles, Dennis, 217
Giles, Rupert
   and class, 2, 93–4, 100
   as demon, 94
   and Jenny Calendar, 1–2, 61–2, 67n11, 74, 145, 158, 192
   and Joyce, 9, 118, 145, 192
   and music, 1–2, 6, 8–9, 11, 39, 44, 57–9, 62, 67n11, 74, 91n1, 107, 118–19, 123–4, 129, 173, 192–3, 230
   and Olivia, 101, 145
   and performance, 6, 88n19, 106–7, 128–9, 173, 190, 193, 196, 199–201, 223, 228–9, 231
   as Ripper, 118–19, 192
   as Watcher, 2, 6, 23, 47, 52, 57, 96, 100, 102–3, 105, 107, 124n30, 180–81, 196, 213, 221; *see also* Buffy
girl power, 9, 151, 155n22, 160–61, 163, 167, 186
Glory, 107, 136
Gokee, Rob, 37, 53
Gorbman, Claudia, 35, 38, 95, 250
Gothicness, 47, 103, 154, 176–7, 198; *see also* music: Goth music
Grad, Rob, 169, 170
Green, Seth, 170
Groening, Matt, 242
Grossberg, Lawrence, 117
Gunn, 28–9

Halfyard, Janet K., 3, 4, 8, 134, 156, 192–4, 223, 233
Halligan, Marion, 108
Hamlet, 91–2
Handelman, Don, 97

Hannigan, Alyson, 175
Hansen, Mark, 98
Harmony, 41–2, 138, 170
Harris, Xander (Alexander); *see* Xander
Hart, Angie, 95
Hartley, John, 203–4
Hatori, Miho, 161–2
Head, Anthony Stewart, 11, 128–9, 195n27, 228
Helford, Elyce Rae, 161, 184
heroes, 23–6, 29
Herrmann, Bernard, 38
Higgins, Dick, 132–3
Hill, Kathryn, 249
Hills, Matt, 129
Holder, Nancy, 7, 67
horror genre, 7, 10, 15–16, 24n16, 36–9, 79, 112, 125, 154, 156–7, 194
humor, 7, 11, 33, 35, 41–3, 45, 54, 61, 93, 96–7, 100–102, 107–8, 145, 174, 176, 192, 197, 200, 203, 210, 212, 221, 229, 235, 240, 244

Indigo Girls, the, 173
Infante, Victor D., 167
Initiative, the, 100, 102
instrumental music, see *Buffy the Vampire Slayer's* music
intermedia, 6, 114, 131–48
intertextuality, xvii, 3, 10, 16, 41, 130, 139, 144, 209–34, 236–7, 249
Interview with the Vampire, 17–18
intratextuality, 9–10, 74n17, 192, 203, 209, 221
Isherwood, Charles, 237

Jackson, Rosemary, 102
Jameson, Fredric, 40
Jasmine, 28
Jenkins, Henry, 129, 132, 140–44, 147
Jonathan, 5, 10
Jonathan Creek, 11
Jones, Steve, 144
Jowett, Lorna, 174

Kaltefleiter, Caroline, 150–52, 154
Kassabian, Anahid, 18, 67, 78, 190, 192, 235, 249–50

Kellner, Douglas, 203
Kendra, 25–6, 185
Kennedy, 175–6
Kermode, Frank, 138
King, John C., xxi–xxii, 4, 46, 169–71, 171
Kiss, 119–20
Klotz, David, 169–70
Knights, Vanessa, ix–x, 4
Koelsch, Stefan, 64
Kohles, Lisa, 177
Kramer, Lawrence, 235–6, 247
Krauss, Alison, 154, 162
Kromer, Kelly, 92
Kruse, Holly, 171

La Bohème; see Puccini, Giacomo
language, 62n3, 82, 87, 93, 95, 99, 101–2, 147, 151–2
   inarticulacy, 61, 93–4
   speech, 64, 81, 85, 157, 174
Larsen, Janet, 64
leitmotif, 9, 33, 35–7, 43, 45, 48–50, 57
Lerner, Neil, 4
Lessig, Lawrence, 140
Lilah, 28
Lilith Fair, 155–6, 245
Little, Tracy, 97
Loesser, Frank, 209, 221
Lorne, 28–9
Lynyrd Skynyrd
   "Freebird", 2, 129, 173

Macherey, Pierre, 41
Madonna, xv, 132, 141–2, 171
magic, 8, 10–11, 22–3, 29, 47–8, 51, 91, 96–100, 102, 105, 107, 119, 122, 145, 159–6, 175, 189, 192, 195–6, 198–9, 200, 217–18, 228, 232, 244, 245
Mann, Aimee, xxi, 129, 154, 169
Marsters, James, 178
Martin, Adrian, 114
Marx Brothers, 235, 247
masculinity, 19–20, 22, 24, 26–7, 29–30, 85, 102, 112n5, 135, 157, 161, 174–6, 216, 246
Masson, Cynthia, 209
Mast, Gerald, 202

Master, the, 24–5, 96, 116, 154n18, 157–8
Mayor Wilkins, 70, 121
McConnell, Kathleen, 181–2
McDonald, Chris, 220
McLachlan, Sarah, 62, 118, 129, 154, 156
melodrama, 36–9, 43, 45, 48, 94, 100, 130, 243
metaphor, 1, 30, 99–101, 115n22,116, 157, 160, 162–3, 165, 178–80, 197–8, 201–2, 207, 213, 215, 217, 241, 245
   "high school is hell", 100, 116, 179, 182
Metz, Christian, 114
Miami Vice, 5–6
Middents, Jeffrey, 3, 209, 216
Midler, Bette, 145–6
Miller, D. A., 237
mimesis, 62, 93, 96–100, 107
mimetic participation, 62–6, 68–9, 72–8
Money, Mary Alice, 131
Monson, Ingrid, 216
morality, 8, 30, 136, 162, 177–82, 185–6, 215
MTV, 8, 114
Muir, John Kenneth, 108, 209, 233
Murphy, Walter, xxiii, 36, 45
Murray, Sean, xxiii, 178n50
musical codes, cultural, xvi–xvii, 7, 11, 15, 18–20, 33–4, 65, 132, 141, 209–10; see also semiotics
music; see also *Buffy the Vampire Slayer*'s music
   audience reception, xvii, 11, 18–19
   character and identity, 8–11, 15–17, 31, 35–6, 39, 49, 56, 113–14, 118–23, 150, 173, 186, 189, 194, 203
   and cool, xxi, 2, 8, 11, 45, 113, 119, 122–7, 130, 168, 170, 172, 183, 216, 246
   embodied meanings, xvii, 62, 65–6, 78
   film music, 34, 36–7, 39, 41, 43, 77, 133
   and gender, 3, 18–20, 22, 24–7, 30, 112–13, 116, 192, 197–8
   and genre, xv, xix, 7, 10, 15–16, 20n11, 27, 33–44, 132, 190, 209–34, 236
   Goth music, 167, 176–9, 186

heavy metal, 167, 171, 177–83, 186, 218, 221
and identification, 11, 67, 78, 115, 117, 123, 191, 200
indie music, see alternative music
and irony, 35–6, 40–44, 71, 75, 212, 229, 232–3, 245
library music, 7, 46, 53, 55
licensing, xxi, 5, 127, 170–71, 178n50
perception and cognition, 61–78
and race, 3, 163, 167, 183–5, 216
record labels, xxi, 168, 170–72
in silent film, 37, 82, 86
and style, 45–60, 117, 127
and taste, 115, 119–22, 127, 130, 166
video, 6, 114, 127, 132, 135–44, 147–8, 177; see also fan fiction
musicals, 3, 10, 11–12, 128, 189–247, 249–50; see also "Once More, with Feeling"
dance, 194, 198–205, 210–12, 214, 239, 241
heterosexual courtship myth, 201–6, 249
modes of address, 191, 206
narrative structures, 189–90, 194–7, 200, 206–7, 239, 242
and parody, 194, 200–201, 204, 229, 239–42, 249
performer-audience relationship, 190–98
and spectacle, 202, 217, 223, 228, 231, 241
as utopian fantasy, 189, 194, 197, 200, 205–7, 210n3, 239
Mutant Enemy, 89
muteness, 82–6, 199
myth, 47, 100, 162, 182, 186, 189–90, 197–8, 201–3, 205

needle dropping, 4, 49
Negus, Keith, 4, 249
Nehamas, Alexander, 35, 41
nerds, 51, 111, 123, 238
Newitz, Annalee, 165
Newman, Kathy, 8–9, 86, 131, 168
No, No, Nanette, 211, 224
noise, 2, 26, 87, 91–2, 94, 96–7, 101

Noxon, Marti, 170, 183, 190, 213

occult, the, 26, 47, 180–81
Olivia, 101, 145
Ono, Kent A., 183–4
opera, 10, 36, 50, 61–2, 74–5, 232–3, 236, 247; see also classical music; Puccini, Giacomo
Overbey, Karen Eileen, 81, 85, 93, 99, 157
Owen, Susan, 160
Oz, 2, 28, 43, 62, 66–7, 70, 119, 120, 123–7, 134–5, 172

Parker, 145
Pateman, Matthew, 21
Patton, Cindy, 135
Penley, Constance, 139–40, 142
Petrie, Doug, 167
Pink Flloyd, 2n3, 173
Platt, Len, 222–3, 231–2
poetry, 61–2, 220
Poniewozik, James, 167, 184
popular music, xxi–xxii, 4, 10–11, 33, 38–9, 42, 51, 111–30, 132, 134–5, 140–42, 146, 154–5, 165–86, 189–90, 198–9, 209
lyrics as commentary, 5, 39, 42, 62, 67, 134, 137–8, 162, 176–7, 184
Porter, Dick, 181
Post, Gwendolyn, 56, 58
postmodernism, 34, 41, 134, 146, 151–2, 167, 236–7, 243
potentials Slayers, the, 28, 106
power, 21n15, 23, 28, 51, 56, 60, 85, 97–9, 100, 103, 105, 159–60, 163, 199, 221, 230; see also Buffy and power; girl power
Preston-Matto, Lahney, 81, 85, 93, 99, 157
production, cultural, 118, 120–21, 123, 125, 129–30
Public Enemy, xv, 4
Puccini, Giacomo, 10, 61, 74–5, 232; see also classical music; opera
Pulp Fiction, 75n18

Ramones, the, 172–3, 201
realism, xxi, 38, 41–2, 97, 113, 151, 190, 194, 197–8, 243, 249

reception, xvii, xix, 11, 18, 84, 115, 139, 141, 146–7, 168n16
Reeves, Jimmie L., 134
Regev, Motti, 119, 125, 130
relationships, romantic, xvii, 9, 21, 28–9, 33, 35, 37, 40–41, 43–4, 46–7, 52, 67, 69–71, 99, 121, 134, 138–40, 142, 144–7, 185, 190, 198–9, 201, 202–5, 207, 213, 220, 245–6
Remencus, Leslie, 3, 166, 168, 178n50
Rent, 231–2, 239
Reynolds, Richard, 26
Riley, 28, 36, 84, 101, 145
Riot Grrrl, 9, 122, 149–63, 166, 172
rituals, xvii, 92, 97, 99, 180, 183, 204, 206
Robinson, Tasha, 138
Rogers, Ginger, 202–3, 210–12
Rolling Stones, the, 18
Rosenberg, Jessica, 150, 152
Rosenberg, Willow; *see* Willow
Rubin, Martin, 217

Saint-Saens, Camille, 7, 11, 82; *see also* classical music
Salzman, Eric, 232
Sandars, Diana, 236–7, 250
Sarris, Andrew, 205
Satre, Jean-Paul, 121
Saturday Night Fever, 10, 42
Saxey, Esther, 139, 140, 144, 146
Schatz, Thomas, 204–6
Schechner, Richard, 101
Schilling, Mary Kaye, 197
Schilt, Kristen, 153, 155
Schultz, Jacques, 196
science, 48, 99–100
Scott, 39, 42, 145
Sells, Laura, 196
semiotics, xvi, 34, 133, 135–6, 148, 236; *see also* musical codes, cultural
Sex Pistols, the, xv, 8
sexuality, 42, 51, 139, 142, 152, 159, 176, 197–8, 214, 217, 245
Shade, Patrick, 92
Shall We Dance, 211–12, 214
silence, xvii, 7, 51, 60, 75, 82, 86–8, 91–108, 112, 192, 249
Silverman, Kaja, 83

The Simpsons, 235, 239–42
Sinatra, Frank, 120–22
sincerity, 43, 69, 245–7
Singin' in the Rain, 203, 213–14
singing, 27, 64, 74, 189, 241; *see also*, *Buffy the Vampire Slayer*'s music; "Once More, with Feeling"
sitcoms, 237, 240, 246–7
slash fiction; *see* fan fiction
Slayage, 3
Sleepy Hollow, 214
Smiths, the, 22
soap opera, xv, xviii, 4, 36–7, 47, 91, 94, 100, 108, 220
Sondheim, Stephen, 190, 205, 209, 221–3, 222, 244–5
songfic, 6, 114, 129–30; *see also* fan fiction
sound design, 7, 11, 38, 87, 95, 104, 135, 192
The Sound of Music, 2, 192, 224
"The Sound of Silence", 165, 205
sound recording, 83–4, 87–8
South Park, 224, 235, 241–3
Spice Girls, the, 161
Spike, 94, 106, 123, 130, 137–8, 178; *see also* Buffy
  and Angel, 30, 61, 121, 139
  and music, 6, 9, 18, 36–7, 43–4, 107, 120, 122, 169–70, 173, 199, 227, 231, 246
  and performance, 107, 120, 122, 190, 196–7, 199–201, 219–20, 232, 246
  as poet, 8, 61, 120n19, 220
  as punk, 8, 18, 120–21, 173, 199, 201, 220
  as Scooby gang member, 28, 94, 206
  as vampire, 17–18, 41, 102, 121–2
  as villain, 105, 120, 178
Stafford, Nikki, 155, 158
Star Trek, 24, 134–41, 176
Star Wars, 174–5
Steiner, Max, 36, 43
Stevens, Doug, xxiii, 3
Stilwell, Robynn, 5–6, 195, 236–7, 240–41, 247
Stravinsky, Igor, 46
subvocalization, 64–5, 66; *see also* voice
Summer Place, A, 43, 128

Summers, Buffy; *see* Buffy
Summers, Joyce, 2n3, 3
Summers, Joyce, 9, 86, 103–5, 118, 145, 159, 192
    Joyce and MOO, 180–81
superheroes, 26, 30, 154, 174, 177
supernatural, the, 6, 11, 21, 23, 26, 28–9, 40, 42–3, 45, 47–8, 83, 95, 103, 106, 113, 115–16, 126, 212
Surridge, Matthew, 210
Sutton, Martin, 213
Swanson, Kristy, 149, 154n18
Sweet, 205, 207, 213–16, 226, 228, 230–31
synchresis, 38, 40
Synder, Principal, 119–20

Tagg, Philip, 4, 7, 10–11, 18–20, 25
Tara, 6, 28, 93, 102, 104, 107, 122, 142, 145, 173, 189–90, 197–8, 200–201; *see also* magic; Willow
Taussig, Michael, 97–8
teen drama, 33, 38, 40, 42
television, 20n11, 33–5, 41, 79–81, 133–4, 166, 174, 180, 183–5, 190, 210, 235–8, 240, 242–3, 245–7, 249
    serials, 33, 35, 88, 144–5, 206, 237
    music, xv–xvi, xviii, 6–7, 22, 24, 36, 48–9, 73, 113–14, 249
    research, xv–xvi, xviii, 11, 133, 249–50
    sound, 79–82, 84–9, 114–15, 133, 135–6, 140
Thornton, Sarah, 116, 124–7
Tonkin, Boyd, 97
Topping, Keith, 194
Travolta, John, 10, 42
Trick, Mr, 185
True, Everett, 174

U2, xxi, 136–7, 141
UPN, 128, 166, 167, 183–4, 191

vampires, 5, 17–18, 21, 30, 41, 47, 70, 86, 112, 116, 120–21, 137, 157, 163, 177–9
Velvet Underground, the, 2, 173, 177
Ventura, Michael, 180
Veruca, 124, 127, 129, 155, 159

VH1, 8, 168
Vicious, Sid, 120, 122, 129n38, 173
Vint, Sherryl, 150
violence, 38, 61–2, 76, 85, 137, 153, 158, 160, 163, 165, 176, 180–83, 185, 219, 241
voice, human, 62, 64, 74, 79–89, 135–6, 154–5, 161, 177, 192, 200; *see also* muteness; subvocalization

Wagner, Richard, 36, 50
Wajnryb, Ruth, 96
Walker, Rebecca, 149
Walser, Robert, 180
Walsh, David, 222–3, 231–2
Walsh, Professor Maggie, 102
Wanker, Thomas, xxiii, 7, 46
Warner, Marina, 97, 102
Warner Bros Television Network (WB), 128, 166–7, 171, 183–5
Warren, 99
Weinstein, Deena, 8
Wesley, 28–9, 30, 127, 128
West Side Story, 250, 222, 224, 230, 237
Whedon, Joss
    and audiences, 128, 138–40, 233
    as composer, 172n32, 190, 197, 209, 210–11, 221–4, 231n48, 244–6
    as creator of Buffy, xxii, 7, 9, 21, 24, 31, 82, 89, 116n13, 131, 138, 165–7, 177, 179, 183, 185–6, 190, 193, 197, 202, 210, 214, 216, 226, 233, 244
    and feminism, 154, 163
    and music, xxiii, 5, 11, 15–16, 67, 71, 73, 114, 154, 168, 170–73, 175, 179, 183–4, 186, 190, 209, 214, 217, 219, 221, 233, 244
    research into, 4, 12
    and silence, 92, 102, 108
Who, the, 2, 173, 185
Wicca, 101, 159n29, 163, 221; *see also* magic; Willow
Wilcox, Rhonda V., 7, 12, 100, 108, 160, 224, 250
Wilkins, Richard; *see* Mayor Wilkins
Williams, Raymond, 133
Williams, Todd, 209

Willow, appearance, 104, 159–60, 172, 206
  and anxiety, 74, 93–4, 104–6, 159
  as computer geek, 47, 159–60
  as Dark Willow, 85, 160, 218
  and magic, 43, 52, 70, 100–102, 107, 122, 145, 159, 189, 244
  and music, 43, 66–7, 122, 127–8, 154–5, 168, 173, 198, 200
  and Oz, 43, 66–7, 125n31, 127, 134–5
  and power, 9, 85, 100, 160
  and Tara, 99, 102, 104, 107, 127, 142, 145, 173, 198–201, 206, 217, 219–20, 228, 244
  and Xander, 37, 52, 57–8, 161, 185, *see also* Buffy and Willow; Oz
Winslade, J. Lawton, 159
Wolfram and Hart, 28, 30
Wood, Michael, 207
Wood, Robin, 167
Wood, Principal Robin, 185

Xander, 95, 130, 207, 217, 245
  and Anya, 101–2, 107–8, 123, 145, 190, 196, 200–206, 210–13, 219, 223, 244–5
  and comedy, 10, 41–2, 52–4, 96n15, 131, 221
  and Cordelia, 9, 52, 54–6, 60–61
  and demonic romances, 10, 42–3, 52
  and music, 8n29, 10, 37, 42–3, 52–6, 107–8, 118, 122, 125, 134–5, 161, 183–4, 201–5, 210–13, 219, 221, 231, 245
  and popular culture knowledge, 112n5, 118, 123–5, 128, 174, 184
  as Scooby gang member, 23, 41, 52, 54–7, 104–5, 170, 189
  see also Buffy and Xander; masculinity; "The Pack"; Willow and Xander; "The Zeppo"
Xena, Warrior Princess, 23n16, 150, 157, 244n13

youth culture, 8, 15–16, 36, 38–9, 40, 45, 93, 111–20, 126, 130, 149–63, 167–8, 172, 174

zines; *see* fandom
Zipes, Jack, 197